Forging Identities in the Irish World

Studies in British and Irish Migration

Series Editors: T. M. Devine, University of Edinburgh, and
Angela McCarthy, University of Otago

Showcasing the histories of migration into and out of Britain and Ireland from the seventeenth century to contemporary times and their impact at home and abroad

From the 1600s to the current day, millions of British and Irish migrants have sought new lives around the world. Britain and Ireland have also received returning migrants and other newcomers of diverse ethnicities. This series will examine the causes, consequences, representations and legacies of these movements on the homelands, the migrants and the destinations in which they settled. The series incorporates not just the inward and outward movement of people, but of ideas, products and objects. It specifically encourages transnational and comparative cross-disciplinary approaches across groups, space and time.

Titles available in the series:

New Scots: Scotland's Immigrant Communities since 1945
Edited by T. M. Devine and Angela McCarthy

Death in the Diaspora: British and Irish Gravestones
Edited by Nicholas J. Evans and Angela McCarthy

Gold Rush Societies and Migrant Networks in the Tasman World
Daniel Davy

Forging Identities in the Irish World: Melbourne and Chicago, c.1830–1922
Sophie Cooper

edinburghuniversitypress.com/series/bims

Forging Identities in the Irish World

Melbourne and Chicago, c.1830–1922

Sophie Cooper

EDINBURGH
University Press

Edinburgh University Press is one of the leading university presses in the UK. We publish academic books and journals in our selected subject areas across the humanities and social sciences, combining cutting-edge scholarship with high editorial and production values to produce academic works of lasting importance. For more information visit our website: edinburghuniversitypress.com

© Sophie Cooper, 2022

Edinburgh University Press Ltd
The Tun – Holyrood Road
12 (2f) Jackson's Entry
Edinburgh EH8 8PJ

Typeset in 10.5/13pt Sabon by Cheshire Typesetting

A CIP record for this book is available from the British Library

ISBN 978 1 4744 8709 2 (hardback)
ISBN 978 1 4744 8711 5 (webready PDF)
ISBN 978 1 4744 8712 2 (epub)

The right of Sophie Cooper to be identified as author of this work has been asserted in accordance with the Copyright, Designs and Patents Act 1988 and the Copyright and Related Rights Regulations 2003 (SI No. 2498).

Published with the support of the University of Edinburgh Scholarly Publishing Initiatives Fund.

Contents

Acknowledgements	vi
Abbreviations	viii
Series Editors' Introduction	x
1 Introduction	1
2 Melbourne and Chicago: An Introduction	28
3 Building Bonds: Secular Club Life	57
4 Church and Club: Religious Parish Life	91
5 Sisters and Schooling: Public and Religious Education	122
6 Different Fighting Styles: Political Nationalism	153
7 St Patrick's Day and the Public Performance of Identity	186
8 Conclusion	220
Bibliography	227
Index	255

Acknowledgements

This is a book about community, and I am lucky to have benefited from the wonderful support and inspiration of countless scholars, colleagues and friends while developing this research. Enda Delaney and Niall Whelehan guided this project during my PhD. I cannot thank them enough for their kindness and generosity. I also want to pay tribute to my MPhil supervisor David Fitzpatrick whose counsel I miss. Angela McCarthy and Tom Devine have been supportive series editors and I thank them, my reviewers and all the editors at Edinburgh University Press for their insightful comments and suggestions. Any mistakes are my own.

Research for this book has been carried out across Britain, Ireland, the United States and Australia. Thank you to all the archivists, librarians and scholars who have helped me along the way with suggestions for potentially exciting research leads and coffee breaks in far-flung libraries on solitary research trips. I would also like to thank everyone involved in digitising archival and newspaper material, particularly that available without a paywall. Comparative and diaspora histories are vital additions to historical knowledge, but I acknowledge the financial pressures that completing them place on researchers. This research was only possible because of the generosity of the William McFarlane Scholarship (Scottish Centre for Diaspora Studies, University of Edinburgh), Simon Fennell Award, King V. Hostick Fund (Illinois State Historical Society), Peter Parish Memorial Award (BrANCH), British Association of Irish Studies, Royal Historical Society and the CUSHWA Center at the University of Notre Dame.

I am writing these acknowledgements in April 2021 – a year into the COVID-19 pandemic – and am very conscious that over the course of writing this book, everyone's world has become a lot smaller. I am incredibly grateful for my Leicester friends who have formed my socially distanced *real people* group over the last year: Svenja, Zoe, Mike, Jan, Hannah and Mat. Inside and outside academia, my friends have been spectacular companions on this journey. In Edinburgh, Sarah L., Anna, Fliss, Joe, Bobbie, Roseanna, the Irish history group, Fi and Ash, Stephen, Anne-Marie, Lisa Marie and Andrew, both Niamhs, Sarah A., Sarah G. and Smarsh and their various partners and small ones have really seen me through. Yorkshire holds many of my favourite people, including Ruth and Maïlys, Luke and Katie, Emma and Emi. Further afield are Kat, Gemma, Danielle, the extended Bramhall family, to name just a few. Through a screen or in real life, you make life that much better!

Wonderful colleagues and friends have given their time to helping this book reach publication. As a precarious academic I have benefited from long discussions with colleagues and mentors at the universities of Edinburgh, Leicester, Newcastle, Northumbria, Strathclyde and much further afield through the joys of Twitter. Despite the structural problems of the university sector, I am so grateful to have worked with the colleagues and students that I have. In the throes of revisions, I am particularly indebted to the generosity of Sarah Laurenson, Bobbie Nolan, Joe Curran, Beth Kitson, Zoe Groves, Maggie Scull and Sarah Sharp for reading chapters, and to Alison Garden for her writing group, which has kept me on track when most needed.

Finally, thank you to all of my family. Mum and Dad, you have encouraged and supported me throughout. Liv and Ed have mocked my enthusiasm while celebrating every milestone. I love you. This work is dedicated to my grandparents, Mo and Jim Cooper and Beryl and Gerry Jones. The Joneses in particular have nurtured a love of history and storytelling since they first introduced me to a microfilm reader aged eleven. Thank you.

Abbreviations

ACA	Archdiocese of Chicago Archives
ADB	*Australian Dictionary of Biography*
ALL	American Land League
ALPML	Abraham Lincoln Presidential Museum and Library
AOH	Ancient Order of Hibernians
BVM	Sodality of the Blessed Virgin Mary
CFL	Chicago Federation of Labor
CHMRL	Chicago History Museum and Research Library
CYMS	Catholic Young Men's Society
DDA	Dublin Diocesan Archives
DIB	*Dictionary of Irish Biography*
DSB	Denominational School Board
GAA	Gaelic Athletic Association
HACBS	Hibernian Australasian Catholic Benefit Society
INA	Irish National Association
INF	Irish National Foresters
INS	Irish National School
IRB	Irish Republican Brotherhood
JAD	Irish Jesuit Archives
LLL	Ladies' Land League
MDHC	Melbourne Diocesan Historical Commission
MLA	Member of the Legislative Assembly
NDA	University of Notre Dame Archives
NLI	National Library of Ireland
NSB	National School Board
PROV	Public Record Office of Victoria
SLV	State Library of Victoria
SPS	St Patrick's Society of Australia Felix

TCD	Trinity College Dublin
UISCC	United Irish Societies of Chicago and Cook County
UILA	United Irish League of America
WCOF	Women's Catholic Order of Foresters

Series Editors' Introduction

Comparative and transnational approaches to migrant groups offer much to scholars of migration. They help, for instance, to alleviate accusations of introspection and parochialism, they provide analytical power through a focus on similarities and differences, and they showcase the ways that homeland origins and destinations remain connected. Within studies of Ireland's diaspora, such approaches comparing cities or regions are still in their infancy. Sophie Cooper's *Forging Identities in the Irish World* therefore breaks new ground in being the first book to focus solely on comparing Irish identities in two global cities. With an eye to the themes of education, nationalism, ethnic and religious associational culture, and public performance on St Patrick's Day, *Forging Identities* explores what it meant to identify as Irish (and especially Irish Catholic) in Chicago and Melbourne in the nineteenth and early twentieth century.

Besides its important comparative and transnational framework, *Forging Identities* is significant in five further ways. First, Cooper explores a range of identities – ethnicity, class and gender. Second, she includes both the migrant and multigenerational descent group. Third, she moves beyond a focus on men alone to also include women and children, lay and religious. Fourth, she situates her analysis within the historiography of urban history, showing how Melbourne and Chicago also changed over time, evolving from small trading posts to vibrant cities. And, fifth, Cooper is alert to broader multidisciplinary approaches to the past, drawing on concepts of mutative identities, culture brokers, and diaspora spaces. These concepts – plus Cooper's own foundational identity concept – allow her to explore multiple influences on identities and to move beyond a focus on male professions of priest, publican and politician, to also include teacher and nun.

To show how churches and schools were instrumental in shaping Irish identity over generations, *Forging Identities* utilises a range of sources including newspapers, religious journals and archives, school records, parish histories, business directories, and ethnic society minutes. Although the focus is primarily on the Catholic Irish, Cooper is also alert to the ways that ethnicity could exist separate from religion in order for Irish migrants to articulate an inclusive identity for both Catholics and Protestants. Future research integrating diverse religious identities will further illuminate Irishness throughout the diaspora to build on this important study.

T. M. Devine and Angela McCarthy

1

Introduction

In February 1884, the Irish communities of Chicago celebrated. John and William Redmond, prominent home rule politicians from Ireland, had arrived in the city on the way back from a lecture tour in Australia. They brought with them John's new wife Johanna, the daughter of a prominent Irish Australian and cousin of William's future wife.[1] The Chicago-based *Western Catholic* proclaimed the decision to stop in the United States and Australia proved that there was 'Unity in Trinity'.[2] Speaking in both Melbourne and Chicago symbolically linked Irish communities across the world, in Ireland and abroad. Despite the enthusiasm of the *Western Catholic*'s editors, historians have been slow to explore the connections within this 'Trinity'. Taking the cities of Melbourne and Chicago as its focus, this book explores the ways that Irish communities encouraged and sustained a collective sense of connection to an idea of 'Ireland' and a wider Irish diaspora. These urban case studies provide broadly similar environments, though each with their own distinctive identity, to explore the tools that Irish people used to promote a sense of community between Irish migrants and their foreign-born children over a period of ninety years. Where James Barrett has written of the Americanisation of ethnic society from the 'bottom up',[3] this book considers the ways that different groups in Melbourne and Chicago society competed and collaborated to sustain a strong sense of ethnic community and belonging. It focuses on the evolution of Irish identities – those predicated on religion, class, and gender – within Melbourne and Chicago, and the ways that individuals engaged with ideas of belonging to a global Irish nation in personal and group contexts.

This book, using the idea of foundational and active identities, seeks to understand the differing but equally important roles of Irish men and women in shaping Irish community life abroad. The distinctive influences of women and men, religious and lay, on Irish community life and identity formation in the United States and Australia have not previously been examined in tandem. *Forging Identities* places children and women alongside men to understand how Irish migrants and their children reached adulthood already ensconced in a network of friendships, associations and memory which entwined religion, ethnicity and class. Jennifer Redmond notes that, while very important, many studies of Irish migrants 'continue to ignore women's specific experiences while claiming to be books about Irish immigrants (not books about Irish men, which indeed they are)'.[4] *Forging Identities* brings women in from the peripheries of St Patrick's Day balls, the attics of domestic servitude and the silent donors to nationalist subscriber lists. These are all important positions. However, they do not fully acknowledge the role of Irish women throughout society in shaping Irish community life from the roots upwards, creating a cultural affinity for children in schools and the family home which in turn could be built upon by male leaders. While men still dominate aspects of this book, this study places men, women and children together to present a fuller image of the worlds that Irish migrants lived in, uniting the middle-class influences of associational culture with the cross-class influences of women in schools, societies and the home.

The diasporic middle classes were an inherently complex group of people encompassing Australian newspaper owners like Samuel and Joseph Winter, sons of an English Protestant convict and an Irish Catholic assisted migrant; Mother Vincent McGirr and Sister Francis Xavier, Sisters of Mercy and the sisters of Catholic historian and botanist Professor John McGirr in Chicago; Tipperary-born John O'Shanassy, the second Premier of Victoria, a draper and a leading supporter of the Catholic Church; and Margaret Haley, teacher and Chicago Teachers' Federation representative.[5] Historians Mary Poovey, Catherine Hall and Leonore Davidoff highlight the varied make-up of the English middle classes and the constant reconstruction of what it meant to be part of the middle class.[6] This variation translates into the Irish case.[7] John Belchem echoes this focus on pluralism in Irish middle-class migrants, tracking divisions between the Irish at the 'apex' of middle-class professional and commercial circles which crossed ethnic boundaries, and those lower down the ladder, members of the merchant and professional classes who were in daily contact with the Irish poor.[8] The diverse needs and motivations of the Irish middle classes in Melbourne and Chicago were partly brought together through voluntary societies and their willing and enthusiastic organising committees.[9] Despite these important positions in encouraging ethnic community, the middle classes are often an understudied element of the Irish abroad, particularly in Australia. Patrick O'Farrell and Jennifer Ridden both consider the Anglo-Irish elites and minor gentry in their studies of the Irish in Victoria. Zoë Laidlaw has similarly studied colonial connections between Britain, the Cape Colony and New South Wales in the early nineteenth century.[10] However, there has been little research done on the 'middling sort' which is the focus of this book. The role of secular and religious ethnic associations in creating and sustaining a multi-generational Irish community in Melbourne and Chicago is therefore explored with reference to a range of clubs and societies with different motivations and audiences.

Building upon previous research into the lived experiences within the Irish diaspora, this book also considers the role of the Catholic Church in uniting ethnic and religious identities. A growing cause for complaint within histories of the Irish diaspora is that they are primarily concerned with Irish Catholics, equating the two identities and ignoring Irish Protestants, particularly those who emigrated before the Famine.[11] While *Forging Identities* is concerned with the structures employed by the Catholic Church to link ethnicity and religion, it also seeks to understand the ways that Irish ethnicity was separated from religion and portrayed as an inclusive identity to be embraced by Catholics and Protestants alike. In the middle-class circles that this book predominantly focuses on, this bonding through ethnicity and class is examined in parallel to the transnational religious connections that were encouraged and profited from by Irish Catholics. In doing so, it relies heavily on Catholic sources which explicitly engage with Irishness, whereas the Protestant perspectives tend to be from more Anglo-American sources. The reasons for this separation will be explored throughout the book but are largely related to the subsummation of middle-class Irish Protestant voices into the wider dominant white Anglosphere. As the nineteenth century drew to a close and the twentieth century progressed, the middle class lost their dominance in diasporic Irish society, with ethnic involvement often becoming more of a symbolic identity or 'leisure activity'.[12] For members of the working classes and their politicians, in contrast, Irishness and Irish Catholicism became a key unifying identity which they sought to dominate. This book does not claim to be an exploration of what it meant to *be* middle class. It instead focuses on the role of the middle class in promoting what it meant to be Irish and how they fought for control of an increasingly vocal and powerful working class.

The rest of this introduction will outline the existing historiography of the Irish in Australia and the United States, discuss the methods,

THE IRISH IN AUSTRALIA AND THE USA

This book is located within the history of the Irish diaspora: the study of those who left Ireland and scattered around the globe principally in the aftermath of the Irish Famine (1845–52). Enda Delaney argues that to 'write the Irish story without the diaspora is to render a partial account'.[13] This book adds to the historiography of Ireland and the ongoing influence of the diaspora in shaping Irish ideas of belonging and nationhood.[14] Critical in understanding the diverse influences to flow in and out of Ireland during the nineteenth century and after is an acknowledgement of the varied experiences of those who joined the diaspora. There was no homogeneity of experience, though the image of the Irish abroad has often been dominated by scholarship of the American urban north. Kerby Miller's landmark examination of life in Ireland and America, *Emigrants and Exiles*, has led to an overriding understanding of Irish Americans as working class, held back by a sense of exile from Ireland and brought together by a primordial identity.[15] Despite this dominance, there has been a growing literature on the Irish abroad over the last forty years, providing a useful framework for this research.[16]

Forging Identities utilises a comparative methodology to test the idea of 'inherently Irish' features of diasporic life. Malcolm Campbell, Regina Donlon, William Jenkins, Donald M. MacRaild and Patrick Mannion have all used comparison to explore similarities and differences in Irish communities spread around the world.[17] These comparisons assist in understanding the importance of varying factors commonly credited with influencing how people saw themselves, and how they were seen and understood by others: family, friends, education, religion, geographical surroundings, the media and the state. Comparison helps to highlight the similarities and divergences within the Irish diaspora. However, it can still restrict the diasporic experience to within the nation state or lead to asymmetrical comparison wherein another country is examined to prove exceptionalism.[18] Campbell has been particularly critical of this with regard to early comparisons of Irish communities within the diaspora.[19] Kevin Kenny suggests a combined use of comparison and transnationalism to explore how particular immigrant groups can 'retain, or develop, diasporic sensibilities that become integral to their emerging, nationally specific ethnic identities'.[20]

Forging Identities explores the similarities and differences, and particularly the successes and failures, of the Irish in Melbourne and Chicago in creating a community based on ethnicity. The Irish in Australia and the United States have frequently been cast as binaries: one middle class and loyal to the British empire and the other working class and vehemently nationalist. As this book will demonstrate, prominent Irish Australians frequently encouraged this dichotomy as a defensive strategy, while Irish Americans like John Mitchel poured scorn on the 'milk and honey' Irish in Australia during the nineteenth century. These cities were host to various Irish identities, related to ethnicity, religion and class, which could connect and conflict with each other. *Forging Identities* explores those differences but also highlights the similarities in the language of belonging, approaches to organising, and celebration of Irish identity.

The scholarship on the Irish in Australia is small but growing. A sustaining belief that distance from Ireland forced an immediate prioritisation of class and allegiance to colonial and Australian identity over an Irish ethnic identity is largely responsible for this dearth. According to this argument, any insistence of continued ethnic identity was futile. The work of Patrick O'Farrell, the foremost scholar on the Irish in Australia, has provided the foundation for this belief.[21] O'Farrell's work primarily focused on the experiences of those living in Sydney and New South Wales, dismissing those in Melbourne as 'Munster peasants' who left their Irish allegiances on the boat. In contrast, this book provides further insight into the diversity of life in nineteenth-century Australia. It counters the sometimes problematic and generalised conclusions that O'Farrell made regarding Irish life in Australian society, joining other, more recent scholarship in broadening understandings of Irish life in colonial Australia.[22] While O'Farrell's scholarship is still important and unrivalled in scope, it has led to the echoing of a similar understanding of the Irish in Australia in many books from an Ireland- or America-based perspective. This reflects a wider problem within the historiography of the Irish diaspora. The use of a small body of nation-based works to inform understandings of the experiences of those living abroad has resulted in illustrating the diversity of the diaspora while concurrently homogenising the experiences of those living within one national border.

More recently, scholars have contributed to an alternative vision of Irish experiences in Australia. Elizabeth Malcolm and Dianne Hall have recently expanded O'Farrell's work to incorporate more complexity of experience. Laurence Geary has studied Irish doctors in Victoria, while David Fitzpatrick and Patrick Coleman have explored connections between the Orange Order in Australia and Ireland.[23] Fitzpatrick has also provided insight into the personal recollections of Irish migrants, using family letters between Australia and Ireland during the nineteenth century as a basis.[24] The use of non-traditional sources has encouraged new research avenues. Susan Arthure takes an archaeological approach, while Dianne Hall and Lindsay Proudfoot have utilised sources such as gravestone inscriptions and cartoons to examine how Irish people saw themselves and were seen in relation to location and race in Australia.[25] However, the lack of geographical specificity in the major books on the subject has led to a persistent image of Irish-Australia steeped in convict history, nativism and English-led Catholicism which has then been spread throughout Irish historiography.[26]

In studying Australia within a colonial context, the Irish have occupied a peculiar place in the historiography of both Ireland and the Empire. Ireland's role as both a partner in the imperial project and a colonised country is complicated and, similar to colonised people who found a way to succeed within an imperial project throughout the world, has led to questions about the power dynamics of colonialism.[27] The historiographical focus has traditionally been on the role of Irish temporary migrants in positions of colonial authority, as civil servants, colonial administrators and in the military. The principal subject of study in these works has been how living and working within the British empire was used to improve social status and how Irish identity was balanced or compromised by different people. Alvin Jackson, Matthew Kelly, Jennifer Regan-Lefebvre and Loughlin Sweeney have explored this balancing of economic mobility and national loyalty, arguing that in cooperating with the mechanisms of empire, Irish, and particularly Irish Catholic, migrants could achieve economic and social mobility while using the language and tools of imperial networks to improve their position and that of Ireland.[28] Important edited volumes have all complicated this narrative further, while research projects aimed at placing Ireland within a global framework prompt new comparative and transnational findings.[29] With an increasing focus on re-examining colonial histories and legacies, this work to explicitly place Ireland within the structures of empire at home and abroad continues to elicit exciting questions and research.[30]

The Irish communities which emerged during and after the Famine were linked through family ties and the increasingly quick technologies of telegram, international post and newspapers. The migrant groups who imagined and constructed Irish community life within Melbourne and Chicago were not static groups of people. Melbourne and Chicago were new and bustling cities, filled with transient peoples and new arrivals. Novel ideas and priorities were introduced constantly, evolving and changing the views of those leading Irish society life, providing shifting avenues for group and individual progress. As more power and communication links flowed into the white settler dominions, culture brokers were able to bypass London and communicate directly with their counterparts in other dominions. Therefore, Melbourne politicians and reformers were frequently in discussions with their counterparts in Ottawa and Toronto with regard to imperial education policy, for example.[31] The British empire was 'a complex communications network through which ideas spread'.[32] The imperial world acted as 'an interconnected zone constituted by multiple points of contact and complex circuits of exchange' and, for English-speakers, one that frequently expanded into the United States.[33]

The Irish diaspora and its religious institutions sought to take advantage of these connections to improve their position in diasporic society and the place of Ireland internationally. This book considers the role of religious orders and organisations in shaping Irish diasporic identity, primarily though not exclusively through the Irish Catholic Church, which facilitated the transfer of information and personnel around the world, including to Australia and the United States. Colin Barr and Hilary Carey have discussed this parallel religious empire as a 'Greater Ireland', particularly after the rise of Cardinal Paul Cullen and what Emmet Larkin has named the 'devotional revolution' which occurred from the 1840s.[34] Barr and Carey note that Greater Ireland was 'a shared cultural space in which a sense of home and shared identity jostled with the varying challenges of the host societies and the inherited divisions of the Irish themselves'.[35] The Irish communities in Melbourne and Chicago were linked to Ireland and throughout the diaspora. How these connections manifested in the creation of an Irish diasporic ethnic identity is the focus of this book.

Unlike the more recent growth of historiography on the Irish in Australia and the wider British empire, Irish migrant groups in the United States have been the subject of a vast and varied literature ever since Oscar Handlin published *The Uprooted* in 1951.[36] While for decades working-class Catholics in the urban north dominated studies, there has been a shift towards a wider understanding of American Irish experiences, mainly Protestants who left Ireland before the Famine and those who settled in the rural and southern states.[37] Within these works there have been explorations of race relations, particularly between the Irish and African-Americans who often worked side by side in badly paid unskilled jobs in the north, and the relationship between poor but free whites and enslaved African Americans in the south. The role of the Irish in the American Civil War has also received the attention of historians, through the examination of ethnic regiments and within the wider Union and Confederate armies.[38] These studies have widened understandings of the Irish experience in the United States during the nineteenth century, the structures that linked Irish migrants, and the forces which shaped perceptions of Irishness abroad. While there are a number of works on the rural American Irish experience, numerous books based within specific cities have provided in-depth studies of communities over multiple generations and classes.[39] These have allowed for repeated re-examinations of how northern urban Irish immigrants were connected and viewed, testing the image of perceived forced exile that haunted Irish immigrants, and the subsequent misery of *Emigrants and Exiles*.[40] This has also been explored in relation to Irish migrants who went further west, further examining whether the ghettoisation and poverty commonly attributed to Irish migrants was a temporary northern-eastern urban phenomenon rather than the plight of Irish migrants throughout the urban north.[41]

Forging Identities has benefited from the incredible work being carried out on Irish women both in Ireland and the diaspora. While Irish women have frequently been left out of more general books on Irish migrant communities, they have been the subject of standalone scholarship. Janet Nolan and Hasia Diner led the way in understanding the lives of Irish women in the United States, while Tara McCarthy and Ely Janis have added much-needed perspectives on Irish women's nationalist and reforming activism more recently.[42] Trevor McClaughlin, Dianne Hall and Elizabeth Malcolm have similarly provided insights from colonial Australia, while Lyndon Fraser and Angela McCarthy have contributed to the study of the Irish female diaspora in New Zealand.[43] This book seeks to place Irish women alongside their husbands, sons and brothers in the formation of Irish community life. The emphasis on Irish female religious orders incorporates scholarship from religious and educational histories too frequently held separate by historians of migration. Maureen Fitzgerald's work on Irish Catholic nuns in New York argues persuasively for the inclusion of these women in studies of reforming and ethnic power. As she notes, convents 'became a primary means through which working class Irish Catholic women gained public power. Moreover, convents provided the Irish Catholic working class with the means to articulate and make manifest its political agendas and social vision.'[44] Mary Beth Connolly and Karly Kehoe, among others, have contributed crucial insights into female Irish religious orders and their role in the diaspora.[45] Too often women religious (as women who have taken religious vows are collectively known) have been rendered 'invisible' both by dominant Protestant and secular narratives of progress and by their own vows.⁴⁶ While Irish Catholic nuns in Melbourne and Chicago were unable to wield the same power as Tammany Hall-backed New Yorkers, the women religious of these cities built and retained power on their charges and congregants. Parish school systems and the Irish religious orders that frequently staffed them created a foundational identity, often unconscious but vital to giving children a sense of location and belonging. This foundational identity could be built upon by male associational culture and the traditional 'culture brokers' of publican, politician and priest when an Irish-descended child reached maturity. For female children, we must also add nun, teacher and union organiser to this list. Cara Delay and Kathleen Sprows Cummings have emphasised the ways that Irish Catholic women worked within and in tension with institutional frameworks of religion and respectability to shape a particularly feminine understanding of Irish Catholicism.⁴⁷ *Forging Identities* takes a similar approach, considering both the explicit and implicit influences on identities traditionally considered to be led by men.

ETHNIC IDENTITY AND THE CITY: METHODOLOGIES AND APPROACHES

Identity is a social construct. It is subjective, it is location-specific and it is intersectional. In other words, people are not just '"human beings" but are also gendered, classed, ethnocized, etc.'.⁴⁸ However, as an analytical term, identity needs to be studied with reference to why, in some contexts, affinities lead to a bonded group based on identity and in others these identity categories are more flexible.⁴⁹ Kathleen Neils Conzen and colleagues argue that 'ethnicity is not a "collective fiction," but rather a process of construction or invention which incorporates, adapts, and amplifies pre-existing communal solidarities, cultural attributes, and historical memories'.⁵⁰ Alan O'Day expands this understanding of ethnicity as a process to include second and later generations through 'mutative ethnicity' whereby ethnic identity is, often unconsciously, adapted to suit the changing needs of daily life abroad. By making it relevant to diasporic life, ethnic identity can be sustained within communities, even among those with weakening lived experience of Ireland. This adaptive ethnicity 'encompasses a persistence, rediscovery or layered form of Irishness among the Diaspora', placing ethnic identity within local contexts.⁵¹ If a 'shared collective memory is a defining feature of a diasporic consciousness', it is vital to explore how a sense of diasporic consciousness of 'being Irish' was 'constructed, represented and internalised' by Irish migrants in Melbourne and Chicago over at least two generations.[52] In response to these influences, ethnic identity is considered a 'result of the dynamic conjunctions of social structures, class conflicts, and cultural patterns in the old country and the new'.[53] *Forging Identities* is based within the communities of Irish-born and Irish-descended people in Melbourne and Chicago: in their schools, in their clubs and in their parades. All of these elements contributed to the ethnic communities which emerged and, in turn, altered the idea of what it meant to be 'Irish' and how engagement with identity could be beneficial. O'Day argues that mutative ethnicity 'is distinct from merely symbolic ethnicity because it is an active part of the everyday life'.[54] Irish identity therefore needs to be examined in a range of contexts to test the idea of inherent 'Irish' values: the transnational influences which changed and shaped diasporic identities and the importance of local settings in filtering these ideas. This is one key advantage of applying a comparative lens to this study.

Forging Identities proposes the concept of a 'foundational identity' to distinguish between unconscious and conscious, or passive and active, engagement with ethnic identity. Foundational Irish identity was based within the parish and considers the impact of being surrounded by people who look and sound like you and your parents on the creation and maintenance of ethnic identity across multiple generations. This term, and its importance within this study, is in part influenced by sociological scholarship on inter-racial and inter-cultural relations, particularly in the United States. According to this scholarship, ethnic or social 'mirroring' is central to the way that members of immigrant groups, and particularly second-generation immigrants, view themselves as an ethnic group.[55] While migrant generations often form their identities with a frame of reference based in their country of origin, later generations form their identities in relation to positive or negative images of their ethnic group.[56] In the nineteenth and early twentieth centuries, the middle classes played an important role in encouraging pride among Irish migrants of all classes, which was frequently articulated through associational culture.[57] Within this study, mutative ethnicity is explored through cultural affinity, encouraged by religious education and parish life. It argues that this cultural affinity was promoted by surrounding Irish-born and -descended children with teachers, religious orders and employers who sounded like their parents. This affinity was more than a passing engagement with Irishness. Instead, Irish heritage and, for most, the Catholic religion became a foundational identity that could be built upon by articulations of Irish or American or Australian nationality. This could be actively ignored, and it was by some. However, for many it provided an often unconscious identity through which all other interactions with a host or immigrant society were viewed. This understanding aligns with Donald MacRaild's argument that though the ethnicity of the Irish 'may have mutated or adapted . . . it continued to be sustained by features of religion, politics and daily life which were inherently Irish'.[58] In this way, this book examines the 'global uniformities' which emerged in Irish communities in Melbourne and Chicago.[59]

Timothy Meagher and John Belchem have joined other scholars in emphasising the need to consider multi-generational influences on migrant communities and social mobility.[60] Meagher has historicised this generational difference in his study of Irish communities in Worcester, Massachusetts, at the turn of the twentieth century. He argues that transformations in Irish-American identity need to be understood over multiple generations as a result of changes in everyday activities, and as part of a community's negotiation of its relations with its neighbours.[61] Ethnic mirroring is an important element in this negotiation, providing the children of immigrants with positive role models who are part of their ethnic community, within the church, school and local economy. As Meagher notes, second-generation Irish Americans moved through a 'chronology of change from accommodation to ethnic revival to the forging of a new, broader group'.[62] This study examines the way that foundational identities provided a lens for how second-generation Irish communities forged this new, broader group, based within an Irish-born community while also embracing their American or Australian identities. While foundational identities were formed in schools and the church, they provided a base layer of commonality which could be built upon to articulate a more political 'Irishness' through associational culture, public performance and nationalism.

While Irish diasporic nationalism, associational culture and political engagement have been the subject of wide-ranging scholarship, the foundational ethnic identity which provided this 'shared collective memory' that defined 'diasporic consciousness' has yet to be explicitly applied to Irish communities in Melbourne and Chicago.[63] Belchem has focused on the ways that generational tensions were largely avoided in Liverpool by the rapid movement of second-generation Irish identification into 'the commemorative memory of the land of their forebears, a sentimental portrayal of the "old sod" promoted by religious and political leaders, ethnic entrepreneurs and commercial impresarios' as well as Catholic schools staffed by Irish religious orders.[64] This book situates these foundational identities as vital to a community's subsequent interactions with more political and civil forms of identity. This base of commonality could then be targeted by community leaders to work towards domestic and international ambitions, political and financial, through active engagement with ideas of Irish ethnicity and identity. The Catholic Church and its predominantly female representatives were instrumental in creating this diasporic consciousness, through representation and ethnic mirroring in schools, clubs and the home. Secular images of Irishness, through civil societies dedicated to ethnic fraternalism and nationalism, were conversely led, in the main, by men. Together these active and passive engagements with Irish community life, also referred to as parish life, created and promoted certain Irish identities in Melbourne and Chicago which could be deployed in public and private.

Where the city geographically *is* for different people is a question that frequently occurs in *Forging Identities*. As urban historians and theorists have noted, the city is a multi-faceted construct.[65] Each city dweller will experience 'the city' differently and imagine it differently. This book focuses upon two cities, but these were spaces in flux. Though people and organisations frequently crossed the expanding city, their everyday worlds were based in their neighbourhoods or parishes. For this reason, the term 'parish life' is used to denote the community structures of associational culture, religion and education. Jay P. Dolan has called the parish 'a window in the wall, through which Catholic life can be observed'.[66] The term is used here in a more general way, though for the same ends. At times the 'parish' was located in an actual parish delineated by the Catholic Church, while at other times it was a neighbourhood or suburb. When required, this local sense of belonging could be expanded to encompass the entire city, as defined by council boundaries, to connect people based on ethnic identity.

Networks play an essential part in exploring community or parish life. David Fitzpatrick's description of networks as 'open and optional rather than exclusive and fully reciprocal', with community best analysed as a product of networks rather than of neighbourhood, is applied.[67] At its core, parish life refers to the infrastructure and institutions that connected Irish and Irish Catholics to each other within the specific city of Melbourne or Chicago, and how these networks were widened to include activities in Ireland and elsewhere in the Irish diaspora. It is used in contrast with the city society, which included people of different ethnic, immigrant and religious backgrounds. Irish parishes interacted with wider city society fluidly, depending on class, gender and timing.

This book explores the ways that different elements of Melbourne and Chicago society encouraged these identity hierarchies and where those hierarchies emerged.

Irish identity is viewed as an ethnic identity within this work, connected to but not dependent on religious identity. Taking this into account, it is possible to explore the secular Irish institutions, usually through engagement with ideas of civil society. Secular society allowed people of Irish birth and descent to self-identify as Irish without conflicting with their religious identity. Avtar Brah's concept of 'diaspora spaces', and the need to consider migrant identity as shaped by both internal and external community influences, is central to this book.[68] Julie Codell argues that '[b]eing in another country offered a freedom from often-restricted identities of home, to which one could return when desired and from which one never entirely left'.[69] Mutual shaping and adaption contribute to the question of what makes an ethnic community. Whether a defensive strategy or not, it was up to Irish migrants to decide whether they engaged with elements of Irish community life. Other elements of community life were less about choice; instead they were a result of religious devotion, family ties or simple geography. The local contexts in which people of Irish birth and descent established a place for themselves and reconfigured their priorities with regard to ethnic and religious identities are inextricably connected to the identities which emerged.

The subjects of this book, the Irish in Melbourne and Chicago, provide a unique comparison of Irish communities. Both cities had similar-sized Irish populations, relative to the total population, and therefore adhere to the ideal comparison of having 'sufficient symmetry or equivalence' while being different enough to highlight patterns or distinctions.[70] Situating immigrant communities within their social contexts, in this case two rapidly growing cities in very different political settings, allows for a deeper interrogation of the transnational influences on diasporic 'Irishness'. Nineteenth-century Melbourne and Chicago have been the focus of significant scholarly work, but despite their many similarities these cities, and the Irish communities they housed, have received little comparative attention.[71] This nation-bound approach does not take into account the influences of differing political and philosophical contexts in altering immigrant identity.

The position of Melbourne and Chicago as 'instant cities' without established native-born elites offers an opportunity to explore the ways that nineteenth-century migrant communities manoeuvred their way up and around the societies they inhabited. Gunther Barth identified the concept of instant cities in relation to San Francisco and Denver: cities that sprang up almost like magic in the mid-century.[72] The concept can be applied to Melbourne and Chicago, two cities which quickly emerged as self-reliant cities based on a boom of natural and human resources and in spite of environmental pressures. This book sees the rapid growth of these communities as different to those within older cities that 'resembled trees that grew haltingly, matured slowly, and decayed imperceptibly'.[73] It is the 'new' cities of Melbourne and Chicago, which had similar periods of growth, explored in Chapter 2, and a lack of entrenched power structures at the beginning of mass Irish Catholic emigration, that form the basis of this book.

The opportunities promised by the economic booms in Melbourne and Chicago during the 1850s and '60s brought many migrants to the expanding cities, directly or indirectly, at a time of increasing nationalist and revolutionary fervour in Europe. The subsequent mixing of different nationalities and generations of immigrants in each city influenced the tone and image of Irish diasporic identity. These 'instant cities' had dominant cultures, but they lacked the entrenched Protestant elites of their older counterparts, and therefore their populations prioritised the position of religion in different ways. Barth hypothesised that in new cities lacking common traditions, social cohesion was fostered by a communal need to order society. The egalitarian opportunities provided by quick success in instant cities meant that people from a diverse range of backgrounds could establish themselves in positions of authority. However, in Barth's study he noted that the egalitarian beginnings of San Francisco and Denver soon reverted to traditional hierarchies of authority based on ideas of class.[74] Lacking traditions of their own, instant cities' inhabitants learned to adapt, piecing together 'a mosaic of practices, largely borrowed from the past, but reflecting in their immediacy and usefulness the creativity of the new cities'.[75] While certain national traditions were transferred abroad, the new and urban contexts provided a certain level of anonymity for those who lived there, and allowed for the opportunity to reshape individual and community identities.

By examining the development of Melbourne and Chicago, from white settlement until the establishment of the Irish Free State, *Forging Identities* provides a new perspective both on the evolution of each city and the connections between the Irish communities living within them. Oliver MacDonagh has researched those living in Melbourne, David Fitzpatrick has edited collections of letters based in Victoria, and Patrick Naughtin has examined the newspapers and networks related to Irish nationalism in Melbourne.[76] *Forging Identities* is the first book which focuses specifically on the Irish communities of Melbourne across the nineteenth century. The Irish in Chicago, conversely, have been the focus of a number of works which frame the questions asked in this book.[77] This scholarship has led the way in understanding the worlds that Chicago Irish people inhabited. Given the prominence of Chicago's Irish nationalists in the 1870s and '80s, when militant nationalism and labour radicalism dominated headlines internationally, much of the work on the city's Irish communities has focused on that time period.[78] This book expands the focus to understand how the impact of early decisions in Chicago's history set the scene for the Irish activism that came to prominence later in the century. Ethnic communities, their churches and institutions, and their fight for public space had long-term and temporary impacts on the shape of each city. The urban space provided particular opportunities for ethnic communities to perform their identities and the power they wielded, through parades, spectacle and physical brick and mortar. Studying Melbourne and Chicago as they developed across almost a century therefore allows for a new consideration of the role of the Irish in shaping these cities.

SOURCES

Forging Identities uses a range of primary source material to build up an image of diverse migrant communities in flux. In her work on emigrant literature, Fariha Shaikh notes that if 'emigration was the bodily experience of moving through space and time . . . then the texts of emigration literature were the objects that mediated this move and produced new ways of thinking about it'.[79] This book seeks to bring the voices of Irish-born and -descended people to the fore in order to understand the ways that 'Irishness' was envisioned both by the people claiming that identity and those who sought to undermine it. As newspapers have been considered 'part and parcel of metropolitan identities', they act as useful mirrors into the key debates and social expectations held by those living in the urban centres of Melbourne and Chicago.[80] A mixture of mainstream newspapers are used, primarily the *Age* and *Argus* in Melbourne and the *Tribune* and *Daily Inter Ocean* in Chicago. These newspapers, aimed at the higher echelons of society, provide conservative and occasionally nativist impressions of the Catholic Irish communities in both cities, providing useful counterweights to the Catholic-produced archival material that also informs this study. As the nineteenth century progressed, newspapers provided an arena for political and social activity, becoming 'more closely associated with public opinion in the popular mind'.[81] While Stephen Vella's warning that newspapers are not 'neutral conduits of information, but rather gatekeepers and filterers of ideas' must be kept in mind,[82] the inclusion of ethnic and religious focused newspapers like *The Advocate* in Melbourne and *Irish American Weekly* and *Western Catholic* in Chicago allows for the consideration of nation-building endeavours from different perspectives and with different, often opposing, motivations.[83]

In addition to these diasporic Irish newspapers, this book also benefits from engagement with Irish newspapers, including the *Freeman's Journal*, which were frequently sent out or franchised abroad. Newspapers influenced the Irish identity formed abroad through editorial choice and public pressure. In this way, newspapers provided a medium through which transnational conversations took place as well as the construction and promotion of ethnic symbolism. Newspaper sources are supplemented by archival records, often collected by the Catholic Church in diocesan archives and by religious orders. Letters published in newspapers help to present the voices of those who did not leave collections of manuscript material. The correspondence and diaries that do exist are largely those of Irish nationalist and community organisers, leaving the 'silent majority' just that, silenced. However, glimpses of the views and priorities of women and the less powerful can be seen in the projects that were funded, the bazaars that were hosted and the societies that were sustained. The types and varieties of Irish community life which filled the society columns of Melbourne and Chicago's mainstream and ethnic newspapers can therefore be used as sources in themselves, supplemented by information found in city directories, school records, parish histories and society minutes.

STRUCTURE

In comparative history, the choice of case studies can emphasise similarity or difference, and these are often chosen explicitly to prove one or the other. Chapter 2 explores the justification of Melbourne and Chicago as case study cities for this book. These cities were established at similar times with an incredibly close proportion of Irish people relative to the total population size. After exploring the history of each city, the chapter places the Irish immigrant community within its local and international contexts. Irish people were on the ground at the start of white settlement, presenting them with important opportunities to influence the shape of each society. These cities should have been the perfect venues for Irish people to assimilate into a broader Melbourne or Chicago identity. However, in both cities specifically Irish identities emerged, evolved and were sustained throughout the nineteenth and early twentieth centuries.

Chapters 3 and 4 use the concept of the 'ethnic parish' to explore how identification with an Irish identity shaped the social lives of those in Melbourne and Chicago. The ethnic parish, and the networks and associations within it, provided interconnected opportunities to articulate Irish identity. Chapter 3 focuses on the secular parish, while Chapter 4 concentrates on the religious. These overlapping parish boundaries allowed for secular and religious understandings of Irish identity to work in tandem, while blurring across gender, class and denominational lines. The religious and secular parishes provided opportunities for socialising, employment and celebration within and outside a specifically Irish circle. This separation of secular and religious is an analytical division not necessarily reflected in the real lives of those studied, but it is useful in examining the different ways that ethnic identity was celebrated and promoted.

The religious parish was a vital point of connection for the Irish abroad and worked alternately in tandem and in conflict with the secular parish. The religious parish was a place for Catholics, particularly Irish Catholics, to meet and work with those of a different class or gender, allowing them to expand their networks outwards. The Irish Famine had encouraged a 'devotional revolution' in Ireland, continuing a process begun in the 1840s which prioritised uniformity and ritual in the Catholic Church.[84] Under Cardinal Cullen of Dublin, the Catholic Church in Ireland was transformed into an ultramontane institution, drawing together the support that Cullen had from the Pope and Roman authorities with the Irish clergy and laity to reform the pastoral provision of the Irish Catholic Church.[85] Cullen was able to achieve this pastoral reform due to the growth of religious orders, often established by wealthy women, who sought to improve the spiritual and welfare provision of the needy and poor of Ireland in the two decades preceding the Famine.[86] The increase in religious order numbers in Ireland in the 1840s was consolidated after the Famine when the rapid decline in the Irish population led to the transformation of the position of the clergy within Irish society. While 33 per cent of Catholics went to Mass in pre-Famine Ireland, this number rose to over 90 per cent by the end of the nineteenth century. Larkin argued that the devotional revolution 'provided the Irish with a substitute symbolic language and offered them a new cultural heritage with which they could identify and be identified'.[87]

This devotional revolution had far-reaching consequences for the development of welfare and educational provision in the diaspora. Chapter 5 focuses on women religious, Catholic education and their influence on ethnic identity formation in the diaspora. The parish school system allowed for the entrenchment of religious communities in Irish diasporic life and was built upon by the promotion of devotional practice which linked middle-class parishioners to each other through charity, social activities and family. By encouraging schoolchildren and young adults to attend Mass, visit the sick and needy in the parish, and read doctrinal books, magazines and pamphlets, Irish Catholics grew up with a sense of community responsibility. Virtue, moral choice and personal development were all intertwined with religious and community devotion. Both cities prioritised a Catholic's virtue and personal development, providing educational facilities and charitable opportunity, improving their social, physical and spiritual position in life and death. These three chapters are primarily concerned with the construction of a foundational Irish identity, built upon ethnic mirroring and frequent contact with ideas of Irish belonging from childhood.

Chapters 6 and 7 build upon the parish lives and networks explored in the previous chapters, examining the ways that Irish community life was articulated as Irish identity through nationalism and public performance. Chapter 6 focuses on Irish political nationalism. Comparison within a wider study of the two communities' cultural and ethnic evolutions allows this study of political nationalism to highlight vital similarities in the creation of diasporic Irish identities: identities traditionally viewed as binaries. Irish nationalism in Melbourne and Chicago worked in tandem and tension with activists in Ireland and was influenced by the evolution of nationalist thought in Ireland and elsewhere in the world. Fearghal McGarry and James McConnel argue that Fenianism was a product of the Irish diaspora 'and cannot be understood without reference to this wider context'.[88] In turn, the transnational connections that funded and promoted activities in Ireland and Great Britain cannot be removed from the diasporic conditions in which Irish nationalism developed.[89]

The local became global through the newspaper reports, lectures and fundraising campaigns which linked Chicago, Melbourne and Ireland. Chapter 7 explores the ways that parish life, nationalist organising and public performance came together in the urban spaces of Melbourne and Chicago by exploring the rhetoric used by leading Irish organisations on St Patrick's Day. The language of belonging and loyalty used at St Patrick's Day dinners and demonstrations brought together the priorities of diverse communities, encompassing educational, religious and political identities within different urban environments. Together, these chapters explore the shifting influences on the promotion and understanding of what it meant to identify as Irish in Melbourne and Chicago during the nineteenth and early twentieth centuries.

NOTES

1. *Irish American Weekly*, 9 February 1884.
2. *Western Catholic*, 2 February 1884.
3. James R. Barrett, *History from the Bottom Up and the Inside Out: Ethnicity, Race, and Identity in Working-Class History* (Durham, NC: Duke University Press, 2017).
4. Jennifer Redmond, *Moving Histories: Irish Women's Emigration to Britain from Independence to Republic* (Liverpool: Liverpool University Press, 2018), p. 4.
5. Geoffrey Serle, 'Winter, Joseph (1844–1915)', *Australian Dictionary of Biography* (ABD).
6. Leonore Davidoff and Catherine Hall, *Family Fortunes*, revised edn (London: Routledge, 2002), p. xxxii; Margaret Poovey, *Uneven Developments: The Ideological Work of Gender in Mid-Victorian England* (Chicago: University of Chicago Press, 1988); Linda Young, *Middle Class Culture in the Nineteenth Century: America, Australia and Britain* (Abingdon: Palgrave Macmillan, 2003).
7. John Belchem, *Irish, Catholic and Scouse: The History of the Liverpool Irish, 1800–1939* (Liverpool: Liverpool University Press, 2007); Craig Bailey, *Irish London: Middle-Class Migration in the Global Eighteenth Century* (Liverpool: Liverpool University Press, 2013); R. F. Foster, *Paddy and Mr Punch: Connections in Irish and English History* (London: Penguin Books, 1995), pp. 281–305.
8. John Belchem, 'The Liverpool-Irish enclave', in Donald M. MacRaild (ed.), *The Great Famine and Beyond: Irish Migrants in Britain in the Nineteenth and Twentieth Centuries* (Dublin: Irish Academic Press, 2000), pp. 126–46.
9. Davidoff and Hall, *Family Fortunes*, p. xxxii; Senia Pašeta, *Before the Revolution: Nationalism, Social Change and Ireland's Catholic Elite, 1879–1922* (Cork: Cork University Press, 1999), p. 4.
10. Jennifer Ridden, 'Britishness as an imperial and diasporic identity: Irish elite perspectives, c.1820–1870s', in Peter Gray (ed.), *Victoria's Ireland? Irishness and Britishness, 1837–1901* (Dublin: Four Courts Press, 2004), pp. 88–105; Zoë Laidlaw, *Colonial Connections 1815–1845: Patronage, the Information Revolution and Colonial Government* (Manchester: Manchester University Press, 2005); Ciaran O'Neill, *Catholics of*

Consequence: Transnational Education, Social Mobility, and the Irish Catholic Elite 1850–1900 (Oxford: Oxford University Press, 2014).

11. William Jenkins, *Between Raid and Rebellion: The Irish in Buffalo and Toronto, 1867–1916* (Montreal: McGill-Queen's University Press, 2013), p. 7; Donald H. Akenson, *Small Differences: Irish Catholics and Irish Protestants 1815–1922. An International Perspective* (Montreal: McGill-Queen's University Press, 1988).

12. Patrick Mannion has considered similar in relation to the Irish in Newfoundland, Nova Scotia and Maine. Mannion, *A Land of Dreams: Ethnicity, Nationalism, and the Irish in Newfoundland, Nova Scotia, and Maine 1880–1923* (Montreal: McGill-Queen's University Press, 2018), p. 8.

13. Enda Delaney, 'Diaspora', in Richard Bourke and Ian McBride (eds), *The Princeton History of Modern Ireland* (Princeton: Princeton University Press, 2016), pp. 490–508; Enda Delaney, 'Our island story? Towards a transnational history of late modern Ireland', *Irish Historical Studies*, 37 (2011), pp. 599–621.

14. Kevin Kenny, 'Diaspora and Irish migration history', *Irish Economic and Social History*, 33:1 (2006), pp. 46–51.

15. Kerby A. Miller, *Emigrants and Exiles: Ireland and the Irish Exodus to North America* (Oxford: Oxford University Press, 1985).

16. Miller, *Emigrants and Exiles*; Kevin Kenny, *The American Irish: A History* (Harlow: Longman, 2000); Enda Delaney, 'The Irish diaspora', *Irish Economic and Social History*, 33:1 (2006), pp. 35–45; David Fitzpatrick, *Oceans of Consolation: Personal Accounts of Irish Migration to Australia* (Cork: Cork University Press, 1994). For an overview, see Delaney, 'Diaspora'.

17. Malcolm Campbell, 'The other immigrants: Comparing the Irish in Australia and the United States', *Journal of American Ethnic History*, 14:3 (1995), pp. 3–22; Malcolm Campbell, *Ireland's New Worlds: Immigrants, Politics, and Society in the United States and Australia, 1815–1922* (Madison: University of Wisconsin Press, 2008); Regina Donlon, *German and Immigrants in the Midwestern United States, 1850–1900* (Abingdon: Palgrave Macmillan, 2018); Jenkins, *Between Raid and Rebellion*; Donald M. MacRaild, 'Crossing migrant frontiers: Comparative reflections on Irish migrants in Britain and the United States during the nineteenth century', *Immigrants and Minorities*, 18:2–3 (1999), pp. 40–70; Mannion, *A Land of Dreams*.

18. Heinz-Gerhard Haupt and Jürgen Kocka, *Comparative and Transnational History: Central European Approaches and New Perspectives* (New York: Oxford University Press, 2009), p. 5.

19. Campbell, 'Other immigrants'; Campbell, *Ireland's New Worlds*.

20. Kevin Kenny, 'Diaspora and comparison: The global Irish as a case study', *Journal of American History*, 90:1 (2003), pp. 134–62.

21. Patrick O'Farrell, *The Irish in Australia: 1788 to the Present* (Randwick: New South Wales University Press, 1987); Patrick O'Farrell, 'The Irish in

Australia and New Zealand, 1870–1990', in W. E. Vaughan (ed.), *A New History of Ireland. VI: Ireland Under the Union, II 1870–1921* (Oxford: Clarendon Press, 1996), pp. 703–24; David Fitzpatrick, 'The Irish in Australia and New Zealand, 1791–1870', in W. E. Vaughan (ed.), *A New History of Ireland. V: Ireland Under the Union, I, 1801–70* (Oxford: Oxford University Press, 1989), pp. 661–81.
22. Chris McConville, *Croppies, Celts and Catholics: The Irish in Australia* (Caulfield: Edward Arnold, 1987); John O'Brien and Pauric Travers (eds), *The Irish Emigrant Experience in Australia* (Dublin: Poolbeg Press, 1991); Oliver MacDonagh, W. F. Mandle and Pauric Travers (eds), *Irish Culture and Nationalism, 1750–1950* (London: Macmillan Press Ltd, 1983); Lindsay Proudfoot and Dianne Hall, *Imperial Spaces: Placing the Irish and Scots in Colonial Australia* (Manchester: Manchester University Press, 2011); Val Noone, *Hidden Ireland in Victoria* (Ballarat: Ballarat Heritage Services, 2012).
23. Laurence M. Geary, 'Australia *felix*: Irish doctors in nineteenth-century Victoria', in Patrick O'Sullivan (ed.), *The Irish World Wide: II: The Irish in the New Communities* (Leicester: Leicester University Press, 1993), pp. 162–79; Patrick Coleman, '"In Harmony": A comparative view of female Orangeism, 1887–2000', in Angela McCarthy (ed.), *Ireland in the World: Comparative, Transnational, and Personal Perspectives* (Abingdon: Routledge, 2015), pp. 110–36; David Fitzpatrick, 'Exporting brotherhood: Orangeism in South Australia', in Enda Delaney and Donald M. MacRaild (eds), *Irish Migration, Networks and Ethnic Identities since 1750* (London: Routledge, 2007), pp. 129–62.
24. Fitzpatrick, *Oceans of Consolation*.
25. Susan Arthure, 'Being Irish: The nineteenth century South Australian community of Baker's Flat', *Archaeologies*, 11 (2015), pp. 169–88; Dianne Hall, '"Now him white man": Images of the Irish in colonial Australia', *Australian Historical Association*, 11:2 (2014), pp. 167–95; Lindsay Proudfoot and Dianne Hall, 'Memory, place and diaspora: Locating identity in colonial space', *Journal of Irish and Studies*, 4:1 (2010), pp. 47–64.
26. Kevin Kenny, for example, argues that imbalance between the sexes weakened ethnic group cohesion in Australia. This gender imbalance was quickly rectified in Melbourne. However, O'Farrell's work and the reliance on his arguments creates an impression of homogenous experience throughout Australia. See Kenny, 'Diaspora and comparison'.
27. Barry Crosbie, *Irish Imperial Networks: Migration, Social Communication and Exchange in Nineteenth-Century India* (Cambridge: Cambridge University Press, 2012); David Fitzpatrick, 'Ireland and empire', in Andrew Porter (ed.), *The Oxford History of the British Empire: The Nineteenth Century* (Oxford: Oxford University Press, 1999), pp. 494–521; Keith Jeffery (ed.), *'An Irish Empire'? Aspects of Ireland and the British Empire* (Manchester: Manchester University Press, 1996).

28. Alvin Jackson, 'Ireland, the Union, and the empire, 1800–1960', in Kevin Kenny (ed.), *Ireland and the British Empire* (Oxford: Oxford University Press, 2005), pp. 123–52; Matthew Kelly, 'Irish nationalist opinion and the British empire in the 1850s and 1860s', *Past & Present*, 204 (2009), pp. 127–54; Stephen Howe, *Ireland and Empire: Colonial Legacies in Irish History and Culture* (Oxford: Oxford University Press, 2000); Kevin Kenny (ed.), *Ireland and the British Empire* (Oxford: Oxford University Press, 2005); Jennifer Regan-Lefebvre, *Cosmopolitan Nationalism in the Victorian Empire: Ireland, India and the Politics of Alfred Webb* (Basingstoke: Palgrave Macmillan, 2009); Loughlin Sweeney, *Irish Military Elites, Nation and Empire, 1870–1925* (Basingstoke: Palgrave, 2019).
29. Jeffery (ed.), *'An Irish Empire'*; Timothy McMahon, Michael de Nie and Paul Townend (eds), *Ireland in an Imperial World: Citizenship, Opportunism, and Subversion* (London: Palgrave Macmillan, 2017); Enda Delaney and Fearghal McGarry, 'Introduction: a global history of the Irish Revolution', *Irish Historical Studies*, 44:165 (2020), pp. 1–10.
30. Shahmima Akthar, '"A public display of its own capabilities and resources": A cultural history of Irish identity on display, 1851–2015' (PhD: University of Birmingham, 2019).
31. Patrick Walsh, 'Education and the "universalist" idiom of empire: Irish National School books in Ireland and Ontario', *History of Education*, 37:5 (2008), pp. 645–60.
32. Regan-Lefebvre, *Cosmopolitan Nationalism*, p. 3.
33. Gary B. Magee and Andrew S. Thompson, *Empire and Globalisation: Networks of People, Goods and Capital in the British World, c.1850–1914* (Cambridge: Cambridge University Press, 2010), p. 16.
34. Colin Barr and Hilary M. Carey, 'Introduction', in Colin Barr and Hilary M. Carey (eds), *Religion and Greater Ireland: Christianity and Irish Global Network, 1750–1950* (Montreal: McGill-Queen's University Press, 2015), pp. 3–29; Emmet Larkin, 'The devotional revolution in Ireland, 1850–75', *American Historical Review*, 77:3 (1972), pp. 625–52.
35. Barr and Carey, 'Introduction'.
36. Oscar Handlin, *The Uprooted: The Epic Study of the Great Migrations that Made the American People* (New York: Little, Brown & Company Ltd, 1951).
37. For an overview of this historiography, see Kevin Kenny, 'Twenty years of Irish American historiography', *Journal of American Ethnic History*, 28:4 (2009), pp. 67–75; Kevin Kenny (ed.), *New Directions in Irish-American Historiography* (Madison: University of Wisconsin Press, 2003).
38. David Gleeson, *The Green and the Gray: The Irish in the Confederate States in America* (Chapel Hill: University of North Carolina Press, 2013); Timothy J. Meagher, *Inventing Irish America: Generation, Class, and Ethnic Identity in a New England City, 1880–1928* (South Bend, IN: Notre Dame Press, 2001); Damian Shiels, *The Irish in the American Civil*

War (Dublin: THP Ireland, 2013); Catherine Bateson, 'The sentiments and culture of Irish American Civil War songs and music' (PhD: University of Edinburgh, 2018).

39. David M. Emmons, *The Butte Irish: Class and Ethnicity in an American Mining Town, 1875–1925* (Urbana: University of Illinois Press, 1990); Margaret M. Mulrooney, *Black Powder, White Lace: The du Pont Irish and Cultural Identity in Nineteenth-Century America* (Lebanon: University Press of New England, 2002); Kevin Kenny, *Making Sense of the Molly Maguires* (Oxford: Oxford University Press, 1998); Mary C. Kelly, *The Shamrock and the Lily: the New York Irish and The Creation of a Transatlantic Identity, 1845–1921* (New York: Peter Lang, 2007); Ronald H. Bayor and Timothy Meagher, *The New York Irish* (Baltimore, MD: Johns Hopkins University Press, 1996).
40. Miller, *Emigrants and Exiles*.
41. R. A. Burchell, *The San Francisco Irish, 1848–1880* (Berkeley: University of California Press, 1980); David M. Emmons, *Beyond the American Pale: The Irish in the West, 1845–1910* (Norman: University of Oklahoma Press, 2010).
42. Hasia Diner, *Erin's Daughters in America: Irish Immigrant Women in the Nineteenth Century* (Baltimore, MD: Johns Hopkins University Press, 1984); Janet A. Nolan, *Ourselves Alone: Women's Emigration from Ireland, 1885–1920* (Lexington: University Press of Kentucky, 1989); Janet A. Nolan, *Servants of the Poor: Teachers and Mobility in Ireland and Irish America* (South Bend, IN: Notre Dame Press, 2004); Ely Janis, *A Greater Ireland: The Land League and Transatlantic Nationalism in Gilded Age America* (Madison: University of Wisconsin Press, 2015); Tara M. McCarthy, *Respectability and Reform: Irish American Women's Activism, 1880–1920* (Syracuse, NY: Syracuse University Press, 2018); Síobhra Aiken, '"Sinn Féin permits ... in the heels of their shoes": Cumann na mBan emigrants and transatlantic revolutionary exchange', *Irish Historical Studies*, 44:165 (2020), pp. 106–30. Useful overviews of the historiography of Irish women in the United States can be found in Bernadette Whelan, 'Women on the move: A review of the historiography of Irish emigration to the USA, 1750–1900', *Women's History Review*, 24:6 (2015), pp. 900–16, and Janet Nolan, 'Women's place in the history of the Irish diaspora: A snapshot', *Journal of American Ethnic History*, 28:4 (2009), pp. 76–81.
43. Trevor McClaughlin (ed.), *Irish Women in Colonial Australia* (St Leonards: Allen & Unwin, 1998); Coleman, '"In Harmony"; Elizabeth Malcolm and Dianne Hall, *A New History of the Irish in Australia* (Cork: Cork University Press, 2019); Lyndon Fraser, 'Irish women's networks on the west coast of New Zealand's South Island, 1864–1922', *Women's History Review*, 15:3 (2006), pp. 459–75; Angela McCarthy, '"In prospect of a happier future": private letters and Irish women's migration to New Zealand,

1840–1925', in Lyndon Fraser (ed.), *A Distant Shore: Irish Migration and New Zealand Settlement* (Dunedin: University of Otago Press, 2000), pp. 105–16.
44. Maureen Fitzgerald, *Habits of Compassion: Irish Catholic Nuns and the Origins of New York's Welfare System, 1830–1920* (Urbana: University of Illinois Press, 2006), p. 3.
45. Mary Beth Fraser Connolly, *Women of Faith: The Chicago Sisters of Mercy and The Evolution of a Religious Community* (New York: Fordham University Press, 2014); Catriona Clear, *Nuns in Nineteenth-Century Ireland* (Dublin: Gill & MacMillan, 1987); Carmen M. Mangion, *Contested Identities: Catholic Women Religious in Nineteenth-Century England and Wales* (Manchester: Manchester University Press, 2008); S. Karly Kehoe, *Creating a Scottish Church: Catholicism, Gender and Ethnicity in Nineteenth-Century Scotland* (Manchester: Manchester University Press, 2010).
46. Fitzgerald, *Habits of Compassion*, p. 8.
47. Cara Delay, *Irish Women and the Creation of Modern Catholicism, 1850–1950* (Manchester: Manchester University Press, 2019); Kathleen Sprows Cummings, *New Women of the Old Faith: Gender and American Catholicism in the Progressive Era* (Chapel Hill: University of North Carolina Press, 2009).
48. Nira Yuval-Davis, *The Politics of Belonging: Intersectional Contestations* (London: Sage Publications, 2011), p. 8.
49. Frederick Cooper, *Colonialism in Question: Theory, Knowledge, History* (Berkeley: University of California Press, 2005).
50. Kathleen Neils Conzen, David A. Gerber, Ewa Morawska, George E. Pozzetta and Rudolph J. Vecoli, 'The invention of ethnicity: A perspective from the USA', *Journal of American Ethnic History*, 12:1 (1992), pp. 3–41.
51. Alan O'Day, 'A conundrum of Irish diasporic identity: Mutative ethnicity', *Immigrants and Minorities*, 27:2–3 (2009), pp. 317–39.
52. Delaney, 'The Irish diaspora'.
53. Kerby A. Miller, 'Class, culture and immigrant group identity in the United States: The case of Irish-American ethnicity', in Virginia Yans-McLaughlin (ed.), *Immigration Reconsidered: History, Sociology, and Politics* (Oxford: Oxford University Press, 1990), pp. 96–129.
54. O'Day, 'A conundrum'.
55. Shaun Wiley, Krystal Perkins and Kay Deaux, 'Through the looking glass: Ethnic and generational patterns of immigrant identity', *International Journal of Intercultural Relations*, 32:5 (2008), pp. 385–98; Stuart Hall and Paul du Gay (eds), *Questions of Cultural Identity* (London: Sage Publications Ltd, 1996).
56. Wiley, Perkins and Deaux, 'Through the looking glass'.
57. John Belchem, 'Hub and diaspora: Liverpool and transnational labour', *Labour History Review*, 75:1 (2010), pp. 20–9. M. Alison Kibler explores

the protests launched against 'stage' Irishmen in *Censoring Racial Ridicule: Irish, Jewish, and African American Struggles over Race and Representation, 1890–1930* (Chapel Hill: University of North Carolina Press, 2015).
58. Donald M. MacRaild, *The Irish Diaspora in Britain, 1750–1939*, 2nd edn (Abingdon: Palgrave Macmillan, 2011), p. 3.
59. Crosbie, *Irish Imperial Networks*, p. 12; C. A. Bayly, *Empire and Information: Intelligence Gathering and Social Communication in India, 1780–1870* (Cambridge: Cambridge University Press, 1996).
60. Belchem, 'Hub'; Meagher, *Inventing Irish America*.
61. Meagher, *Inventing Irish America*, pp. 9–10.
62. Ibid.
63. Delaney, 'Irish diaspora'.
64. Belchem, *Irish, Catholic and Scouse*, p. 18.
65. Henri LeFebvre, *The Production of Space*, trans. Donald Nicholson-Smith (Oxford: Basil Blackwell, 1991); Richard Dennis, *Cities in Modernity: Representations and Productions of Metropolitan Space, 1840–1930* (Cambridge: Cambridge University Press, 2008).
66. Jay P. Dolan, *The American Catholic Experience: A History from Colonial Times to the Present* (Garden City: Doubleday & Co., 1985), p. 159.
67. David Fitzpatrick, 'The Irish in Britain: Settlers or transients?', in Patrick Buckland and John Belchem (eds), *The Irish in British Labour History: Conference Proceedings in Studies* (Liverpool: University of Liverpool Press, 1993), pp. 1–10.
68. Avtar Brah, *Cartographies of Diaspora: Contesting Identities* (London: Routledge, 1996), pp. 16, 181; Mary J. Hickman, Nicola Mai and Helen Crowley, *Migration and Social Cohesion in the UK* (Abingdon: Palgrave Macmillan, 2012).
69. Julie Codell, 'Introduction', in Julie Codell (ed.), *Imperial Co-Histories: National Identities and the British and Colonial Press* (London: Associated University Presses, 2003), pp. 15–28.
70. Kenny, 'Diaspora and comparison'; J. Matthew Gallman, *Receiving Erin's Children: Philadelphia, Liverpool, and the Irish Famine Migration, 1845–1855* (Chapel Hill: University of North Carolina Press, 2000), p. 17.
71. James Belich focused on the two cities in connection, using Melbourne and Chicago, along with London and New York, to analyse the reach of the expanding Anglo-World during the long nineteenth century. However, Belich's work does not focus on the people within the cities, nor their role in shaping the society or being shaped by them. James Belich, *Replenishing the Earth: The Settler Revolution and the Rise of the Anglo-World, 1783–1939* (Oxford: Oxford University Press, 2009).
72. Gunther Barth, *Instant Cities: Urbanization and the Rise of San Francisco and Denver* (Oxford: Oxford University Press, 1975), p. xxi.
73. Barth, *Instant Cities*, p. xxii. Harold L. Platt alters Barth's thesis, renaming Chicago a 'shock city', focusing on the environmental problems brought

about by rapid industrialisation. Platt, *Shock Cities: The Environmental Transformation and Reform of Manchester and Chicago* (Chicago: University of Chicago Press, 2005); Graeme Davison, *The Rise and Fall of Marvellous Melbourne* (Melbourne: Melbourne University Press, 1979), p. 6.
74. Barth, *Instant Cities*, pp. 156–63.
75. Ibid., pp. xxii–xiv.
76. Oliver MacDonagh, 'The Irish in Victoria, 1851-91: A Demographic Essay', in T. D. Williams (ed.), *Historical Studies: Papers Read Before the Irish Conference of Historians* (Dublin: Gill and Macmillan, 1971), pp. 67–92; Patrick Naughtin, 'The Green Flag at the Antipodes: Irish Nationalism in Colonial Victoria during the Parnell Era, 1880–91' (PhD: University of Melbourne, 2011); Patrick Naughtin, '*The Melbourne Advocate*, 1868–1900: Bastion of Irish nationalism in colonial Victoria', in Ciara Breathnach and Catherine Lawless (eds), *Visual, Material and Culture in Nineteenth-Century Ireland* (Dublin: Four Courts Press, 2010), pp. 223–33; Fitzpatrick, *Oceans of Consolation*.
77. Lawrence J. McCaffrey, Ellen Skerrett, Michael F. Funchion and Charles Fanning, *The Irish in Chicago* (Urbana: University of Illinois Press, 1987); Melvin Holli and Peter d'A. Jones (eds), *Ethnic Chicago: A Multicultural Portrait* (Grand Rapids, MI: Wm B. Eerdmans Publishing, 1995); Patricia Kelleher, 'Class and Catholic Irish masculinity in antebellum America: Young men on the make in Chicago', *Journal of American Ethnic History*, 28:4 (2004), pp. 7–42; Mimi Cowan, 'Immigrants, nativists, and the making of Chicago, 1835–1893' (PhD: Boston College, 2015).
78. Michael F. Funchion, *Chicago's Irish Nationalists, 1881–1890* (New York: Arno Press, 1976); McCaffrey et al., *The Irish in Chicago*; Gillian O'Brien, *Blood Runs Green: The Murder That Transfixed Gilded Age Chicago* (Chicago: University of Chicago Press, 2015).
79. Fariha Shaikh, *Nineteenth-Century Settler Emigration in British Literature and Art* (Edinburgh: Edinburgh University Press, 2019), p. 6.
80. Miriam Dobson and Benjamin Ziemann (eds), *Reading Primary Sources: The Interpretation of Texts from Nineteenth- and Twentieth-Century History* (London: Routledge, 2009), p. 13.
81. Hannah Barker, *Newspapers and English Society 1695–1855* (London: Routledge, 2014), p. 197.
82. Stephen Vella, 'Newspapers', in Dobson and Ziemann (eds), *Reading Primary Sources*, pp. 192–208.
83. Benedict Anderson, *Imagined Communities: Reflections on the Origin and Spread of Nationalism*, revised edn (London: Verso, 1991), pp. 42–3.
84. Larkin, 'Devotional revolution'.
85. Emmet Larkin, 'Paul Cullen: The great ultramontane', in Dáire Keogh and Albert McDonnell (eds), *Cardinal Paul Cullen and his World* (Dublin: Four Courts Press, 2011), pp. 15–33.

86. Maria Luddy, 'Women and philanthropy in nineteenth-century Ireland', *Voluntas: International Journal of Voluntary and Nonprofit Organizations*, 7:4 (1996), pp. 350–64; Clear, *Nuns*, p. xvi; Irene Whelan, 'Religious rivalry and the making of Irish-American identity', in J. J. Lee and Marion R. Casey (eds), *Making the Irish American: History and Heritage of the Irish in the United States* (New York: New York University, 2006), pp. 271–85.
87. Larkin, 'Devotional revolution'.
88. Fearghal McGarry and James McConnel (eds), *The Black Hand of Republicanism: Fenianism in Modern Ireland* (Dublin: Irish Academic Publishing, 2009), p. xix.
89. David Brundage, *Irish Nationalists in America: The Politics of Exile, 1798–1998* (Oxford: Oxford University Press, 2019), p. 5.

2

Melbourne and Chicago: An Introduction

In the early 1830s, the areas that would become the vibrant cities of Melbourne and Chicago were small trading posts. On the side of Lake Michigan and at the nexus of three rivers, Chicago was a hub for Native American and French-Canadian traders, while Port Philip, as Melbourne was then known, was the home of members of the Kulin Nation and the site of occasional excursions by British settlers based in Van Diemen's Land. Within two decades, both areas would explode into settlements of largely migrant European populations, becoming 'instant' or 'shock' cities during the 1850s: urban centres which quickly emerged as self-reliant cities based on a boom of natural and human resources and in spite of environmental pressures.[1] Irish immigrants arrived at the cusp of this transformation in the 1840s and continued to flow in throughout the nineteenth century, ensuring the existence of vibrant and vocal multi-generational Irish communities with a firm grasp of the industrial, political and social worlds of each city. This chapter explores the evolution of Melbourne and Chicago as urban centres and as homes for the Irish populations discussed in this book. In doing so, it considers the similarities and divergences of two cities which boomed, economically and demographically, emerging as important locations within the histories of the British empire, Australia and the United States by the end of the century.

Chicago or Chigagou, the 'wild garlic place', was the home of the Potawatomis in the early 1830s, where they carried out a thriving fur trade with the Sacs, Foxes, Ottawas and Chippewas as well as Europeans and Americans.[2] The first non-Native American settler in the area was Quebecois Jean Baptiste Point du Sable in the 1770s, followed by the establishment of the American military settlement Fort Dearborn in 1803 and its rebuilding after the War of 1812. Conflict between the

American military and Sac chief Black Hawk over Illinois lands in 1832 led to retribution on all indigenous peoples in the area in the form of land treaties, while glimpses of fertile land inspired the movement of vast numbers of Europeans and Americans from elsewhere in the United States to the banks of Lake Michigan.[3] White settlement in Melbourne began in 1835, when John Batman led a group of Europeans from Hobart in Van Diemen's Land. Prior to this, members of the Kulin Nation, mainly the Boonwurrung, Wathauroung and Wurundjeri People, occupied the area. After the so-called Batman Treaty of 1835, the only treaty ever extended to Aboriginal people in Australia by representatives of the British Government and one which, at least at face value, promised to protect the indigenous landholders, the area became known as Batman Hill, latterly Melbourne, within the Port Philip District.[4] After white settlement, a mixture of violence, missionary entreaties and municipal by-laws meant that Aboriginal members of the Kulin Nation were slowly pushed out of the city limits. By 1860, settler and indigenous life had become so segregated that it was possible for European visitors to the area to construct Melbourne as a 'white' city.[5]

The future prominence of Chicago was signalled in 1836 when the Illinois State Legislature authorised the digging of the Illinois and Michigan Canal, bringing the first large influx of immigrants to the area.[6] The next year, Chicago was incorporated as a city and by 1840 it had become home to around 4,500 people, overwhelmingly white men. Melbourne was officially incorporated as a city ten years after Chicago, in 1847. The turning point for Melbourne's population was the discovery of gold in rural Victoria in July 1851. As word spread of the potential riches to be found, gold prospectors streamed in. Between September 1851 and December 1852, the ground of Victoria yielded 4.6 million ounces of gold and brought between five and seven thousand people a month to Victoria's shores over the following two years, peaking in September and October 1852 when 16,000 and 19,000 people arrived respectively. While the majority of these arrivals headed straight to the goldfields of Ballarat and Bendigo, a failure to strike gold frequently sent prospectors back to Melbourne in the hopes of alternative employment.

The mid-nineteenth century signalled the advent of a new type of city: cities without a long history which benefited from an immediate prioritisation of industry and industriousness. Melbourne and Chicago had their settler roots in the land expansion of the 1830s and developed rapidly at the same time as Ireland's rural and Catholic population began to emigrate in large numbers. In the middle decade of the nineteenth century, Chicago's population increased by 250 per cent while

Melbourne's increased fourfold. As this huge expansion of European settlers occurred, the indigenous landholders were pushed out by treaty and through violence. By the 1880s, Melbourne and Chicago were the 'second cities' of their respective nations, with strong industrialised economies and some of the largest urban populations in the English-speaking world. The beginning of the twentieth century witnessed a tussle for continued prominence in their respective nations. Melbourne briefly succeeded, becoming Australia's capital city after Federation in 1901 and remaining in that coveted position until the more 'neutral' Canberra was awarded the prize spot in 1927. Chicago's position as the United States' railway hub ensured its continued importance in the nation, while its prominence in gangland activities drew the eyes of the world to its streets throughout the first decades of the new century.

YOUNG AND VIBRANT CITIES

Both of these burgeoning cities were host to transient populations. When building the city's institutions did not provide enough opportunities, Chicago's labouring population followed construction work out into wider Cook County, and the surrounds of Illinois and neighbouring states. Similarly, Melbourne was a stopping point for many of the travellers who arrived in the area, a place to buy essentials before heading to the goldfields, or to return to when faced with failure. Despite this, as the 1850s continued, Chicago and Melbourne's populations became more stable. David Galenson estimates that Chicago's young male society witnessed a 14 per cent turnover rate during the 1850s, the lowest in the main urban centres of the United States.[7] In Australia, the declining yields from the Victorian goldfields saw some prospectors return to their homes while others set sail for San Francisco and other goldfields. More journeyed back to Melbourne and began to build the emerging city. This stability was further aided when, also attracted to the job opportunities, more women arrived in each city. Irish emigration in the aftermath of the Famine was a 'unique European emigration', with Irish women emigrating in the same numbers as men.[8] In the second half of the nineteenth century, 1.9 million men and 1.8 million women emigrated from Ireland.[9] By the twentieth century, higher numbers of women were leaving Ireland than men.[10] Changes in landownership patterns in Ireland led to a decrease in status for women, particularly those without dowries, and therefore a rise in single women. Faced with increased chances of dependence on older siblings or the convent, Irish women left to find jobs and, to a lesser extent, husbands, abroad.

While men outnumbered women in rural districts, single women tended to remain in the urban environment, where there were more possibilities for quick and respectable employment and lodgings with families and other single women. This would become a source of concern for emigration societies preoccupied with the moral health of migrant women, with many explicitly recruiting women to settle in more rural areas.[11] Earlier in the century, in an attempt to even out the single-male influx that had accompanied the gold rushes, 21 per cent of assisted migrants from the United Kingdom were Irish women compared to Irish men who accounted for 9 per cent between 1848 and 1856. This preference for women was reflected in every national group from the United Kingdom; the British and colonial legislatures' attempt, according to Robin Haines, at 'social engineering'.[12] Despite these opportunities, the networks and prospects for employment and marriage were better in urban centres than in rural districts and women overwhelmingly rejected the encouragement to settle in rural areas, continuing a trend of male-dominated rural Victoria and female-dominated urban space. In Melbourne, Irish-born women marginally outnumbered their male counterparts in the city and every suburb between 1857 and 1921.[13] This near equity in numbers of Irish men and women in both Melbourne and Chicago enabled the creation of multi-generational Irish communities abroad, where Irish men and women could marry each other and raise families while retaining their Irishness.

These were *young* cities dominated by young people. The cities flourished, with the majority of their citizens under the age of thirty.[14] In 1850 they accounted for 30,113 of Cook County's 43,385 inhabitants.[15] In Victoria four years earlier, the mean age of the population was 23.6 years – 25.7 for men and 20.3 for women – increasing to 24.5 in 1854 before declining each decade until 1891, when a peak mean age of 25.6 was reached.[16] By 1911, 57 per cent of Melbourne's population was under thirty years of age.[17] As one contemporary visitor to Melbourne observed, 'the population of a young colony has not, as a rule, many aged people: it is mostly composed of the young and healthy of both sexes: such only are fitted, and such only selected by emigration agents to perform the hard work of colonization.'[18] For young people, Melbourne and Chicago provided opportunities for entertainment, employment and marriage. The dominance of childbearing-aged people, particularly as the cities grew, led to a need for infrastructure: churches to get married in and for babies to be baptised, schools and hospitals, and saloons and dance halls for entertainment. In both cities, the Catholic Church fought to provide much of this initial infrastructure, particularly as the numbers of Irish Catholics leaving Ireland for new opportunities in the United States and Australia began to rise. This battle for control will be explored in future chapters.

By 1921 the Irish-born population of Chicago and Melbourne had aged and declined in number. The exact numbers of Irish-born people in Melbourne after 1891 are difficult to judge – the 1901 census was not published, and in 1911 and 1921, Irish birth was only noted at state level. At a micro-level, Irish birth was lumped in with 'British Isles' and British nationality. In 1911, however, there were 41,477 people of Irish birth in Victoria, decreasing from 61,512 in 1901. By 1921 they only accounted for 27,242 of Victoria's 754,724 total population and were largely aged above forty.[19] The new Commonwealth of Australia (established in 1901) passed the Immigration Restriction Act, effectively creating a White Australia policy.[20] Although this policy did not exclude Irish migrants, there was a general decrease in the numbers heading to 'Marvellous' Melbourne. Similarly, until 1924, Irish migrants were exempt from immigration quotas into the United States. However, the First World War slowed international migration generally.[21] When Irish people did choose to leave the emerging Irish State, they increasingly headed to Britain.[22] While the Irish communities of Melbourne and Chicago had been refreshed with new and young arrivals throughout the nineteenth century, by the first decades of the twentieth century they were increasingly made up of Irish-born elders and second-generation youngsters. As later chapters will explore, this had important effects on the associational culture and nationalism of Melbourne and Chicago's Irish communities.

Table 1 Population of Melbourne and Chicago with percentage increase[23]

	Melbourne	% Increase	Chicago	% Increase
1840/1	4,479	—	4,470	—
1850/1	23,143	417	29,963	570
1860/1	114,998	397	109,260	265
1870/1	204,741	78	298,977	174
1880/1	282,947	38	503,185	68
1890/1	425,892	50	1,099,850	119
1900/1	496,079	16	1,698,575	54
1910/11	588,971	19	2,185,283	29
1920/21	765,865	30	2,701,705	24

MIGRANT COMMUNITIES

Migration was a constant feature of each city, forcing their societies to adapt to and incorporate the new influences that arrived on ships, trains and carts each year. It is impossible to consider migration as a static or one-off event. As the populations of Melbourne and Chicago doubled between census years, immigrants and their children found similarities and differences, worked together and pushed back against each other, to find their own space and community abroad. The massive increase of Irish-born people living outside Ireland was originally prompted by the Great Famine of 1845–52. Prior to the peaks of the 1850s, 48 per cent of the assisted migrants arriving in New South Wales and Victoria were Irish, despite them making up only 30 per cent of the United Kingdom's population.[24] Similarly, before the Famine Irish people contributed around one-third of all immigrants into the United States.[25] The devastation wrought by the Famine led to a dramatic decline in Ireland's population, the forced removal of starving tenants often in family units abroad by Irish landlords, and the emptying of British and Irish poorhouses into foreign cities. The change in rural Irish Catholic landownership and emigration patterns, and the forced establishment of Irish communities abroad, enabled future chain migration and new networks within the growing Irish diaspora.[26] Though Ireland's close neighbours England and Scotland received large numbers of Irish people, it was the United States which received the highest proportions of Irish immigrants. Buoyed by stories of financial opportunities and success, the United States was home to 48 per cent of Irish-born people living outside of Ireland by 1861, compared to the 3.5 per cent to be found in Australia. By 1870 this had risen respectively to 60.5 per cent and 6.8 per cent.[27]

The 'founding fathers' of Chicago were French Canadians and native-born Americans, though the Canadians soon gave way to European immigrants. By 1852, just over half of Chicago's population was foreign-born, almost two-thirds of whom were from the Germanic states and around one-third from Ireland.[28] They were joined by small numbers of immigrants from Britain, France and Scandinavia. While Italians had been present in Chicago from 1850, they only made up a handful of the city's population until the great wave of southern European immigrants arrived in the 1880s.[29] The same was true of free African Americans, a very small community until the Great Migration of 1910–50.[30] Chicago's ethnic make-up was mixed, but Germans and Irish people competed for numerical dominance and primacy in the job market throughout the first four decades of the city's existence. In Melbourne, the distance from Europe, the colony's position within the British empire, and the immigration control that those two factors allowed for, ensured the dominance of white migrants from Britain and Ireland from the 1840s. The gold rushes brought Chinese labourers to the colony, and a promise of opportunity increasingly encouraged the migration of small numbers of African Americans, Germans and Scandinavians, and other colonised subjects from across the British empire as the decades progressed.[31]

While emigrants from Britain and Ireland dominated Melbourne society, Chicago was an ethnically plural city which gained new immigrant groups each year. These new arrivals joined American-born children of immigrants, creating multi-generational migrant communities which varied in occupation and financial status. The Superintendent of the US Federal Census in 1850 observed that these close Irish communities led many Irish parents to report their American-born children as 'natives of Ireland'. He noted that

> Foreigners associate so exclusively together, and are socially so generally separated from the natives for a long time, that their feelings of alienship are inseparably connected with their families, and their children as well as with themselves, and they do not always discriminate between locality of birth, parentage, blood, origin, even religion, and sometimes they merge all into one class, calling all Irish, &c., who are sons of Irish soil, because they have a common blood, origin, or religion.[32]

Despite this emphasis on Irish community, Irish populations spread themselves through both cities instead of settling in Irish enclaves as in other cities.[33] By the 1870s, working and living alongside people of a different nationality was a common experience and the 'myth of ethnic segregation simply did not hold true' in either city.[34] As Louise Carroll Wade has noted, even Chicago areas like the Irish-dominated Bridgeport were ethnically mixed.[35] The Irish in Chicago and Melbourne lived side by side with their non-Irish peers, though they may have chosen to associate socially based upon ethnicity. The reasons for this will be explored later in this chapter.

Despite the large disparity in absolute numbers of Irish people arriving in the United States and Australia, Melbourne and Chicago attracted remarkably similar proportions of Irish immigrants until the 1880s (see Table 2).[36] The Irish-born populations of Melbourne and Chicago varied in character but, until 1891, not in size relative to city totals. While it may seem irrelevant to compare an Irish-born community of 70,000 to one of 29,000 (as in 1890/1), a look at the information in

Table 2 demonstrates the importance of comparison. Despite a diverging number of Irish-born people in each city after the 1870/1 censuses, one important element remains similar: the position of the Irish-born in proportion to the larger population. Class remained an important way of separating city populations by ethnicity and occupation, and this was true for both Melbourne and Chicago in the first decades of the twentieth century.[37]

The 'Irish' community as a whole cannot be quantified due to the lack of census material, but the 1890 census notes 149,795 white people living in Chicago with both parents born in Ireland, with an additional 33,547 with at least one Irish parent.[38] While the census records 70,000 Irish-born people living in Chicago in 1890, consideration of the Irish 'community' should take into account American-born children and adults who were raised by Irish parents and in Irish-staffed schools and churches. In Chicago, this would increase the 'community' size by 113,500 or 16.7 per cent. A similar extrapolation of the Irish community, additional to the Irish-born population, can be made in Melbourne. Of course, not all Irish-born or second-generation Irish actively involved themselves with 'Irish' diasporic life, but these figures are useful when illustrating the numbers of people involved in moments of Irish public life, for example on St Patrick's Day.

Table 2 Irish-born population in Melbourne and Chicago, 1850–90[39]

	Melbourne Irish-born	Irish-born as % of Melbourne's population	Chicago Irish-born	Irish-born as % of Chicago's population
1850/51	4,584	19.8	6,096	20.3
1860/61	17,495	15.2	19,889	18.2
1870/71	28,878	14.1	39,988	13.4
1880/81	25,753	9.1	44,411	8.8
1890/91	29,469	6.9	70,028	6.4
1920/21	N/A	N/A	56,786	2.1

MAKING IT IN/TO THE CITY

Scholarship on the Irish in Australia and America has focused on geographical and occupational backgrounds as a motivating factor in differing journeys of adaption and interaction abroad. Oliver MacDonagh and David Fitzpatrick have argued that the preponderance of migrants, particularly farmers from the more prosperous areas of Kilkenny, Tipperary, east Limerick, east Clare and north Cork, along with the

Ulster border counties, led to a less radical Irish diasporic community in Australia.[40] America's post-Famine migration was more mixed, leading to a greater number of poverty-stricken, Irish-speaking migrants from Connaught and Munster, which had an opposite effect on the political outlooks of Irish migrants in the United States. While Melbourne received migrants from a range of backgrounds, overall, Irish migrants to Melbourne left Ireland with a higher social status than those who migrated to Chicago.

Melbourne and wider Victoria were 'synonymous with fame and fortune', and in 1852 and 1853 more British and Irish emigrants bought tickets to Melbourne than to any other place in the world.[41] The people that bought these tickets had the resources to travel and made a choice to chase the possibility of wealth, bringing the second sons of wealthy families and experienced businessmen to the city as well as less financially secure fortune hunters. However, while some paid around £6 to get to the port of Williamstown, roughly five miles from Melbourne, most British and Irish migrants to Melbourne did so with some assistance from the Colonial Land and Emigration Commission. Between 1831 and 1850, only one in three emigrants to Australia paid their own fare.[42] The rise in workhouse intake during the 1840s and 1850s, particularly during the Irish and Scottish famines, meant that new schemes had to be dreamed up, with the Australian colonies promoted as a fitting place to send the poor of the United Kingdom.

The high proportion of Catholics in Irish workhouses was reflected in an increase of Catholic arrivals during the mid-nineteenth century, encouraged by assisted emigration schemes, which meant that until 1890 many parishes only had to pay an emigrant's fare to the point of embarkation, usually Liverpool, whereas they had to pay for an American emigrant's entire voyage.[43] Assisted migration may have acted as a cost-saving measure for parish authorities, but most potential migrants were still required to pay an expensive deposit and buy their own travelling clothes in order to avail of government assistance to Australia. Instead, a pattern of friend and family chain migration, which exempted migrants from government restrictions, was the preferred option for those reaching Victoria. When a group of Members of the Legislative Assembly (MLAs) suggested restricting the numbers of Irish Catholics recruited for assisted passage, Martin Hood MLA refuted the idea. Hood argued that discriminating against recruiting Irish Catholics via agents would be pointless as four-fifths of those who sent home for their friends, and therefore were not in need of government encouragement, were Irish Roman Catholics.[44] The colony received the lowest percentage of assisted migrants from 1850, dropping from 86 per cent in 1848 to 35 per cent in 1852.[45] During the 1850s these assisted migrants could be recruited by emigration agents, who would travel around the United Kingdom and provide information about the wonders of the British colony, or they could be put forward by 'sponsors' already in Australia. The schemes had the perceived extra advantage of tempering the 'influx' of Chinese migrants who had arrived in Victoria with the finding of gold. While Melbourne society had elements of anti-Irish and anti-Catholic sentiment, it focused its hatred and fear on the 'race weaker than themselves': the male Chinese workers.[46] However, the swift growth of the city outpaced its infrastructural progress.

Fitzpatrick has argued that Irish immigrants headed to Australia tended to be 'economic outcasts whom "modernization" had left with cash but without a life-line'. After the Famine, the Irish tradition of splitting land between a family's sons was overturned; younger sons lost their expected land inheritance and therefore often the chance to marry well.[47] These younger sons were in clear contrast with the majority of Irish immigrants to the United States, those left without cash but little altered social status. However, recent research has uncovered that a disproportionately large number of immigrants to Illinois were from the 'northern *half* of Ireland (not Ulster alone)' during the Famine. Even during the chaos of the Famine, migrants from Antrim, Armagh, Derry and Down tended to be more skilled than those from elsewhere in Ireland, with around 50 per cent migrating as labourers opposed to the higher rate of 70 per cent elsewhere in Ireland.[48] While the poorer counties of Donegal, Roscommon and Cavan undermined this northern bias toward more skilled work, Tyler Anbinder and Hope McCaffrey's research indicates a migration stream from Ireland to Illinois with increased financial capabilities and family connections. Understanding the social backgrounds of migrants is often more important than examining their county of origin, particularly in regard to exploring the social position that the middle classes adopted in Melbourne and Chicago, where the formal county associations of New York were noticeably absent from parish life.[49] Poor Irish immigrants were often more readily accepted by their non-Irish societal peers than by their Irish social betters.

The Irish-born contingent of each city rose rapidly until the 1870s. While the reasons for the downturn in migration to Melbourne and Chicago vary, and the death of earlier Irish-born settlers should be taken into account, there was a strong link to the economy. The Panic of 1873 was influenced by an international agricultural depression and affected Ireland badly in the short and long term, culminating in a period of hunger and rural unrest in Ireland between 1878 and 1881. As the colony of Victoria was not negatively affected by the depression, the active downturn in the number of Irish-born residents was linked in part to the 1872 restructuring of the United Kingdom's Colonial Land and Emigration Commission and its reduced role in state-assisted migration.[50] In Chicago, 1877 was the worst year of the economic collapse, leading to wage reductions and job losses, vital information transmitted to Ireland through newspapers, family letters and religious anti-immigration societies.[51]

Although opportunities to go abroad were decreasing, Ireland in the late 1870s was in dire need of its traditional 'safety valve' of emigration. The agricultural depression of 1878–81 had important consequences for the cause of Irish nationalism: the Land War and an upsurge in tenants' rights agitation occurred at the same time as increased popularity for the Irish Parliamentary Party and Charles Stewart Parnell.[52] As Irish emigration to both America and Australia was dependent on chain migration, the depression of the 1870s impacted the ability of family and friends to pay for potential emigrants' passage. The subsequent economic improvement of the 1880s signalled a recovery of, and increase in, the number of Irish-born in Chicago and Melbourne. For those destined for Chicago, this coincided with the growing importance of Chicago internationally and locally, including a rise in fortunes in Irish nationalist activities in the United States. This improvement of status and economic opportunity led to rising internal migration into Chicago as well as internationally.[53] The economic recovery of Ireland and Britain coincided with increased migration into Melbourne, while the decline of Melbourne's economy, brought about by wild land speculation, maritime strikes and the shrinking of foreign investment, led to a reversal of its previous population and wealth boom.[54] Ireland's economic recovery would not last very long and, by 1911, one-third of those born in Ireland lived outside of the country.[55] Irish emigration reached a height of 915 persons to Australia and 21,758 to the United States in 1913. The outbreak of the First World War slowed international travel exponentially, reducing the total numbers of people emigrating from Ireland to 980 in 1918. By 1920, international travel had restarted but in much smaller numbers than before the war, and subsequently decreased steeply. In 1917, thirteen people emigrated from Ireland to Australia.[56]

INDUSTRY

Mud is a word frequently applied to Chicago and Melbourne in their early years of settlement. When Ellen Clacy arrived in Melbourne in 1852, she described 'Mud and swamp – swamp and mud'. While Melbourne's inhabitants had begun to build institutions and organise the town, the discovery of gold had 'completely upset everything and everybody, and put a stop to all improvements about the town'.[57] Men involved in building the town's infrastructure fled to the goldfields, leaving a resource-rich but labour-poor community squelching through the mud. Similarly, Chicago's position next to Lake Michigan and in swamplands made mud a constant problem. In 1856, Chicago's streets had yet to be artificially elevated 'above the swamp which the almost indecipherable laws of commerce had made the site of a great city. An air of newness was over everything.'[58] In the mid-century there was a real risk that the people of Chicago would literally sink in their homes and on their roads if not for the work of immigrant labourers. This artificial elevation was still not completed by the turn of the century, continuing the need for new supplies of cheap labour.

Due to Chicago's rapidly expanding industries there were constant labour shortages, leaving Chicago's manufacturers beholden to its immigrants and separating the city from established cities like Philadelphia and Boston. While nativist politics gained in popularity throughout the United States during the 1850s, they failed to take hold of Chicago politics for long. The only Know-Nothing (American Party) Mayor of Chicago, Levi Boone, was elected in 1855, and for a time there were sympathetic newspapers 'willing to nurse the bigotry and intolerance that gave them voice'.[59] Boone and his city council enacted laws requiring that the city only hired native-born Americans and that beer licences were raised in price, alienating Germans who worked in and owned the city's breweries, and the Irish and German labourers who sought employment and entertainment in them.[60] The subsequent political collaboration between Irish and German communities in Chicago resulted in the unseating of Boone within a year, and the reminder that '[f]rom the very first Chicago has been indebted to foreign-born citizens'.[61] The native-born American population was in the minority. It could ill afford to alienate the workforce that it relied upon to create the city's infrastructure, especially when the city was still firmly, or not so firmly, at its foundational level.

In the mid-1850s, Melbourne's economy crashed as the goldfields yielded less precious metal. The reduction of gold discoveries by

1855 turned attention and, importantly, labour resources back to the expanding Melbourne, with incredible results. By 1861, Melbourne had become 'the largest as well as the most glamorous city on the continent', with thriving cultural establishments, including Irishman Redmond Barry's brainchild, Melbourne Public Library.[62] Melbourne's community builders sought to transfer British institutions to the colonial city, creating a sense of order and familiarity across the world.[63] Graeme Davison argues that the founders of urban Australia were 'not from the villa-owning classes, but from those mobile sections of the British working class that had contributed most to the urbanisation of Britain itself'.[64] Labour radicalism mixed with the working-class roots of urban Australia to create a Melbourne concerned with social reform, in theory if not action. Beginning in 1854 with the Eureka Stockade,[65] Melbourne and the other cities of Victoria were host to a series of strikes and reforms leading to the perception of the colony as a 'working man's paradise'.[66] In 1856, Melbourne workers in the building trades achieved the eight-hour day, joined by the coachbuilders and irons trades over the next few years.

In the short term, Melbourne's transient population was a burden to be carried through the charity of more geographically and financially stable members of society. A 'Canvas Town' emerged on the banks of the River Yarra. Though initially a temporary camp area, by 1854 the area had two schools, one Presbyterian and one Catholic.[67] The Canvas Town later became known as Emerald Hill, a reflection of the Irish demography of its inhabitants. Small export industries, wheat and wool, were re-established, expanded, and the economy recovered quite rapidly. Utilising the economic markets of the British empire between 1865 and 1888, Victoria's wheat output increased sevenfold, half of which was exported. Its wool output roughly tripled in the same period, over 90 per cent of which was exported.[68] These industries would lead to Melbourne's meteoric rise to 'Marvellous Melbourne' in the 1880s and through its protectionist economic stance, exempted it from the recessions that afflicted much of the rest of the Western world during the 1870s.[69] The 1880s were a time when trade and social ties were consolidated to make Melbourne 'marvellous'. The emigration of free settlers, people who possessed a desire to help themselves and had certain economic and social resources, were hailed as the reason for Melbourne's success and served 'to animate "Marvellous Melbourne" in the coming generation'.[70] Melbourne continued to rise in stability and international importance until the 1890s, when the economy based upon land speculation and foreign investment imploded.[71]

Chicago's position by Lake Michigan and within the canal and rail complex helped its economic boom. However, it was the Civil War that cemented Chicago's place within the United States' power hierarchy. Initially greeted with horror, it soon emerged that for Chicago the Civil War would provide 'a wonderful stimulus to its commerce and manufactures'.[72] Rail link improvements during the 1850s meant that by the time war broke out, Chicago was established as the western terminus of the trade rail route from New York via New York State, Ohio and Pennsylvania. Through the canal network, the city's transport reach also extended down the Mississippi River. The war brought an increased demand for Chicago's resources, and its position as a transport hub meant that troops, munitions and supplies could be moved to any part of the country with relative ease. Additionally, the Civil War stimulated the progress and use of machinery in the area as production continued apace despite the reduction of previously available manpower.[73] Chicago's entrepreneurs established industries to cater for the Union's troops: stockyards to sell and buy animals, slaughterhouses to kill them and salting factories to preserve the meat before it was loaded onto railroad lorries. Further industries emerged using the by-products of these animals, and soap and candle makers set up shop near the stockyards. By the end of the Civil War, the Chicago Union Stockyard District provided employment for thousands of people, which continued over the next century.[74] These industries, the Stockyards and associated slaughterhouses, as well as towns like Pullman which were directly related to the railroads, meant that the population of Chicago doubled in each census year during the nineteenth century. This shock city exploded with people and with them came a smelly, noisy city where human and animal tussled for space.

An early historian of Chicago, Bessie Louise Pierce, observed that the growth of Chicago as an influential American and global city was the result of several factors, 'but it was accelerated by the faith of all these Chicagoans in the future of their city, a faith so assertive and boastful that it became contagious'.[75] This self-esteem had existed from Chicago's early days, usually in competition with the seeming ease and overindulgence of established cities like Boston and Philadelphia. Chicago's inhabitants believed that the city's rise to prominence was 'the natural outcome of a realistic evaluation of the city's progress', a product of their society's youth, enterprise and energy.[76] This self-belief was tested to its fullest on 8–9 October 1871, when the Great Chicago Fire, skipping over a Chicago River layered with animal fat from the stockyards, wiped out an area four miles long and three-quarters of a mile across in central Chicago. With close to 17,500 buildings burnt down, 100,000 homeless and between 120 and 300 dead, Chicago's municipal government and charitable institutions had to come together to avoid a breakdown in order and a slowing of the city's progress on the global stage. Newspapermen and contemporary observers proudly proclaimed that Chicago's men and women rose to the challenge with the 'motto on a shingle stuck up amid the ruins long before they had cooled, "All gone but wife, children, and energy."'[77] The supposed cause of the fire, Mrs O'Leary's infamous cow, caused a brief resurgence in anti-Irish comment but, as immigrant neighbourhoods were some of the worst hit and more labour was needed to repair the damage, Chicago continued to welcome more workers from across the country and further afield.[78] Over the next decade Chicago became a home for labour radicalism, culminating in the 1886 Haymarket bombing and the 1893 Pullman Strike. The involvement of newly arrived immigrants in these activities, combined with the prominence of Irish physical-force nationalists in the city, stirred up anti-immigrant sentiment in the final decades of the nineteenth century. However, the more established Irish and Germans, those who had arrived in earlier periods of immigration, retained control of city politics and policing. The economic recession slowed the population explosion during the 1870s; however, the 1880s brought about economic recovery and new employment opportunities. By the time of the 1890 census the city's population had increased by another 119 per cent. Labour and ethnic unrest continued into the new century alongside increasing city-level corruption.[79]

By 1891, Melbourne was almost half the size of Chicago, and bigger than St Louis, Cincinnati and San Francisco. James Belich argues that 'Relative to host populations, [Melbourne] was even more remarkable than Chicago' and both were named among 'the marvels of the world'.[80] The Australian economy decreased by 30 per cent between 1891 and 1895, an economic position that was further condemned by a decade-long drought across eastern Australia.[81] The Federal Conventions of the late 1890s ended in the establishment of the Commonwealth of Australia, and Melbourne became the temporary capital city of the newly federated country.[82] This brought the eyes of the world to the city, and would have important repercussions for the Irish, and particularly the Irish Catholic Church, in Melbourne. While Chicago's race riots of the 1910s brought negative press to the city, migrants continued to flock in due to the economy's steady growth.[83] The history of Chicago was one of reinvention and rejuvenation, and though the position of immigrants fluctuated, they were afforded more opportunities to declare their national identities and move throughout society than in older and more entrenched cities.

IRISHNESS, EMPLOYMENT AND CLASS

In nineteenth-century Chicago, there were certain jobs which attracted Irish people more than others. Kevin Kenny has noted that the 'Irish provided most of the muscle and brawn' of canal building and were a cheap, expendable labour force throughout the United States.[84] As such, Irish men dominated Chicago's labour industry and Irish women the city's domestic service between 1850 and 1880.[85] They followed a trend visible throughout the United States. In 1860, around 60 per cent of gainfully employed adult Irish immigrant males held unskilled jobs compared to 15 per cent of native-born Americans. The construction of 'skilled' or 'unskilled' work is problematic and wrapped up in perceptions of class and respectability. These terms, used by census enumerators and therefore difficult to dismiss, ignore the range of skills involved in labouring and domestic service. For example, while the agricultural backgrounds of many Irish immigrants meant that they were more suited to non-skilled manual work than Germans and Americans, this also meant that they dominated as teamsters, car-men and draymen.[86] Irish people also dominated manual labour jobs in Melbourne, though they did not become prominent union leaders until the 1870s, when more skilled workers arrived from Ireland and the Australian-born children of Irish immigrants began to reach adulthood.[87] In both cities, occupational networks were created, bringing people together based upon occupation, ethnicity and geographical base. Those involved in the railway industry were focused in the north and west of Melbourne, and Emerald Hill's proximity to the River Yarra created 'an uninterrupted vista of foundries, factories, and stores of all descriptions' related to the river and harbour trades.[88]

This spread of Irish people across multiple industries and locations discouraged Irish ethnic clustering, while the white skin of most Irish migrants meant that bureaucratic ghettoisation never emerged in the same way that it did for Chinese people in Melbourne or African Americans in Chicago. In 1870 and 1880, 52 per cent of working Irishmen and women in Chicago worked in the 'Personal and Professional Services', predominantly as labourers or domestic servants, and were overrepresented in the unskilled and semi-skilled labour markets.[89] Domestic servants frequently 'lived in' with their employers, forcing Irish women to live in neighbourhoods with few Irish homeowners. The employment opportunities for English-speaking Irish women in Melbourne and Chicago allowed women to remain single if they desired and supported them when eligible men were not to be found.[90] Domestic service and later teaching were principal occupations for Irish women in both cities, though as Chapter 5 demonstrates, religious life also beckoned for some. Letters and money from abroad, particularly from older sisters, aunts and cousins, further encouraged the mixed emigration of Irish sons and daughters.

Irish people were dominant in 'unskilled' jobs, but they also found powerful positions in skilled occupations and those concerned with law and order. This allowed for class-based community action and cross-class influence when required. For many, this class-based community action became particularly relevant in the 1870s. The immigrant labour that arrived in response to Chicago's fire-inspired construction boom became an unemployment problem when the city's economy was struck by international recession in 1873. The Panic of 1873 'constituted the city's first great crisis of hegemony', as Chicago's working class reacted against the growing industrial society leaders, separating employers from producers, and slowing production through 'widespread strikes and quasi-insurrectionary rebellion of the immigrant working class during the 1877 railroad strikes'.[91] These strikes set the stage for a newly unionised Chicago, inspired by international socialism and largely led by German labour revolutionaries. This increase in labour radicalism coincided with a change in immigrant nationalities in the city, with southern Europeans joined by an expansion in the Ukrainian and Polish communities during the 1880s.[92] While the skilled trades had organised in the 1850s in Melbourne and pushed for the eight-hour day, in the 1870s Melbourne's unskilled labourers unionised. By 1879 there were seventeen eight-hour trades in Melbourne, and by 1888, forty-six.[93] This increased unionisation culminated in a number of strikes during the 1880s, which continued into the early twentieth century and the creation of a powerful Labor Party in the city.[94]

By the mid-1860s, Irish people had found alternative ways of exercising influence in each city, largely through entry into the professions, police and politics. Irishmen made up 36 per cent of Chicago's union leadership in 1864 and expanded their influence across ward and, later, city politics as the nineteenth century progressed.[95] Contacts within the government were utilised to benefit the ethnic community, politically and financially. The corruption that late nineteenth-century Chicago became known for was used advantageously by its Irish citizens.[96] John O'Shanassy, Charles Gavan Duffy and Bryan O'Loghlen all became state premiers in Victoria, raising Irish-born and Catholic men to the highest political office of the state and placing them alongside the most influential men in the British empire. While Dianne Hall and Elizabeth Malcolm have highlighted the religious and anti-Irish discrimination experienced by these men,[97] their rise undermines both the contemporary argument that Irish Catholics were unable to govern themselves, and the historiographical argument of Patrick O'Farrell that the Irish in Melbourne were largely 'Munster peasants' without their own leaders.[98] Outside of business elites, Irish people, particularly Trinity College Dublin-educated, were over-represented in the colony in law, medicine and journalism, as they were throughout the British empire.[99]

In addition to politics, Irishmen claimed power and prestige in each city through the police. In 1866, Irish-born men made up an estimated 27 per cent of policemen in Chicago. As a sign of their growing influence, six out of the eight men in the city's detective department were of Irish descent, as were three captains and two sergeants in the force. In certain districts in the city, Irish-born men accounted for five of six police officers.[100] As a typical police officer in Chicago could make between six and seven hundred dollars a year, it was a dangerous but lucrative occupation, which had the added perk of lengthening the arm of the often-corrupt city political machine. As will be seen later, occupational and ethnic networks and associations often overlapped and aided their members, helping to provide job opportunities and social security while also contributing to ethnic stereotyping and suspicion. Similarly, ex-members of the Royal Irish Constabulary and British Army shaped the Victorian police force. Due to the promotion of Irish policing traditions as the ideal within the British colonies, Irish officers were encouraged to move around the empire, exporting Irish training as well as 'ideas about policies and procedures, [and] uniforms'.[101] Irish networks were actively encouraged within the police forces of the empire. By 1874, 82 per cent of the police officers in Victoria were Irish-born.[102] Therefore, at the same time as Irish people were characterised as drunken troublemakers,[103] they were also providing the hard edge of law and order at a policing and legislative level. Irish men and women found a place and networks within each stratum of Melbourne and Chicago society influencing the shape of the new city and the social priorities therein.

RELIGION

While this book seeks to explore 'Irish' community life and identity in Melbourne and Chicago, it is primarily focused on Irish Catholics and the role of the Catholic Church as an institution. Irish Protestants existed in both cities and, at times, held important roles in the associational culture of Irish life abroad. However, during the 1850s, 83 per cent of the Irish in Australia were Catholic, and 80 per cent in America.[104] These figures reflect a similar denominational make-up to Ireland at the time: 80.9 per cent in 1834 before dropping to around 77 per cent from 1861.[105] The influence of the devotional revolution and reduction of religious oppression in Ireland led to a surge in regular Mass attendance as the nineteenth century progressed. By 1911, 75 per cent of Irish people were Catholic, with the proportion rising in what would become the Irish Free State after Partition where, in 1936, 93.5 per cent of the population was Catholic.[106]

The Catholic Church in Chicago was one of a multitude of nationalities: Irish, German, Polish and French, to name a few. Catholics dominated the Irish, Germanic and Polish populations of the city, though each also had Protestant elements. They coexisted alongside Jews from Bavaria, Scandinavian Lutherans and native-born American and British Protestants in the city. The Catholic Church in Melbourne was a much more English-speaking affair, dominated by an Irish laity and clergy with a few English exceptions.[107] Protestants were also noticeable in the lists of notable Irish in Victoria. Across Victoria, Protestants outnumbered Catholics roughly three to one in all census years. The migration of Trinity College Dublin-educated men and extended families sending out all their second and third sons to the colony meant that among the key figures of Melbourne, and Melbourne Irish society, both Protestant and Catholic Irish people were represented. At times this led to a more inclusive ethnic associational culture in Melbourne, but this cross-denominational cooperation was increasingly swayed by class allegiances, with Irish Protestants more likely to associate with other Protestants or class peers than Irish Catholics. A similar separation emerged in Chicago, but the Protestant Irish population was seemingly much smaller and definitely much less vocal in the city than in Melbourne or in Canadian cities such as Toronto.[108] The Catholic Church and the role of the Irish within each city's hierarchy, religious orders and laity are important considerations in the formation of Irish community life in Melbourne and Chicago.

Power was wielded by Irish Catholics in both cities. All three of Melbourne's Catholic archbishops from 1848 to 1963 were Irish-born, as were four of Chicago's five Catholic (arch)bishops between 1844 and 1902. This Irish prominence was reflected through the clergy and religious orders of both cities. By 1890, Chicago was the largest Catholic centre in the Midwest, second only to New York City in the whole of the United States. Members of the Irish Catholic laity also frequently rose to the status of mayor, politician, magistrate and merchant. While

Melbourne's municipal governments were dominated by Irish Catholics from the 1850s, Chicago gained its first Irish Catholic mayor in 1893, when John P. Hopkins took office. In 1905, Irish American Edward Dunne, the son of two Irish nationalists whose families had been exiled after the 1798 and 1848 rebellions, was elected.[109] These men were followed in the office by another seven Irish-American Catholics. The close nature of religious parish life and political power in both Melbourne and Chicago ensured a continued connection between Catholic social life and politics well into the twentieth century. As later chapters will demonstrate, the priorities of Irish Catholicism would be promoted at every level of Melbourne and Chicago society from an early stage. This book's focus reflects the dominance of the Catholic Irish and the nature of archival materials relating to Irish communities in both cities.

CONCLUSION

Although they are almost 10,000 miles apart, the stories of Chicago and Melbourne mirror one another to a striking degree, both in terms of their dramatic evolution from small settlements into booming hubs and major players in a global context, and in the heritage of the Irish communities within them. Melbourne and Chicago had similar beginnings in terms of economic and population booms, as well as a philosophical outlook based on individual endeavour and the uniqueness of their city. These cities, which adhere to Gunther Barth's concept of an 'instant city', were in competition for respect and acceptance from their older counterparts, and their populations walked a tightrope of industry and civility. These new urban contexts allow for the exploration of the different influences on identity formation within diasporic Irish communities. The Irish had been part of the original European settlement of each locale, and elements of the Irish-born communities of Melbourne and Chicago established themselves throughout society, taking with them different understandings of what it meant to be Irish or American or Australian, and where religion fitted into that identity. At times, Irish Catholic communities were considered a threat to the progress of the city and were subject to nativist attacks. However, for the majority of the later nineteenth century, Irish Catholics and Protestants were accepted elements of white society. The comparison between Irish communities in Melbourne and Chicago provides a unique examination of the tools used by Irish immigrants to create a world for themselves abroad, enabling the shaping of a diasporic Irish identity and engagement with Ireland through remittances and political example and pressure.

In the aftermath of the Famine, poor rural workers migrated to the rapidly transforming urban worlds of Chicago and Melbourne as labourers. They housed transient communities who moved around the city and surrounding areas in search of work. However, as the cities grew and stabilised, the Irish populations developed distinctive community cultures which evolved across different generations and were subject to constant competition on the basis of class, religion and nationalist feeling. Other networks existed in each city which consolidated ethnic links and associations. These included occupational networks which took advantage of and encouraged the dominance of both Irish men and women in certain occupations and fields: manual labour, domestic service and, at the more powerful end of the spectrum, politics and the police and fire services of both Melbourne and Chicago. This gave the Irish middle classes a power base which could be extended across society and politics, still enduring a century later, which would have been much more difficult to achieve had the Irish not been present in the cities as early as they were.

Melbourne and Chicago emerged within very different international contexts. At the most basic level, Melbourne was part of a Crown Colony and as such loyalty had to be demonstrated to Queen and empire. Chicago, conversely, was a city within a country which had achieved its system of republican governance through war with Britain. These contexts brought differing civil restrictions and opportunities for the Irish abroad. A key difference in image was between the immigration policies of the United States and Victoria. While the United States was portrayed as a haven for 'the huddled masses', Australia was very firmly part of the British empire, and for most of the nineteenth century attracted immigrants predominantly from Britain and Ireland. Due to distance and chain migration, it was possible for people from across Europe to reach the United States, whereas only a select group of people – white and British – were actively encouraged and supported in their quest to reach Australia. This also meant that English-speaking Irish people were at a distinct occupational advantage linguistically compared to many immigrants in Chicago in a way that they were not in Melbourne, where most migrants spoke English. These different immigration dynamics altered the group relationships within each society, though both were united in the early twentieth century by nativism and subsequent migration restrictions.

Despite these divergences, Melbourne and Chicago were both instant cities, and their quick rise to wealth and prominence gave their inhabitants a sense of self-confidence and fluidity. There were opportunities for social advancement, religious toleration and political control in

Melbourne and Chicago that did not exist in older, more established cities like Sydney and New York. Their inhabitants were also conscious of a sense of competition with their older neighbours, encouraging an image of an ambitious, less refined younger sibling, determined to make their mark. The Irish utilised social networks often based around religion and occupation to claim control and space for themselves enabled by their early arrival in each city. The similarities in Irish population size relative to total population provide a further foundation for the comparison of the Irish identities and communities which emerged in Melbourne and Chicago during the second half of the nineteenth century.

By the end of the nineteenth century, there were substantial similarities between the United States and Australia in terms of urbanisation, manufacturing and economic volatility, as well as the role of Irish people within labour activism.[110] All of these elements influenced the reception of different groups of immigrants in the cities, as well as where the Irish were placed in the hierarchy of acceptance. Occupational and political links enhanced the connections made during social events and on Sunday mornings, and often enabled the introduction of new members to organised ethnic fraternalism. The next chapter explores the secular life of Irish men and women in Melbourne and Chicago. Though the religious and secular lives of Irish communities overlapped, Chapter 3 analyses the ways that connections were made with other Irish people through common ethnic heritage as opposed to religion, which is the focus of Chapter 4. Secular ethnic fraternity was vital in forming an accessible 'Irish' identity abroad, shaping the image of Ireland which would be promoted by the influential middle classes and be reflected or reacted to in other areas of society.

NOTES

1. Barth, *Instant Cities*, xxi; Platt, *Shock Cities*.
2. William Cronon, *Nature's Metropolis: Chicago and the Great West* (London: W. W. Norton & Co., 1991), p. 27.
3. Ibid., p. 27.
4. Richard Broome, *Aboriginal Victorians: A History Since 1800* (Crows Nest: Allen & Unwin, 2005), p. xxiii.
5. Penelope Edmonds, *Urbanizing Frontiers: Indigenous Peoples and Settlers in 19th Century Pacific Rim Cities* (Vancouver: UBC Press, 2010), p. 152; Sophie Cooper, '"English, yet essentially un-English": Female constructions of imperial belonging in Melbourne, 1850–1870', in Sutapa Dutta (ed.), *British Women Travellers: Empire and Beyond, 1770–1870* (London: Routledge, 2019), pp. 189–204.

6. Ryan Dearinger, *The Filth of Progress: Immigrants, Americans, and the Building of Canals and Railroads in the West* (Berkeley: University of California Press, 2016). Chapters 3 and 4 specifically focus on the role of Irishmen in this civil-engineering progress.
7. David W. Galenson, 'Economic opportunity on the urban frontier: Nativity, work, and wealth in early Chicago', *Journal of Economic History*, 51:3 (1991), pp. 581–603.
8. Lawrence McCaffrey, 'Irish-American dimension', in McCaffrey, Skerrett, Funchion and Fanning (eds), *The Irish in Chicago*, pp. 1–21.
9. Maria Luddy, *Women and Philanthropy in Nineteenth-Century Ireland* (Cambridge: Cambridge University Press, 1995), p. 13.
10. Diarmaid Ferriter, *The Transformation of Ireland, 1900–2000* (London: Profile, 2005), p. 120.
11. Diner, *Erin's Daughters*, pp. 39–40.
12. Robin F. Haines, *Emigration and the Labouring Poor: Australian Recruitment in Britain and Ireland, 1831–60* (Basingstoke: Macmillan Press Ltd, 1997), pp. 32–3.
13. Victorian Census, 1857, 1861, 1881, 1891: no statistics could be found for 1871 or 1901. Australian Commonwealth Census, 1911, 1921.
14. Simon Sleight has emphasised the representation of Melbourne as both a young city and a city of youth in his work *Young People and the Shaping of Public Space in Melbourne, 1870–1914* (London: Routledge, 2013), p. 13.
15. *Seventh Census of the United States*, 1850 (Washington, DC: Robert Armstrong, 1853).
16. *Census of Victoria, 1861* (Melbourne: John Ferres Government Printer, 1861); *Census of Victoria, 1871* (Melbourne: John Ferres Government Printer, 1871); *Census of Victoria, 1881* (Melbourne: John Ferres Government Printer, 1884); *Census of Victoria, 1891* (Melbourne: Robert S. Brain Government Printer, 1892).
17. *The First Commonwealth Census, 1911* (Melbourne: J. Kemp Government Printer, 1911).
18. Charles Rooking Carter, *Victoria, the British 'El Dorado' . . . a field for emigration* (London: E. Stanford, 1879), pp. 45–6.
19. Australian Census, 1921.
20. James Jupp, *From White Australia to Woomera: The Story of Australian Immigration* (Cambridge: Cambridge University Press, 2002), p. 8.
21. Kenny, *The American Irish*, pp. 181–2.
22. Ferriter, *Transformation of Ireland*, pp. 120–1.
23. Population figures alter due to boundary changes in 'city and suburbs' in both cities. 1841 Melbourne census figure, reported in 'Census of Port Phillip', *Geelong Advertiser*, 17 July 1841; *Census of Victoria, 1854* (Melbourne: John Ferres Government Printer, 1855); Victorian Census

1861, 1871, 1881, 1891; Australian Commonwealth Census 1911; *The Second Commonwealth Census, 1921* (Melbourne: H. J. Green Government Printer, 1921). The figures for Melbourne or 'Greater Melbourne' include the Melbourne city and suburbs. *Sixth Census of the United States*, 1840 (Washington, DC: Norman Ross Pub., 1990); *Seventh Census of the United States*, 1850 (Washington, DC: Robert Armstrong, 1853); *Eighth Census of the United States*, 1860 (Washington, DC: Government Printing Office, 1864); *Ninth Census of the United States*, 1870 (Washington, DC: Government Printing Office, 1872); *Tenth Census of the United States*, 1880 (Washington, DC: Government Printing Office, 1886); *Eleventh Census of the United States*, 1890 (Washington, DC: Government Printing Office, 1892); *Thirteenth Census of the United States*, 1910 (Washington, DC: Government Printing Office, 1910); *Fourteenth Census of the United States*, 1920 (Washington, DC: Government Printing Office, 1920). The population increases are also related to the changing city limits in 1863.

24. Marjory Harper and Stephen Constantine, *Migration and Empire* (Oxford: Oxford University Press, 2010), p. 53.
25. David Noel Doyle, 'The Irish in North America, 1776–1845', in J. J. Lee and Marion R. Casey (eds), *Making the Irish American: History and Heritage of the Irish in the United States* (New York: New York University Press, 2006), pp. 171–212.
26. Miller, *Emigrants and Exiles*; David Fitzpatrick, 'Emigration, 1801–70', in W. E. Vaughan (ed.), *A New History of Ireland, Volume V: Ireland Under the Union, 1: 1801–1870* (Oxford: Clarendon Press, 1989), pp. 562–622; Cormac Ó Gráda, *The Great Irish Famine* (Cambridge: Cambridge University Press, 1995).
27. Fitzpatrick, 'Emigration, 1801–70'.
28. For specific statistics, see Cowan, 'Immigrants, nativists', pp. 264–5.
29. Dominic Candeloro, 'Chicago's Italians: A survey of the ethnic factor, 1850–1990', in Melvin Holli and Peter d'A. Jones (eds), *Ethnic Chicago: A Multicultural Portrait* (Grand Rapids, MI: Wm. B. Eerdmans Public Co., 1995), pp. 229–59.
30. Marcia Chatelain, *South Side Girls: Growing Up in the Great Migration* (Durham, NC: Duke University Press, 2015), p. 3. Despite the small numbers of African Americans in Chicago, 1862 saw a race riot break out after an Irish American refused to serve an African American in Bridgeport. John B. Jentz and Richard Schneirov, *Chicago in the Age of Capital: Class, Politics, and Democracy during the Civil War and Reconstruction* (Urbana: University of Illinois Press, 2012), p. 64.
31. Caroline Bressey, 'Surfacing black and brown bodies in the digital archives: Domestic workers in late nineteenth-century Australia', *Journal of Historical Geography*, 70 (2020), pp. 1–11; Marilyn Lake and Henry Reynolds, *Drawing the Global Colour Line: White Men's Countries and*

the International Challenge of Racial Equality (Cambridge: Cambridge University Press, 2008), pp. 15–46.
32. US Federal Census, 1850.
33. Oliver MacDonagh, 'The Irish in Australia: A general view', in Oliver MacDonagh and W. F. Mandle (eds), *Ireland and Irish-Australia: Studies in Cultural and Political History* (London: Croom Helm, 1986), pp. 155–74.
34. Dominic A. Pacyga, 'To live amongst others: Poles and their neighbors in industrial Chicago, 1865–1930', *Journal of American Ethnic History*, 16:1 (1996), pp. 55–73.
35. Louise Carroll Wade, *Chicago's Pride: The Stockyards, Packingtown, and Environs in the Nineteenth Century* (Urbana: University of Illinois Press, 1987), p. 145.
36. These figures are compiled from census data. In 1891, Government Statist Henry Hayter received permission to pulp all the individual household schedules to avoid handing personal information over to police officers searching for wanted criminals. Terence H. Hull, 'The strange history and problematic future of the Australian census', *Journal of Population Research*, 24:1 (2007), pp. 1–22.
37. Malcolm and Hall, *New History*, p. 303; US Federal Census, 1920.
38. US Federal Census, 1890.
39. Victorian Census 1851, 1861, 1871, 1881, 1891. The figures for Melbourne or 'Greater Melbourne' include the Melbourne city and suburbs: Melbourne statistics were formulated using census statistics from 'Melbourne Proper', Richmond, E. Colingwood, Sandridge, Emerald Hill, Smith, Hotham (only 1861), Hotham (not 1891), Fitzroy, Prahran, St Kilda (not 1881), Brighton (not 1881), Brunswick, Hawthorn, Kew (not 1891), St Yarra (not 1871 or 1881). Though these categories were used in summaries, they were not always used in all tables each census year. US Federal Census 1850, 1860, 1870, 1880, 1890: the population increases are also related to the changing city limits in 1863.
40. MacDonagh, 'The Irish in Australia'; David Fitzpatrick, 'Irish emigration in the later nineteenth century', *Irish Historical Studies*, 22:86 (1980), pp. 126–43.
41. Graeme Davison, 'Gold-rush Melbourne', in Iain McCalman, Alexander Cook and Andrew Reeves (eds), *Gold: Forgotten Histories and Lost Objects of Australia* (Cambridge: Cambridge University Press, 2001), pp. 52–66.
42. K. S. Inglis, *The Australian Colonists: An Exploration of Social History 1788–1870* (Melbourne: Melbourne University Press, 1974), p. 18.
43. George Nadel, *Australia's Colonial Culture: Ideas, Men and Institutions in Mid-Nineteenth Century Eastern Australia* (Melbourne: F. W. Cheshire, 1957), p. 25; Haines, *Emigration and the Labouring Poor*, pp. 25–30.
44. *Victorian Hansard*, 10 March 1857.
45. Haines, *Emigration and the Labouring Poor*, pp. 23, 198.

46. *Victorian Hansard*, 14 January 1857.
47. Fitzpatrick, 'Irish emigration'.
48. Tyler Anbinder and Hope McCaffrey, 'Which Irish men and women immigrated to the United States during the Great Famine migration of 1846–54?', *Irish Historical Studies*, 39:156 (2015), pp. 620–42.
49. John T. Ridge, 'Irish county societies in New York, 1880–1914', in Ronald T. Bayor and Timothy J. Meagher (eds), *The New York Irish* (Baltimore: Johns Hopkins University Press, 1996), pp. 275–300.
50. Harper and Constantine, *Migration and Empire*, pp. 51–2.
51. Dominic Pacyga, *A Biography: Chicago* (Chicago: University of Chicago Press, 2011), p. 86; Fitzpatrick, 'Emigration, 1871–1921'.
52. Paul Bew, *Land and the National Question in Ireland, 1858–82* (Dublin: Gill & Macmillan, 1978).
53. O'Brien, *Blood Runs Green*, p. 15.
54. Davison, *Marvellous Melbourne*, pp. 13–15.
55. Ferriter, *Transformation of Ireland*, p. 23.
56. Central Statistics Office, 'Life in 1916 Ireland: Stories from Statistics Emigration' Table 1.9 Estimated emigration classified by destination, 1912–1920 and 2011–2015, using Emigration Statistics of Ireland in House of Commons Parliamentary Reports, Population and Migration estimates CSO. Available from https://www.cso.ie/en/releasesandpublications/ep/p-1916/1916irl/people/emigration/#d.en.97639 [accessed 23 April 2021].
57. Ellen Clacy, *A Lady's Visit to the Gold Diggings of Australia in 1852–53* (London: Hurst & Blackett, 1853), pp. 23–9.
58. Willis John Abbot, *Carter Henry Harrison: A Memoir* (New York: Dodd, Mead & Company, 1895), p. 45.
59. John F. Flinn, *History of the Chicago Police: From the Settlement ... The Mayor and Superintendent of the Force* (Chicago: Police Book Fund, 1887), p. 63.
60. Michael F. Funchion, 'Irish Chicago: Church, homeland, politics, and class – The shaping of an ethnic group, 1870–1900', in Holli and Jones (eds), *Ethnic Chicago*, pp. 57–92. There are few occupational statistics based on nationality for the 1850s and 1860s. By 1870, 587 of Illinois' 848 brewers were German.
61. Flinn, *Chicago Police*, p. 63.
62. Davison, 'Gold-rush Melbourne'.
63. Cooper, "English, yet essentially un-English".
64. Graeme Davison, 'Colonial origins of the Australian home', in Patrick Troy (ed.), *A History of European Housing in Australia* (Cambridge: Cambridge University Press, 2000), pp. 6–25.
65. Led by Peter Lalor, brother of James Fintan Lalor, the Eureka Stockade took place in the goldfields of Ballarat and became a focus point for labour and dissenting history in the colony.

66. Andrew Brown-May, 'A charitable indulgence: Street stalls and the transformation of public space in Melbourne, c. 1850–1920', *Urban History*, 23:1 (1996), pp. 48–71.
67. Emerald Hill would later become 'South Melbourne'.
68. Belich, *Replenishing the Earth*, p. 317.
69. Davison, *Marvellous Melbourne*.
70. James Grant and Geoffrey Serle, *The Melbourne Scene 1803–1956* (Melbourne: Melbourne University Press, 1956), p. 86.
71. Stuart MacIntyre, *A Concise History of Australia* (Cambridge: Cambridge University Press, 1999), p. 129.
72. Edward James Taaffe, Howard L. Gauthier and Morton E. O'Kelly, *Geography of Transportation*, 2nd edn (Englewood Cliffs, NJ: Prentice-Hall, Inc., 1996), p. 97.
73. Elias Colbert and Everett Chamberlain, *Chicago and the Great Conflagration* (Cincinnati, OH: J. S. Goodman & Co., 1872), pp. 113–16.
74. Ann Durkin Keating, *Chicagoland: City and Suburbs in the Railroad Age* (Chicago, IL: University of Chicago Press, 2004); Dominic A. Pacyga, *Slaughterhouse: Chicago's Union Stock Yard and the World It Made* (Chicago, IL: University of Chicago Press, 2015).
75. Bessie Louise Pierce, *A History of Chicago, Volume II* (Chicago, IL: A. A. Knopf, 1940), p. 34.
76. Carl Abbott, 'Civic Pride in Chicago, 1844–1860', *Journal of the Illinois State Historical Society*, 63:4 (1970), pp. 399–421.
77. Colbert and Chamberlain, *Chicago*, p. 319.
78. Kerby A. Miller, Ellen Skerrett and Bridget Kelly, 'Walking backward to heaven? Edmond Ronayne's pilgrimage in Famine Ireland and Gilded Age America', in Enda Delaney and Breandán Mac Suibhne (eds), *Ireland's Great Famine and Popular Politics* (London: Routledge, 2016), pp. 80–141.
79. Pacyga, *Chicago*, pp. 180–213.
80. Belich, *Replenishing the Earth*, p. 2; Davison, *Marvellous Melbourne*, p. 231.
81. MacIntyre, *Concise History*, pp. 129–31.
82. Kristin Otto, *Capital: Melbourne when it was the Capital City of Australia, 1901–27* (Melbourne: Text Publishing, 2009).
83. Harold L. Platt, *The Electric City: Energy and the Growth of the Chicago Area, 1880–1930* (Chicago, IL: University of Chicago Press, 1991), p. 98.
84. Kevin Kenny, 'Labor and labor organizations', in J. J. Lee and Marion R. Casey (eds), *Making the Irish American: History and Heritage of the Irish in the United States* (New York: New York University Press, 2006), pp. 354–63.
85. US Federal Census, 1870 and 1880.
86. Patricia Kelleher, 'Class and Catholic'.

87. Keith Pescod, 'Irish participation in Victoria's union movement, 1850–1900', *Australasian Journal of Irish Studies*, 11 (2011), pp. 7–27.
88. James Francis Hogan, *The Irish in Australia* (London: George Robinson & Co., 1888), pp. 37–9.
89. US Federal Census, 1870 and 1880.
90. Andrew Urban, *Brokering Servitude: Migration and the Politics of Domestic Labor During the Long Nineteenth Century* (New York: New York University Press, 2017).
91. Jentz and Schneirov, *Chicago in the Age of Capital*, p. 9.
92. Holli and Jones (eds), *Ethnic Chicago*.
93. John Rae, 'The eight hours day in Victoria', *The Economic Journal*, 1:1 (1891), pp. 15–42.
94. Nick Dyrenfurth, '"A terrible monsters": From "employers to capitalists" in the 1885–86 Melbourne Wharf Labourers' Strike', *Labour History*, 94 (2008), pp. 89–111.
95. Jentz and Schneirov, *Chicago in the Age of Capital*, p. 59.
96. James L. Merriner, *Grafters and Goo Goos: Corruption and Reform in Chicago* (Carbondale: Southern Illinois University Press, 2008), pp. 40–1; McCaffrey, 'The Irish-American dimension'.
97. Malcolm and Hall, *A New History*, pp. 280–8.
98. O'Farrell, *The Irish in Australia*. O'Shanassy was from Tipperary, Duffy from Monaghan and O'Loghlen from Dublin.
99. Geary, 'Irish doctors in nineteenth-century Victoria'; Jarlath Ronayne, *First Fleet to Federation: Irish Supremacy in Colonial Australia* (Dublin: Trinity College Dublin, 2002), pp. 227–9; Crosbie, *Irish Imperial Networks*, pp. 18, 68.
100. *Chicago Tribune*, 1 January 1866; Richard C. Lindberg, *To Serve and Collect: Chicago Politics and Police Corruption from the Lager Beer Riot to the Summerdale Scandal, 1855–1960* (Carbondale: Southern Illinois University Press, 1998), pp. 15–16.
101. Georgina Sinclair, 'The "Irish" policeman and the empire: Influencing the policing of the British empire – commonwealth', *Irish Historical Studies*, 36:143 (2008), pp. 173–87.
102. Donald H. Akenson, *The Irish Diaspora: A Primer* (Toronto: P. D. Meany Co., 1996), p. 145.
103. O'Farrell, *Irish in Australia*, pp. 80–2.
104. David N. Doyle, 'The Irish in Australia and the United States: Some comparisons, 1800–1939', *Irish Economic and Social History*, 16 (1989), pp. 73–94.
105. Akenson, *Irish Diaspora*, p. 29.
106. Tom Inglis, *Moral Monopoly: The Rise and Fall of the Catholic Church in Modern Ireland* (Dublin: University College Dublin Press, 1998), p.19.
107. Victorian Census, 1881 and 1891.

108. William J. Smyth, *Toronto, The Belfast of Canada: The Orange Order and the Shaping of Municipal Culture* (Toronto: University of Toronto Press, 2015); Jenkins, *Between Raid and Rebellion*.
109. Richard Allen Morton, *Justice and Humanity: Edward F. Dunne, Illinois Progressive* (Carbondale: Southern Illinois University Press, 1997), p. 1.
110. Campbell, *Ireland's New Worlds*, p. 139.

3

Building Bonds: Secular Club Life

The first half of the nineteenth century saw 'respectable society along British lines' spread around the world and come into 'contact with the specific fluidities of local conditions'.[1] When Irish migrants first reached Melbourne and Chicago in the 1830s and 1840s, they were not entering into the hierarchical and settled populations of Boston or, to a lesser extent, Sydney. Instead, their early arrival gave them a place at the table when it came to establishing what respectable society would look like in their locality. This is not to say that Irish migrants were unquestioningly accepted into wider local and national ideas of respectability. Elizabeth Malcolm and Dianne Hall have demonstrated the anti-Irish and anti-Catholic prejudice felt by Irish migrants in the Australian colonies, and David N. Doyle writes that Irish people were pressured to 'Americanise' in greater proportions in the Midwest than further east.[2] However, the economic and social opportunities of fluid societies such as Melbourne and Chicago allowed for the growth of a 'middle crust' who sought to represent their compatriots from a position of power.[3] To aid this, associations predicated on Irish birth or heritage were established early on in both Melbourne and Chicago, serving both defensive and inclusive purposes. They aimed to unite Irish people against prejudice, misfortune and the threat of violence, while also allowing members of Irish communities to join with recognised markers of middle-class culture. These ethnic associations provided networks which would expand into occupational, nationalist and religious circles, in terms of membership and ideas.[4] In addition to explicitly ethnic associational life, Irish workers took advantage of clubs with high Irish memberships to facilitate ethnic networks and boundaries in Melbourne and Chicago.

The associational culture of Melbourne and Chicago evolved at different rates over the nineteenth century. While most histories of the

Irish in the United States and Australia focus on the development of secular club culture in the years after 1880, this chapter emphasises the importance of each city's early development in shaping how ethnic associational culture emerged and sustained over multiple decades. The role of Famine Irish migrants had a significant impact on the types of associational culture that developed, while the maturation of the children of Famine migrants in the 1860s and 1870s had an important impact on the shape and accessibility of middle-class life and ethnic associational culture as the century drew toward a close.[5] How effective these associations were depended on their appeal and protection of Irish people and their ideas of ethnic culture. As understandings of ethnic identity and community boundaries fluctuate constantly, this multi-generational approach provides important insights into how local and international contexts influenced Irish diasporic ethnic life over a ninety-year period.[6]

The multi-generational appeal of certain ethnic societies, indicated by the involvement of men aged twenty-five to seventy, alludes to the varied and evolving interests and needs of prospective members. Tanja Bueltmann argues that ethnic associationalism was 'intrinsically linked' to ethnic identity and was a vital vehicle for those interested in maintaining it.[7] Some societies managed to adapt to the changing needs of Melbourne and Chicago's populations, demonstrating to their members the material benefits of engaging with 'imaginings' of identity.[8] Social organisations were established to achieve certain goals: professional improvement, financial security in cases of joblessness or death, entertainment or exercise. They helped migrants ameliorate or overcome the loneliness which accompanied geographical and cultural dislocation. Membership of an ethnic society did not preclude membership of other voluntary associations based around class, religion and occupation, but it did present an opportunity to speak for and address a group of people based on their heritage. This group of people, however, was inherently male. Though women were understood to be the keepers of ethnic identity, they are 'mostly absent in the power structure of immigrant organisations'.[9] Men led civil society and dominated the articulation of public Irish identity. While women are largely excluded from the narrative of civil society, especially until the twentieth century, they are not absent from either community activism or ethnic identity formation. These efforts will be explored in later chapters.

This chapter examines the overlaps in organisation and organising committee to explore the ways that diasporic Irish society was brought together, under an umbrella of ethnic identity, across class and generation.

It questions why *these* ethnic clubs were created and how they developed over time with reference to local and transnational Irish connections. John Belchem's concept of 'culture brokers' is central to understanding the influence of middle-class Irish migrants over the less fortunate in superimposing 'a wider "invented" affiliation' to ethnic Irishness.[10] By focusing on the middle classes and associational culture, it utilises the idea of civil society as a middle ground existing between the imposition of the state and 'the prescription imposed by the ritual and custom of tightly organized kin and quasi kin networks'.[11] The middle class was not a homogenous group, nor did it emerge fully formed in each city. This was trial and error, and the emergence of dominant voices in conflict and concordance with other elements of Melbourne and Chicago society can provide important insights into how community boundaries were set and contested over the first few generations of Irish diasporic community life. Secular club life is used to denote associational culture which maintained a separation from religious institutions, the focus of Chapter 4. This did not preclude overlap in membership, activities or motivation in reality. Similarly, the study of secular ethnic club life across multiple generations cannot be understood without reference to wider class movements.

The chapter is organised by time period. The first section focuses on the establishment of associational culture in each burgeoning city. In Melbourne, this time period saw the growth and dominance of the St Patrick's Society of Australia Felix (SPS). In Chicago, conversely, a variety of clubs were established and quickly fell out of favour due to poverty and shifting priorities. The American Civil War brought transition and a move toward nationalist political organising; this postwar period (1866–78) is the focus of the second section, a time when there was a surge in interest in fraternalism internationally, coinciding with the growth of working-class solidarity and industrialisation in both Melbourne and Chicago. The third section is influenced by Irish nationalist shifts, with the outbreak of the Land War, hope for home rule, and a growing focus on cultural nationalism in Irish associational culture. The final section (1900–22) considers the influence of labour activism and nationalism on apparently apolitical and secular ethnic associations, bringing the impacts and tensions of revolution, war and ideas of belonging together. Secular Irish organisations influenced who was perceived to belong to the wider Irish community and who did not. Therefore, the persistence of associations with mixed denominational membership provides an important insight into the role of religious institutions in shaping Irish identity abroad.

1840–1865

In Melbourne and Chicago a priority of the newly settled professional elite was to establish a club life predicated on ethnic fraternity and continuing social mores of home. Echoing the mobilisation of associational culture as political pressure by Daniel O'Connell in Ireland, 1842 witnessed the establishment of organisations dedicated to showing Irish pride in both cities. Daniel O'Connell's Repeal Association extended to Chicago, where an association was established under the presidency of William B. Egan, a physician and recorder. At least sixty men signed the association's charter in December 1842, when a Committee of Ways and Means was established and Repeal Wardens elected.[12] Of the twenty committee and warden member names recorded in newspaper articles of the time, three would become grocers, three police constables, two Justices of the Peace and one a brewer by 1844, demonstrating the powerful position of those who established 'respectable' society in Chicago.[13] The St Patrick's Society of Melbourne, established the same year, also reflected the city's 'middle crust', with an original committee consisting of the town's professional elite: doctors, merchants, councilmen and clerks.[14] There were crossovers with other voluntary organisations in the cities: Charles McDonnell and James Carney were respectively the Secretary and Treasurer of both Chicago's Repeal Association and the Catholic Library Society by 1844.[15] How these overlaps were utilised and separated, particularly with reference to religious influence, determined understandings of Irish belonging in the diaspora. In transient cities which numbered fewer than 5,000 inhabitants, connections and networks were fundamental to the smooth running of society, even when cross-community cooperation was vital to the city's growth and success. In addition to establishing social contacts, clubs and associations were deemed positive for social cohesion and offered a taste of home for those far from it.[16] These organisations were therefore important not only to the establishment of respectable society but to an internationally recognisable society itself.

Just as the Repeal Association arrived from Ireland, other transnational understandings of citizenship and belonging emerged. In Chicago this took the form of city-wide militias which contributed to civil society as well as reflecting Chicago's settler status and perceived need for defence. The Montgomery Guards were the first Irish militia formed, later joined by the Shields Guards and the Emmet Guards. The naming of these militia units dually demonstrated the established heritage of the Irish within America and their continuing importance within Chicago society. Though militia units were ethnic organisations, and were used widely in events of national significance to the Irish in America, they were established primarily to demonstrate loyalty to their adopted home and capacity for citizenship. Belonging to a militia had additional benefits to demonstrating acceptance to the martial environment of a city. In both the United Kingdom and the United States, working- and middle-class men used involvement in militias to improve their social standing and respectability.[17] Members and officers of these militias were better off financially, and socially superior to other Irish immigrants who did not participate in similar endeavours.[18] However, these militias were dependent on the economic well-being of their men.

Between 1850 and 1860, the Irish-born population of Chicago trebled, with the Irish Famine bringing huge numbers of unskilled and poverty-stricken migrants. As Sven Beckert notes, capital and culture require one another and cannot be extricated from each other.[19] By 1860, when around 60 per cent of employed adult Irish migrant men in the city held jobs classified as unskilled, the Emmet and Montgomery Guards had 'succumbed to the pressure of hard times, and was now practically among the things of the past'.[20] When the American Civil War broke out, only the Shields Guards, a company composed mostly of mechanics, skilled workers, were regularly drilling 'with Irish energy'.[21] The other units had to be revitalised. While belonging to a militia brought status and structure, it also required time to drill and financial resources to buy and maintain a uniform. Not everyone had these resources or the desire to give them up.

Melbourne did not witness the widespread establishment of militias. However, its population was not immune to threats of intimidation and violence. The SPS was established in July 1842, reflecting, if not being representative of, the mixed denominational make-up of the Irish in Melbourne at the time with a committee of nine Episcopalians, five Presbyterians and five Roman Catholics.[22] In its first month, the Society attracted a membership of 127 who were willing to pay the 5s. entrance fee and 12s. annual fee.[23] In a town with a total population of around 4,500, Irish people making up around a quarter of that, this was a dominant proportion of Melbourne's 'middle crust'. The SPS original committee emphasised its non-sectarian foundations, proclaiming that it was dedicated to encouraging Irish national feeling, 'the relief of the destitute, the promotion of education, and generally, whatever may be considered by its members best calculated to promote the happiness, the honor, and prosperity of their native and adopted land'.[24] Dual loyalties, to Ireland and adopted homeland, were again the priority of early ethnic associational culture.[25]

Though part of the town's emerging elites, the committee members of the 1840s were also young men with rapidly shifting allegiances. Wider political disputes, usually surrounding municipal elections, fed into the SPS, pulling the mixed-denominational committee apart and leading to a war of words in Melbourne's newspapers which would last for years.[26] The SPS took on a more explicitly Catholic shape with the new leadership of Catholic Vicar-General Fr. Patrick Geoghegan and grocer-draper John O'Shanassy in 1843. This coincided with the establishment of an Orange Lodge under the leadership of original SPS committee member and town clerk, John C. King.[27] Geoghegan's joint position in the SPS and as the highest-ranking Catholic priest in the Port Phillip area, combined with the Society's donation of £1,000 toward the erection of St Patrick's Church, encouraged greater tensions between Protestants and Catholics.[28] These tensions found an outlet on 12 July over the following three years.

The twenty-five-year-old O'Shanassy organised the first formal hurling match in the town in 1843, ostensibly for the enjoyment of the town's young Irish men and women. However, the timing of the planned match, to be held on Batman's Hill on 12 July, was deemed suspicious, and the town's authorities, fearing violence, cancelled the Orange march. Similar hurling matches were arranged on 12 July in 1844, 1845 and 1846, angering the town's Protestant newspaper editors.[29] Matches in the 1840s were organised between Irish counties and were accompanied by county-specific heckling in the newspapers, contrary to Patrick O'Farrell's argument that Irish regionalism was left on the journey out to Australia.[30] Unlike the cultural recreation that would be at the heart of sports in future years, these matches were primarily concerned with demanding territory and protection for Irish people. Tensions between the SPS and the Orange Lodge were brought to a head in 1846 when a riot broke out and shots were fired into the gathered Irish crowd from the Orange refuge of the Pastoral Hotel.[31] The British Government stepped in and passed the Party Processions Act (1846), ensuring that such riots would not hamper Melbourne society's progress and peace in the future. While Richard Davis notes that the Orange Order was usually considered English or Scottish as opposed to Irish in the colonies, this was still presented as an imported Irish problem in Melbourne's newspapers.[32] The SPS became an easily recognisable contrast to the town's Orange Order, the focus of anti-Irish and anti-Catholic sentiment, but also a positive beacon of Irish success.

In 1846 the Society was accused of 'training [people] to flourish a shillelagh, and to band together in mock hurling matches, to intimidate those whom they choose to denounce as their enemies'.[33] However, its committee sought to adapt in order to survive, prioritising the Society's secular and cultural efforts. Geoghegan resigned his position as Chairman, religious harmony became the focus of speeches, and the Society was repackaged as a respectable voice of the growing city's middling sort. By 1858 Melbourne's SPS numbered 135 members, had an established position in the city's hierarchy, and brought together members of the professional elite.[34]

Melbourne's first Irish society adapted to meet the needs of some, if not all, of its Irish population, moving from riotous and youthful to respectable and stable within a decade and maintaining its dominance throughout the societal upheaval of the gold rushes in the 1850s. Chicago, conversely, was a conglomeration of ethnic societies. This was largely a reflection of middle-class priorities and the affluence of each city's Irish population more generally. While Melbourne had its poor Irish, the city generally benefited from restricted Famine-era immigration due to steep fares and government sponsorship of those considered 'worthy' migrants. Those that made it to the Australian colonies were also assisted by state-funded emigration schemes, which meant that many arrived with some capital and guidance in finding a job and new home.[35] Chicago became home to starving labouring classes and nativism, particularly in the form of the American Protective Association (Know-Nothings) who elected their first Mayor of the city in 1855.[36] Though the working and middle classes remained broad and fluid in the 1850s, Patricia Kelleher argues that 'it had enough coherence for working-class men to serve as a negative reference point for men who hoped to consolidate an elevated class status'.[37] For many upwardly mobile Irish Catholics, the improvement of the Catholic Church and the claiming of public space for Irish Catholics was a higher priority than establishing a civil society based around ethnic associations.[38] The lower-middle and labouring classes, therefore, established the most prevalent forms of non-militarised Irish associational culture in Chicago life during the city's early years: self-improvement and benefit societies.

The Chicago Hibernian Benevolent Society was established in 1852 and chartered three years later.[39] In 1855, the Hibernians had a membership of 'several hundred' and claimed to encourage brotherhood among Irishmen regardless of political, religious or geographical background.[40] They were joined in 1860 by the United Sons of Erin Benevolent Society.[41] Each society had a mixture of occupations on their executive committees, primarily labourers, foremen, clerks and merchants, and these men remained with the societies over multiple decades.[42] Benefit societies fostered middle-class values of respectability and economic self-sufficiency. Their memberships, including committee members, frequently overlapped with nationalist organisations, indicating organising committees dually concerned with improving the position of the Irish in Ireland and in Chicago, raising issues of self-respect and ownership of city space.[43] Benevolent societies helped migrants to find jobs, aided families monetarily in cases of death or sickness, and provided a venue for social events. They also linked those in the middle class, or who aspired to be, with those they were helping to help themselves, aiding the creation of an identifiable ethnic community which spanned the city. During the 1840s and 1850s, while Chicago's Irish population was largely poor and newly arrived, there was a dependence on the ethnic parishes of the Catholic Church and informal community networks to respond to poverty, nativism and violence.

Tracking the venues for ethnic club meetings can help to understand the position of migrant populations within wider society and the status of organisations in shaping ethnic boundaries. Despite a temperance movement growing in Ireland and out into the diaspora during the 1840s and early 1850s, 'single men from all classes found a common bond in pub culture'.[44] This was not just about bringing members together with food and drink. These pubs were often owned and run by Irish people, helping to improve their finances and open the door to potential members. The Melbourne SPS moved from its original venue of Timothy Lane's public house, The Builders' Arms, to its own dedicated hall in July 1849.[45] The separation of Victoria from New South Wales in 1851 brought new requirements of the city, most importantly a venue for the new Victorian Legislative Council. In the absence of any other large hall in the city, politicians turned to the SPS committee to request the use of theirs. The rent of the hall improved the Society's finances while simultaneously emphasising the importance of the Irish community in the colony's progress. The rent allowed for the opening of a school, while a circulating library of 450 books was built and the Society held lectures and debates throughout the 1850s.[46] The early financial success of members of Melbourne's Irish society, and the decision to invest in stone and mortar on behalf of Irish civil society, continued the good fortune of the SPS and the position of Melbourne's Irish middle class.

By 8 October 1857, the Legislative Council of Victoria was settled into its new purpose-built home and the SPS was free to reopen its hall with a public dinner comprising of 'several distinguished public men, not only Irish, but English, Scottish, and American'. The mixture of ethnicities welcomed into the St Patrick's Hall led the *Age*'s reviewer to comment that 'the entertainment may thus, to a considerable extent, be considered as a display of Australian Nationality'.[47] As the *Age* usually joined the *Argus* in their anti-Irish sentiment, this consideration of Irish and Australian nationality as linked demonstrates the high position of the SPS in the esteem of Melbourne society by the late 1850s. While Irish people, particularly Irish Catholics, were over-represented in unskilled labour and domestic service, 'these occupations never engrossed the main body of Irish immigrants'.[48] Alongside the anti-Irish and anti-Catholic sentiment which continued throughout the nineteenth century, Irish men were also over-represented in law, politics, journalism and medicine from 1850. Tipperary-born John O'Shanassy was the colony's second Premier, Monaghan-born Charles Gavan Duffy had offered the colonial legislature a real taste of Westminster showmanship, and Cork-born Redmond Barry led many of the city's most esteemed institutions.[49] There was a strong Irish middle class in Melbourne bringing together Protestants and Catholics, and this diverse group of culture brokers was central to the city's economic and cultural success.

Chicago's Irish population was in a less affluent position, and with a fluctuating collection of ethnic organisations, saloons continued to be the main venue for association meetings until the 1880s when the St Patrick's Society was meeting in the Grand Pacific Hotel.[50] James Barrett argues that most immigrants 'came to understand their new world less through such [middle-class] formal programs than through informal contacts ... in streets, churches, and theaters'.[51] The ongoing reliance on hotels, bars and saloons as venues for such a variety of Irish associational culture underscores the open nature of ethnic socialisation in Melbourne and Chicago, and melding of the formal and informal elements of ethnic life. Without this strong and visible Irish middle class with its accompanying ethnic associations and civil institutions, Chicago's Irish had to wait for another opportunity to claim a place in the city and nation's foundation story.

This opportunity came on 15 April 1861 when Abraham Lincoln called for 75,000 men to join the fight against Confederate rebellion. Members of Chicago's Irish middle classes rushed to show their dual loyalty. Irish volunteer units were quickly raised, mirroring those in New York and other eastern cities.[52] New York's Irish Brigade was assembled by Young Irelander-hero Thomas Meagher, but without resident heroes of Irish nationalism, Chicago turned to James Mulligan. Mulligan, a prominent lawyer of Irish parentage, organised the 23rd

Illinois regiment, or the Irish Brigade of the West, using the cause of Irish freedom to recruit men from Chicago.[53] A newspaper advertisement in April 1861 called on the Irish of Chicago, 'For honor of the Old Land, rally. Rally for the defence of the new'.[54] Despite a promising start, the War Department rejected their offer of service. Confronted with cries of discrimination on racial and political lines, Mulligan went directly to Washington, DC and secured the government's acceptance.

A second Irish-Catholic regiment, the 90th Regiment or 'Irish Legion', was formed by Fr. Dennis Dunne of St Patrick's parish in 1861 and 1862.[55] Though the Irish Brigade and Irish Legion had Catholic links, Mulligan recruited based upon Irish ethnicity not religion. These ethnicity-based brigades served two main purposes. For men like Captain J. C. Fitzgibbon of the 14th Michigan Infantry they were places of refuge. Fitzgibbon asked that his entire company be transferred to the 23rd as the men they were serving with 'are partially American and bigoted Protestant. In Almighty God's name, if you can possibly do it, get us transferred to you, where we can be with and amongst our own race and people.'[56] For others, Irish brigades presented an opportunity to prove Irish martial traditions or loyalty to America and the Union.[57] Instead of a multi-generational organisation dedicated to ideas of respectability, Chicago continued to rely on short-term organisations dedicated to serving the requirements of the time.

In Chicago, the Civil War and the consequent movement and death of young men threw the city's associational culture into turmoil. The Civil War had brought new industries, legal and illegal, to the city, leading to an economic boom and, subsequently, a more tightly structured Irish middle class.[58] By the end of the war in 1865, Chicago was home to the middle-class St Patrick's Society and the predominantly lower-middle and working-class Fenian Brotherhood.[59] As in the 1840s, membership of multiple ethnic organisations was commonplace, helping to connect benevolent societies with nationalist activities, and education with voluntarism. Dual loyalties continued to shape Irish associational culture in the city, through men like L. H. O'Connor, a clerk, who was both Corresponding Secretary of the United Sons of Erin and the District Center of the Fenian Brotherhood.[60] O'Connor acted as a conduit between those involved in the Catholic Church-endorsed United Sons of Erin and the Church-condemned Fenian Brotherhood, crossing dividing lines in ambition for Irish charity and politics while retaining his status within civil and ethnic life. Chicago's secular parish in its early history was defined by military training, through ethnic militias and nationalist organisations. These associations expanded during the Civil War, when militia leaders and Irish nationalists joined with people who had never participated in ethnic associational culture to form Irish regiments.

In the early decades of settlement, ethnic associations in both cities sought to supplement the work of religious charities in providing food, shelter and information to newly arrived immigrants from Ireland. This work had the twofold effect of helping Irish people to support themselves and improve the reputation and standing of the Irish within Melbourne and Chicago. Members of secular ethnic associations positioned themselves as loyal Americans and Australians, arguing that their Irish identity aided their loyalty to their new homes. Experience of community-based ethnic organisation, in all its guises, granted Irishmen with 'clear evidence of the value to dispossessed and disaffected people of collective expression'.[61] However, the success of these organisations depended heavily on the resources available to each Irish community. In Chicago there was greater strain on money, time and status. What was available was often directed at short-term endeavours or into transnational efforts such as the Catholic Church. It was only in Melbourne, with its relatively stable middle class and a flexible economy, that ethnic organisers had the time and resources to adapt to the changing needs of the city. As the 1860s drew to a close, established societies such as the St Patrick's Society and the Hibernian Benevolent Society continued to cater socially to city and professional elites and charitably to those less fortunate. Ethnic fraternalism expanded to involve friendly societies, sports clubs and building societies, opening the doors further to working-class and lower-middle-class-led endeavours.

1866–1878

The late 1860s witnessed an international move toward fraternalism, heralding a rise in formally organised ethnicity-based societies. The middle classes tended to be at the forefront of this fraternalism. However, working-class agency combined with a growth of labour solidarity and nationalism to promote a range of Irish imaginings of ethnic belonging. Irish immigrants had been active in the politics of Melbourne and Chicago during the first decades of each settlement. As the 1860s drew to a close, children born or raised abroad reached adulthood. This new generation of Irish Americans and Australians grew up in the fluid spaces between different waves of migrants, providing them with opportunities to act as 'intermediaries' between an 'older generation of cosmopolitan Irish émigrés' and those who had arrived during the Famine years and its aftermath.[62] The 1870s also saw a widening of opportunities to gain qualifications in trade and the professions. This opened new avenues of collective action to Irish immigrants and their children, often regardless of religious background, in the form of labour unions such as Knights of Labor and the Federated Seamen's Union of Australasia.[63] Community organisers sought new ways of uniting the wider Irish populace as class divisions separated commercial society in Melbourne and Chicago. Benevolent and building societies organised around ethnicity but split on class lines were complemented by the growth in popularity of more amusing pastimes. In Melbourne this was the growth of Gaelic games while in Chicago, Irish nationalist organisations also encouraged cultural activities.

The epicentre of Irish identity formation and ethnic associational culture differed significantly in Melbourne and Chicago. While ideas of respectability were shared in both cities and continued to influence the emergence of a club life, the working classes held much more power in Chicago than in Melbourne during the 1860s and 1870s. This dominance sustained because of the disruptions of the American Civil War and the Chicago Fire of 1871, and ethnic societies continued to compete with each other, emerging and declining based on generation and immigrant cohort. Without these disruptions, it took until the 1880s and the growth of working-class union organising for Melbourne's Irish middle-class authority regarding Irish public identity to wane. In the meantime, the SPS provided a strong voice in defence of Melbourne's Irish community, particularly as ethnic tensions began to rise.

After almost two decades of relative peace between the 'green' and 'orange' communities, the 1867/8 state visit of Prince Alfred to Australia led to a surge in Orange Order activity in the state's capital. Melbourne's Orange Order celebrated the prince's visit by hanging a large transparency of William III crossing the Boyne and the motto 'This we will maintain' from the Protestant Hall.[64] Fearing trouble, local authorities entreated the Orangemen to remove the banner, but when they failed, a large crowd of 'Ribbonmen' gathered in front of the building singing 'The wearing of the green' and threw stones at the banner. In response, shots were fired from the hall, injuring a number of young people who had joined in the singing 'evidently out of fun, and with the intention of making a noise, rather than taking part in a political demonstration'.[65] A nine-year-old boy died from his wounds.[66] The SPS maintained its non-sectarian stance, but used its prominent position in Melbourne society to present a clear opposition to the actions of the Orange Order, just as in 1846. This time the SPS's representatives were presented as Melbourne's calm and respected elders. The SPS's mixed religious make-up lent further support to arguments of Irish colonial loyalty and celebration of Irish culture in its most inclusive sense, in stark contrast to the Orange Order.

Having had an early and strong presence in the city, the Irish were able to benefit from an established society in a way that other ethnic groups could not. The Irish Catholic newspaper, the *Advocate*, was established in 1868 and worked alongside Irish civil life in Melbourne to connect members of societies within Victoria with each other and with those in Ireland. In July 1869, the SPS opened a registry office for newly arrived migrants. Based at St Patrick's Hall, a central and well-known institution, the registry was designed to connect newly arrived Irish immigrants with Irish members of the middle class, thereby joining different parts of society together in ethnic solidarity.[67] While new immigrants, men and women, were encouraged to use the office in order to avoid 'being entrapped into disreputable situations', potential employers could use it to protect themselves from 'being imposed upon by unsuitable servants'.[68] The SPS also pledged to send information back to Ireland regarding the state of the labour market in Victoria, to act as agents for Irish people in Victoria who wished to 'bring out friends from home', and to make enquiries concerning missing compatriots.[69] In establishing the registry office and information service, members of the SPS were echoing patterns followed by immigrant and ethnic societies across the world, focusing on providing an educational function and helping newcomers.[70] The balls and meetings that the Society held throughout the year presented opportunities to meet, to socialise and to mirror patterns of civil society and business networking that were fundamental to the establishment of a stable society in the eyes of the middle classes. Connecting new migrants to old had the dual effect of establishing the SPS as the leading voice of multiple generations of Irish people and refreshing its membership just when its founders were reaching their later years. While the Society provided its members with benefits, including a subscription fund which could be accessed in times of sickness or death, the St Patrick's Hall provided a venue where shared cultural experiences, memories and interests could be used as a foundation for judgements on character and trust.[71] Membership of the SPS, therefore, provided advantages for Irish people throughout the city and across different classes.

While they could not benefit from the position of Melbourne's SPS, Chicago's Irish middle classes also sought respectable ethnicity-based pursuits in a concerted effort to counteract racialised portrayals of Irish people as uneducated, drunk and violent. Temperance societies re-emerged after a lull in the late 1850s and 1860s, and they were accompanied by other 'improving' pursuits such as the Chicago Irish Literary Association (also referred to as the Irish Literary Society), which was established in 1868. Connecting their reforming manifestos, the Literary Association's president, John J. Fitzgibbon, paid tribute to the founder of the Father Mathew Total Abstinence and Benevolent Association temperance society in his welcome speech, noting that the Literary Association was also 'established for the welfare, culture, and literary advancement of its members' and was strenuously non-religious.[72] By 1872, the *Chicago Post* commented that the Literary Society included 'the most ultra of the Chicago Irish element. Protestants, Presbyterians and Catholics [who] mingle fraternally and advocate the independence of Ireland.'[73] This society emphasised the intellectual position and history of the Irish in Chicago and the world while also contributing to political nationalist awareness and activities.[74] These connections were supported through business networks such as the company Fitzgibbon & Scanlan, co-owned by the Association's Fitzgibbon and prominent Irish nationalist businessmen the Scanlan brothers. These men linked the secular literary society with Irish political nationalism, continuing the boundary crossing of earlier endeavours.[75] However, non-religious organisations like the Literary Association were usually short-lived or fluctuated in the official record in Chicago, either falling from visibility or morphing into a religious association in everything but name, due to the changing priorities of their organisers and the lack of investment in encouraging multi-generational participation.

Middle-class society life in Chicago was disrupted by the fire of 1871. That year, the recently established St Patrick's Society disappeared from city directories. It had among its committee, city elders, school inspectors and aldermen.[76] While these men retained their influence in Chicago, they redirected their energies into Catholic charities and Irish political nationalism in the aftermath of the fire. In their wake, the Ancient Order of Hibernians (AOH) reached the city. While the AOH has become synonymous with Irish associational culture, it does not feature in Chicago's directories until 1875, two years after the Panic of 1873 sent the city into an economic depression.[77] This growth of Catholic Church-organised and related associational culture will be more fully explored in Chapter 4. However, the late emergence of the AOH, at a similar time to elsewhere in the Midwest,[78] may have been due to the alternative options for Irish people already in existence in Chicago. The Hibernian and United Sons of Erin benevolent societies provided the insurance element, and the militias, church and the St Patrick's Society and Fenian Brotherhood provided the social. In the aftermath of the fire, the Chicago Relief and Aid Society took charge of distributing financial compensation, while societies like the St Vincent de Paul Society took over the spiritual and domestic aid. After the immediate destruction was taken care of, a new society was required. The AOH took on this need, permeating occupational and community life in Chicago from that time.

As the new and existing middle classes in Melbourne and Chicago fought to maintain their position as spokespeople of each city's Irish population, they were confronted by the needs and power of Irish people outside of their immediate circles. Connections between Ireland and abroad, and travel between the two, largely determined the priorities of Irish associational culture. Trinity College Dublin (TCD) graduates made up a large proportion of the professional population of Melbourne from its earliest times.[79] These men were connected by training and family, sometimes referred to as the 'Irish cousinage', and though there were not enough of them to establish distinct clubs, they remained united through their recreational activities.[80] TCD graduates participated in Melbourne elite culture, while many also had the resources to travel back to Ireland. For aspiring lawyers, this travel was partly a journey of necessity. Being called to the Irish Bar helped to avoid Victoria's residency law, and many recent migrants bounced between Melbourne and Ireland until they were qualified to work in the colony.[81] While travel within the United States was common for Chicago's professionals, occupational requirements did not induce the same international travel nor continued connections with Irish alma maters. This was largely because of the occupational demography of the city's Irish population who, if they were in the professional classes, were American-trained by the 1870s. Instead of a professional class going back and forth through necessity to bring news from Ireland, Chicago relied upon visitors from Ireland on fundraising or speaking tours, a luxury that few extended to Australia. Divergences in the springs of influence also occurred because of the emphasis on Catholic Irish identities in Chicago compared to Melbourne's more secular ethnic civil society.

Sport was used to link Irish people to their fellow immigrants in Australia and also to temporary inhabitants of the city. Cricket and rugby were popular games for Ireland's middle class, and this popularity was transferred into the wider empire.[82] Sport in Ireland developed 'as a shared culture across time and place', influenced by both Gaelic tradition and Ireland's place within the British empire.[83] As members of the British empire, Irish people in Melbourne and Ireland embraced traditionally British sports like cricket, and used them to connect with each other, to an Irish identity and to a wider imperial identity. One letter to the editor of the *Advocate* from 'Shamrock' asked why there was not an Irish national cricket club established in Melbourne. They were able to list at least eleven potential players who would 'be well able to uphold the glory' of the 'green isle' against 'all comers', suggesting John O'Shanassy and Tyrone-born politician Captain Charles McMahon as sponsors.[84] The enthusiasm for an Irish cricket team with the support of prominent Irish-Australian politicians suggests a cross-generational and cross-class interest in cricket when there was no public cry for Gaelic games. These matches between descendants of different corners of the United Kingdom were promoted as an opportunity for spectators to show ethnic pride in a good-humoured way, avoiding the political and violent tensions brought about by earlier competition. In 1860 O'Shanassy had commented, 'It was a novelty to him to witness a game of cricket . . . and he hoped that at some future time, he would be able to show them on that ground the Irish national game of hurling.'[85] He would not have to wait for long.

The Gaelic games of hurling and football had suffered under the strict coercion laws which outlawed mass meetings in Ireland, to the extent that one scholar has deemed the playing of hurling across most of Ireland as 'well-nigh extinct' by the 1870s.[86] In its absence, athletics grew as a key pastime from the 1850s, particularly in Dublin where it was spearheaded at TCD, and later the Irish Champion Athletic Club, established in 1871. The resurgence of hurling in a codified form began with an increase in interest in the game in Dublin, specifically in TCD, the academic home of many of Melbourne's leading Irish men. In 1870 a set of rules entitled *Laws of Hurling* was drawn up and publicised by the Dublin University Hurley Club.[87] This was followed by a revised set in 1879, when the Irish Hurley Union was established.[88] These trends in Trinity and their reflection in Melbourne can be attributed to the influence of TCD-educated Irish Australians who spearheaded the change, pre-empting the international codified revival of the sport in 1884. This was reflected in Melbourne's Irish celebrations, on St Patrick's Day, St Stephen's Day and the Queen's Birthday picnics.[89] As well as providing a link to Ireland, hurling presented opportunities to visit other Victorian cities, helping to encourage a constant recalibration of what it meant to be Irish and Australian. In September 1877, Melbourne Hurling Club went to Geelong for the first formal inter-city match in twelve years.[90] Gaelic games worked alongside civil organisations like the SPS to perform and promote a distinctive Irish identity, connecting 'ancient' sporting traditions to diasporic camaraderie, and crucially, separate from 'British' sports like rugby and cricket.⁹¹ Inter-city matches provided an opportunity for Irish people to come together, claim public space, stadiums and newspaper columns, and join in activities promoting cultural nationalism.

The resurgence of Gaelic games in a formal setting did not reach Chicago until long after the establishment of the Gaelic Athletic Association in Ireland in 1884, though there were occasional matches at Clan na Gael events, for example in 1874 when the Irish Rifles played the Clan's team after a lecture on 'The Genius of Irish Liberty'.⁹² In the absence of specifically *Irish* sporting endeavours, Irish nationalist organisations presented working-class Chicagoans with opportunities for support and education. These organisations led to an increase in ethnic fraternal visibility in Chicago. For many, they were places to meet with other Irish-born and -descended men to socialise, and build upon existing familial, friendship and occupational networks. They were located in different areas of the city with numerous branches, allowing for the continuation and complementing of parish life. In April 1868, the flooring gave way in Healy's Hall, 543 Archer Avenue, during a Fenian meeting. Patrick Ryan was killed and at least nine others were injured.⁹³ All the men injured lived in and around Archer Avenue in the Bridgeport area of Chicago, working as labourers or in the more skilled occupations of teamsters, carpenters and one as a soap manufacturer, a by-product of the local slaughterhouses.⁹⁴ The injuries, which were multiple and debilitating, reduced the incomes of an entire stretch of Archer Avenue families. Even without failing floorboards, for the large proportion of Chicago's Irish population who worked in labouring occupations, the risk of injury and fatality was high. Membership of benefit and fraternal societies, and the kinship networks provided by nationalist organisations based in the local community, provided monetary, medical and caring support for those without extended familial networks. Though many of these organisations were short-lived, they presented opportunities to bond with neighbours outside the church, school and stockyards, helping to build up multi-generational bonds locally, if not city-wide.

While pursuing political nationalist aims, which will be explored further in Chapter 6, the Fenian Brotherhood also sought to provide alternative reforming and educational entertainments for its members. The Fenian Dramatic Club was one product of this provision. The first drama put on by the men and, notably, women of the club was 'Robert Emmet'. According to reviews, it seems that community rather than quality was the priority.⁹⁵ The educational opportunities provided for by the Fenian Dramatic Club could also be found in other societies in

Chicago. The working and lower middle classes were mirroring the educational motivations of earlier ethnic organisations, while the networks between Fenian Centers presented transient members with access to support systems and social activities. The ethnic organisations that emerged in Melbourne and Chicago were responding to the needs and demands of their populations. In Melbourne, the SPS was complemented by the growth of Gaelic games in a top-down effort to unite different strands of Irish society. In Chicago, with its larger and more vocal working class, ethnic organisation emerged at a local level. It would take until the 1880s for it to be united across the city.

Land and labour agitation grew in importance during the 1870s, finding an audience intent on reducing social inequality in the industrialising cities of Melbourne and Chicago. The Chicago Fire, for example, brought hardship but also presented new opportunities for Irish labourers, who were in great demand, and contractors who could make fortunes and rise in influence quickly.[96] These new middle classes came from different backgrounds but frequently entered politics as aldermen, a position which 'exerted enormous control over the expansion of the city' and its workers.[97] Irish-born Arthur Dixon had made his fortune by 1870, when he had a personal estate of $5,000. In addition to working as a freight agent, Dixon acted as an election inspector.[98] In the 1880s he brought together the middle-class elements of his life as both an alderman and as president of the re-formed Irish Literary Association.[99]

Organisers in each city used the inequality in Ireland to unite Irish workers. While this was a progression of working-class-led activity in Chicago, it led to a disruption of middle-class control in Melbourne. Irish working-class organisers sought to establish societies based upon ethnicity, thereby placing the 'Irish within, not apart from, the wider working class'.[100] Up until this point, Melbourne's ethnic associations had placed their members within the wider middle class and norms of respectability. With the advent of stronger unionisation in Melbourne, there was a concerted effort to find an Irish voice within the working class. Concurrently, political nationalist organisations provided social outlets for their members while connecting them back to Ireland and with similar organisations around the world. Political and cultural nationalist societies rose in prominence during the 1880s, providing an ethnic focus for members of the Irish diaspora of different classes and political outlook. However, while there was a greater spread of ethnic associations in Melbourne and Chicago, the use of ethnic newspapers and a rising lower middle class facilitated the consolidation of a visible Irish ethnic associational culture. Existing personal relationships were encouraged through cross-city annual meetings, frequent letters and newspaper editorials. Successful ethnic organisations, such as the SPS in Melbourne, continued to adapt, encouraging new generations of Irish immigrants to find their place within the mix of older Irish and their foreign-born descendants. This allowed for a recalibration of what Irish identity meant in recognition of the new challenges faced by the Irish diaspora.

1879–1900

The 1870s were dominated by the working classes in Chicago and middle classes in Melbourne. The 1880s saw a shift in both cities. Middle-class organisations dedicated to political improvement, in Ireland and abroad, were established as new affluence and political influence were wielded in Melbourne and Chicago. Successful middle-class organisers altered their focus to maintain their position in the civic life of both cities, leaving the everyday organisation of diasporic Irish life to those in the lower middle and working classes. The boom in population in both cities had led to city sprawl, spreading Irish communities across large distances. The establishment of the tram system in Melbourne in the mid-1880s and the elevated transit (or 'L') in Chicago in the early 1890s helped to bring these disparate societies together. In previous decades, elite societies provided for newly arrived immigrants through charity. Labour agitation and the rise of trade union activity led to an increase in Irish labourers and clerks organising into friendly societies and paying into insurance funds which could be transferred between city and country. This growth in friendly society membership was reflected internationally, with a crucial upsurge in society numbers in Ireland in the aftermath of the British Friendly Societies Act of 1875.[101] How continuity and cooperation were encouraged in the daily lives of the Irish in Melbourne and Chicago in the midst of political, class and religious division is crucial to understanding the sustenance of diasporic Irish civil society.

The Irish famine of the late 1870s prompted the Land War in Ireland and new arrivals of migrants from the south and west of Ireland. Chicago's middle classes, relatively absent from non-religious aid during the 1850s, sought to establish a voice of compassion and care in the latter years of the 1870s. Chicago's St Patrick's Society was reconvened in 1878 with a new focus on the 'question of Irish colonization and in caring for the Irish immigrant' under William Onahan.[102] While members of the St Patrick's Society were involved in nationalist activities, Onahan remained firm on excluding Irish politics, outside of support for home rule achieved by constitutional means, from the Society's meetings.[103] The St Patrick's Society quickly shifted to reflect its president's position as a leading Catholic layman, retiring its secular ethos as well.[104] Instead, the Irish-American Club, established in 1880, brought together the city's leading men and served a more secular purpose for Chicago's Irish and Irish-descended elites.[105] Its membership roll included 'nearly every prominent Irish-American resident of Chicago' and was open to anyone who believed in the right of Ireland to be governed by and for its own people as an independent nation, serving as a stepping stone to higher economic and political power through the utilisation of ethnic networks. With regard to party politics, the Democratic Party still garnered most of Chicago's Irish support, though Irish-American loyalties were sought through the Irish-American Republican Club which rose to national prominence during the 1880s.[106] Though nominally an Irish-American society, the Republican Club reached out to those from different ethnicities who shared its aims.[107] Ethnic heritage was used as a focus for domestic political change, with speakers using Irish history for American ends. This was an opportunity for those of Protestant and Catholic Irish backgrounds to come together in joint loyalty to America and their Irish compatriots within that American society.

Despite differences of opinion regarding Irish politics, there was a concerted effort to create a central hub for Irish club life in Chicago. The Irish-American Council and United Irish Societies of Chicago and Cook County (UISCC), established in 1876, served this purpose alongside ethnic newspapers based in New York and Chicago. The city's organisations tended to be local and run by working and lower-middle-class culture brokers. The UISCC existed to bring these local parish-based associations together with the wealthy and influential.[108] Less affluent organisations could access the influence of the Irish-American Club's middle-class and elite members and, in turn, they could access potential voters, workers and enforcers. While the everyday meetings of Irish life in Chicago may have been spearheaded by clerks and labourers, the city-wide organisations maintained a similar occupational demographic throughout Chicago's history, from the Repeal Association to the Irish-American Club. Each man was prominent in Irish nationalist activities and Chicago industrial and civic life, furthering the bonds built in a variety of Irish nationalist associations and professional life.

Class connections presented new opportunities for secular celebrations of Irish identity and political aspirations, as Irish Catholic religious affiliation became more accepted and secure in the face of greater hostility to other ethnic and racial groups in each city. In Chicago, connections made within secular and religious ethnic organisations were supplemented by the patronage of Democrat politicians who provided Irish voters with jobs on the city payroll.[109] In Melbourne, there was a similar unification of disparate organisations across class lines. Branches of the Land League/Irish National League were established during the early 1880s, and its citizens gave generously to Irish constitutional and humanitarian relief efforts throughout the decade. There was a desire to learn about Irish events and history, and knowledge was provided by the *Advocate*, Catholic organisations and public institutions like the Melbourne Public Library, which by 1887 had 2,500 volumes categorised as 'Ireland'.[110] As the 1880s continued, and the possibility of Irish home rule increased, club life in Melbourne reflected and supported this. The Celtic Club was formed in Melbourne in 1887. It took seven months before the Club had permanent lodgings, by which time the membership roll comprised 196 city and country members, including twenty clergymen of different faiths and thirty-seven members of the learned professions.[111] These men represented Melbourne's middle-class life and business, and provided a connection between the priorities of the established SPS and newer organisations concerned with Irish nationalism.

While the SPS and the Celtic Club epitomised Melbourne's civil society, the 1880s also witnessed the growth of an Irish working-class voice in Melbourne and with it more connections between club life and religious affiliation. Melbourne's SPS could no longer provide the services required by the expanding Irish working class, especially those who needed security not charity. A gap emerged that needed to be filled. The Irish National Foresters (INF) Benefit Society was established in 1886 and was specifically aimed at men aged between sixteen and forty years of age, who 'must be Irishmen or of Irish descent, of good moral character and industrious habits'.[112] The objectives of the INF were to provide monetary support to members and their families in case of sickness and help with burial expenses for the member or predeceased wife. Surgical and medical aid was to be provided for members, their wives and children, as well as for the widowed mothers of unmarried members.[113] The 1860s and 1870s saw the rise of working-class fraternalism in the United States, and the economic downturns of the 1880s brought about the same in Melbourne. In 1879, it was estimated that 80 to 90 per cent of Australia's manual workers were members of friendly societies. The INF operated within a wider trend of working-class collective action, with workers supporting themselves and families financially while membership of the organisation also encouraged connections within a specific locale and ethnic community.

The membership rolls of the INF's Henry Grattan Branch, based in Carlton and named after the eighteenth-century Irish politician, show that this was a club dominated by the labouring and lower middle classes. Though the leadership was often of the higher occupational level of clerk, in 1891 most of the new members declared their occupation as 'labourer'.[114] As the 1890s continued, and Victoria's economic depression deepened, working men needed the security brought by social connections and benefit societies. In 1892, a clergyman in Richmond, close to the Carlton base of the Henry Grattan Branch, observed that most working men in his parish were, on average, about £4 in arrears with rent.[115] The INF operated a system of electing members, requiring a new member to be proposed by an existing member, or at least to have access to the platform, and have that proposal seconded in an open meeting.[116] The INF provided financial and medical support to Irish workers while also presenting highly mobile Irishmen with access to social networks based on ethnicity. In 1891, Melbourne organisers of the INF decided to join with other branches in Australia to affiliate with the organisation in Ireland, Great Britain and Africa.[117] Movement across and through different diaspora hubs was acknowledged through transferable memberships of these organisations. Utilising the ethnic community within a city allowed new arrivals to Melbourne to use existing familial and friendship networks to find support within society.

The Henry Grattan INF meetings were held at the Commercial Hotel, a popular pub on Drummond Street run by Matthew Rahilly.[118] Rahilly had emigrated from Liverpool to Melbourne in September 1859 as a nineteen-year-old labourer and, on reaching Melbourne, 'evinced a practical interest in Catholic and Irish national affairs', including involvement in St Patrick's Day parades in 1887 and 1888 as well as the INF.[119] Through his connections with Irish associational life, Rahilly was able to provide a friendly venue and supplement his income.[120] Just as Timothy Lane had offered the Builders' Arms to the SPS in the 1840s, Irish secular parish life benefited the local economies of Irish people as well as helping to create a sense of ethnic community within the wider city. The spread of local branches into the suburbs also helped to make membership of an ethnic association more relevant to the everyday interactions of Irish people in Melbourne. After decades of domination by the SPS, the economic depression of the 1890s forced a change in Irish civil society and the use of tools, resembling those used in the 1840s, to reach out to new generations of immigrants.

The Gaelic Revival had an impact in both cities. As Nicholas O'Donnell began Irish language classes in Melbourne, a Philo-Celtic Association was established in Chicago.[121] A group of fifty Irish GAA players undertook an 'American invasion' tour in 1888, hoping to fundraise for the GAA and interest members of the diaspora in a planned 'international Gaelic festival' in 1889.[122] While the fundraising effort failed, the tour did lead to a growth of Gaelic games in Chicago. The Emmets and the Shamrocks, Gaelic football clubs, were established in Chicago's West Side in 1888. Patrick Coughlin, a founder of the Emmets, cited the growing Irish cultural revival and Irish nationalism as reasons for the club's establishment.[123] Chicago hosted the first American GAA-affiliated league in the United States in 1890, and three years later there were ten Gaelic football teams in the city, including the Davitts, the O'Connells and the Wolfe Tones.[124] While the Irish-American Club involved men of rank and influence, the GAA attracted working men. Two years later, the Chicago *Tribune* was reporting the results of Gaelic games played at 39th Street.[125] The presence of Irish sporting life in the mainstream and traditionally conservative *Tribune* instead of in the ethnic press indicates a growing acceptance of the place of Irish cultural life within Chicago, and its widespread appeal to multiple generations of Irish-born and -descended people who now lived and operated within wider American society.

The 1880s had witnessed a widening and streamlining of Irish ethnic associational culture in both Melbourne and Chicago. Just as the UISCC connected disparate motivations and class loyalties, the Melbourne *Advocate* helped coordinate Irish activities which were spread across location and class. Although working-class organisation had disrupted the dominance of the middle-class SPS in Melbourne, and the Irish-American Club had given an elite sheen to Chicago's efforts, organisers in both cities utilised existing networks, overlapping memberships and ethnic newspapers to connect increasingly disparate clubs. The organising committees of these clubs also helped to maintain consistency of message. This reflected the growing associationalism of Irish cultural life in Ireland, where the Gaelic Revival met political nationalism and labour radicalism during the 1880s and 1890s.

1900–1922

Political and labour organising dominated secular associations in the first decades of the twentieth century. As Melbourne and Chicago both became political hubs – Melbourne as the temporary capital city of the Commonwealth of Australia, and Chicago as the 'second city' of the United States – Irish people took a leading role. While the Irish accounted for a fifth of Chicagoans in 1900, they had a disproportionate impact on the city.[126] In Melbourne, Irish people played a leading role within labour, political and religious activity. However, this leading role was increasingly subsumed into wider organisations, without an explicitly Irish brand, where Irish people were able to quietly shift the priorities of organisations with high Irish memberships in their favour, while focusing their attention on Irish religious and nationalist organisations when the need arose.

The Irish gained dominance in Chicago through the Democratic Party and labour activism, most obviously through the Chicago Federation of Labor (CFL) and associated Chicago Teachers' Union. John Fitzpatrick, who had arrived from Athlone at the age of eleven, led the CFL from 1902, bringing together his labour activism with his Irish nationalism. Under Fitzpatrick's presidency, the CFL issued condemnations of British activities in Ireland throughout the Irish Revolutionary Era (1912–23).[127] The stockyards and packing houses provided other Irish workers with ethnic unity alongside their class solidarity. Knights of Labor assemblies were led by Irish women like Elizabeth Flynn Rodgers from the late nineteenth century, while striking women workers from Libby, MacNeill & Libby packhouse formed a labour club named after Maud Gonne in late 1900.[128] While labour organisations such as these had wide appeal, much further than just Irish workers, the influence of Irish men and women within them can be seen. In the Chicago Women's Trade Union League, for example, women spent Sunday evenings at each other's homes singing 'mostly Irish songs because many of the girls were Irish'.[129]

Labour activism and politics became a home for Irish people in Melbourne as well, though increasingly faith and class solidarity became opposing positions. Irish-Melbournians found leadership roles in the Australian Labor Party from its establishment in 1901.[130] However, the First World War saw tensions between labour and Catholic organising erupt when, largely Irish, members of the Catholic Federation were expelled from the Labor Party in 1915.[131] As connections between religious and ethnic identity increased, there was a sharp decline in secular ethnic organising. As the next chapters will explore, sustaining Irish identity depended on ethnic influencers of all ages, and through multiple generations. Institutions operated by Irish Catholic religious orders, especially schools, were fundamental to this. The growing closeness in Irish and Catholic identities was therefore unsurprising as Melbourne entered the twentieth century.

Throughout the nineteenth century, the SPS had dominated secular Irish sociability in Melbourne. Its members proudly held on to the status and respectability afforded by association with the oldest Irish organisation in Victoria.[132] By 1862, it had expanded its reach and appeal to new generations of members by establishing local benefit societies in addition to its social association.[133] During the early twentieth century, it was giving out loans to its members and became embroiled in a row with the British Medical Association over the rights of friendly societies.[134] In this it was joined by other benefit societies such as the Hibernian Australasian Catholic Benefit Society (HACBS) and INF.[135] Despite the best efforts of the SPS to expand its membership, including the establishment of a ladies' auxiliary, it struggled to entice a younger membership in the face of more activist benefit and Catholic societies.[136] While the SPS remained an important element of Melbourne's civil society in the early twentieth century, it was increasingly less relevant to the needs of most Irish Australians and therefore lost much of its dominance in the communication of Irish identity.

In Chicago, the Irish-American Club closed its doors in the early 1890s. It was replaced by the Sons of St Patrick and a new St Patrick's Society during that decade, though these organisations largely focused on hosting dinners for the short time that they were in existence. The Irish Fellowship Club took up the banner in 1902, attempting to 'emulate' the earlier Irish Literary Society and Irish-American Lyceum Club, which had emerged in the late 1890s.[137] It held weekly lunches with musical performances and guest speakers, presenting a strong and respectable Irish middle class to counter publicly the nepotism of Chicago politics. While Irish-American middle-class organisations provided a constant presence in Chicago associational life, there was a noticeable reduction in the explicit provision for Irish migrants. While the Illinois St Andrew's Society funded an old people's home, free of charge, for Scottish migrants, and old age care was provided for Norwegians, Swedish, Danish, Bohemian and German Chicagoans, there were no explicitly Irish homes.[138] Presumably they were welcomed into the Catholic homes. Similarly, while practically all immigrant groups maintained ethnic welfare societies in 1918, no Irish organisations were recorded in the city directory.

The gradual evolution of Irish secular associational life into explicitly Catholic or nationalist organisations occurred in both Australia and the United States. Timothy Meagher notes that in the 1910s, the Irish associations of Worcester, Massachusetts, increasingly became part of a 'militantly Catholic, patriotically American, pan-ethnic, American

Catholic people, with themselves as leaders of this new group, arbiters of this new identity'.[139] A quest for respectability still permeated across ethnic associational culture. However, power, money and political status could also force acceptance within American and Australian societies. In addition to networks across both cities, organisers in Melbourne and Chicago connected with those across the diaspora and in Ireland. The direction of Irish diasporic associationalism was further united by the sending of delegates to international Irish race conventions. These brought members of the diaspora together to fundraise, to decide on political and cultural messaging, and to help strengthen international relationships.[140] Just as the growth of public transport facilitated greater cooperation between Irish communities in cities like Melbourne and Chicago, diasporic organisations were brought together through steam travel and the telegraph.

CONCLUSION

Secular parish life was contingent on personal networks building upon connections made in Ireland and abroad, at university, in shared interests and through occupation. These networks could be expanded throughout the city and internationally by membership of elite organisations, such as the Melbourne SPS and the Irish-American Club, and through the issuance of invitations to prominent national and international speakers. The members of these clubs sought to improve and maintain the status of Irish people within Melbourne and Chicago, and specifically cement professional bonds between individuals involved in committee positions. They were frequently based on cross-denominational cooperation, permitting an inclusivity of Irish ethnic associational culture at a middle-class and elite level of society. It was only with the growing affluence and stability of the late 1870s and 1880s that club life afforded the opportunity to encompass a range of denominational allegiances in the cities, and then only in the more affluent areas of each city. The surge in Irish nationalist activity and reduction of migration in the twentieth century forced Irish clubs to reconsider their priorities.

Societies aimed at decreasing social inequality operated within more local parish surroundings, and it is perhaps less surprising to see the influence of the Catholic Church. Based within a parish or suburb, these organisations created the sense of an ethnic community, providing social and financial support while linking men from similar geographical and occupational backgrounds to their local pub or hall. Relying on a system of recommendations, these societies took into account the transient nature of life for many Irish labourers during the nineteenth and early twentieth centuries. Affiliation with branches in different states and countries provided a transnational and fluid system of support for often young, migratory workers, necessary in the 1840s and the 1880s, both decades of high migration domestically and internationally. The SPS attempted to expand recruitment of younger generations by branching out into benefit societies based in localities. While this did not necessarily work, it did allow the oldest Irish society in Victoria to continue its presence in Melbourne. In the place of explicitly Irish societies came Irish dominance of labour organisations, drawing power away from the middle classes and placing it into the hands of the working classes and Catholic parishes.

Engagement with a diasporic Irish community identity altered between the 1840s and 1922, with power changing hands reflecting wider class and political shifts. However, there was always a strong 'middle crust' of clerks, police officers and publicans to connect Irish associational culture across each city. While Irish Protestants made up an important element of this 'middle crust' in both cities, their presence in ethnic organising was focused upon in different ways. In Chicago, their inclusion in specifically Irish societies was often used to highlight the cosmopolitanism and free-thinking nature of a cultural organisation like the Literary Association. In Melbourne, conversely, cooperation between Irish Catholics and Protestants was a mainstay of subscription-based organisations until the 1870s, due to financial pressures and the demographics of its Irish community. In later decades, Protestants from all backgrounds were included in Melbourne's Irish nationalist organising but increasingly excluded from associational culture which performed Irishness predicated on Catholicism. Melbourne and Chicago had a variety of organisations which appealed to different generations and sections of each city's Irish inhabitants. These shifted over time, including and excluding parts of each city's 'Irish' community depending on the priorities of their committees. Ethnic organisations complemented membership of other fraternal societies, allowing Irish and Irish-descended people in Melbourne and Chicago to work within and benefit from both class and cultural structures. While secular club life was dominated by men, women were vital in shaping this civil society through their roles of teacher, nurse and organiser, roles that will be explored further in the next two chapters.

NOTES

1. Kristen McKenzie, *Scandal in the Colonies: Sydney and Cape Town, 1820–1850* (Melbourne: Melbourne University Press, 2004), pp. 5–6.
2. Malcolm and Hall, *New History*; David N. Doyle, 'The Irish in Chicago', *Irish Historical Studies*, 26:103 (1989), pp. 293–303.
3. O'Farrell, *The Irish in Australia*, p. 15; McCaffrey, 'The Irish-American dimension'.
4. McCarthy, *Respectability and Reform*. McCarthy has explored the connections between labour and suffrage activism and Irish ethnic associations.
5. Michael F. Funchion, 'The political and nationalist dimensions', in McCaffrey, Skerrett, Funchion and Fanning, *The Irish in Chicago*, pp. 61–97; Malcolm and Hall, *New History*, pp. 293–304. Similar occurred in New York according to Patrick McGrath, 'Secular power, sectarian politics: The American-born Irish elite and Catholic political culture in nineteenth-century New York', *Journal of American Ethnic History*, 38:3 (2019), pp. 36–75.
6. Conzen et al., 'The invention of ethnicity'.
7. Tanja Bueltmann, *Clubbing Together: Ethnicity, Civility and Formal Sociability in the Scottish Diaspora to 1930* (Liverpool: Liverpool University Press, 2015), pp. 5–6; Belchem, 'Liverpool-Irish enclave'.
8. Enda Delaney and Donald M. MacRaild, 'Introduction', in Enda Delaney and Donald M. MacRaild (eds), *Irish Migration, Networks and Ethnic Identities since 1750* (London: Routledge, 2007), pp. vii–xxii.
9. Marlou Schrover and Floris Vermeulen, 'Immigrant organisations', *Journal of Ethnic and Migration Studies*, 31:5 (2005), pp. 823–32.
10. Belchem, 'Liverpool-Irish enclave'.
11. R. J. Morris, 'Introduction: Civil society, associations and urban places: Class, nation and culture in nineteenth-century Europe', in Graeme Morton, Boudien de Vries and R. J. Morris (eds), *Civil Society, Associations and Urban Places: Class, Nation and Culture in Nineteenth-Century Europe* (Aldershot: Ashgate Publishing, 2006), pp. 1–16; Ernest Gellner, *Conditions of Liberty: Civil Society and its Rivals* (London: Hamish Hamilton, 1994).
12. *New-York Freeman's Journal and Catholic Register*, 10 December 1842.
13. *General Directory and Business Advertiser of the City of Chicago for the Year 1844* (Chicago: Ellis & Fergus Printers, 1844), henceforth Chicago City Directory, 1844.
14. Edmund Finn, *The Chronicles of Early Melbourne, 1835 to 1852, Historical, Anecdotal and Personal* (Melbourne: Fergusson & Mitchell, 1888), p. 643.
15. Chicago City Directory, 1844.
16. Hilde Greefs, 'Clubs as vehicles for inclusion in the urban fabric?

Immigrants and elitist associational Practices in Antwerp, 1795–1830', *Social History*, 41:4 (2016), pp. 375–95.
17. Catherine Hall, *Civilising Subjects: Metropole and Colony in the English Imagination 1830–1867* (Chicago: University of Chicago Press, 2002), p. 387; Belchem, *Irish, Catholic and Scouse*, p. 127.
18. Cowan, 'Immigrants, nativists', pp. 93–4, 102.
19. Sven Beckert, 'Institution-building and class formation: How nineteenth-century bourgeois organized', in Morton, de Vries and Morris (eds), *Civil Society, Associations and Urban Places*, pp. 17–38.
20. Kelleher, 'Class and Catholic'; A. T. Andreas, *History of Chicago from the Earliest Period to the Present Time in Three Volumes*, vol. 2 (Chicago: A. T. Andreas, 1884), p. 161.
21. Andreas, *History of Chicago*, p. 161.
22. Finn, *Early Melbourne*, p. 646.
23. *Port Phillip Patriot and Melbourne Advertiser*, 15 August 1842; Finn, *Early Melbourne*, p. 646.
24. *Port Phillip Gazette*, 2 July 1842.
25. *Melbourne Times*, 2 July 1842.
26. Finn, *Early Melbourne*, p. 647; *Port Phillip Gazette*, 15 April 1843; *Port Phillip Gazette*, 28 October 1843.
27. Finn, *Early Melbourne*, p. 646; Tas Vertigan, *The Orange Order in Victoria: Origins, Events, Achievements, Aspirations, and Personalities* (Melbourne: Loyal Orange Institution of Victoria, 1979).
28. *Melbourne Times*, 27 August 1842.
29. *Melbourne Courier*, 16 July 1845; *Port Phillip Patriot and Melbourne Advertiser*, 12 July 1845.
30. O'Farrell, *Irish in Australia*, p. 197.
31. *Argus*, 24 July 1846; *Port Phillip Patriot and Melbourne Advertiser*, 16 July 1846. This riot and its aftermath will be explored in more detail in Chapter 7.
32. Richard P. Davis, 'Loyalism in Australasia, 1788–1868', in Allan Blackstone and Frank O'Gorman (eds), *Loyalism and the Formation of the British World, 1775–1914* (Woodbridge: Boydell Press, 2019), pp. 223–40.
33. *Argus*, 22 December 1846.
34. *Age*, 7 April 1858.
35. MacDonagh, 'The Irish in Australia'.
36. Lindberg, *To Serve and Collect*, pp. 3–12.
37. Kelleher, 'Class and Catholic'.
38. The national religious parish system was established in Chicago in 1844 and will be the focus of Chapter 4.
39. *The Chicago City Directory, and Business Advertiser* (Chicago: Robert Fergus Book & Job Printer, 1855). Henceforth Chicago City Directory, 1855.

40. Pacyga, *Chicago*, p. 31.
41. *Chicago Daily Times*, 19 March 1855; T. M. Halpin, *Chicago City Directory, for the Year 1861–62* (Chicago: Halpin & Bailey Publishers, 1861). Henceforth Chicago Directory, 1861.
42. Chicago Directory, 1861; *Chicago City Directory, for the Year 1863–4* (Chicago: Halpin & Bailey Publishers, 1863); *Edwards' Chicago Business Director: Embracing a Classified List of all Trades, Professions and Pursuits in the City of Chicago, for the Year 1866–7* (Chicago: Edwards, Greenough & Deved, 1866); *Edwards' Chicago Business Director: Embracing a Classified List of all Trades, Professions and Pursuits in the City of Chicago, for the Year 1868–9* (Chicago: Edwards & Co. Publishers, 1868); *Edwards' Chicago Business Director: Embracing a Classified List of all Trades, Professions and Pursuits in the City of Chicago, for the Year 1869–70* (Chicago: Edwards & Co. Publishers, 1869), supplemented with information from the US Federal Census, 1860 and 1870.
43. Kelly, *The Shamrock and the Lily*, p. 146.
44. Ben Schrader, *The Big Smoke: New Zealand Cities, 1840–1920* (Wellington: Bridget Williams Book, 2016), p. 90; Matthew Allen, 'Sectarianism, respectability and cultural identity: The St Patrick's Total Abstinence Society and Irish Catholic temperance in mid-nineteenth century Sydney', *Journal of Religious History*, 35:3 (2011), pp. 374–92.
45. Finn, *Early Melbourne*, pp. 653–4.
46. Finn, *Early Melbourne*, p. 654; *Age*, 7 July 1856, 8 April 1857, 28 November 1857.
47. *Age*, 8 October 1857.
48. MacDonagh, 'The Irish in Australia'. See Malcolm and Hall, *A New History*, for consideration of anti-Irish and anti-Catholic stereotyping and prejudice throughout the nineteenth century.
49. Malcolm and Hall, *A New History*, p. 280.
50. *Rand McNally & Co.'s Pictorial Guide to Chicago: What to See and How to See It* (Chicago: Rand McNally & Co., 1886).
51. James R. Barrett, *The Irish Way: Becoming American in the Multiethnic City* (London: Penguin Books, 2012), p. 3.
52. Shiels, *Irish in the American Civil War*.
53. Kelleher, 'Class and Catholic'.
54. *Chicago Tribune*, 20 April 1861.
55. James B. Swan, *Chicago's Irish Legion: The 90th Illinois Volunteers in the Civil War* (Carbondale: Southern Illinois University Press, 2009), p. 11; Theodore J. Karamanski, *Rally 'Round the Flag: Chicago and the Civil War* (Oxford: Rowman & Littlefield Publishers, 2006), p. 78.
56. Edward C. Russell of Knox County, Illinois, assured Mulligan that he could provide good references if he could join the Irish Brigade, 28 January 1862; Capt. J. C. Fitzgibbon to Mulligan, 10 February 1862

(Chicago History Museum and Research Library, Mulligan Papers, Box 1). Original emphasis.
57. Susannah Ural Bruce explores these blended and changing motivations in '"Remember your country and keep up its credit": Irish volunteers and the Union Army, 1861–1865', *Journal of Military History*, 69:2 (2005), pp. 331–59.
58. Jentz and Schneirov, *Chicago in the Age of Capital*, p. 25.
59. Chicago Directory, 1863 and 1866.
60. Chicago Directory, 1861; *Daily Inter Ocean*, 3 January 1866, 5 May 1866.
61. Kyle Hughes and Donald MacRaild, *Ribbon Societies in Nineteenth-Century Ireland and Its Diaspora: The Persistence of Tradition* (Liverpool: Liverpool University Press, 2018), p. 227.
62. McGrath, 'Secular power, sectarian politics'; Funchion, 'Political and nationalist dimensions'.
63. Pescod, 'Irish participation'; Richard Schneirov, *Labor and Urban Politics: Class Conflict and the Origins of Modern Liberalism in Chicago, 1864–97* (Urbana: University of Illinois Press, 1998), pp. 17–24; McCarthy, *Respectability and Reform*, pp. 35–7.
64. John Milner and Oswald W. Brierly, *Cruise of H.M.S. Galatea, Captain . . . the Duke of Edinburgh in 1867–1868* (London: 1869), pp. 245–7.
65. *Australasian*, 30 November 1867; *Illustrated Australian News for Home Readers*, 20 December 1867.
66. Milner and Brierly, *Cruise of H.M.S. Galatea*, pp. 245–7.
67. *Advocate*, 28 November 1868.
68. *Advocate*, 19 June 1869.
69. Ibid.
70. Peter Clark, *British Clubs and Societies 1580–1800: The Origins of an Associational World* (Oxford: Oxford University Press, 2000), p. 304.
71. The court case of Dr McCarthy, who sued the St Patrick's Society for wages owed after he was removed as the Society's chief medical officer in 1869, brought this aspect of provision into the public arena. *Age*, 13 December 1869; *Argus*, 24 December 1869.
72. *Irish American Weekly*, 12 June 1869.
73. *Chicago Post*, 19 August 1872.
74. *Daily Inter Ocean*, 15 July 1870.
75. Mortimer, Michael, Edward and John F. Scanlan; Charles Ffrench (ed.), *Biographical History of the American Irish in Chicago* (Chicago: American Biographical Publishing Co., 1897), p. 366; Chicago Directory, 1870.
76. Chicago Directory, 1866, 1868 and 1869.
77. Chicago Directory, 1875.
78. Donlon, *German and Irish*, p. 135.
79. By 1891, TCD (48) ranked third, behind the University of Melbourne (243) and Cambridge (56), in the number of graduates living in Victoria.

The Royal Ireland University produced eleven graduates and Queen's University Ireland, six. Victorian Census, 1891.
80. Ronayne, *First Fleet to Federation*, p. 14.
81. John Waugh, *First Principles: The Melbourne Law School, 1857–2007* (Melbourne: Melbourne University Publishers, 2007), pp. 17–22.
82. Alan Bairner, 'Ireland, sport and empire', in Jeffery (ed.), *An Irish Empire?*, pp. 57–76.
83. Paul Rouse, *Sport and Ireland: A History* (Oxford: Oxford University Press, 2015), p. 4.
84. Kathleen Thomson and Geoffrey Serle, *A Biographical Register of the Victorian Legislature: 1859–1900* (Canberra: ANU Press, 1972), p. 135.
85. The match was played between Victoria and New South Wales. *Age*, 6 February 1860.
86. Marcus de Búrca, 'The Gaelic Athletic Association and organized sport in Ireland', in Grant Jarvie (ed.), *Sport in the Making of Celtic Cultures* (Leicester: Leicester University Press, 1999), pp. 100–11.
87. Art Ó Maolfabhail, 'Hurling: An old game in a new world', in Jarvie (ed.), *Sport in the Making of Celtic Cultures*, pp. 149–65.
88. Trevor West, *The Bold Collegians: The Development of Sport in Trinity College, Dublin* (Dublin: Lilliput Press, 1991), p. 57.
89. *Advocate*, 28 December 1872; Ó Maolfabhail, 'Hurling'.
90. *Geelong Advertiser*, 17 September 1877.
91. Frances Harkin, '"Where would we be without the GAA?": Gaelic games and Irishness in London', *Irish Studies Review*, 26:1 (2008), pp. 55–66.
92. *Daily Inter Ocean*, 26 July 1874; *Daily Tribune*, 9 August 1874.
93. *Irish Citizen*, 2 May 1868; *Daily Illinois State Register*, 24 April 1868; in this report, thirty or forty men were wounded.
94. Information from *Irish Citizen* supplemented by the Chicago Directory, 1868 and 1869.
95. *Irish Republic*, 20 July 1867.
96. Ellen Skerrett, 'The development of Catholic identity among Irish Americans in Chicago, 1880–1920', in Timothy J. Meagher (ed.), *From Paddy to Studs: Irish-American Communities in the Turn of the Century Era, 1880–1920* (New York: Greenwood Press, 1986), pp. 117–38.
97. Ibid.
98. US Federal Census, 1870; *Daily Inter Ocean*, 16 April 1867.
99. *Lakeside Annual Directory of the City of Chicago* (Chicago: Chicago Directory Company, 1880); *Daily Inter Ocean*, 18 September 1874; *Chicago Daily Tribune*, 13 March 1881.
100. Delaney and MacRaild, 'Introduction', p. xi.
101. Anthony D. Buckley, '"On the club": Friendly societies in Ireland', *Irish Economic and Social History*, 14 (1987), pp. 39–58; Dan Weinbren and Bob James, 'Getting a grip: The roles of friendly societies in Australia and Britain reappraised', *Labour History*, 88 (2005), pp. 87–103.

102. Andreas, *History of Chicago*, vol. 3, p. 614.
103. William Onahan to B. Callaghan letter, 25 November 1881 (Box 5, William J. Onahan Papers, ADMN/C5920/601, Chicago Archdiocesan Archives (CAA)).
104. Andreas, *History of Chicago*, vol. 3, p. 614.
105. *Irish Nation*, 7 January 1882; Andreas, *History of Chicago*, vol. 3, p. 410.
106. Patricia Kelleher, 'Young Irish workers: Class implications of men's and women's experiences in Gilded Age Chicago', *Éire-Ireland*, 36:1&2 (2001), pp. 141–65; Steven P. Erie, *Rainbow's End: Irish-Americans and the Dilemmas of Urban Machine Politics, 1840–1985* (Berkeley: University of California Press, 1990), p. 59.
107. *Chicago Tribune*, 3 March 1880. US Federal Census, 1880 and *The Lakeside Annual Directory of the City of Chicago, 1882* (Chicago: Chicago Directory Co., 1882); *The Lakeside Annual Directory of the City of Chicago, 1889* (Chicago: Chicago Directory Co., 1889).
108. *The Lakeside Annual Directory of the City of Chicago, 1885* (Chicago: Chicago Directory Co., 1885); Kelleher, 'Class and Catholic'.
109. Erie, *Rainbow's End*, pp. 54–9.
110. Hogan, *The Irish in Australia*, p. 30.
111. Hugh Buggy, *Celtic Club: A Brief History, 1887–1947* (Melbourne, 1948), p. 2.
112. *General Laws of the Irish National Foresters' Benefit Society: Executive Council of Australasia* ('The Reformer' Printing Company, 1888).
113. *General Laws*, 4.
114. Henry Grattan Branch, Irish National Foresters form of declaration for new members, 1899–1903 (Box 2/0/INF 5, Melbourne Diocesan Historical Commission (MDCH)). Davison, *Marvellous Melbourne*, pp. 192–3.
115. Davison, *Marvellous Melbourne*, p. 21.
116. *General Laws*; INF notebook, c. 1889 (Box 2/0/INF 3, MDCH).
117. *Advocate*, 31 October 1891.
118. *Age*, 9 December 1880.
119. *Inward Overseas Passenger Lists (British Ports)*, Microfiche VPRS 7666, Public Record Office of Victoria (PROV); *Australia, Death Index, 1787–1988* (Ancestry.com); *Advocate*, 20 May 1920; St Patrick's Society marshal in parade, *Argus*, 18 March 1886; district president of St Patrick's Society and marshal in parade, *Argus*, 19 March 1887.
120. Rahilly's links to the Catholic Church were reflected throughout his family. Of the nine surviving children of the fourteen born to Matthew and his wife Elizabeth, three daughters became nuns, two in Melbourne and one in Tasmania. *Advocate*, 1 April 1916; 'Mr Matthew Rahilly', *Advocate*, 20 May 1920. Sister Ildephonsus (Sisters of Charity, East Melbourne), Sister Eustace (Hobart), Sister Canisius (Sisters of Mercy, Nicholson Street).

121. Val Noone, *Nicholas O'Donnell's Autobiography* (Ballarat: Ballarat Heritage Service, 2017); *Irish American*, 27 May 1895.
122. *Freeman's Journal* (Dublin), 20 August 1888.
123. Ibid.
124. *Chicago Tribune*, 22 October 1891, 27 February 1893; George B. Kirsch, Othello Harris and Claire E. Nolte, *Encyclopedia of Ethnicity and Sports in the United States* (Westport, CT: Greenwood Publishing Group, 2000), p. 176.
125. *Chicago Tribune*, 10 September 1894.
126. Doyle, 'Irish in Chicago'.
127. David Brundage, 'American labour and the Irish question, 1916–23', *Saothar*, 24 (1999), pp. 59–66; James Barrett, *Work and Community in the Jungle: Chicago's Packinghouse Workers, 1894–1922* (Urbana: University of Illinois Press, 1990), pp. 191–2; Suellen Hoy, 'The Irish girls' rising: Building the women's labor movement in Progressive-Era Chicago', *Labor*, 9:1 (2012), pp. 77–100; Robert L. Reid (ed.), *Battleground: The Autobiography of Margaret A. Haley* (Urbana: University of Illinois Press, 1982).
128. Hoy, 'Irish girls' rising'; McCarthy, *Respectability and Reform*, pp. 46–54.
129. Hoy, 'Irish girls' rising'.
130. Malcolm and Hall, *New History*, pp. 300–5.
131. Patrick O'Farrell, *The Catholic Church in Australia: A Short History, 1788–1967* (London: Geoffrey Chapman, 1969), p. 211.
132. *Advocate*, 23 June 1917.
133. *Advocate*, 16 February 1922; *Advocate*, 11 August 1906; *Tribune*, 23 December 1915.
134. *Advocate*, 14 February 1920; *Advocate*, 15 July 1920.
135. *Advocate*, 1 December 1900; *Advocate*, 25 January 1908; *Advocate*, 29 March 1919.
136. *Advocate*, 1 April 1920; *Advocate*, 14 February 1920; *Advocate*, 16 February 1922.
137. Michael F. Funchion, *Irish American Voluntary Organisations* (Westport, CT: Greenwood Press, 1983), pp. 173–4.
138. *Chicago Social Service Directory* (Chicago, IL: Burmeister Printing Co., 1918).
139. Meagher, *Inventing Irish America*, p. 4.
140. Gerard Keown, 'The Irish Race Conference, 1922, reconsidered', *Irish Historical Studies*, 32:127 (2001), pp. 365–76; Brundage, 'American labour'.

4

Church and Club: Religious Parish Life

On Friday 15 November 1850, a grand parade made its way through the streets of Melbourne. The parade ended four days celebrating Victoria's separation from New South Wales, and brought together the city's social, political and religious leaders and organisations. In front of the Mayor and Members of the Legislative Council marched six hundred children. This 'immense assemblage of children' was made up solely of pupils and teachers from Melbourne's Catholic schools and was described as being 'full of promise to the future "Victoria"'.[1] These Catholic children marched alongside the SPS and the Father Mathew Total Abstinence Society, positioning current and future representatives of Irish and Catholic religious and secular communities at the forefront of the new colony's foundational story. The prominent position of Catholic children in the parade, and the lack of remark on the involvement of Protestant children, indicates the fluidity of the hierarchy of religion in the Australian colonies during the mid-century. Parish schools operated within a wider religious parish life, emphasising the connections between religion, ethnicity and community from childhood to late adulthood. While Chapter 5 will focus on the role of education in moulding multi-generational identities, this chapter explores the emergence and development of associational religious parish life in Chicago and Melbourne.

The religious parish was a vital point of connection for the Irish abroad and worked alternately in tandem and in conflict with the secular parish. The influence of the laity in promoting religious parish life cannot be ignored. This chapter utilises the methodologies of Sarah Roddy and William Jenkins, concentrating on the efforts of the Irish laity to spread Catholicism outside of the church walls and bring Catholic families together in devotion.[2] By focusing on the Irish Catholic parishes of Melbourne and Chicago, it examines the transnational links that the Irish laity brought with them to the diasporic parish. These lay endeavours were particularly important in Melbourne during the 1850s, when there were a total of thirteen priests caring for eight missions in Victoria.[3] Catholics in Chicago were slightly better provided for but, in both cities, the laity took on a role in religious parish life that priests and religious orders could not.

Investment in religious schools, churches, convents and hospitals, referred to as 'brick and mortar Catholicism' by Ellen Skerrett,[4] demonstrably claimed space within the city for Irish Catholic communities while providing a focus for religious parish life. Though often led by the laity, activities still took place within the structures of the religious parish, giving the clergy 'an in-built advantage' in their desire to control their parishioners' activities.[5] This chapter examines some of the processes through which the image of, and loyalty to, the religious parish were encouraged and adapted by the clergy, religious communities and the laity. It is an investigation of the structures of parish life, and how Irish Catholic communities adapted to the different challenges they faced in Melbourne and Chicago. It is largely based within the parish and not the diocese, focusing upon the weekly interactions that shaped the everyday lives and identities of Irish Catholics in Melbourne and Chicago. The source material denotes the different ways that Catholics in both cities interacted with their parishes. In an ethnically plural city like Chicago, the name of a community's church identified its congregation's ethnicity and class.[6] This chapter therefore relies heavily on parish histories in Chicago, indicating the strong ties that bound generations of the same family to the local and national church. In Melbourne, conversely, where Irish people made up almost the entire Catholic Church laity, there was a greater identification with the wider city, and then suburb and the class of people that lived therein. The record of parish life can therefore be found in the city's newspapers and city histories instead of parish histories. This comparison emphasises the importance of the local contexts of each city, the ethnic pluralism or homogeneity of each parish, and the common strands of influence from the Irish origins of its congregation. This chapter is split into three sections. The first (1830–65) details the growth of Catholic social provision in each city. The second (1865–80) focuses on the increased role of women and the working classes in religious associational culture, while the final section (1880–1922) explores the impact of papal encyclicals emphasising separate provision for Catholics on the nature of Catholic organising in both cities. Tensions between Irish nationalist organising and religious control can be seen to varying degrees throughout the later sections as the prioritisation of 'Irish' and 'Catholic' is fought over.

1830–1865

The early years of Melbourne society were marked by religious cooperation and compromise. The New South Wales Church Act of 1836 had diminished the power of the Anglican Church in the Australian colonies, ensuring that one religion was not overtly financially or legally protected by the state. Early settlers in Melbourne were keen to make the most of this state-protected denominational acceptance. Protestants and Catholics spent the 1830s and 1840s working together to build up Melbourne's infrastructure, donating to the erection of each other's religious schools and chapels.[7] While there were moments of sectarian upheaval, for the majority of the first two decades of colonial Melbourne, its inhabitants could not afford to separate themselves based on religion. When Father Geoghegan, the man who established the first Catholic mission in Melbourne in 1838, attempted to make the SPS an Irish Catholic society, the resultant tensions were greeted with changes in Geoghegan's approach. Religious practice became a private and personal activity until Ireland's bishops responded to the laity's requests for religious leaders to supplement the efforts of Geoghegan and his thirteen priests in 1849.

The Catholic diocese of Chicago was established in November 1843 and welcomed its first bishop, Irish-born William Quarter, in 1844. Quarter's arrival signalled the creation of a parish system in Chicago that would alter Catholic interactions with the rest of Chicago society until the 1960s. Quarter's decision to separate the English-speaking from non-English language churches distinguished Chicago's Catholic Church from other US cities. His justification was that the church was a place of calm, recollection and community, and part of this was communion in a parishioner's native language. The 'national parish' system was therefore reflected out from the church into schools and clubs, and through the religious orders who arrived to staff them. The first separate church was for the city's German-speaking population, and was soon followed by French Canadian, Polish, Bavarian and later Italian congregations. The English-language parishes were quickly dominated by Irish migrants and clergy, helping to create ethnic and linguistic links between priest and parishioner. An Irish Catholic religious community based around nationality, connected to but outside of Sunday Mass, was encouraged by the arrival of Irish women religious to run parochial schools, hospitals and orphanages in 1846. These women, and their male teaching counterparts, worked to promote a sense of transnational community: bridging the ocean between Ireland and Chicago via Rome. Through their position in institutions utilised by the whole community – men, women, children – across society's class divisions, the American Irish Catholic Church was therefore able to influence new generations of Irish and Irish-American Catholics, linking ethnic and religious identities within an American immigrant church.[8] The dominance of English-speaking Irish Catholics in Chicago's hierarchy was often a cause for concern for other ethnic groups, and in 1848 German Catholics petitioned for a German-speaking bishop after Quarter's death. They were successful in the appointment of James Van de Velde as the city's second bishop but Van de Velde's lack of popularity with Irish congregations soon saw a return to Irish-American dominance.[9]

The Catholic laity in Melbourne actively petitioned for religious representation, as did their compatriots from the Protestant faiths. Anglican requests were answered first when Charles Perry, consecrated as Bishop of Melbourne in Westminster Abbey in 1847, arrived in the city the following year.[10] James Alipius Goold was soon named Catholic Bishop of Melbourne, arriving in 1849, at which point Perry refused to acknowledge his counterpart's equal position as 'Bishop of Melbourne'.[11] The competition between the Catholic and Protestant bishops signalled a change in the religious harmony of the growing city. While Geoghegan had acted in defence of his parishioners' civil and religious liberties, Goold sought to protect the authority of his position and his church in the city.[12] The arrival of and backlash to Earl Grey's so-called Irish orphan girls – 4,000 Irish teenagers and young women sent from Ireland's workhouses to Sydney, Melbourne, Adelaide and Hobart – presented Goold with his first opportunity to rally Irish people around a common cause.[13] In 1850, Melbourne's City Council wrote to Queen Victoria and her government representatives to protest the use of the Immigrant Fund to send girls of 'abandoned character ... the sweepings of Irish workhouses' to Melbourne.[14] Goold organised a public meeting in support of the "orphans".[15] He endeavoured to connect the Irish in Melbourne to each other, to himself and to those who remained in Ireland, through religion and common experience of life in Ireland. Irishmen of different denominational backgrounds spoke for the Irish women's character and goodness, and Goold took on the role of witness for their Catholic devotion.[16] Instead of being stranded and turning to prostitution, Goold noted that the women had been brought into Melbourne's Catholic communities. He had personally given Confirmation to sixty-five of them, and the majority 'complied with their religious duties'.[17] Goold promoted himself as a link between the Irish Catholic populations of Melbourne, Victoria and Ireland while bonding his representatives and congregation to his religious and ethnic identities and heritage.

Goold was able to expand these connections between Ireland and Melbourne, and as the years progressed he was able to provide support and the promise of community to Irish people before they had even left Ireland. Within his papers are a noticeable number of letters of introduction from Cardinal Cullen in Dublin.[18] Letters of introduction, based upon Irish Catholic religious networks, at episcopal and clerical levels, helped new immigrants form bonds with prospective countrymen, while emphasising the homogeneity of Victoria's lay Catholic Church. Goold also sought to have his parishioners' national background reflected from the pulpit after 'indiscreet language [was] used by the clergyman, who is a native of England, and having reference of the country and habits of the congregation, who are all Irish'.[19] While Irish-born clergymen may have aided ethnic community building in Catholic parishes, the arrival of more clerics also transferred territorial loyalties from Ireland into an Australian context.[20] These tensions were mediated through the Catholic hierarchy in Ireland, further emphasising the transnational ties between the Catholic Church in Ireland and Victoria. This would be an ongoing feature of the Catholic Church in Melbourne, particularly during the First World War.

By the end of the 1850s, the Catholic parishes in Melbourne and Chicago were sufficiently staffed and supported for the laity to begin organising religious associations of their own. In 1858, the parishioners of the Holy Family Parish in Chicago established the city's first St Vincent de Paul Society.[21] It operated using a system of two or three men who called on parishioners for contributions, in the form of money or provisions, for the poor of the community. Four ladies then 'constituted a committee to visit the poor to prevent imposition, and give the deserving tickets for supplies'.[22] This organisation was primarily focused on helping the poor of the community, bringing together slightly wealthier members of the parish with the less fortunate to improve the state of life for all Irish Catholics. A year later, Melbourne's Catholics also turned their attention to community improvement, though not charity, establishing the Catholic Young Men's Society (CYMS) under the guidance of Father Bleasdale.[23] Originally established in Limerick in 1849, the aim of the Society was the 'fostering, by mutual union and co-operation, and by priestly guidance the spiritual, intellectual, social and physical welfare of its members and in obedience to and under the guidance of the Hierarchy'.[24] Though principally concerned with the spiritual welfare of its members, the CYMS also included a vital educational element in its meetings. Transnational connections between Ireland and Australia were quickly spread through migration and club life, emphasising the continued ties uniting Irish people across the world.

The CYMS leaders were training Catholics, who were largely Irish, to become active citizens of Melbourne society. Evening classes were provided alongside social and physical activities in the Sacred Heart schoolroom, linking parish elementary education provision with a wider need for societal improvement. The CYMS acted as 'a Catholic version of a mutual improvement society, like the Mechanics Institutes'.[25] The 1857 expansion of the franchise to all men in Victoria increased this need. While the franchise was withheld from their compatriots in Ireland, those in Victoria had to rise to the challenge of responsible government, demonstrating that Irish Catholics could 'exercise the powers they held, not only with integrity and independence, but with knowledge and intelligence'.[26] Just as elementary religious education was primarily concerned with the creation of good citizens, Melbourne's Catholics were cognisant of providing separate educational opportunities to its adults. In this way, they were supporting the arguments presented by Melbourne-based promoters of Irish home rule, that Irish people were able to organise and promote responsible government within the British empire. An examination of the 1863–4 CYMS membership list indicates that this desire for the promotion of Catholic young men was achieved. That year, Melbourne's CYMS included James Francis Hogan, later nationalist MP for Tipperary, Samuel Winter, who helped to establish the *Advocate* newspaper and later edited the Melbourne *Herald*, and prominent magistrates John and James Rowan.[27] The CYMS was training proud Catholic Irish and Irish-Australian men who rose to be leading and influential professionals in Australia and Ireland.

While the CYMS provided an outlet for many of Melbourne's Catholic young men, another improvement society was sought to encourage men to save and therefore protect themselves and their families from the changing whims of an industrialising city, especially within an economy based upon speculation. In response to this need, members of the CYMS organising committee established the St Francis' Benefit Society in 1864.[28] Goold was heavily involved in the Society's establishment, considering it to be a viable alternative to 'objectionable societies with signs and passwords'.[29] Organisations such as the CYMS and St Francis' Benefit Society combined with the separate schooling of Catholic children by Irish religious orders to form a clear group of adults in the 1870s and 1880s who promoted Irish and Catholic culture and heritage. This cultural affinity could then be built upon, primarily by Irish and Irish-descended men, to encourage engagement with Irish ethnic fraternalism and nationalism within Melbourne. This active participation with political Irish nationalism was enabled by the foundational connections of religious education and parish life which provided a common experience based within Irish diasporic life.

St Francis' Church, next to the Bishop's house, acted as a hub for the CYMS and other Catholic activities, bringing parishioners together from across Melbourne. This was Melbourne's Catholic Church, near to the Fitzroy Sisters of Mercy convent and a short walk from the State Library of Victoria, religious and secular representations of Melbourne's Irish-led reforming endeavours. It was at the other side of Melbourne's epicentre from the Anglican Church, creating a clearly delineated Catholic space which would soon become the site of its cathedral. As the 1860s progressed, new branches of the CYMS extended into the suburbs, following the exodus of Catholics from the centre of Melbourne. The movement of weekly meetings of the CYMS and other religious organisations into the suburbs encouraged parishioners to socialise with other Irish people from the same Melbourne suburb, and often class and occupational background, as them. Though these branches slowly encouraged Irish parishioners to base themselves in their suburbs, St Francis' Church continued to act as a central base for ethnic and religious celebrations and occasions, helping to facilitate a common Irish and Catholic city-wide parish to marshal the activities of each suburb and club, family and individual voter.

A similar spread of religious society life across different areas of the city occurred in Chicago. By 1861, there were seven conferences of the Society of St Vincent de Paul in Chicago, helping to tie people to their local parishes as well as with the wider city.[30] The committee membership of these conferences overlapped with the leadership of the Hibernian Benevolent Society and the Benevolent Society of the United Sons of Erin, uniting the laity in their ethnic and religious identities, as well as providing a group of community leaders across Chicago. Despite these connections across Irish associational culture, the members of the Society of St Vincent de Paul were 'principally laborers and mechanics – the true and ever faithful friends of the poor and friendless'.[31] This was an example of working-class Irish people helping out their peers while they were in a financial position to do so. As detailed in the previous chapter, many Irish immigrants were reliant on a precarious labour market, and participation in such organisations during times of relative wealth could help a family when they were in financial difficulties. As these conferences were based within the national parish, there was a further connection to the local Irish Catholic community as a support network to be relied upon in times of need.

While the laity may have led the committees of these societies, they were organised with the aid of parish clergy, enabling the communication of clerical values to the laity. This, according to Brian P. Clarke's work on Irish Catholics in Toronto, was in order to avoid tensions between a clergy wary of lay activism and an enthusiastic congregation.[32] Seizing on the desire for religious social and devotional organisations, and supported by the arrival of more religious communities, Chicago's Catholic churches began to establish sodalities to unite their parishioners from school age to adulthood. The Married Men's Sodality was established in the Holy Family Parish in 1859, and 'was from the beginning the mainstay of the parish ... the right hand of the pastor in carrying on his wonderful work'.[33] The married men's organisation was soon followed by the 'Congregation of the Consolers of Mary', a school sodality based in Sacred Heart school in 1860. This was complemented by the Young Ladies' Sodality in 1861 and St Anne Sodality (the Married Ladies' Sodality) in 1862.[34] Similar organisations emerged in Chicago's other parishes and schools, uniting parish congregations around their church and ethnicity. As the next chapter will explore, support for the work of female religious orders prompted women-led Catholic organising networks which could be translated into more formal structures, like sodalities, within the religious parish. It was only after the Sisters of Mercy had arrived and began to expand their provision in Melbourne that Irish Catholic women began to forge their own organisations: the earlier arrival of female religious orders in Chicago and the networks that emerged through schooling and fundraising gave the women there an impetus and confidence to demand their own space within the parish.

These sodalities encouraged devotion and community bonds: while membership of a sodality promised protection of a person's soul during life and death, it also required collecting funds from other parishioners, visiting sick members, attendance at funerals, and charitable services. These activities brought members together in religious and charitable endeavour and helped local clergymen to establish a clear parish community, financially and spiritually. Sodalities encouraged a sense of interdependence, particularly for women left without their husbands and brothers during the American Civil War. In 1861, the Sisters of Mercy were renamed the 'soldiers of Mercy' when they travelled to

Missouri and then to the *Empress*, a hospital ship of the United States Sanitary Commission, to tend to the wounded, further encouraging their reputation as the 'church's shock troops'.[35] When an Irish Brigade for Chicago was raised, James Mulligan asked the Irish Sisters of Mercy to accompany it to tend to its injured.[36] They returned to Chicago in May 1862 and their work was continued by the Daughters of Charity, who closed their school the following month to go and tend to the sick in Philadelphia. Women religious at home visited sick and wounded Confederate prisoners in Camp Douglas, a camp commanded by Colonel Benjamin Sweet, a parent at the Sisters' St Xavier's Academy.[37] The laity also played their part in supporting the religious community during the Civil War, organising bazaars and fundraiser concerts. In April 1864 a 'grand union fair' was held in Bryan Hall for the benefit of the city's orphans.[38] The following year, the 'ladies of the parish' were again called upon to support the Society of St Vincent de Paul's fair, which lasted two weeks and included visits from four hundred St Patrick's school boys and 120 boys from the orphan asylum on one day.[39] These were opportunities for Chicago's Catholics to fundraise for their institutions, but considering the amount of dancing and musical entertainments, they were also opportunities for members of gender-segregated organisations to come together to enjoy themselves.

In both Melbourne and Chicago, events like balls and bazaars may have encouraged mixing, but they were organised for specific parish institutions and by parish-based societies, parishes that were separated by nationality. These events were concerned with Irish Catholics meeting Irish Catholics from elsewhere in the city, further encouraging identification and socialisation with a particular Irish and Catholic community. Connections were based within networks of middle-class Catholics and then expanded upwards and downwards to create a sense of unity within the Irish Catholic parish. Despite this vertical and cross-class interaction, the status quo of Chicago and Melbourne's parish power structures was maintained through familial and economic ties. An examination of the leading voices in both cities' Irish Catholic parishes reveals intergenerational connections between active middle-class Catholic families, the Catholic education system and the cloister. An Irish Catholic family could therefore improve its social standing through effective engagement with the religious parish within the city and further afield.[40] As the years progressed, the leaders of Chicago's Catholic female religious orders were products of its American, and Irish, schools and sodalities. The leaders of Melbourne's convents tended to be arrivals from Ireland until the 1930s, largely as a consequence of the colonial focus of the

Irish Catholic Church's convent training schools. However, Australian-born Irish Catholic women religious filled the ranks of religious orders, continuing existing middle-class influences within the Catholic parish and remaining connected to lay life through their family members.[41]

In Melbourne, Catholic organisations prioritised respectability politics and the raising of Catholic status through education, whereas Chicago Catholics organised around charitable giving. This was, at least in part, due to the differences in state structure in the early decades of each city. Melbourne was influenced by the state social provision in Britain and Ireland which expanded in the 1830s and 1840s. While colonial authorities shied away from the establishment of workhouses, there were networks of cross-denominational private charities in addition to public benevolent asylums, magistrates' 'poor-boxes' and municipal relief funds.[42] This burgeoning, but often quite informal, state provision was met with a Catholic Church whose religious and lay hierarchy prioritised the improvement of the middle class before the poor, as demonstrated in the next chapter. In Chicago, conversely, the Catholic Church hierarchy worked within an environment with little state social provision and a generally much poorer congregation. The emphasis, therefore, was on Catholic-led provision of care and charity. This was all reflected in the shape of the religious parish, as will be seen in Chapter 5, and influenced which associations emerged over time.

1865–1880

Irish Catholic institutions had spread across both Melbourne and Chicago by 1865, taking the religious and social priorities of the Catholic hierarchy into the everyday worlds of its Irish communities. While the Catholic Church provided social and educational opportunities for Irish men and women in Melbourne and Chicago, there was an emphasis on Irish women, both as 'the occasions of sin' and as providers of succour. This condemnation of women who did not conform to ideals of domesticity had become central to Irish society in the aftermath of the Famine, and was reflected in the emergence of Magdalen laundries and female reform institutions in both Melbourne and Chicago during the 1860s.[43] While the Irish origins of these reform institutions cannot be ignored, their emergence in Melbourne and Chicago coincided with increasingly stable populations and a growing 'middle crust' focused on reputation in the late 1860s. Members of each society's middle class and professional elite sought to improve the international recognition of their city, moving away from their frontier foundations and the resultant crime and poverty. Irish-born religious orders were supplemented numerically by local girls and women who had benefited from schooling within the ethnic religious parish and the growing welfare provision within each city. Irish institutions were therefore adapted for these urban requirements, just as they had been introduced in Ireland from French contexts.

Women were regarded as the primary providers of moral and religious education in the young. If this provision did not come from nuns, it was provided by mothers, aunts and sisters, as Chapter 5 will explore.[44] Religious education was imperative for women of all classes in Melbourne and Chicago's parishes. While the religious community expanded, the laity were called upon to actively counter the threat of poverty and loss of 'virtue' within Irish society abroad. Thomas Harmon noted in 1916 that a parish priest is dependent 'to a great extent upon the co-operation and moral support of his parishioners; the willing hands and the hearty support of early settlers'.[45] The Irish Catholic Church, therefore, though controlled by the clergy and engaged middle class, was able to influence the lives of Catholics throughout Melbourne and Chicago. Using social and charitable activities and the presence of Irish-born and -trained religious representatives, the priorities of the local Catholic Church and the Irish Church could be linked.

For those who did not or could not attend a Catholic school during the week, the Sunday School Association was established in Chicago in the late 1860s, encouraging children and young adults to continue their education within the church. The Sunday School Association served another purpose: investing members of the parish in the improvement of all. Each year, two men were assigned in each district 'to go from house to house' to collect one dollar per family for the upkeep of Sunday schools and the distribution of Catholic literature to those in need. In return, subscribers received a copy of the monthly educational publication, *The Messenger*, and four Masses were said each month for the spiritual well-being of the members.[46] Organisers of the Sunday School Association provided support for their students in spiritual matters as well as educational, attending all the public functions of the schools, including processions on First Communion and Confirmation days. Described as 'a most devoted bodyguard for the children', these adults provided students with community networks linked to the Church, parish and professional society.[47] For many middle-class parishioners, they 'had to identify as Catholics and Irish, but Irishness could be a taken-for-granted background social fact. This privileged Catholicism.'[48] One way to improve the position of the wider Irish population of Chicago was through charitable activity, a popular option for the middle classes around the world during the later decades of the nineteenth century.

It was not just men who collaborated between cassock and congregant to improve the standing of Irish Catholic priorities and institutions in the city. Laywomen supported their local Catholic institutions financially through bazaars and fundraising committees in both cities. Annette Shiell has argued that the charity bazaar model was brought to Australia by the Irish Sisters of Mercy, continuing a 'philosophy and strategy of fundraising' which had been developed by the Order in the 1820s and 1830s.[49] The increasing movement of religious parish life from the central hub into the suburbs was reflected in bazaar organisation. As the majority of Melbourne's Catholics were Irish, there was no need to refer to church name to denote the national allegiances of the congregation. Instead, the suburb became the local base for parish activities, linking women who would have seen each other on a weekly basis at church and on the street.[50] The *Advocate* facilitated this sense of parish organisation and unity after 1868. Bazaars were held to help the various religious communities pay off debts incurred when expanding their buildings and institutions, with suburban committees joining together to support a rotating number of charities based in different areas of the city.[51] In this way, parish communities were still linked centrally to work toward a fairer and more respectable Melbourne.

Studying the lists of women involved in Catholic charity bazaars during the late 1860s and 1870s illuminates a core group of laywomen, mainly married to leading Catholic politicians and professionals present in the rolls of Melbourne's SPS. As well as being connected through social and religious ties, these women were linked to the work of women religious in the community, often between teacher and parent or pupil. Women were involved in the Melbourne Ladies' Benevolent Society, and collections were made in all the Catholic churches in the city and suburbs for the support of their work in 1871.[52] While women were involved in the creation of community spirit, their work also aided the subversion of Protestant-inspired state legislation. In the midst of government funding debates in 1879, the Sisters of Mercy declared that all 'proceeds of Bazaars, &c., are most faithfully divided by the Sisters of Mercy, between the two departments of the Institution, Girls and Boys, and subscribers are earnestly requested to specify ... that this division may be made'.[53] Equal donations to the education of Catholic children of both genders were required in order to ensure that government grants continued to the religious institution.

The Great Fire of 1871 brought new challenges for Chicago's

inhabitants, and the Catholic Church therein. Catholic parishes in the centre of the city were faced with burned-down churches, orphanages and schools, displaced children and families, and a serious shortage of money to replace the hard-saved cash that had allowed for the infrastructural expansion of the previous fifteen years. One descendant of a St Mary's parishioner noted that her father and his friend, 'prudent far-seeing young men', had run into the burning church to rescue the parish records.[54] The local church was the keeper of family histories and the links between family and community. In a time when marriage and baptism records were needed to claim Civil War pensions, this salvaging of church records was particularly vital. Despite the hardships brought about by the Chicago Fire, parishioners sought to restore the Church's institutions. When the Good Shepherd nuns and their wards were left without a home, those who could donated stone and lumber to help rebuild the city's institutions in the absence of monetary support. Catholic lay charities also continued to distribute relief through previously established charitable associations linked to the Church. Though the Chicago Relief and Aid Society (CRAS) helped those affected financially, its committee was firm in its position that only residents who could prove themselves completely destitute or those who had lost the homes that they *owned*, were eligible for financial aid: many were left without help.[55] In the meantime, Good Shepherd Sister Martha 'became so familiar a figure to the citizens of Chicago' due to her walks 'travel-stained and weary, but ever cheerful and contented'.[56] As the CRAS' 'contributions to helping destitute women were ... negligible', women's aid organisations and women religious worked hard to improve the position of the women and children of the city.[57] The way that the nuns dealt with their reduced circumstances was applauded, continuing the work that they had become famed for during the Civil War.

The Society of St Vincent de Paul continued to grow throughout the city in the aftermath of the fire, and by the end of the decade there was a conference in every parish. These conferences were instrumental in bringing together Irish Catholics, those providing aid and those in need, as well as spreading charity around the city. Working alongside other Catholic and community organisations allowed the Society to spread its influence into the city's schools, charities and homes. The St Vincent de Paul members attempted to fill some of the void left by CRAS, 'distributing words of consolation and also inducing the Catholic portion of them to send their children to both Sunday and day school, any of whom are destitute are supplied with books and the schooling paid for'.[58] By 1872, the Society of St Vincent de Paul conference in Bridgeport recorded an attendance of three hundred boys at its Sunday school.[59] Socially, people continued to be affected by the chaos of the Chicago Fire. Those who had been forced from their homes by the fire spent the winter surviving in 'scantily covered board shanties', with life further complicated by a labourers' strike, a horse sickness and 'now the excessive cold with the thermometer frequently 30° below zero'. The Society of St Vincent de Paul helped the needy with donations of food, wood and occasionally money. However, the quarterly report of the Holy Family Parish demonstrates the Society's preoccupation with education, complaining that despite its best efforts, 'our little library is quite neglected and probably less attention is paid to the mental and spiritual improvement of the poor than in older cities where the members of the Society are not under the necessity of working hard for the support of themselves and families'.[60] In addition to charitable giving, subscriber lists for stained-glass windows, altars and buildings fill the official parish histories of Chicago, creating a familial connection to the expansion of the Church's institutions.

As the population of Chicago continued to expand, more religious orders arrived from Ireland, directly or otherwise. With these new arrivals came the opportunity to expand the provision offered to the Catholics of the city and to adapt to the needs of people who were flooding into the city. In 1876, the Ladies of the Immaculate Heart of Mary opened St Joseph's Home for 'young working girls and those coming to the city without friends or means'.[61] Juvenile bands were established in parish schools, uniting younger generations with their older co-parishioners, to march and parade as part of the parish. One such band was the Emerald Cadets, who 'dressed in tight-fitting green jackets, black trousers, brown leather belts and caps of military type, such as the soldiers of '61 were. They were equipped with real muskets.' While older boys could join the Emerald Cadets, younger students were encouraged to join the Crusaders, who drilled with tin swords.[62] In the midst of accusations of loyalty to a foreign prince in the Vatican,[63] these cadet units showed religious and ethnic loyalty to the United States, and particularly the Union, in a similar way to the ethnic militias that paraded on St Patrick's Day and reminded others of the Irish Catholic sacrifice in the Civil War. The 1879 Silver Jubilee of the definition of the Immaculate Conception brought all of these elements of the Holy Family Parish together, a process that had begun the year previously when the first cornerstone of the parish's Sodality Hall was laid, under an ethnic religious banner instead of a purely ethnic one.[64]

In Melbourne, this explicit connection between ethnicity and religion also continued, particularly in organisations aimed at younger generations. The St Francis' Benefit Society had evolved into the Hibernian Australasian Catholic Benefit Society (HACBS) by 1871, bringing branches together from across the Australian and New Zealand colonies.[65] This transnational organisation linked Irish people together through bureaucracy and centralised conventions, while providing a ready-made support network across Australasia for those on the move. Societies such as the HACBS provided a source of financial support, but were also important in encouraging a linked Irish, Australasian and Catholic identity. Within the HACBS this was achieved through opportunities to participate in ethnic public ceremonies, and to 'cherish the memory of Ireland' through engagement with Irish history and culture.[66] The CYMS, meanwhile, encouraged the study of Irish history 'to obviate the reproach of indifference, to cultivate a spirit of individual independence and self-respect'.[67] Catholic associations encouraged debate and education, preparing the politicians, journalists and voters of the future to think for themselves, but based on a core set of values of Catholic education and devotion. The *Advocate* and the political debates on Ireland and Victorian religious education that were presented therein continued the efforts of young men's sodalities, the CYMS, the HACBS and similar associations based in and around the parish. These lay and clerical endeavours also contributed to the emerging transnational links with Irish nationalist organisations in Ireland and elsewhere in the diaspora. After Goold declared that Catholic parishioners needed to separate themselves from mixed friendly and oath-bound societies at the risk of excluding 'themselves from participation in the benefits derivable from communion with the Romish Church', there was a greater need for interaction with proudly Catholic societies.[68]

Melbourne's Irish Catholics did not only fundraise for their own institutions. They also participated in efforts to improve the status of the Catholic Church around the world, particularly in Ireland. Visiting priests engaged in speaking tours of Australia to fundraise for building efforts, encouraging a sense of linked churches as when Rev. Peter Byrne preached a sermon in St Francis' Church in aid of St McCartin's Church in Monaghan.[69] Closer to home, Catholics were encouraged to take heed of the building work taking place in Ireland and to donate to local building funds. In one sermon, Cardinal Wiseman noted that in Ireland, 'Wherever he went, notwithstanding the poverty of the people, he saw churches, colleges, and religious houses erected.' Another cleric reminded his audience that 'the parting words of the good old father and mother were – "Go abroad, my children, and prosper but *mind your religion.*"'[70] Melbourne's answer to this was St Patrick's

Cathedral. Dedicated in 1851, it was finally consecrated in 1897 after years of partial use. Not only was St Patrick's a powerful reminder of the strength and presence of Catholics in the city, its patron saint, and the Daniel O'Connell statue which was erected in front of the cathedral in 1891, was a reminder of the linked Irish and Catholic identities of its builders and funders.[71]

The years after 1865 had witnessed the expansion of the Catholic Church's resources and organisations in Melbourne and Chicago. Parishes were increasingly separated by class and occupational connections, encouraged by lay charitable activities, religious schooling and extracurricular religious organisations. The ethnic homogeneity of the Catholic Church in Melbourne encouraged a new focus on geographical suburbs. St Kilda was known for its wealthy parishioners and was home to a number of Irish politicians, whereas Collingwood and Richmond became working- and aspiring middle-class Irish centres. In Chicago, parishes and their congregations also had their own identities. The Holy Family Parish was the largest and second-oldest parish, encompassing large swathes of Chicago's near west side. It welcomed some of the city's most powerful and wealthy Irish Catholics, whereas the Nativity of Our Lord was in the centre of South Halsted Street, a working-class community on the cusp of the stockyard neighbourhoods. The 1870s had left both cities with a more vocal working class as a result of labour disputes and increased educational provision. This manifested differently in each city, but common themes of increased ethnic and class solidarity emerged in both.

1880–1922

For all Irish people, the 1880s were a time of heightened political and cultural nationalism channelled into transnational community action. For Catholics, Pope Leo XIII's *Arcanum on Christian Marriage*, issued on 10 February 1880, warned of the dangers of mixed marriages and the formation of associations that led to these connections, mixed schooling as well as mixed socialising.[72] Influencing the parish lives of those in Melbourne and Chicago, the *Arcanum* codified a trend of separation that had begun the previous decade. The religious education debates of the late 1870s and 1880s, which will be explored further in the next chapter, encouraged a more defensive Irish and Catholic community in Melbourne, echoing the ethnically and religious linked Irish Catholic communities in Chicago. In both cities, their Catholic parishes were inherently Irish, through migration patterns or through an early established plan of national parishes. As Irish nationalism became a more potent force throughout the Irish diaspora, the Catholic Church came into conflict with political organisations and priorities. How the Catholic Church in Melbourne and Chicago adapted to these new tensions – tensions brought about by a sustained encouragement of ethnic and religious links over the previous forty years – will be the focus of this chapter's final section and expanded upon in later chapters.

The Sodality of the Blessed Virgin Mary (BVM) was the largest sodality in Melbourne's Catholic Church. With at least five hundred members, it brought young Catholic men together to assist the archbishop and other senior clergy in their religious and charitable duties throughout the city.[73] Considering that the uniform of the sodality was black tie or 'academical robes' and many of the names recorded at one meeting correspond to members of the Legislative Assembly, this sodality sought members from the professional classes. Joseph Rowan and Frank Gavan Duffy are just two of the ex-students of the Jesuits' St Patrick's College and former CYMS members who emerge in their rolls.[74] Just as women religious encouraged a feeder system from convent school to convent, religious schools also instilled in Catholic boys a continuing dedication to the Catholic Church and its associations into adulthood. The social standing of many sodality members meant that imperial loyalty was still an important consideration in public ceremony. While at one sodality dinner, Dr Kenny proposed the first toast to 'their Holy Father the Pope', this was clearly not a usual option. It was only because 'the dinner was exclusively a Catholic one in a Catholic college [St Patrick's]' that the toast to their 'temporal ruler', the Queen, was subordinate to their spiritual ruler.[75] Jesuit schools such as St Patrick's College were used to instil imperial as well as religious priorities in their students, and connections with Catholic schools in England and Ireland were encouraged, particularly with Stonyhurst College. The parish school system linked Irish Catholic men to each other and their faith throughout life. Even if they did not actively engage with the religious parish's extracurricular activities, friendships and occupational links maintained some link to their religious identity. Those from the upwardly mobile middle classes could be expected to transfer these priorities into their professional and political lives.

Members of the clergy in Melbourne belonged to, and were welcomed into, leading social circles, and, in turn, lay members were recognised by the Catholic hierarchy. One way that the laity were recognised was through the award of papal knighthoods, such as the Order of St Gregory the Great. Patrick O'Brien, JP was a wine and spirit merchant who had arrived in Port Phillip in 1840, and was a founder and trustee of the SPS and an MLC for Kilmore, Kyneton and Seymour. In 1886 he gave £1,000 to the St Patrick's Cathedral fund, and in recognition of his long service to the Catholic cause he was invested as a papal knight, a member of the Order of St Gregory the Great.[76] His wife was also an active member of the Catholic Church's fundraising committees, often noted in reports for chairing the Hawthorn suburb's stalls.[77] The O'Briens were just one example of the crossing of religious, political and societal elites within Melbourne and Chicago society. The professional classes could benefit socially from engagement with the Catholic Church, and senior clergymen could further their religious endeavours financially by mingling with the laity. However, this was not purely power brokers working together for mutual improvement since bishops and senior clergymen were often from similar social and geographical backgrounds to Melbourne's professional classes and could gain intellectual and nostalgic stimulation from each other. Middle-class religious networks were therefore self-sustaining and mutually beneficial. The political and cultural ambitions held by individuals in those circles for Irish and imperial Irish identity were therefore transmitted through secular and religious parish life to the wider Irish community.

While primarily concerned with religious devotion, connections between Irish Catholic religious facilitated social and political action through faith. The spread of religious educators throughout Melbourne's suburbs both separated parishes and united them under a city-wide Catholic community. Just as bazaars brought Melbourne's Catholics together in charitable endeavour, so too did the networks of religious men and women throughout the city. In August 1882, members of the Children of Mary Sodality[78] at St Peter's and St Paul's school in Emerald Hill concluded their twelve months' prayer for the 'peace and prosperity of Ireland with a general communion and procession'. Branches of this sodality throughout Melbourne and wider Victoria had brought together four thousand 'monthly communicants' from Melbourne's convents, the Christian Brothers, and all the children and pupils under their care, for monthly Mass.[79] The Sodality of the BVM at St Patrick's College also veered into political matters when it held debate evenings.[80] School sodalities were central to the unification of Catholic children from across schools and institutions and wider Victoria. These sodalities were designed for children and adults who had been taught by religious orders to aid the continued interaction of Catholic children with the Catholic Church, and specific religious communities, localities and schools.

Chicago's Irish Catholic Church was, by 1880, in a position to expand its care and guidance due to the city's economic recovery and the arrival of more religious communities. The Holy Family Parish took the opportunity to establish a sodality for working boys in 1880, and a female counterpart was organised in 1891 at the St Joseph's Home for Friendless Girls.[81] Seven years later, the Holy Family Parish sought to encourage devotion in the parish's children who were unable to attend parish schools. From the first Monday in Lent 1887, all Catholic children over the age of twelve were required to attend lessons to prepare for their First Holy Communion. Girls and boys, and working girls and boys, were all instructed separately at different times and in different venues.[82] Devotional Catholicism 'influenced the way Catholics thought about themselves and the world in which they lived', and with more religious communities available, the parish took on the role of internally monitoring the morals and social lives of their parishioners more thoroughly.[83] Part of this expansion was enabled by the exponential increase of Irish religious women in Chicago's parishes. Between 1880 and 1890, the figure jumped from 128 to 349 in specifically Irish female religious communities.[84] In the same decade, Chicago's population increased by 119 per cent and, though the city's religious orders could not keep up with this expansion, they opened more parish schools and reform institutions in an attempt to stem the threat of poverty and heresy.

Just as sodalities aimed to expand and unite the devout congregations of Melbourne, the CYMS united its suburban branches to form the Victorian Catholic Young Men's Societies Union in 1886.[85] The Richmond branch filled a potential void in its members' lives by meeting on Wednesday nights for lectures, and then on Tuesdays and Fridays for 'off' meetings at which 'Every inducement is offered', with a selection of amusements including a reading room, cards, draughts, boxing and fencing, as well as the use of a gymnasium and piano.[86] The CYMS aimed to fulfil a 'great need in the life of a young man', both spiritually and educationally, providing the tools needed to aid their personal and economic betterment.[87] The laity also attempted to improve the lives of those in the city who could not afford the black tie of the sodality of the BVM. In the eight months after opening in October 1887, the St Vincent de Paul's Home for Men in Fitzroy noted that they had sheltered and fed '4653 poor men of all classes and creeds'.[88]

These charitable institutions helped to combat the potential enticement of secret, oath-bound societies linked to Irish separatism that remained a very unlikely threat to Melbourne society, and the more realistic social evils brought by wild economic speculation and failure. In 1889, at a presentation to Fr. Aylward for sixteen years' service to St Joseph's in Collingwood, reference was made to the religious societies established in the parish over that time. Among them were the Christian Doctrine Society, the Society of St Vincent de Paul, the CYMS, the Apostleship of Prayer, the Altar Society and HACBS.[89] These organisations demonstrate the mix of religious, national and social activities which helped the Irish Catholic Church intercede in most aspects of the lives of those who chose to associate and take advantage of the provisions of Irish Catholic life. Engagement with their Catholic identity was therefore beneficial to the Irish in Melbourne. Middle-class networks helped to reinforce respectability and existing connections formed in religious schools and secular organisations based on Irish ethnicity. Sodalities helped to spread Catholic identity across the classes, supporting the benefit societies of HACBS and INF. Throughout the 1890s, social events were used to strengthen these ties. The 1894 HACBS social, for example, brought together representatives of the SPS, CYMS, League of the Cross Society and INF, along with ladies of the parish.[90] In 1897, the role of women in the official associational culture of the parish was highlighted when the first conference of branches of the HACBS Ladies' Auxiliaries, six branches in total, was held in Melbourne.[91]

The religious press acted as an 'important educator of the people' outside the parish school, increasing the importance of editorial choices in shaping identity.[92] The *Western Catholic* became Chicago's foremost Irish Catholic journal in 1872. Pastorals from Cardinal Cullen of Dublin were frequently published, as were articles devoted specifically to Irish Catholicism. Its pages were filled with Irish news, life, landlordism and nationalism.[93] Newspapers were vital in the creation of an Irish Catholic voice, both in promulgating views and priorities and forcing a reaction between Irish and non-Irish communities. By covering Irish events, history and (re)printing letters and editorials, Irish people were able to create 'their own transnational public sphere' as well as international networks.[94] The *Western Catholic*'s Irish focus was possible because of the preponderance of German-language newspapers which also blended ethnicity with religion. In Melbourne, the *Advocate* and, later, the *Tribune* provided this newspaper community. Through ethnic and religious newspapers, the Catholic clergy could encourage their parishioners to 'campaign' for Catholic issues, particularly in relation to supporting the parish school system.[95] Archbishop Mannix took this control to heart when he bought the *Advocate* in 1919. Combining newspaper influence with the weekly opportunities of parish priests and women religious to 'cajole and convince' their parishioners, the Catholic hierarchy were able to approach their parishioners at a local and city level.

These avenues for contact could be used by parishioners as well as the clergy. By the 1880s, Irish people in Chicago were secure in their position as the dominant ethnic group of the Chicago diocese. The presence of another Irishman in the archbishopric and the number of Irish religious communities in the city had encouraged a linking between leading Irishmen in the city and their religious leaders. The St James' Parish, established in 1855, had close familial and civil links with the Sisters of Mercy's St Agatha Academy and Mercy Hospital, providing the parishioners with influential connections. After the parishioners heard that they may not get the priest they had hoped for, they travelled up Wabash Avenue to Archbishop Feehan's house to request a meeting. Finding Feehan absent, they left a respectful but direct letter suggesting that if he could not appoint Fr. D. J. Riordan, their choice, he should 'appoint some other good and zealous priest who would be in harmony with the people of the Parish'.[96] The men who signed this letter included prominent and wealthy businessmen like Michael and John Cudahy as well as bookseller Bernard Callaghan and labourer Dennis O'Connell.[97] All sixteen of the men who signed the letters had 'Irish' surnames, and cross-referencing their names demonstrates the overlapping religious, ethnic and nationalist concerns of these men. Michael Cudahy, John Guerrin and Bernard Callaghan were noted as attending an 1879 anti-rent gathering supporting Irish land reform.[98] Guerrin, a doctor, was also the chairman of the Chicago Committee for the Irish National League Convention in 1886, a committee that included four of the sixteen above signatories.[99] The connections of these men, in just one of Chicago's Catholic parishes, illustrate some of the ways that parishioners' lives crossed over, on religious, national and geographical issues. With these priorities, it is clear that the desired-for 'harmony' within the parish related to the wish for an Irish priest to reflect the Irish make-up of the parish.

The Catholic laity in Chicago followed an international trend when they decided to establish a separate organisation dedicated to the social progress of their parishioners. The Ancient Order of Hibernian Benefit Association of the State of Illinois filed a certificate of organisation in 1881.[100] By 1884 there were thirty divisions of the Ancient Order of Hibernians (AOH) within Chicago, and a further four in the soon-to-be Chicago districts of Brighton Park, Pullman and Cummings.[101] There were also eight divisions of the Hibernian Rifles in the area.[102] Joining the work of the AOH in 1883 were the Illinois Catholic Order of Foresters, established by leading Irishmen, Deputy Sheriff P. J. Cahill and Hon. John F. Scanlan.[103] Patricia Kelleher has argued that Americans, and therefore Irish Americans, perceived acceptance by their own cultural group, ethnic and occupational, 'as a criterion for access to the higher rungs of the social ladder'. The challenge for ambitious Irishmen was to maintain 'support networks that included but also transcended their immediate group, by striving to increase their cultural group's prestige, and by exhibiting a style of manliness that commanded respect from all sides'.[104]

Organisations like the AOH blended these networks of militia, benefit and entertainment. By 1888, all the Holy Family Parish sodalities had their own libraries and reading rooms, making their Sodality Hall 'the heart or center of social activities of the parish'.[105] Ethnic societies based within the national parish allowed for cross-class networking, and in 1894, the opportunity was extended to the women of Chicago when the Women's Catholic Order of Foresters (WCOF) was established, providing life insurance for most female members for the first time.[106] The WCOF was an alternative to the growing secular women's labour and temperance unions that were uniting working women in the city, particularly white immigrant women, from the late 1880s.[107] Irish and Irish-American women emerged in leadership positions within Chicago's labour assemblies, eventually leading strikes.[108] Catholic organisations aimed at women complemented and competed with the secular, political and socialist unions that the Church saw as threats to society and family values. These Catholic organisations linked people throughout the parish, across class boundaries, and provided them with financial support and relative independence. This was of particular use during the economic depression of the 1890s, which the Irish community was 'better able to weather' than other groups due to the diversity of occupations.[109] While others struggled through the 1890s, Chicago's Irish community continued to spread into the middle classes.

The parishes within Melbourne and Chicago were fundamental in creating Catholic identity in the cities. As these were the places that Irish immigrants and descendants lived, where they filtered the different influences of diasporic life through their ethnic, class and occupational points of reference, there was an implicit connecting of Irish and Catholic identities. Melbourne and Chicago both benefited from an improvement in public transport in the years after 1882, enabling increased movement between central and more suburban parishes.[110] Individual parish associations were brought together for bazaars and central committee meetings, complementing the connections between members who were often involved in multiple organisations. The 1880s saw the maintenance of Catholic parish organisations begun in the 1850s and 1860s, but also benefited from the international increase of fraternalism, reflected in both religious and secular parish life. Ethnic and religious separation of Irish Catholic communities had been encouraged for thirty years, and the codification of this in the Pope's *Arcanum* collided with the increase in Irish nationalist activity. At times, these ethnic and religious connections were utilised for political gain, while at others they were in direct conflict. These conflicts and connections will be the focus of the next chapter.

The number of Australian Catholics born in Ireland dropped from half in the 1870s to a fifth in the 1900s.[111] As the new century began, both Irishness and Catholicism needed to become relevant to new generations of Irish Australians who had no lived experience of Ireland. Education played a vital role in this, both in formal school settings and in adult social environments. In 1901, the Australian colonies joined together under federal rule. With this change in legislative status came a rebranding of certain organisations. The HACBS organisation was networked into the global AOH, with the American AOH suggesting that HACBS might encourage closer connections across organisations through an Australian name change. The 1903 general meeting emphasised the close ties of ethnicity and religion in Australia, offering 'practical encouragement' to the teaching of Irish history in Catholic schools and condemning the 'Stage Irishman' trope in Australia in solidarity with actions by the AOH.[112] Victoria retained its dominance of HACBS within Australia and New Zealand, and the day-to-day activities of HACBS in Melbourne parishes did not change drastically.[113] The ladies' branches of the HACBS met every fortnight.[114] However, in mixed events, women continued to take a subordinate role throughout the early twentieth century, principally performing musical accompaniments while male representatives presented reports on their behalf.[115]

In December 1911, the Catholic Federation was formed, bringing together delegates from Victoria's Catholic societies to present a unified front for Catholic religious, civil and social interests in Australia.[116] Catholic rights formed the basis of social activism as well as labour activism, both within and in contention with the Labor Party.[117] The Catholic Federation, which numbered around 40,000 members in 1914, represented a wider push for Catholic rights particularly related to education, under the supervision of vocal Archbishop Daniel Mannix, who arrived in 1913. As Colin Barr notes, the Catholic parish and particularly the parish school became a vital vehicle for embedding Irish identity and knowledge in new generations. It was the parish school and surrounding parish associations that 'accounts for the endurance of a coherent diasporic Irish Catholic identity long after significant Irish migration had ceased'.[118] The role of education in shaping multi-generational Irish identity and community will be further explored in the next chapter.

While Australian bishops were accused of socialism, Chicago's Irish Catholic communities briefly flirted with socialist thought before their rising class position realigned their priorities.[119] However, the role of social Catholicism did increase after 1900, particularly as Irish communities became increasingly middle class or 'proto-middle class in politics and aspirations'.[120] This renewed interest in ideas of respectability accompanied the rise of temperance in Catholic and labour organisations from 1890, and in 1902 the Knights of Columbus banned alcohol from their functions, a decision that was adopted by the AOH two years later.[121] Irish Catholic engagement with temperance movements fluctuated based on local contexts. Just as in the 1850s when Fr. Mathew's cause was undermined by nativist threats to German and Irish business, the threat of Prohibition and support of Catholic Al Smith meant that enthusiasm for temperance also ended by 1920.[122]

The rising tide of anti-Catholic feeling that occurred in both Melbourne and Chicago during the 1910s, alongside the continued fight for Catholic educational funding, brought Irish Catholic organisations more closely together. While Irish Catholics in both cities rose in socio-economic terms, their religion ensured a persistent sense of religious defensiveness, and thus a sustained Catholic parish community. A distinctly Irish Catholic club life worked alongside parish schools staffed by Irish-descended teachers and under an inherently Irish Catholic hierarchy. It was through the parish that local and transnational priorities came together and adapted to the needs of new generations of Irish-identifying Chicagoans and Melbournians.

CONCLUSION

The Catholic Church provided a foundational point of commonality and acted as a moral and comforting force for the Irish communities in both cities, aided in large part by the Irish background of many of its members and leaders. As Ciara Breathnach has emphasised in her study of the Irish in Otago, for the Catholic Church to truly embed in a community, it must have a receptive population.[123] In both Melbourne and Chicago, there had been repeated requests to Ireland for spiritual support in the 1840s: the Irish Catholic Church was therefore responding to an existing Catholic audience instead of purely a mission of conversion.[124] The desire to expand the Irish Catholic Church was enabled by an active laity, encouraged by sodalities, charities and benefit societies. During the early years of the Catholic Church of Melbourne and Chicago, religious parish life emerged in varying ways. The key difference was where this 'parish' was envisioned to be. In Chicago the parish was based largely on local geography, dictated by the national parish system, linking ethnicity with religious allegiance from the 1840s. The early arrival of women religious from Ireland encouraged this centring of life around local provision. Melbourne's Catholic Church was limited by a lack of clerical and religious personnel in its founding years. Instead, Irish Catholics in Melbourne made the most of the resources that they did have by focusing their activities around St Francis' Church. This central concentration was enabled by the ethnic homogeneity of the Melbourne Catholic Church, subconsciously linking Irish and Catholic religious life while allowing for the secular defence of Irish virtue and goodness.

While based in differing abstract locales, the religious parishes in Melbourne and Chicago were linked by their dependence on active middle-class community leaders who built upon familial and professional networks. In both cities, the organisers of religious parish life were also connected through ethnic secular life, through the SPS in Melbourne and organisations such as the Hibernian Benevolent Society in Chicago. Irish religious and ethnic parish life therefore enjoyed and relied upon a symbiotic relationship between members and organisers, contemporaneously encouraging the continuation and evolution of a sense of Irish diasporic community.

The extent to which the local Catholic Church supported, and restricted, ethnic and secular fraternalism influenced the types of organisations which emerged at different times. If the bishop said that 'good' Catholics should not mix socially with non-Catholics, this was only sustainable if the Church provided alternatives. These substitutes were inspired by the Irish roots of the religious and lay communities that shaped the religious parish life in both cities. While the Catholic Church in Melbourne and Chicago has received scholarly attention based on geography, comparison of the parish lives that emerged in both cities allows for further understanding of personal influence and institutional structures.

The Irish backgrounds of the religious communities and clergy in Melbourne and Chicago allowed for the surrounding of Australian- and

American-born congregations with a community lineage intimately related to Ireland. As such, the national parish, locally and city-wide, bonded Catholics to each other and to Ireland. The position of Irish religious women in the daily lives of schools and sodalities, as well as in institutions like hospitals, helped to provide a consistent ethnic mirroring throughout Catholic life. Where women encouraged their students to join the convent, organise bazaars and participate in religious education, men were encouraged to continue their religious devotion through connections and associations resembling the secular civil society of each city. Men and women benefited from engagement with the Catholic parish in terms of rising social status and community support. Their involvement with a particularly Irish Catholic church life in Melbourne and Chicago helped to sustain links with Ireland and Catholic communities elsewhere in the diaspora. While this foundational engagement with Irish identity and community was spearheaded by women, these links could be built upon by male political nationalist leaders.

NOTES

1. *Argus*, 19 November 1850.
2. Sarah Roddy, *Population, Providence and Empire: The Churches and Emigration from Nineteenth-Century Ireland* (Manchester: Manchester University Press, 2014); Sarah Roddy, 'Spiritual imperialism and the mission of the Irish race: The Catholic Church and emigration from nineteenth-century Ireland', *Irish Historical Studies*, 38:152 (2013), pp. 600–19; Jenkins, *Between Raid and Rebellion*, pp. 114–32.
3. George Goodman, *The Church in Victoria During the Episcopate of Charles Perry, First Bishop of Melbourne* (Melbourne: Seeley & Co. Ltd, 1892), p. 154.
4. Ellen Skerrett, 'Chicago's Irish and "brick and mortar Catholicism": A reappraisal', *US Catholic Historian*, 14:2 (1996), pp. 53–71.
5. R. V. Comerford, 'Deference, accommodation, and conflict in Irish confessional relations', in Barr and Carey (eds), *Religion and Greater Ireland*, pp. 33–51.
6. Eileen McMahon, *What Parish Are You From? A Chicago Irish Community and Race Relations* (Lexington: University of Kentucky Press, 1995).
7. Frances O'Kane, *A Path is Set: The Catholic Church in the Port Phillip District and Victoria: 1839–1862* (Melbourne: Melbourne University Press, 1976), pp. 4–5.
8. Sheridan Gilley, 'The Roman Catholic Church and the nineteenth century Irish diaspora', *Journal of Ecclesiastical History*, 35:2 (1984), pp. 188–207.

9. Charles Shanabruch, *Chicago's Catholics: The Evolution of an American Identity* (South Bend, IN: University of Notre Dame Press, 1981), pp. 10–11.
10. A. De Q. Robin, 'Perry, Charles (1807–1891)', *ADB*.
11. J. R. J. Grigsby, 'Goold, James Alipius (1812–1886)', *ADB*.
12. O'Kane, *A Path is Set*, p. 1.
13. Trevor McClaughlin, *Barefoot and Pregnant? Female Orphans who Emigrated from Irish Workhouses to Australia, 1848–50* (Melbourne: Genealogical Society of Victoria, 1991), pp. 1–23.
14. *Geelong Advertiser*, 13 April 1850. The *Argus* continued the attacks on the 'poor, stunted, ignorant creatures' over the next weeks, 20 April 1850.
15. April 1850, Goold diary (MDHC).
16. *Geelong Advertiser*, 20 April 1850.
17. June 1850, Goold diary (MDHC).
18. Cullen to Goold, Dublin, 14 September 1852, 15 November 1864 (Goold Papers, MDHC).
19. 15 July 1853, Goold diary (MDHC).
20. Christopher Dowd, *Rome in Australia: The Papacy and Conflict in the Australian Catholic Missions, 1834–1884* (Leiden: Brill, 2008), pp. 244–5.
21. Thomas M. Mulkerins, *Holy Family Parish Chicago: Priests and People* (Chicago: Universal Press, 1923), pp. 18–20.
22. Mulkerins, *Holy Family*, pp. 18–20.
23. D. F. Bourke, *A History of the Catholic Church in Victoria* (East Melbourne: Catholic Bishops of Victoria, 1988), p. 74.
24. Paul Sargent, *Wild Arabs and Savages: A History of Juvenile Justice in Ireland* (Oxford: Oxford University Press, 2013), p. 63.
25. Patrick Morgan, *Melbourne before Mannix: Catholics in Public Life 1880–1920* (Ballarat: Connor Court Publishing, 2012), p. 17.
26. *Age*, 10 May 1859.
27. John W. Howard, *The First Thirty Years' Rise and Progress of the Hibernian Australasian Catholic Benefit Society* (Melbourne, 1896), p. 58.
28. John Howard and Edward Nolan were involved in the establishment of both the CYMS and the St Francis' Benefit Society. By July 1869, there were an estimated 220 members of the benefit society. *Advocate*, 17 July 1869.
29. Howard, *First Thirty Years*, pp. 14–15.
30. Chicago Directory, 1861.
31. *Irish American Weekly*, 17 October 1863.
32. Brian P. Clarke, *Piety and Nationalism: Lay Voluntary Associations and the Creation of an Irish-Catholic Community in Toronto, 1850–1895* (Montreal: McGill-Queen's University Press, 1993), pp. 3–6.
33. Mulkerins, *Holy Family*, p. 548.
34. Ibid., pp. 24, 454, 565, 579.

35. Suellen Hoy, *Good Hearts: Catholic Sisters in Chicago's Past* (Urbana: University of Illinois Press, 2006), p. 37.
36. *Chicago Tribune*, 18 September 1861.
37. Hoy, *Good Hearts*, pp. 41–2.
38. Mulkerins, *Holy Family*, p. 43.
39. *Daily Inter Ocean*, 15 October 1865, 4 November 1865.
40. Mulkerins, *Holy Family*, pp. 471–3; Connolly, *Women of Faith*, pp. 15–18; Andreas, *History of Chicago*, vol. 1, p. 523; John E. McGirr, *Life of the Rt. Rev. Wm. Quarter, D.D.: First Catholic Bishop of Chicago* (orig. 1849, reprinted St Mary's Training School Press, 1920). For one Melbourne example of many, see Matthew Rahilly mentioned in Chapter 3.
41. Sophie Cooper, 'Something borrowed: Women, Limerick Lace and community heirlooms in the Australian Irish diaspora', *Social History*, 45:3 (2020), pp. 304–27.
42. Christina Twomey, 'Gender, welfare and the colonial state: Victoria's 1864 *Neglected and Criminal Children's Act*', *Labour History*, 73 (1997), pp. 169–86.
43. Nolan, *Ourselves Alone*, p. 36.
44. Martha Kanya-Forstner, 'Defining womanhood: Irish women and the Catholic Church in Victorian Liverpool', in Donald M. MacRaild (ed.), *The Great Famine and Beyond: Irish Migrants in Britain in the Nineteenth and Twentieth Centuries* (Dublin: Irish Academic Press, 2000), pp. 168–88.
45. Thomas L. Harmon, *Fifty Years of Parish History: Church of the Annunciation, Chicago, Ill., 1866–1916* (Chicago: D. B. Hansen & Sons, 1916), p. 26.
46. Mulkerins, *Holy Family*, p. 464.
47. Ibid., p. 459.
48. Kelleher, 'Class and Catholic'.
49. Annette Shiell, *Fundraising, Flirtation and Fancywork: Charity Bazaars in Nineteenth Century Australia* (Newcastle: Cambridge Scholars Publishing, 2012), pp. 68–70.
50. *Advocate*, 6 March 1869, 26 June 1869.
51. Ibid.; *Advocate*, 21 December 1872, 28 September 1878.
52. *Advocate*, 30 September 1871.
53. *The St Patrick's College Gazette*, December 1879 (Jesuit Archives Dublin).
54. Julia Mary Doyle to Harry Koenig, 10 June 1951 (Madaj Collection, Box 1, Archdiocese of Chicago Archives (ACA)).
55. Maureen A. Flanagan, *Seeing with their Hearts: Chicago Women and the Vision of the Good City, 1871–1933* (Princeton, NJ: Princeton University Press, 2002), p. 15.
56. Mary Foote Coughlin, *A New Commandment: A Little Memoir of the Work Accomplished by the Good Shepherd Nuns in Chicago During a*

Half Century, 1859–1909 (Chicago: Sisters of the Good Shepherd, 1909), pp. 64–5.
57. Flanagan, *Seeing with their Hearts*, pp. 21–2.
58. 'Report of St Stephen's Conference, From October 1, to December 31, 1871' (St Vincent de Paul Society Administrative Records – Minutes – ADMIN/M3300/964, ACA).
59. 'Report of the Conference of St Bridget, Chicago, 1 January 1872', ibid.
60. 'Report of Holy Family Conference, For the Year ending December 31, 1872', ibid.
61. Mulkerins, *Holy Family*, pp. 107, 151.
62. Ibid., pp. 452–4.
63. John T. McGreevy, *Catholicism and American Freedom: A History* (New York: W. W. Norton & Company, 2004), pp. 102–3.
64. Mulkerins, *Holy Family*, pp. 139–40.
65. The Irish-Catholic Benefit Society (originally the St Francis' Benefit Society) amalgamated the Catholic Benefit Society with the other Irish benefit societies in 1871, resulting in the HACBS name.
66. Bourke, *Catholic Church*, p. 74.
67. Howard, *First thirty years*, p. 10.
68. *Ballarat Courier*, 15 July 1873.
69. *Advocate*, 26 June 1869.
70. *Ibid.*, 5 December 1874.
71. *Sydney Morning Herald*, 1 June 1891.
72. Thomas C. Hunt, 'The impact of Vatican teaching on Catholic educational policy in the United States during the late nineteenth century', *Paedogogica Historica*, 24:2 (1984), pp. 437–60.
73. *Age*, 10 July 1886.
74. *Advocate*, 2 July 1887.
75. Ibid., 20 August 1887.
76. *Freeman's Journal* (Sydney), 30 April 1887; Thomson and Serle, *Biographical Register*, p. 153.
77. *Advocate*, 26 June 1869; *Age*, 9 May 1881.
78. *Manual of the Children of Mary for the Use of All Establishments, Schools and Orphan Asylums of the Sisters of Charity* (Toronto: P. J. Kennedy & Sons, 1867), p. 11.
79. *Advocate*, 26 August 1882.
80. *St Patrick's Gazette*, December 1879 (JAD).
81. Mulkerins, *Holy Family*, p. 456.
82. Ibid., p. 159.
83. Dolan, *The American Catholic Experience*, p. 220.
84. Sophie Cooper, 'Irish migrant identities and community life in Melbourne and Chicago, 1840–1890' (PhD, University of Edinburgh, 2017), p. 163.
85. Bourke, *Catholic Church*, p. 74; *Irish-Australian Almanac*, 1888.

86. *Catholic Magazine* (January 1890), p. 28.
87. Bourke, *Catholic Church*, p. 74.
88. *Advocate*, 16 June 1888.
89. Ruth Trait, 'Rev. Patrick Joseph Aylward 1849–1898', *Footprints*, 15:2 (1998), p. 33.
90. *Coburg Leader*, 24 March 1894.
91. *Argus*, 10 May 1897.
92. Dolan, *American Catholic Experience*, p. 246.
93. *Western Catholic*, 5 March 1881.
94. Cian McMahon, *The Global Dimensions of Irish Identity: Race, Nation, and the Popular Press, 1840–1880* (Chapel Hill: University of North Carolina Press, 2015), pp. 4–5.
95. Timothy Walch, 'The Catholic press and the campaign for parish schools: Chicago and Milwaukee, 1850–1885', *US Catholic Historian*, 3:4 (1984), pp. 254–72.
96. Letter to Archbishop Feehan, Chicago, 30 September 1883 (HIST/H3300/63 – Historical Records – Various Bishops, ACA).
97. US Federal Census, 1880.
98. *Daily Inter Ocean*, 29 December 1879.
99. 'Circular, Chicago Committee to Eugene Kelly', 7 January 1886 (John Devoy Papers, MS 18,048(1), National Library of Ireland (NLI)).
100. *Daily Illinois State Journal*, 22 July 1881; Frank L. Reynolds, 'The Ancient Order of Hibernians', *Illinois Catholic Historical Review*, 4:1 (1921), pp. 22–33. William Curran attended the Anti-Rent Gathering supporting Irish land reform in 1879. *Daily Inter Ocean*, 29 December 1879.
101. Chicago's city limits were expanded in 1889, annexing large parts of the South Side into the city.
102. *Third Annual Directory of Ancient Order of Hibernians of the United States, Containing the names and addresses of all national state, county, and division officers: 1884–1885* (Sweetman's Book & Job Printing House, 1884), pp. 50–5.
103. Ffrench (ed.), *American Irish*, pp. 83, 167.
104. Kelleher, 'Class and Catholic'.
105. Mulkerins, *Holy Family*, p. 161.
106. Ibid., pp. 714–16.
107. Lara Vapnek, *Breadwinners: Working Women and Economic Independence, 1865–1920* (Urbana: University of Illinois Press, 2009), pp. 60–1.
108. Hoy, 'The Irish girls' rising'; McCarthy, *Respectability and Reform*.
109. Skerrett, 'Development of Catholic identity'.
110. Improvements to the Chicago cable car system began in 1882, while the Melbourne cable tram system opened in 1885.
111. O'Farrell, *Catholic Church*, p. 160.
112. Ibid., p. 4.

113. *Hibernian Australasian Catholic Benefit Society: 2nd Biennial Meeting of Deputies from States of Australia and New Zealand* (Sydney: Finn Brothers, 1903).
114. *Advocate*, 5 October 1907.
115. *Independent* (Footscray), 28 May 1904; *Standard* (Port Melbourne), 10 October 1908; *Advocate*, 9 January 1909.
116. O'Farrell, *Catholic Church*, pp. 197–8.
117. Ibid., pp. 210–11.
118. Colin Barr, *Ireland's Empire: The Roman Catholic Church in the English-Speaking World, 1829–1914* (Cambridge: Cambridge University Press, 2020), p. 475.
119. Shanabruch, *Chicago's Catholics*, p. 152.
120. Doyle, 'The Irish in Chicago'.
121. John F. Quinn, *Father Mathew's Crusade: Temperance in Nineteenth-Century Ireland and Irish America* (Amherst: University of Massachusetts Press, 2002), p. 185.
122. Ibid., pp. 190–1.
123. Ciara Breathnach, 'Irish Catholic identity in 1870s Otago, New Zealand', *Immigrants & Minorities*, 31:1 (2013), pp. 1–26.
124. Gerard Connolly, 'Irish and Catholic: Myth or reality? Another sort of Irish and the renewal of the clerical profession among Catholics in England, 1791–1918', in Roger Swift and Sheridan Gilley (eds), *The Irish in the Victorian City* (London: Croom Helm, 1985), pp. 225–54.

5

Sisters and Schooling: Public and Religious Education

The 232 children resident in Chicago's Lake Avenue St Joseph's Orphan Asylum on census night did not know their parents or their parents' nativity. Most, according to the 1880 census enumerator, had been found in the street at a young age with few identifying details. Despite this, most had Irish names. Kate McCormick and Maggie Comerford played alongside Nellie Mulligan and Bridget O'Connell, and Eugene Hanifan slept beside Michael Denehy and Willie Powers. The entire adult population of the orphanage was from Ireland: thirteen Sisters of St Joseph of Carondelet, two male servants and one elderly priest. These Chicago children were given Irish names, raised by Irish people, and presumably continued on to be part of Irish communities into adulthood. Similar could be expected of the children who attended Immaculate Conception School on North Franklin Street, where five of the six Sisters of St Dominic were born in Ireland or had Irish parents, or those attending St Joseph's School on Emerald Avenue where that was true of all seven Sisters.[1] These were Catholic and Irish institutions transferred abroad and once there altered the growing Irish community in ways that might not be immediately recognised. Religious-run schools and institutions created a structure for parish life, and through the incorporation of confirmation classes and sodalities, the religious life of children continued into adulthood, taking and expanding the bonds of friendship, loyalty and identity across generations.

Studies of Irish community connections have traditionally focused on the 'culture brokers' of priest, politician and publican. However, this excludes important figures of authority who featured in the everyday lives of the Irish diaspora in Melbourne and Chicago: female members of religious orders and women teachers. In addition to schools, these women established the social services for the poor in Melbourne and

Chicago. The great migration from Ireland during and in the aftermath of the Famine prompted the Irish Catholic Church hierarchy and supporters to make efforts to ensure that their increasingly dispersed parishioners could still access religious services and the structures that encouraged continued religious devotion.[2] Women religious played a large role in this diasporic endeavour: teaching Catholic children in parish and private schools, running orphanages, hospitals, and institutions for the elderly and those considered social delinquents. While male religious orders benefited from a greater public presence and freedom to speak their minds on political and cultural matters, the impact of women religious in shaping ethnic identity and community life has been downplayed or ignored. Though infrequently dwelt upon by scholars, their Catholic identities outweighing their Irishness, this chapter considers the influence that female religious orders had on linking Irish and Catholic identities in Melbourne and Chicago during the nineteenth century. It presents the role of women religious in supporting the development of parish schooling alongside legislative debates regarding the funding and role of education in Melbourne and Chicago during the nineteenth and early twentieth centuries.

Between 1830 and 1922, schooling acted as an international trigger point for debates around citizenship, taxation and the place of religion in teaching. Education is considered a key ingredient in creating and sustaining a devout Catholic community. Religious education and the consequent moral and economic progress of children was related to the entire local Irish Catholic community's position within wider society. As Mary Hickman has highlighted, educational reform in the nineteenth century Anglosphere was primarily concerned with building political subjects and was therefore a tool of state construction.[3] Both Melbourne and Chicago were new cities and populated by young people during the second half of the nineteenth century. As Mary Hatfield notes, 'family and school [should be viewed] as interconnected sites for identity formation'.[4] Most parents paid a fee toward their children's education until the final decades of the nineteenth century, though schoolteachers in Melbourne and Chicago were all encouraged to give free education to orphans and children of indigent parents. The involvement of religious orders allowed for free or highly subsidised education without needing to pay staff salaries. It also allowed the Catholic Church to organise its parishioners based on priorities of class and ethnicity, and to retain control of their religious education.

The leaders of the Catholic Church in Ireland in the aftermath of the Famine felt that 'the full reinstatement of its authority lay in achieving untrammelled control over the management of all educational institutions patronized by the Catholic laity'.[5] This concern for the education of Catholic children spread around the world. It was supported by religious orders trained to teach, encouraged by directives from the Vatican, and was enforced at different times by threats of excommunication and other spiritual downfalls. The schoolroom remains an important place in the shaping of children's minds and hopes: a place where non-familial adults have influence on future paths taken. Melbourne and Chicago, growing rapidly and in harsh conditions during the nineteenth century, were environments where Protestant-inspired ideals of human autonomy and liberalism reigned. Catholics conversely saw 'moral choice and personal development as inseparable from virtues nurtured in families and churches'.[6]

Catholic ritual was instilled from a young age in these educational institutions, helping to create a Catholic adult population which prioritised religious devotion and community over individual liberty. Schools were linked to churches, both physically and socially, and the provision of sodalities and other social organisations linked to the Church meant that children could be surrounded by the priorities of faith, family and – with such large numbers of Irish religious in the diaspora – mother country. For 'liberal' Catholics and non-Catholics, this immersion represented a threat to the prosperity and peace of their new nation. The education debates provide an insight into each society's position on citizenship, religion and loyalty. Irish women, in their position as teachers, lay and religious, helped to bond children, and therefore new generations of Irish descendants, into communities based on Irish and Catholic identities.[7] This chapter is organised around demographic shifts and key legislation. While previous chapters focused on the male-dominated Irish associational culture which emerged in Melbourne and Chicago, this chapter explores the debates which ensured the daily interaction of children and parents with ideas of ethnic and religious belonging through their teachers.

1830–1860

For organisers in Melbourne and Chicago, the priority for the first thirty years of settlement was the establishment of an educational system. Melbourne and Chicago were settler towns where single men and women dominated and children had to wait for potential teachers to arrive. What did emerge were rudimentary structures with wealthier children prioritised over poorer ones. While state education systems were slowly established, the Catholic Church sought alternatives which would help to 'protect' Catholic children from entering 'secular' schools, which were often heavily influenced by Protestant teachings. This section focuses on the ways that settlers in Melbourne and Chicago worked together, and in tension with each other, to produce an educated citizenry. Melbourne's state education system was a product of the city's position within the British empire. White settler educationalists looked to their experiences growing up in Britain and Ireland as inspiration, and later corresponded with their counterparts in other English-speaking areas of the empire, particularly in British North America, for reforming ideas. Central to the educational reforms in the Australian and Canadian colonies was the Irish National School (INS) system. Established in 1831, the INS system was the product of efforts to mediate tensions between Protestant and Catholic leaders and communities in Ireland. In Ireland, schools were administered by a Board of Education made up of local representatives of business and religion.[8] In order to satisfy the spiritual concerns of religious representatives, religious instruction was provided separately to the secular school day, and only with the permission of parents. As such, it aimed to improve the educational progress of all Irish children, while promoting non- or un-denominational education. In reality, the INS system created a country of denominationally separated schools and children.

Authorities in New South Wales first looked to Ireland and the national school system as a way of financing and administering their schools in 1836. The small numbers of clerics and the lack of Catholic religious orders in the Port Philip District, subsequently Victoria, until 1856 encouraged, *or necessitated*, cross-community schooling. The National Education Board Incorporation Act of 1851 established a version of the INS system as Victoria's state-funded education system. Schools would receive a portion of state money, relative to the size of the school, and in the case of denominational schools relative to the size of the religious population, to pay the salaries of teachers. It differed from Ireland in its administration. A Board of Education (NSB) oversaw national (and non-denominational) schools and a Denominational School Board (DSB) administered religious schools. The differing size and population distribution of Victoria and Ireland was a significant reason for this variation: Victoria's landmass is roughly three times the size of Ireland's and with far fewer large towns.[9] Therefore, while denominational schools prospered in more densely populated areas, national schools were established in places where denominational difference could be sacrificed for an education of any kind.[10] The school boards effectively had different remits and largely focused either on rural or on urban areas. By the end of 1851, the NSB only controlled eleven of 135 schools operating in the colony.[11]

Despite the widespread control of the DSB in Victoria, the dual-board system went from being a 'real boon to the community' to a flawed system which suffered from poor quality of teaching, irregular pay and a lack of oversight within two years.[12] A Select Commission was established in 1852 to investigate the system's flaws. However, there was little actionable improvement in response to the Commission's negative observations.[13] The main result was the introduction of upper schools and advanced subjects such as languages for children aged ten and above by the DSB in 1854.[14] The Catholic Church dominated the DSB schools, and Archbishop Goold looked to Ireland for religious teaching support in this expansion. In requesting an increase in Irish clerics and religious orders, Goold consolidated the links between the Catholic religion and Irish nationality of most of his parishioners. Anti-Catholic attacks, led by the *Age* newspaper, linked Irish and Catholic prejudices in the minds of both opponents and proponents of the DSB. *Age* journalists participated in stereotyping Irish people, and particularly Irish Catholics, as unquestioning devotees of their priests, a popular image within the British and American press.[15] Using examples of Irish corruption in the United States, the religious and educational priorities of Irish Catholics were seized upon to blame the Irish immigrant population for political divisions in the colony.[16] In an effort to respond to anti-Catholicism and new pressures on the DSB, the Sisters of Mercy, temporarily stationed in Western Australia, were the first to respond, arriving in March 1857. They were joined six years later by the Sisters of the Good Shepherd, a French order based in Ireland.[17]

Illinois passed its first school law in 1833, providing for an elected school commissioner to apportion funds among teachers in Chicago and further afield. The city's first purpose-built school opened in 1835 and a Board of Inspectors was elected in May 1837.[18] Over the next ten years, Chicago's state school system was reorganised repeatedly, with school districts emerging to cater for the expanding population. The arrival of King's County-born bishop William Quarter in 1844 led to an immediate Catholic investment in education. Quarter established a school in his own house and the College of St Mary [of the Lake] opened a month after his arrival. In other communities, the Church funded the construction of schools in simple frame structures. The Irish Sisters of Mercy arrived from Pittsburgh in 1846 and 'spearheaded a separate school system' for Chicago's Catholic immigrant children.[19] While later arrivals of women religious from Germany and other Catholic countries helped to expand the Church's welfare provision within Chicago, for the first ten years Irish Catholics dominated the city's provision.

The first five women religious to arrive were Sisters of Mercy originally from Ireland. These women, the oldest of whom was twenty-four, soon established themselves within Chicago. The women became recognisable as the 'Walking Nuns', emphasising a particular brand of religious service brought from Ireland: obedience and humility balanced with meaningful service.[20] Recruiting from within the United States quickly began and by the outbreak of the Civil War the Sisters of Mercy had accepted a hundred members into their convent and built the city's first permanent hospital, while concurrently establishing and running parochial schools, select fee-paying academies and orphan asylums. Amid stories of Irish women running bars or drunkenly fighting,[21] women of the habit provided Irish Catholics with an image of moral agency. Mother Superior Mary Agatha O'Brien noted, a year after their arrival, that

> Our Schools are already numerous – every moment that can be spared from religious exercises – the Sisters are occupied in teaching the poor, or in instructing the ignorant in their catechism, or teaching protestants (many of whom visit us) that Faith and doctrine of the Catholic Church, or else, in visiting the Sick.[22]

In visiting the sick, these women took their lives in their hands, and often lost them. The cholera outbreak of 1854 led to the death of four Sisters of Mercy, including O'Brien, a devastating loss for the small community.[23] Later that year, the Sisters opened St Agatha's Academy in memory of their Mother Superior. They opened a Magdalen asylum in 1858, soon transferring its control to the four newly arrived Irish Sisters of the Good Shepherd.[24] The charity demonstrated by the Sisters of Mercy connected them to their parishioners, encouraging the expansion of the religious community and the work that they could do. The Sisters of Mercy were joined by the Sisters of the Holy Cross in 1856, Sisters of St Joseph's Carondolet (1858), Sisters of Charity (1858) and the Religious of the Sacred Heart (1859), providing support for parochial schools that male religious could not compete with.[25] The Irish brothers of the Dutch Jesuit Province and the Irish Christian Brothers had an important presence; however, male religious orders did not have the numbers or mission statement to construct 'a miniature welfare state' as the Irish women in the city did.[26] When male religious orders were based in schools, they focused their efforts on post-elementary education and most boys' schools were run by lay teachers during the 1860s. Women religious, conversely, staffed their own schools as well as the hospitals and refuges that they administered.[27] Irish-born and -descended women were therefore the most frequent representatives of a joint Irish and Catholic identity in the everyday lives of Chicago's immigrant Irish communities, more approachable than the priest and more ubiquitous.

The *Western Tablet* argued that the 'real object of education is to give children resources that will endure as long as life endures; habits that will ameliorate, not destroy'.[28] In the eyes of nuns and parents throughout the diaspora, to read and write was to rise.[29] If Irish and Irish Catholic children could read and write, they could manage their household accounts and they had the opportunity to find permanent white-collar work instead of the drudgery and uncertainty of labouring. They therefore had the potential to financially and politically support their family, their wider community and, crucially, the Catholic Church's endeavours. To educate an Irish Catholic child in Irish Catholic schools was to improve the future chances of that child and their entire community.

The Catholic Church in Victoria was almost homogenously Irish, placing Irish Catholic politicians at the forefront of education debates in Victoria.[30] In Chicago, conversely, the Catholic Church was ethnically and linguistically plural from its beginning. However, a distinctly Irish Catholic system of schooling emerged when, to avoid conflict and misunderstandings between priest and parishioner, Quarter adopted a system of separating parishes, and parish life, based upon ethnic heritage. The national parish system was reflected in the parish school system, concurrently joining Catholic children in a shared devotion to their faith while separating them from each other on ethnic lines. German immigrant children were taught in German by German teachers, and Irish children were taught by English-speaking Irish religious orders, continuing an Irish Catholic Church tradition of using English not Irish in services.[31] Free schools were offset financially by the establishment of private and fee-paying day and boarding schools run by women religious and attended by girls of all religious backgrounds.[32] This system meant that itinerant immigrant workers such as John Onahan, who could not afford the $120 that the nuns would have charged to educate each of his daughters privately, could still place his children in a religious-run parish school.[33]

Women religious helped the women and children of Chicago, but they also worked to improve the infrastructure of the Church. In 1855 the 'lady teachers and pupils' of St Agatha's Academy presented Quarter's successor, Bishop O'Regan, with 'a purse containing $100, in gold, to aid in building his house'.[34] They were helping to raise the profile of the

Church in Chicago, using their links within the parish to tie the bishop to his congregation. Similarly, in 1859 the lay members of Holy Family Parish donated $1,004 within ten weeks for stained-glass windows.[35] Ellen Skerrett has argued that 'churches and schools became important symbols of respectability and commitment' for the Irish Catholics who first established parishes in Chicago.[36] The support of the parish therefore 'became a prime objective of Irish immigrants as they moved up the social ladder'.[37] As poor Irish people continued to arrive in Chicago, Irish parishioners were forced to balance charitable activity with ambitions for an institutional presence for the Catholic Church in the city: schooling played an important role in those ambitions.

The early arrival of the Sisters of Mercy in Chicago coincided with the arrival of poor Famine migrants, and they were therefore free to establish missions for the neediest. In Melbourne, however, the later arrival of women religious meant that plans to provide for the city's poor were superseded by the wishes of Archbishop Goold and the growing Irish middle class. The Sisters of Mercy were instructed to provide selective education for the young ladies of the city, as 'being ignorant, [the young ladies] were to be considered the poorest of the poor'.[38] Goold was primarily concerned with providing religious and educational instruction to the daughters of Victoria's growing Catholic elite. In this he reflected the view of Dublin's Cardinal Cullen, who believed that 'each class ought to be educated for the sphere of life in which they have to move' and that wealthy Catholics should be educated separately to their poorer co-religionists.[39] Between 1854 and 1857, children in Victoria had benefited from an increase in the number of female teachers, but their opportunities to learn were still dependent on the whims and resources of inspectors in the area. Where religious orders were unavailable, religious schools were staffed by lay teachers and, depending on the area, visited infrequently by local clerics. The introduction of lay and religious female teachers 'constituted an unprecedented female invasion of the public sphere of men' and provided young Australian and Irish-Australian children, especially girls, with new role models outside of the home.[40] The Irish Catholic Church was concerned with maintaining the status quo. However, within the diaspora, education was also seen as a tool for social uplift.[41] The dominance of Irish women within the ranks of Catholic schoolteachers resulted in an educational environment tied to Ireland and Irish identity, acting as a subtle daily reminder to students of their religious and ethnic heritage, while the presence of women in habits in the streetscape expanded this reminder into the growing city.

In July 1854, INS inspector Arthur Davitt and his wife Ellen arrived from Ireland to act as principal and senior mistress of Melbourne's newly built Model School and Training College.[42] Several other teachers arrived from Ireland soon after to train Australian-based teachers, bringing with them a reliance on INS Books, described by one regional paper as 'very popular, excellent, and remarkably cheap school books' with a 'world renowned' superiority.[43] These school books were approved by the Anglican and Roman Catholic archbishops of Dublin, had most references to Ireland removed and focused on the preservation of Britain's social hierarchy and order.[44] By 1859, 169 teachers had been trained at the Model School, 130 deemed worthy of classification for NSB appointments.[45] The influence of the INS system on Melbourne's school system met the Irish influence of the Catholic Church in the denominational schools, allowing for two elements of Irish life to make their way into the Victorian education system: Protestant-inspired non-denominational state control and Catholic Church control through education. The dominance of Irish immigrants within Melbourne's Catholic Church provided for the unconscious promotion of ethnic identity through education.

A dual system of schooling emerged in Melbourne and Chicago during the 1850s. As parish schools increased in number in Chicago, so did the state school system. These schools were overseen by the Office of Superintendent of Schools, but each school remained independently governed, allowing for an ethnic state school system to emerge parallel to the denominational school system. Despite public school expansion, few Irish children attended public schools; by 1860 only 4 per cent of Chicago's public-school children had been born in Ireland.[46] While Hickman has argued that the Catholic Church in England used education to strengthen children's Catholic identity at the expense of weakening their Irish identity, in Chicago, the outcome was a strengthening of both identities.[47] The Irish background of the educators was vital to this. However, the sense of difference felt by Irish Catholic children, and Irish Catholics more generally, was aided by an antagonistic press and nativist politics within the United States. As the number of Irish Catholics in the United States grew during the 1850s and began to gain political and cultural power, supportive newspaper editors declared that they could 'by gradual and legitimate action recover Ireland' as well as 'engraft its own nature and sympathies on the future people and history of America'.[48] The national parish system in Chicago helped to create a close-knit, supportive and increasingly powerful community for Irish Catholics. However, that same system separated the Irish from other

Catholics and led to the perception that they were a threat to American, and Protestant, ways of life.

Parents, politicians and religious leaders worked together to establish parish schools based within and around their communities. For most Irish people this meant creating Irish Catholic schools staffed by Irish teaching orders and funded by those who could pay. Irish women were therefore instrumental in creating a cultural affinity through daily, or at least frequent, interaction with their students and the imparting of Irish and Catholic priorities. The involvement of Irish religious orders helped parents to have some choice in the education provided to their children. While the first priorities of Irish parish schools were faith, elementary education and community loyalty, commitment to those left in Ireland was also an inherent element of parish life, connecting the parish to a space beyond city and national borders. This commitment was understood differently in each city. However, financial support and a pledge to educating future generations in the diaspora better than previous generations united communities across the diaspora.

As the 1850s concluded, violent disputes erupted in Boston and New York City regarding the teaching of the King James Bible in schools.[49] Catholics in Melbourne and Chicago based their concerns about the public school system on the inability to ensure that they were truly secular. Instead of removing all religious elements from schools, there was a continued dependence on Protestantism for resources and guidance. If the public school system could be monitored and all elements of Protestantism could be removed, alongside Catholicism and Judaism, prominent Catholic clerics such as the Bishop of Demerara, John Hynes, could see its use in helping the social progress of Catholics.[50] However, this was a class-based debate. The Catholic hierarchy in Melbourne and Chicago were mainly concerned for Catholics without financial and social resources – those who remained the majority. It was their souls that remained in question and at the mercy of political and theological disputes. For those with wealth there were options. Charles Gavan Duffy, for example, sent his son Frank to England from Melbourne for a Stonyhurst education.[51] Catholic parishioners continued to support their local parochial school financially and with labour when required. Though the financial burden was borne and shared, the payment of both a school tax and parochial school fees was a matter of consternation which would erupt more clearly in the 1860s.

Education was a product of the Irish Catholic community and this brought children and parents together with politicians and religious; to improve one generation through learning was to potentially improve older and future generations of Irish Catholics in Chicago. In Melbourne the entire education system was rooted in Ireland in some way. While there were non-Catholic denominational schools, Irish Catholics did not need to compete with any other nationality within the Catholic parish system; it was the Catholicism of parochial schooling that appealed, not its nationality. The national school system was based on the Irish system and people found similar benefits and flaws in it in Melbourne as they did in Ireland. In Chicago, Catholics were able to establish a school system parallel to the state school system and split on national lines in the 1840s due to an engaged bishop and the early arrival of Irish nuns. In Melbourne, conversely, the later arrival of a bishop and even later arrival of teaching orders required an initial state solution which acknowledged the mixed make-up of the city's founding population and was based upon Irish educational reform. Irish people in both Melbourne and Chicago took it upon themselves to create systems of education that challenged the presumed dominance of Protestant and liberal thinking, and encouraged systems of support based around ethnicity and religion. Despite this, Melbourne remained a colonial city within the British empire, while Chicago's Irish communities asserted ownership over an increasingly Irish-American city.

1860–1872

Melbourne and Chicago continued to attract large numbers of immigrants during the 1860s. The post-Famine migration from Ireland was split equally between genders, leading to an explosion in the numbers of school-aged children in the 1860s. During that decade the number of boys in Victoria under the age of fourteen increased at ten times the rate of boys and men over that age. Therefore, while the population of Victoria increased by a third in the decade after 1861, the number attending schools trebled.[52] Likewise, in Cook County, the children of school age jumped from 19 per cent of the total population to 27 per cent between 1860 and 1870.[53] As a result, the educational provision in both cities had to increase. Concurrently, the Pope published his *Syllabus of Errors*, which guarded against the mixing of Catholics and non-Catholics. The nationalist awareness which was resurging in Ireland during the decade was exported to Melbourne and Chicago through migration, aided by the spread of Irish and Irish Catholic religious orders. This helped parochial schools to function while worrying those who supported public school systems, particularly Protestants who feared the international reach of the Catholic Church. This section considers how changing funding systems influenced Irish Catholic identity formation in each community. It explores how Catholic religious representatives and their lay counterparts used state education reform to forge a clear and distinct place for themselves in Melbourne and Chicago society.

While priests in the immigrant church have been described as 'neighborhood chieftains', religious sisters, who were subordinate to priests, 'were spiritual authorities of immense significance for the children in their classrooms and objects of reverent respect in the larger community'.[54] As the nineteenth century progressed, girls increasingly outnumbered boys among those enrolled in Ireland's national schools, and these women filled the schools of Melbourne and Chicago as teachers, nuns and mothers hoping for similar educational opportunities for their children.[55] While increasing numbers of women religious arrived from Ireland, the established communities were joined by local girls who had benefited from their educational influence. The reputation of the Sisters in improving the lives of each city's poor and despised encouraged new postulants, as did the routinised behaviour of convent school life.[56] These women, and their Irish background, influenced the communities they ministered to, both in their spiritual and their ethnic identity. The feeder system, from school to cloister, was a matter of satisfaction and community creation for families and local historians alike. The Holy Family Parish official history, for example, lists eleven pages of the names of women who had entered the Sacred Heart Sisters from the parish and its schools.[57] Boys did not tend to spend as long in schools as their sisters and therefore, for men, secular parish life was in direct competition with the religious. For Catholic girls, who tended to stay in school for a longer time, everyday life included increased female interaction with the religious authority of women in the parish.[58]

Schools in close proximity to Catholic churches were a prerogative of Chicago's Catholic hierarchy, particularly aided by the national parishes, which led to multiple schools within a few blocks of each other. By 1861 the numbers attending these schools were being supplemented by an additional 5,180 students attending Sunday schools attached to Roman Catholic churches.[59] Four years later, 82 per cent of Chicago's parishes had elementary schools, making up 16.5 per cent of students enrolled in schools city-wide.[60] Attendance at the local parish school ensured that 'Home and school functioned in harmony', in opposition to a public school system which sought to homogenise the backgrounds of students. Catholic supporters of separate schooling promoted the parochial school as a place 'where children would learn the ethnic truth.'[61]

Irish religious orders, lay teachers and volunteers from the St Vincent de Paul Society staffed these day, boarding and Sunday schools, further linking the representatives of ethnicity and religion, Irish and Catholic, with the wider parish community. New generations of Irish teachers, lay or religious, enabled and encouraged ethnic mirroring within parish schools, subliminally creating an inter-generational cultural affinity to Ireland. As English speakers, opportunities within the public school system continued for Chicago's Irish Catholics as the nineteenth century drew toward a close. Outside of official schooling, children attended neighbourhood clubs with the children of other Irish immigrants where they were taught by Irish or Irish-American teachers.

In both cities, the subject of double taxation for the parents of students attending non-state-funded schools remained at the forefront of discussions. Daniel Reily, a representative at the Illinois Constitutional Convention, argued that 'Millions of Irish who for centuries were suffering under the penal law, and paying tithes to a church they could not accept as a religious teacher come to America for freedom of conscience.'[62] He called for a freedom of conscience amendment to the Illinois Constitution which would provide state funding for all schools or none. Though Reily's amendment was defeated, his argument that Catholics should have protection from economic discrimination as well as religious persecution would continue to be raised. The subject of economic discrimination was also raised in Melbourne that year, in 1862, when the Victorian Legislature passed the Common Schools Act. The dual-board system was ended after a decade of debates with the establishment of a single Board of Education composed of members representing the principal churches, to oversee the state-funded schools in Victoria. At the time, the DSB controlled 460 of the 647 state-funded schools in the colony.[63] A choice was given to all DSB schools: transfer to the single-board system and receive state funding, but under the proviso that religious teaching be separated from the four and a half to five hours of secular instruction provided per day.[64] The Catholic Church in Melbourne opted out. A decision was made to charge fees for private school tuition and to offset the costs of keeping poor schools running for little tuition by fundraising through donations and community events.[65]

The work of the Sisters of Mercy in Melbourne was a firm step forward for Catholic education in the city. However, when Archbishop Cullen of Dublin declared in 1863 that priests could not send teaching candidates to be trained in the non-denominational Model Schools, and that no teacher trained in one could be employed in a Catholic school, the Irish-controlled Melbourne church followed suit.[66] The

Church's campaign against 'mixed education' required the importation of more seminary- and convent-trained teachers into Melbourne's Catholic parochial school system. The French and English Sisters of the Good Shepherd arrived in 1863 and 1864, and their numbers were soon supplemented by daughters of Irish Catholics from the colony.[67] The Society of Jesus (Jesuits) arrived in 1865 to establish and take control of schools for boys, and they were joined by the Christian Brothers three years later. While the Sisters of Mercy were inspired by the specifically Irish contexts of their community's foundations, and undoubtedly brought these influences to their pupils, it was with the male teaching orders' arrival that a specifically political Irish influence was brought into Melbourne's schools.

Joseph Lentaigne SJ and William Kelly SJ were the first Irish Jesuits to arrive in Melbourne and immediately took over the running of St Patrick's School, originally founded by the SPS. Lentaigne's position as the first Irish Provincial (1860–3) and his experience teaching at many of Ireland's top Catholic schools denotes the importance of Melbourne's Catholic children in the eyes of the Irish Catholic Church's hierarchy. The inclusion of Kelly, who had been expelled from Maynooth for his public support of the Young Irelanders, in this first mission also indicated the strongly Irish nationalist strand to the education that Melbourne's Catholic boys would receive. With the arrival of Superior Fr. Joseph Dalton SJ a year later, the Jesuits were able to instil a joint sense of Irish and Catholic loyalty in Melbourne's Catholic population that would reach across the classes. It quickly became more vocal and united with the establishment of the *Advocate* newspaper in 1868. The Christian Brothers would later help to cement this sense of difference from wider society through the education of the sons of Melbourne's poorer families. These men slowly took control of the management of the city's Catholic male schools and orphanages. The Jesuits, in particular, were vital in ensuring the role of Irish politics and tradition in Australian Catholicism.[68] The Irish Jesuits worked within the parish system to complement community institutions that the laity had established, resulting in an Irish Catholic society that was being attacked from the outside and supported from within. While Melbourne's Irish Catholics were not detached from Protestant society, they were creating a separate sphere which they were increasingly comfortable inhabiting.

While ethnic representation within the national parish was useful for the promotion of an Irish and Catholic identity, Catholics could also use their new contexts to press the municipal government. Educational provision was the priority for Chicago's Catholics, leading to cross-community cooperation on the Board of Education and within the public school system. The prime motivator for this action was the financial support of religious schools. In this there were opportunities for intra-faith cooperation, principally with the Germans. There were potential allies across the Catholic Church, meaning that a united Irish voice was not essential, nor aspired to, for change to be achieved. Just as in Melbourne, there were debates about religious education within Irish Catholic communities, especially at a civic level, where professional and personal networks were built upon engagement with city-wide reforming efforts. This left the option open to those who believed in secular state education to work from within the system to achieve it.

The involvement of Irish Catholics in the public school system, as inspectors, teachers and cleaners, has led to the conclusion that, while Chicago's schools were not 'completely devoid of instances of anti-Catholicism', there was intra-religious cooperation regarding the education of Chicago's schoolchildren.[69] Catholic social and business leaders, such as James Carney, Charles McDonnell, Thomas Brennan and James Ward, were all involved in the Chicago Board of Education from the start.[70] In addition to involvement in the Board of Education, these men participated in specifically Irish improvement endeavours. McDonnell, a school superintendent in the late 1860s, had been a founder of the city's Repeal Association and attempted to establish an Irish Emigrant Aid Society in 1869. These men were joined within the teaching ranks by increasing numbers of Irish National School-educated women, and later their American Catholic parish school-educated daughters.[71] For many of Chicago's Catholics, education was the key to social progress and moral fortitude, whether it took place in a Catholic school or a public one.

By March 1867, children attending school made up one-sixth of Melbourne's population.[72] They were a sizeable and important element of society.[73] The Catholic Church was shaping the minds of many of these 'youngsters' but the promise of future devotion could not offset the expenses incurred in educating them, particularly as the 'proportion of so-called destitute children was rapidly, and even alarmingly, increasing in the schools from year to year'.[74] A petition presented to the Legislative Assembly in March 1869 argued that Catholics did not receive a fair share of the annual vote in the Assembly in aid of elementary education, and as a result the views of Catholics were under-represented in education decisions. The clergy and laity who signed the petition noted that they ran forty-six schools, attended by 2,561 pupils, without any financial support from the Board of Education. In this way they were 'annually deprived, for Educational purposes at about twelve thousand pounds (£12,000) sterling'. If the Catholic Church's schools had access to that money, they could 'give a sound primary education to the children of their communion'.[75] The petition was prompted by a proposal to remove grants given to schools who opted out of the Board of Education's control, if they had been established before January 1869. Catholics in Melbourne believed that they were being financially punished for the Church's quick response to the Common Schools Act.

As parish schools gained the resources to provide secondary education, middle-class parents became increasingly concerned with the ability of schools to help their children pass civil service and law school examinations. While working-class parents tended not to take advantage of higher levels of education which required the payment of additional school fees, the upwardly ambitious middle classes paid for their children to have the opportunity to join the professional and governing classes of the city. However, they were confronted by poor examination results in the Catholic college established by the Jesuits, in contrast to the results of pupils attending the Anglican, Presbyterian and Wesleyan colleges in Melbourne.[76] Ciaran O'Neill has noted the tendency for the sons of the Irish Catholic middle classes to choose occupations based upon 'consolidation and a preference for positions and professions with existing status in society'.[77] Students had to pass their examinations in order to have the opportunity to progress socially in Melbourne and achieve respectability and status. Presented with lower success rates in the Jesuit College, parents had to balance ethnic and religious loyalties with value for money and upward social progression. The threatened removal of students from Catholic schools based on poor exam results and entrance into Protestant schools demonstrates a prioritisation of results over religious and ethnic identity from some parents. Lacking the ethnic nepotism and political machines of some American cities, Melbourne's Irish Catholics were, to a larger extent, dependent on good grades and social contacts to progress up the political and social ladder.

The 1860s witnessed the establishment and expansion of a separate community-funded system of schooling for Irish Catholic children in both Melbourne and Chicago. In Melbourne this was the product of decades of debates. The survival of religious schools without the benefit of previously available funds required the efforts of newly arrived Irish Catholic teaching orders. Chicago's parallel system of education had existed since 1844, aided in large part by the early arrival of its women religious and diverse population. Though Chicago's education system progressed for decades without experiencing the tensions of eastern cities, 'double taxation' became a cry of discrimination against the Irish Catholic community, just as it did in Melbourne. Those choosing Catholic-controlled religious schools in both cities faced coded accusations of backwardness and unthinking clerical devotion which would undermine the freedoms provided by living in a new city which did not have an established religion. Melbourne and Chicago had distinct educational systems but both witnessed a growth of Catholic religious control in Irish Catholic parish life during the 1860s complemented by an awareness of community links between ethnicity and religion. While the link between Irish and Catholic identities had previously existed in both cities, the debates of the 1860s and 1870s brought the public image of these two elements closer in Melbourne while encouraging Chicago's Irish to seek support from their co-religionists. In both cases, education continued to be seen as the primary opportunity for the potential improvement of the child, community and city.

1872–1890

Women religious from Ireland were, by 1870, providing education, care and moral reprobation for all levels of Irish society. In doing so they were also promoting the idea of Irish Catholic generosity and selflessness to the wider society in Melbourne and Chicago. The educational reforms of the 1860s and early 1870s were reconsidered in Melbourne and Chicago during the next fifteen years, with debates centred around the idea of free and compulsory elementary education for all children. These debates prompted the Catholic parish to respond on religious and ethnic grounds, in order to maintain a coherent multi-generational Irish Catholic identity and community. The new laws increased the financial burden on Catholic families and communities, as well as the pressure on the Catholic teachers who staffed the schools, particularly as a series of Vatican decrees were issued emphasising the undesirability of mixed schooling. However, the increase in the numbers of Irish Catholic children attending school had the positive effect of bringing local Irish Catholic communities together to fundraise for their schools. These events emphasised the Irish and Catholic identities of the parishioners and utilised the skills that were used to raise funds for other Catholic endeavours and Irish national causes. While men may have supported the schools financially and politically, lay women used their fundraising capabilities to support their religious orders, particularly women religious.

The Victorian Parliament continued to host debates on religious education, though this resulted in little change and instead encouraged the drawing of political lines based on religious and liberal sentiment. Charles Gavan Duffy compared the debates to those which had taken place in the House of Commons fifty years previously regarding Catholic emancipation.[78] The anti-Catholic sentiment that had filled the *Age* for decades met the *Advocate*'s narrative of international discrimination against Irish and Catholic people to create a community voice which linked respect, nationality and religion.[79] Inequality through education was the central concern of the framers of the Victorian 1872 Education Act, who argued that education should be secular, compulsory and free, and that the public school system should be managed by a new Department of Education.[80] Although Melbourne's Irish community included successful and wealthy Catholics, it also encompassed a large proportion of society who could not afford to pay for private and secondary denominational education for their children. These people were dependent on government and Church-aided education, while educating their children could have the effect of removing extra wages from the household. Under the new law, children aged between six and fifteen were required to attend school for no fewer than sixty days in each half-year, with certain exemptions, or their parents risked a fine of five to twenty shillings or could be imprisoned for up to seven days.[81] It was therefore the parents who could least afford to lose the wages of their children who risked being fined for non-attendance. In this way, opponents argued that the legislation 'effectively removed the common law parental right to determine whether or not a child should be given a formal education'.[82] As Melbourne's Catholics were predominantly Irish, the religious school debates were framed as a continuation of anti-Catholic oppression, similar to Daniel Reily's argument in Chicago. Despite this, the Education Act 1872 (Victoria) was passed, removing state funding from non-government schools and centralising the public school system.

The 1872 Education Act precipitated the arrival of the Presentation Sisters from Limerick in December 1873, in addition to more Jesuits and Christian Brothers. Highlighting the local and transnational links between Melbourne's Irish parishioners and Ireland, Fr. Corbett welcomed the Sisters to St Kilda with 'an interesting and touching account of the departure of the Nuns from Limerick for their distant new home from a Limerick Paper'.[83] A select day school was soon established, providing 'a thorough education' for the young ladies in the suburb under the control of nuns who were also 'young, highly educated, and of respectable parentage'.[84] The Presentation Sisters arrived in direct response to the passing of the Education Act. Defending against a perceived attack on the spiritual welfare of Catholic children, they had left 'friends and home for us and for our children, and therefore we owe them, on our own part, and as sponsors for those children'.[85] They were one of five religious orders, male and female, that worked in Melbourne until 1882. These women, respectable and educated, were aiding women and children from across the city, not just Irish or Catholics, thereby extending their influence outside of the Catholic parish. While the Irish women religious of the city received thanks and interest from non-Catholics in Melbourne, the male religious courted scandal. These men, along with Archbishop Goold and Irish Catholic politicians, became the focus of anti-Catholic feeling related in part to their primary role as educators and influencers.

In the aftermath of the 1872 Education Act, parish schools relied on fees, donations and community fundraisers to support themselves. These fundraising events served to bring parish life closer, with Irish Catholics working together to provide the education they wanted for their children, who now went to school together as well as being neighbours and seeing each other at ethnic clubs and social events. Despite this increased financial pressure on Catholic schools, the number in Melbourne ballooned. These schools, and the female teachers within them, were educating children from a range of backgrounds, as well as educating them at different levels, as post-elementary schooling along with music and languages were charged for. As the school numbers expanded, more religious orders arrived from Ireland. Their arrival meant that control of religious educational provision expanded and changed while remaining in Irish and Catholic hands. In 1881 the Catholic Diocesan Synod warned that 'The enemy never slept, and it might be that they would sleep, and the enemy might gain an advantage over them; hence if they grow slack in the war against secular education the faith might possibly perish in this country.'[86] This was a battle to protect Catholicism, one that was presented as part of a battle that the Irish had fought for centuries in Ireland.

The issue of state-funded religious schooling was settled when Illinois' new constitution was enshrined in law. The 1870 Constitution provided for a system of free education for children aged between nine and fourteen.[87] It was the hope of legislators that by providing free and early education 'the spirit of evil is curbed and crime proportionally diminished'.[88] To aid this moral advancement, an 1872 amendment declared that the educational instruction in free public schools should not 'in any manner, be hindered or clogged by any sectarian teachings'.[89] There was no chance of combining the school systems to allow for religious teaching in public schools or for state funding of denominational schools. The 1872 amendment made it clear that Catholic priorities were not the same as those of the government. Religious education was deemed to hinder improvement, and the discordant responses of the ethnic and mainstream press highlighted the antipathy felt by proponents of the different education systems. What made a good citizen in Catholic minds diverged from the state, and representatives of each viewed the other as hampering progress and promoting backwardness in a new democracy.

Though parochial schools had not benefited from state funds before the 1870s, the knowledge that there was little potential for future funding was perceived as a slight against Catholic Americans. For Irish Catholics, America was hailed as a place for educational and occupational progress, a country where they could overcome the repression of their religious education system at home. The 1872 amendment was woven into a wider story of discrimination alluded to by Daniel Reily ten years previously. Compulsory education was met with similar suspicion. When raised in the Illinois Legislature in 1873 and 1874, it was greeted by the Irish Catholic press as a threat to the liberties promised to all Americans by the Bill of Rights. The *Chicago Post* argued that compulsory schooling was good training 'for the franchise of the citizen; to make the man entirely competent for the duties of self-government'.[90] While Catholics in Chicago believed in the opportunities provided by education, the prospect of funding a separate system of religious schools with the added burden of thousands of extra students galvanised community pressure on legislators to resist compulsory school policies. In 1873 the Irish Catholic Benevolent Union resolved, along with the German Catholic Central Association, that the public school system, in 'ignoring all supernatural authority, and making God, the first knowledge, the last thing to be learned, is a curse to our country and a floodgate of atheism and of sensuality, and of civil, social and national corruption'.[91]

Compulsory education became even more dangerous for Catholics after the 'Instruction of the Propagation of the Faith' of 1875, which declared that public education 'was opposed to Catholicism since it excluded all religious instruction and thus constituted a great evil if children were allowed to be exposed to it'. Bishops were instructed to use every means in their power to prevent Catholics from all contact with public schools.[92] That year President Ulysses Grant urged Congress to pass a constitutional amendment banning government aid to religious schools, and to enforce taxation on Catholic Church-owned property. In this, Grant argued that the government was curbing the 'tyranny' of the priesthood in American cities.[93] The amendment was blocked by

Democrats in the Senate but the public support of the President for such anti-Catholic sentiment was indicative of the wider problem faced by Catholics in the United States. The *Pomeroy's Democrat* warned that the Catholic Church's policy of separate schooling was 'its death' due to the financial burden placed upon Chicago's poor Catholic communities.[94] Unable to afford to pay both private school fees and municipal school taxes, poorer families had to 'forfeit their right to every particle of it [school tax] unless they send their sons and daughters to the common schools. This they cannot conscientiously do, in view of the sectarian tendencies and hostile character of many of them'.[95] The *Western Catholic*'s relocation to Chicago in 1872 allowed Archbishop Feehan to use its wider circulation, across parish boundaries, to raise the issue of Catholic education in the 1880s.[96] He specifically called for a centralised school board for parish schools in the city, attempting to raise religious schools to a similar administrative level as state schools. Just as in Melbourne, the double taxation of Catholic families who wished to send their children to Catholic schools disproportionately targeted the labouring classes in Chicago, who lacked the resources to have a choice but required the social opportunities brought by education.

In 1876 Chicago's Catholic parochial school system was educating 15,000 of Cook County's 138,282 potential students, a small but significant proportion, insufficient to present a threat of tyranny.[97] In 1883 the Illinois Congress enshrined compulsory education for twelve weeks in each school term for children aged between eight and fourteen years old.[98] The need for more parochial schools to cater for the children affected by compulsory schooling was seized upon as a community project requiring the response of both priest and laity. It resulted in 'the most rapid construction of parochial schools in the nation's history'.[99] Chicago's Catholic schools may not have directly influenced the majority of the city's students. However, their alumni filled the public school system as teachers. For the daughters of Irish immigrants, teaching replaced domestic service as the respectable occupation of single Irish women during the late nineteenth and early twentieth centuries.[100] Public schools afforded 'excellent education at slight cost and supplied a large number of Catholic girls with responsible and moderately profitable posts as teachers'.[101] As the Irish national parish primarily operated through English, Irish Catholic women were ideally suited to teaching in multi-ethnic public schools. Consequently, Catholic schools like St Patrick's Girls' High School trained their students to become 'self-supporting teachers who could also make significant contributions to their family's economic well-being'. In doing so, they also ensured a continued presence of Irish

Catholics in the daily lives of Chicago children who attended public school.[102] Irish-descended women provided post-elementary education within the public school system, enabling the maintenance of Irish cultural affinity and ethnic representation begun in elementary school and emphasised across parish life through their teachers. Further education for women was encouraged, providing an alternative to convent life and helping Irish and Irish-descended families to become upwardly socially mobile through their daughters, aunts and sisters.

Fundamentally, Irish Catholics were caught between economic, social and religious pressures: the pressure to provide a good and affordable education for their children, to observe the Church's teachings, to adhere to peer pressure, and to make use of the social and ethnic networks available to them. By taking advantage of the religious education provided by their parish, Catholics opened themselves up to negative comments regarding the power of the priest over their vote, which in turn led to accusations of disloyalty to the United States and the British empire. By supporting these schools financially, the labouring and middle classes who sent their children to parish schools were taxed doubly. However, in sending their children to public schools they risked rejecting a potential future community employment opportunity for many Irish children, in politics and in education. For many, religion and moral education could not be separated. Catholic organisations were willing to work with those of the Protestant faiths to protest against the increased intervention in private matters by the state.[103]

The education debates of the 1870s and 1880s led to a recalibration of the identity hierarchy within Chicago and Melbourne. While Chicago's Irish Catholics had traditionally linked their ethnicity and religion, during this time their religion was prioritised as the Catholic community came together to protest against compulsory education. In Melbourne, conversely, the debates of the 1870s and 1880s took on an increasingly ethnic tone. In both cities, the religious education debates were framed by the Irish Catholic ethnic and religious press as a continued attack on Catholic Irish people who had suffered from the imposition of Protestant teachings in education in Ireland, and while seeking the religious freedom of the 'new world', were again confronted by an ascendancy dedicated to undermining the social progress of their children. Debates about religious education and the place of religious as opposed to political and societal freedom overlapped with wider themes of nationalism, both national and diasporic, and social activism in both cities. As such, the continued existence and funding of religious schools became inextricably linked to themes of belonging and citizenship.

1890–1922

As the 1880s drew to a close and the nineteenth century entered its last decade, these community bonds continued to cause conflict with the wider non-Catholic communities in Melbourne and Chicago. But they also helped to create a stronger parish life, based on ethnicity and religion, which could be engaged with both domestically and internationally. By 1890 the education question had still not come to a conclusion that Catholics found appropriate. Melbourne Catholic archbishop Dr Carr commented to Dublin's archbishop Dr Walsh that 'The school question affords the only grievance we feel. It entails the necessity of supporting our own separate schools while we have to constitute to the support of the state schools.'[104] Many Catholic parents still had to pay a double tax for religious education, but Carr's words reflect the image presented by prominent Irish Catholics in Melbourne: that they benefited from the opportunities of living within the empire as a state with responsible government. Education was the tie that bound Irish Catholics to each other, and the arrival of more Irish Catholic religious communities as the century came to a close provided an alternative for Catholic children, while surrounding them with fellow Irish and Irish Australians who held faith and heritage in high regard.

Pope Leo XIII declared in 1884 that the Catholic Church 'has always expressly condemned mixed or neutral schools; over and over again she has warned parents to be ever on their guard in this most essential point.'[105] Though the dispute over compulsory and state-funded education was multi-denominational in both cities, disagreements were often blamed on the Catholic Church. Proponents of religious schooling in Chicago were accused of attempting 'to Coerce American Catholics into a Dangerous Foreignism' and split the allegiance of American children.[106] Indictments of disloyalty were aimed at Catholics from the growing American Protestant Association or Know-Nothing Party as the 1880s progressed, taking over from the government's attempts to federally influence school systems. This show of loyalty to the Union became particularly important in 1890 during the thirty-fifth anniversary commemorations for the Grand Army of the Republic. The Chicago district of Englewood decided to host the memorial services at the district's Protestant churches, in direct tension with the Catholic Church's stance on mixing. The Board of Education ordered that all children in Englewood's public schools attend the memorial services, regardless of faith: 'The children were warned that they must not be absent, under pain of having a black mark opposite their names, which would interfere with their record of average attendance.'[107] In response, the Catholic clergy demanded in a letter to the Board of Education that the services be held in the non-denominational schoolhouses instead. If this was not possible, they declared that 'if the Catholic children are withheld from the services, the Church must not be blamed for being un-patriotic and un-American'.[108]

The previous year the Baltimore Congress of Catholic Laymen had emphasised that 'the world should know that loyalty to God means loyalty to the State'.[109] Perceptions of loyalty were at risk, but there was also a financial threat. A renewed compulsory education law, known as Edward's Law, had been passed in 1889, threatening guardians with a fine of twenty dollars if their charges failed to attend school for less than sixteen weeks in a school year: the memorial services counted toward this.[110] The fight for separate schooling for Catholic children away from the influences of individualistic Protestants was to continue for decades in Chicago's Catholic Church. However, the ethnic parish system and the close community structures that it encouraged provided Irish Catholics with a multitude of avenues in which to access and criticise the government, including across the Catholic faith.

By 1900, Chicago's Irish Catholic community was noted for its cohesiveness. Though it had spread across the city, wherever 'they settled, they built churches'.[111] With these churches came more school-building projects.[112] The distinctly Irish nature of the English-speaking Catholic schools was emphasised during the 1900s when a campaign to teach Irish history was launched by Archbishop Quigley, the Irish History Society of South Chicago and the Ancient Order of Hibernians. By 1909 Irish history was taught in twenty-six parish schools.[113] A similar initiative was undertaken by the HACBS, which offered prizes to Catholic school students for essays on Irish history.[114] The influence of religious orders in Melbourne's Catholic schools continued into the twentieth century. Of the 452 teachers in Melbourne's Catholic parochial school district, 249 were members of religious orders in 1905. In the thirty-one Catholic colleges and high schools, three-quarters of teaching staff were members of religious orders, many from Ireland.[115] Interest in Irish history and literature was further encouraged through the student newspapers which emerged in Catholic high schools during the late nineteenth and early twentieth centuries, providing students with an active role in promoting Irish interests.[116] The arrival of new Catholic ethnic groups at the turn of the century led to new levels of competition in Melbourne and particularly in Chicago. The older Irish and German Catholic migrant groups were confronted by new arrivals of eastern and southern European Catholics, alongside the arrival of an American-born German archbishop.[117] This push for a particularly Irish brand of Catholicism in Chicago was therefore partly about reasserting Irish Catholic power within the Church as well as more generally in the city.

The beginning of the First World War led to a rise in nativism and suspicion of the Catholic Church as a 'foreign' institution in Australia and the United States.[118] The new Chicago archbishop George Mundelein sought to prepare Catholic students for American life by establishing a new school board, which ruled in 1916 that all students had to use the same textbook written in English.[119] The school board declared that 'we intend to take the hyphen out of the parochial schools in Chicago'.[120] The education question also continued to cause rifts in Melbourne society. As O'Farrell notes, instead of 'seeing the decorous shelving of the education question' at the outbreak of the First World War, 'a Catholic campaign more intense and aggressive than any since the 1870s' was waged.[121] The Catholic Federation of Victoria, enthusiastically encouraged by archbishop Daniel Mannix, worked alongside the Victorian Catholic Workers' Association for Catholic educational rights, coming into conflict with the Labor Party and wider patriotic feeling.[122] The battle would continue long into the twentieth century.

By 1922, both cities had entrenched dual systems of elementary schooling, with parochial schools being funded largely by the local parish. Irish pride and memories of persecution were consistently appealed to throughout the nineteenth and early twentieth centuries to sustain Catholic attention on religious educational rights.[123] In both cities, Irish and Irish-descended women continued to make an impact through parochial and public schooling. Schoolteachers like Margaret A. Haley and Julia Flynn were vital to the expanding public school systems and became important leaders in suffrage and labour union organisations in Chicago and Melbourne.[124] The increasing number of educated Irish-descended women entering the teaching profession helped to provide new role models for future generations and moved more Irish families into the middle classes, garnering them increased social, economic and political clout.

CONCLUSION

The education of children was a central issue for Irish migrants. The second half of the nineteenth century witnessed the expansion of public and parochial schools in Melbourne and Chicago, and by the century's final decades the two cities provided both elementary and secondary schooling to children of all backgrounds for the first time. While hailed as social progress, the widening of educational opportunity also brought tensions about funding and the denominational mixing of children. The position of the Catholic Church was clear; it had a social mission to provide moral and educational instruction to the next generations of Catholics, and therefore Catholic parents were risking their children's moral and spiritual future if they were sent to public schools which, in the eyes of many Catholics, as government institutions had a strong Protestant influence. In response, the Catholic Church and laity in both Melbourne and Chicago sought alternative resources with which to educate their children. In this they benefited from the expansion of Irish Catholic teaching orders during the nineteenth century, providing a labour source which did not require the finances of the state government. These women and men allowed for the entrenchment of religious communities in Irish diasporic life, and for the influence of Irish and Catholic teachers on new generations of Irish descendants.

Melbourne and Chicago both benefited from the legislative prioritisation of education early in their histories. However, the Catholic Church's capacity to cope with these demands altered the future path of each city's educational system. Religious education instilled a sense of difference in Irish Catholic children, aiding the creation and continuation of Irish and Catholic community identity. While Irish male religious orders did run schools for boys, they focused their efforts on post-elementary teaching, often leaving elementary teaching to lay teachers or nuns. It was Irish female religious orders who had daily interactions with schoolchildren in Melbourne and Chicago, building upon the familial home to encourage a sense of cultural affinity with Ireland, an identity that was inextricably linked to the national parish and religion. Irish and Irish-descended women in Melbourne and Chicago were responsible for the creation and advancement of a foundational identity which connected ethnicity and religion. In doing so, they shaped particular areas of each city physically through schools and hospitals, in addition to the mental and social bonds of the parish. As Catholics who could afford to often sent their children to private schools, domestically or back in Europe, Irish women in religious orders and in public schools were responsible for the spread, unconscious or otherwise, of Irish and Irish Catholic priorities throughout the labouring and middle classes. They created an ethnic community which could then be built upon by the religious, secular and nationalist leaders who emerged in Melbourne and Chicago.

NOTES

1. US Federal Census, 1880.
2. Gilley, 'Roman Catholic Church'.
3. Mary Hickman, *Religion, Class and Identity: The State, the Catholic Church and the Education of the Irish in Britain* (Aldershot: Avebury, 1995), p. 40.
4. Mary Hatfield, *Growing Up in Nineteenth-Century Ireland: A Cultural History of Middle-Class Childhood and Gender* (Oxford: Oxford University Press, 2019), p. 13.
5. David Dickson, Justyna Pyz and Christopher Shepard, 'Introduction and Acknowledgments', in David Dickson, Justyna Pyz and Christopher Shepard (eds), *Irish Contexts in the Origins of Modern Education* (Dublin: Four Courts Press, 2012), p. 1.
6. McGreevy, *Catholicism and American Freedom*, p. 36.
7. David Fitzpatrick, '"A share of the honeycomb": Education, emigration and Irishwomen', *Continuity and Change*, 1:2 (1986), pp. 217–34.
8. Donald H. Akenson, *The Irish Education Experiment: The National System of Education in the Nineteenth Century* (London: Routledge, 1970, repr. 2012), p. 224; Walsh, 'Irish National School Books'; Thomas Mangione, 'The establishment of the Model School system in Ireland, 1834–1854', *New Hibernia Review*, 7:4 (2003), pp. 103–22.
9. Victoria's area is 91,749.1 square miles compared to Ireland's 32,595.
10. Children were also focused in different areas due to the demographic make-up of newly settled areas. The goldfields, for example, did not house many children in the 1850s as it was mainly young single men who went to find their fortune. The centre of Melbourne, conversely, was the home of many children and families.
11. Edward Sweetman, Charles R. Long and John Smyth, *A History of State Education in Victoria* (Melbourne: Critchley Parker, 1922); T. L. Suttor, *Hierarchy and Democracy in Australia: 1788–1870* (Melbourne: Melbourne University Press, 1965), p. 261.
12. *Argus*, 21 June 1852.
13. Sweetman et al., *State Education*, p. 53.
14. Carole Hooper, 'Access and exclusivity in nineteenth-century Victorian schools', *History of Education Review*, 45:1 (2016), pp. 16–27.
15. Michael de Nie, *The Eternal Paddy: Irish Identity and the British Press, 1798–1882* (Madison: University of Wisconsin Press, 2004), p. 91.
16. *Age*, 17 June 1859; Dianne Hall and Elizabeth Malcolm, '"English institutions and the English race": Race and politics in late nineteenth-century Australia', *Australian Journal of Politics & History*, 62:1 (2016), pp. 1–15.
17. Anon., *Some of the Fruits of Fifty Years: Ecclesiastical Annals ... Since the Erection of Each* (Melbourne: A. H. Massina & Co., 1897), p. 16.

18. Andreas, *History of Chicago*, vol. 1, pp. 206–9.
19. Kathleen A. Brosnan, 'Public presence, public silence: Nuns, bishops, and the gendered space of early Chicago', *Chicago Historical Review*, 90:3 (2004), pp. 473–96.
20. Ibid.
21. Newspapers frequently listed the ethnicity of those arrested for public disorder; McGreevy, *Catholicism and American Freedom*, p. 94.
22. Sister Mary Agatha (St Francis Xavier Academy for Young Ladies, Chicago) to the President of the Society for the Propagation of the Faith at Lyons, 4 December 1847 (Madaj Collection, Box 1, ACA).
23. *Daily National Intelligencer*, 31 July 1854.
24. Suellen Hoy, 'Caring for Chicago's women and girls: The Sisters of the Good Shepherd, 1859–1911', *Journal of Urban History*, 23:3 (1997), pp. 260–94.
25. Andreas, *History of Chicago*, vol. 2.
26. John Belchem, 'The Irish in Britain, United States and Australia: Some comparative reflections on labour history', in Patrick Buckland and John Belchem (eds), *Irish in British Labour History: Conference Proceedings in Irish Studies* (Liverpool: University of Liverpool Press, 1993), pp. 19–27.
27. Chicago Directory 1868 and *The Lakeside Annual Directory of the City of Chicago, 1878–9* (Chicago: Donnelly, Loyd & Co., 1878).
28. *Western Tablet*, 14 February 1852.
29. Hoy, *Good Hearts*, p. 6.
30. *Age*, 17 June 1859, 2 July 1859.
31. Gilbert J. Garraghan, *The Catholic Church in Chicago, 1673–1871* (Chicago: Loyola University Press, 1921), pp. 112–14, 123–4; Larkin, 'Devotional revolution'.
32. Brosnan, 'Public presence'.
33. John Onahan to William Onahan, 30 May 1852 (Onahan Collection, Box 1, ACA).
34. *Leader*, 10 March 1855.
35. Mulkerins, *Holy Family Parish*, p. 57.
36. Ibid.
37. Whelan, 'Religious rivalry'.
38. Maree G. Allen, *The Labourers' Friends: Sisters of Mercy in Victoria and Tasmania* (Melbourne: Hargreen Publishing Company, 1989), p. 34.
39. Joseph Doyle, 'Cardinal Cullen and the system of national education in Ireland', in Keogh and McDonnell (eds), *Cardinal Paul Cullen and his World*, pp. 190–204.
40. Marjorie R. Theobald, *Knowing Women: Origins of Women's Education in Nineteenth-Century Australia* (Cambridge: Cambridge University Press, 1996), p. 131.
41. Fitzpatrick, 'Honeycomb'.
42. Warwick Eunson, 'Davitt, Arthur (1808–1860)', *ADB*.

43. *Portland Guardian and Normanby General Advertiser*, 11 July 1859.
44. John Logan, 'The national curriculum', in James H. Murphy (ed.), *The Oxford History of the Irish Book, Volume IV: The Irish Book in English* (Oxford: Oxford University Press, 2011), pp. 499–517.
45. Eunson, 'Davitt'; Max Waugh, 'The national system of education in Victoria, 1849–1862: Sir Richard Bourke and the Irish connection', in Philip Bull, Frances Devlin-Glass and Helen Doyle (eds), *Ireland and Australia, 1798–1998: Studies in Culture, Identity and Migration* (Sydney: Crossing Press, 2000), pp. 102–12.
46. Mimi Cowan, '"We know neither Catholics, nor Protestants, nor Free-Thinkers here": Ethnicity, religion, and the Chicago public schools, 1837–94', in Barr and Carey (eds), *Religion and Greater Ireland*, pp. 187–205.
47. Hickman, *Religion, Class and Identity*, p. 173.
48. Reprinted in *Western Tablet*, 28 February 1852.
49. McGreevy, *Catholicism and American Freedom*, p. 7.
50. Hynes to Goold, 23 December 1858 (Hynes to Goold correspondence, File 1, MDHC).
51. H. A. Finlay, 'Duffy, Sir Frank Gavan (1852–1936)', *ADB*.
52. Geoffrey Blainey, *A History of Victoria* (Cambridge: Cambridge University Press, 2013, 2nd edn), p. 59.
53. US Census Summaries, 1860 and 1870.
54. James P. McCartin, *Prayers of the Faithful: The Shifting Spiritual Life of American Catholics* (Cambridge, MA: Harvard University Press, 2010), p. 9.
55. Janet A. Nolan, '"The nun who stopped traffic" and "the Patrick Henry of the classroom": Justitia Coffey, Margaret Coffey, and Chicago's school wars', *Radharc*, 5/7 (2004–6), pp. 33–52; Nolan, *Servants of the Poor*, p. 2.
56. Cooper, 'Something borrowed'.
57. Harmon, *Church of the Annunciation*; Mulkerins, *Holy Family*.
58. Nolan, *Servants of the Poor*, pp. 85–6.
59. Chicago Directory, 1861.
60. James W. Sanders, *The Education of an Urban Minority: Catholics in Chicago, 1833–1965* (Oxford: Oxford University Press, 1977), pp. 4, 12.
61. Ibid., pp. 46–7.
62. 'Proceedings of the [Illinois State] Convention', *Sangamo Journal* (Illinois), 17 March 1862.
63. Waugh, 'National System'.
64. Akenson, *Irish Education*, p. 227.
65. Cooper, 'Something borrowed'.
66. Desmond Bowen, *Paul Cardinal Cullen and the Shaping of Modern Irish Catholicism* (Dublin: Gill and Macmillan, 1983), pp. 133–8; Susan M. Parkes, '"An essential service": The National Board and teacher

education, 1831–1870', in Brendan Walsh (ed.), *Essays in the History of Irish Education* (Abingdon: Palgrave Macmillan, 2016), pp. 45–83.
67. Allen, *Labourers' Friends*, p. 40.
68. David H. Murphy, 'Irish Jesuit schooling in Victoria, Australia', *Irish Journal of Education*, 25:1/2 (1991), pp. 52–8.
69. Cowan, '"We know neither Catholics"'.
70. Ibid.
71. Nolan, *Servants of the Poor*, p. 24.
72. *Argus*, 22 August 1868.
73. Carter, *Victoria, the British 'El Dorado'*, pp. 82–3.
74. 'Legislative Assembly', 20 August 1868, *Victorian Hansard* VI, p. 754.
75. *Advocate*, 20 March 1869.
76. Fr. Dalton to Fr. Moore, 6 September 1870 (MSSN/AUST/236/13, JAD).
77. O'Neill, *Catholics of Consequence*, p. 156.
78. *Victorian Hansard*, XIV, p. 40.
79. *Advocate*, 19 March 1870.
80. Sweetman et al., *State Education*, p. 65.
81. Education Act 1872 (Vic), 36 Vic. No. 447, pts. 13 & 14. Simon Sleight notes that only twenty-five officers were employed throughout Victoria to implement the Education Act's compulsory declaration. Sleight, *Young People*, p. 51.
82. Ann R. Shorten, 'The legal context of Australian education: An historical exploration', *Australia New Zealand Journal of Law Education*, 1:1 (1996), pp. 2–32.
83. *Advocate*, 7 February 1874.
84. *Advocate*, 17 January 1874, 24 January 1874.
85. *Advocate*, 9 October 1875.
86. *Advocate*, 23 May 1885.
87. Illinois Constitutional Convention, *The constitution of the state . . . July 2d, A.D. 1870* (Springfield: Western News Co., 1870): Article VIII relates to Education.
88. *Journal of the Constitutional Convention of the State of Illinois. Convened at Springfield, December 13, 1869* (Springfield: State Journal Printing Office, 1870), p. 522.
89. Ibid.
90. *Chicago Post*, 30 January 1873.
91. *New York Herald*, 18 October 1873.
92. Hunt, 'Vatican teaching'.
93. McGreevy, *Catholicism and American Freedom*, pp. 92–3.
94. Quoted in *Daily Inter Ocean*, 28 January 1876.
95. *Pomeroy's Democrat*, 4 March 1876.
96. Walch, 'The Catholic press'.

97. Ibid.; *Twelfth Biennial Report of the Superintendent of Public Instruction of Illinois: 1877–1878* (Springfield: Weber & Co. State Printers, 1879), p. 57.
98. 'Compulsory Education Act', *Laws of the State of Illinois Enacted by the Thirty-Third General Assembly* (Springfield: H. W. Bokker, 1883), pp. 167–8.
99. Martin R. West and Ludger Woessmann, '"Every Catholic child in a Catholic school": Historical resistance to state schooling, contemporary private competition and student achievement across countries', *Economic Journal*, 120:546 (2010), pp. 229–55.
100. Diner, *Erin's Daughters*, pp. 96–7.
101. *Sunday Times*, 31 October 1875.
102. Nolan, *Servants of the Poor*, p. 24.
103. McGreevy, *Catholicism and American Freedom*, p. 118.
104. Carr to Abp Dr Walsh (Dublin), 20 September 1889 (uncatalogued, DDA).
105. West and Woessman, '"Every Catholic child"'.
106. *Daily Inter-Ocean*, 1 November 1890.
107. *New York Tribune*, 30 May 1890.
108. *New York Tribune*, 30 May 1890.
109. *New York Herald*, 13 November 1889.
110. Shanabruch, *Chicago's Catholics*, p. 60.
111. Ibid., pp. 41–2.
112. *Illustrated Souvenir of the Archdiocese of Chicago: Commemorating the Installation of the Most Reverend Archbishop George W. Mundelein, D.D., February 1916* (Chicago: R. H. Fleming Publishing Company, 1916).
113. Shanabruch, *Chicago's Catholics*, pp. 114–15.
114. *Geelong Advertiser*, 20 August 1910.
115. *Freeman's Journal* (Sydney), 23 December 1905.
116. Chicago Regional Community Papers, Sisters of Mercy Heritage Center (SMHC).
117. Shanabruch, *Chicago's Catholics*, pp. 119–27; Pacyga, *Chicago*, pp. 186–9.
118. *Advocate*, 28 December 1918.
119. Shanabruch, *Chicago's Catholics*, p. 187; Edward R. Kantowicz, 'Cardinal Mundelein of Chicago and the shaping of twentieth-century American Catholicism', *Journal of American History*, 68:1 (1981), pp. 52–68.
120. Shanabruch, *Chicago's Catholics*, p. 188.
121. O'Farrell, *Catholic Church*, p. 210.
122. Ibid., pp. 204–12.
123. Barr, *Ireland's Empire*, p. 474.
124. Reid (ed.), *Battleground*; McCarthy, *Respectability and Reform*; Marjorie Theobald, 'Women, leadership and gender politics in the interwar years: The case of Julia Flynn', *History of Education*, 29:1 (2000), pp. 63–77.

6

Different Fighting Styles: Political Nationalism

The language of nationalism redefined the immigrant experience, contributing to the continuous invention and reinvention of diasporic priorities and identities, and crucially, allowing Irish migrants to define themselves in terms of ethnic pride and new world loyalty. By focusing on certain motifs within Irish nationalism, such as exile, republicanism or political autonomy, migrants could be both Irish and Australian or American, allowing them to continue to be different without 'feeling as if they were outsiders'.[1] The reasons for involvement in Irish diasporic nationalism were varied, but historians of the Irish diaspora often focus on ideas of counteracting humiliation, loneliness and aspirations to respectability. Motivations shifted depending on local concerns, the availability of passion-rousing visiting lecturers, and events in Ireland. In both Chicago and Melbourne, the strength of community organising structures largely steered the direction of nationalist fervour.

This chapter explores the role of the middle class in leading and facilitating nationalist ambitions in Melbourne and Chicago, echoing the work of John Belchem on 'culture brokers' in Liverpool.[2] Male leaders dominate this chapter, as they do the historiography on nationalism and politics across the world. Traditionally, Irish women have been dismissed from discussions on nationalism; dominant (male) narratives argued that the toils of everyday life left them with little time or inclination for abstract ideals like nationalism, or portrayed women as naïve donors to subscription lists and little more.[3] However, as the previous chapter noted, women had a central role to play in forming foundational links within the Irish diasporic community. These connections were built upon for different, but related, ends by men. Within political nationalist organising, women were important participants and fundraisers, often working behind the scenes to facilitate the events that are now associated with the men whose names went into the newspapers.[4]

Nineteenth-century Irish nationalism was filled with gendered ideas of nationhood and the quest for respect, either abroad or in Ireland. It focused on men fighting for the honour of Ireland, to release her (as Ireland is typically portrayed) from England's shackles in the United States, or to restore Ireland to her true potential as a self-governing loyal part of the empire in Australia.[5] These ideas were encouraged within arenas usually only open to men, the Ladies' Land League presenting a visible anomaly in the nineteenth-century history of Irish nationalism. The 'push' factors of British misrule and lack of employment opportunities, which led Irish men to leave Ireland, were exacerbated for women. Women were additionally affected by the embedding of patriarchal society in Ireland in the aftermath of the Famine, when landownership patterns and decreasing marriage opportunities led to the exodus of Ireland's women.[6] These systems were echoed abroad, leading to nationalist agitation 'rooted in the homosocial world of the fraternal association and the saloon'.[7] The overlapping membership of different nationalist organisations within Melbourne and Chicago led to stronger fraternal links but could also result in the confusion and dilution of ideologies. The social advantages of joining Irish nationalist organisations could therefore outweigh the ideological differences, prioritising ethnicity over politics.

Previous chapters have outlined how foundational identities, based in cultural and ethnic affinities, were created and encouraged within middle-class diasporic communities in Melbourne and Chicago through education, religious and secular parish life, and political debate. This chapter examines how community leaders utilised this cultural affinity to promote Irish political nationalist activities, whether armed rebellion, moral force or constitutional change. In doing so, it explores the connections that evolved between middle-class leaders and their labouring-class counterparts in Ireland, Melbourne and Chicago. The term 'nationalism' incorporates a diverse range of motivations and activities, bringing together people of different classes, religions and moments of migration. How those of Irish birth and descent articulated their relationship with Ireland, and their vision of Irish governance, depended on their class allegiances as well as a range of other influences. This social imagining of Ireland and its political potential was a key uniting force for Irish diasporic organising. This chapter is organised to reflect key shifts in nationalist organising in Ireland and abroad. As Malcolm Campbell notes, Irish nationalist organising in Australia and the United States was distinct until the mid-1860s, largely reflecting their differing political contexts. As Irish Catholic community organising became stronger and more influenced by the working and lower-middle classes after 1880, Irish-Australian nationalism began to more closely resemble the Irish-American experience.[8] After 1900, there was another shift in domestic and transnational nationalist organising and this is explored in the final section. This chapter brings the national picture put forward by Campbell into the specific city contexts of Melbourne and Chicago.

1840–1860

In decimating Irish society between 1845 and 1852, the potato blight completely transformed Irish nationalism abroad. The Famine fundamentally altered the way that British control of Ireland was viewed worldwide and how land was distributed and farmed in Ireland. Republicanism in Ireland 'went into hibernation' during the 1850s while people recalibrated ownership patterns and familial structures.[9] The focus of Irish political nationalism therefore shifted out to the newly reshaped diaspora. The Famine provided a cause and an image of British repression and systematic cruelty, even genocide, for nationalist leaders to unite around, and the failure of the Young Irelander rising in 1848 aided the promotion of this message after its leaders were flung across the globe.[10] Eyes were briefly sent to Van Diemen's Land when Young Irelanders like John Mitchel and William Smith O'Brien were transported from Ireland. On escaping the Australian colonies, they continued to North America and Europe, carrying the rapt attention of the Irish diaspora with them.[11] Bringing people from across Ireland, and from a mix of religious and class backgrounds together, the legacy of the Young Irelander movement was the creation of a distinctive Irish history written to 'nourish collective memory and reinforce allegiances and obligations to the nation'.[12] The emphasis on an Irish national identity based principally in cultural and historical arguments, not religion or language, allowed for the possibility of engagement with a range of images of nationalism as the nineteenth century progressed.

Most of the Young Irelanders transported to Australia left as soon as they could, lest they catch 'the contagion of respectability' and decide that they could live happily within the British empire, like Kevin Izod O'Doherty did.[13] However, the promise of new opportunities, wealth and excitement drew others to Melbourne's shores. Charles Gavan Duffy, politician and editor of the *Nation*, growing tired of the lack of nationalist sentiment in Ireland in the aftermath of the Famine, sought a new home in Melbourne in 1854, as did Peter Lalor, the younger brother of land reform advocate James Fintan Lalor.[14] Without relatively easy travel to and from Ireland, following the departure of most heroes of Young Ireland, Melbourne society prioritised making sense of the chaos that accompanied the gold rush. A similar lull in nationalist activity occurred in Chicago. The Chicago Repeal Association, explored in Chapter 3, had been one of the principal organisations in the growing town of the 1840s. However, support for O'Connell's cause declined after his death in 1847 and Chicago's Irish population began to respond to the more pressing needs, physical and emotional, of Famine migrants. As a result, nationalist organisations in the city disappeared.[15]

John Mitchel's arrival in 1856 signalled the growth of Chicago's influence as a centre for Irish diasporic nationalism. Mitchel's choice of Chicago for a lecture stop reflects both the growing nationalist sentiment in the city and its potential fundraising opportunities. He was the first ex-Young Irelander to reach the city on a lecture tour, but not the last. Though the message veered between separatism and home rule, lecture tours became an important tool used by Irish nationalists throughout the nineteenth century. They allowed political leaders to concurrently raise money for personal and ideological activities, and to elevate the profile of their message. Chicagoans attended these lectures for their sense of occasion, and the accompanying parties, as much as for their nationalist rhetoric; a particularly enticing mix for a young population trapped in a daily toil to survive in a new city and chaotic economy.

Visiting Irish nationalist lecturers only arrived in Melbourne in great numbers in the 1880s, due to the distance and cost of travel. However, while Melbourne may have lost access to the majority of its Irish nationalists, it retained other transported agitators who influenced Irish-Australian thinking and identity. Earlier in the century, New South Wales had been the final destination for around eight hundred transported Irish radicals, United Irishmen and Defenders, who were joined by Chartists and other nonconformists from across the United Kingdom.[16] This mix of free thinking had more of an impact on Melbourne society and the formulation of early Irish Victorian identity than the Young Irelanders who left. The Eureka Stockade of 1854 is connected in the popular mind to Irish-Australian identity and, though it occurred in the goldfields of Ballarat, Eureka informed Melbourne society immensely.

The state enforcement of gold diggers' licence fees and the release without charge of an ex-convict and hotel proprietor who kicked a drunken Scottish digger to death led to accusations of local administrative corruption and the influx of troops into the area. The diggers began to organise in response, with leading Chartists working with agitators from other backgrounds to combat the increased militarisation of the goldfields. Together they formed the Ballarat Reform League, promoting moral force tactics of resistance over physical force.[17] In mid-November 1854, Governor of Victoria Charles Hotham ordered all available troops in Victoria to Ballarat, 'a decisive step towards conflict'.[18] This radical labour protest gained its reputation as an Irish protest when an advance guard of troops marched through an Irish area with bayonets. Though the troops had been met with derision throughout their march, the Irish who lived in Eureka Lead threw stones at the soldiers and subsequently the regiment's drummer boy was shot and killed. Retribution was expected, and on 2 December, four hundred soldiers ambushed a reduced group of 150 diggers before dawn. Five soldiers and thirty diggers were killed, with a hundred more arrested. The next night, soldiers fired indiscriminately into tents which had lights on illegally; three more people were killed.[19]

Historians have hailed the 1854 Eureka Stockade as a nationalist moment, with Irish people challenging the British establishment.[20] This connection was largely due to the choice of 'Vinegar Hill', the site of one of the final battles of the 1798 United Irishmen rising, as a password for those entering the stockade.[21] The involvement of Peter Lalor, brother of Young Irelander James Fintan Lalor, as leader of the 'rebels', also infers some influence of Young Irelander principles relating to popular sovereignty and land rights.[22] Eureka was a moment of convergence which, in the words of T. L. Suttor, 'sealed in blood the marriage between Irish Catholics and social and political radicalism in Australia: this is Young Ireland's and Eureka's chief bequest to Australia.'[23] However, Eureka was not a united Irish rebellion against British troops due to ethnic pride or a response to the exertion of British power over Irish. British commentators also discouraged the view of Eureka as a diasporic Irish rebellion, blaming 'foreigners' for the uprising.[24] Instead, it was part of a wider radical stream of thought brought about by the mix of people in Victoria at that time, where Chartists mixed with Dissenters, and Young Irelanders mixed with trade unionists.

The Eureka Stockade's Irish nationalist credentials are contentious, and this uncertainty has dogged the image of Irish nationalism in Melbourne during the mid-century. Patrick O'Farrell argued that for most Australian Irish, 'involvement in Irish causes was a luxury they could not afford'.[25] Similarly, Keith Amos notes that 'there seemed to be little point of conspiring for an Irish freedom 14,000 miles away'.[26] However, the absence of an Irish political nationalism recognisable in the United States does not equal a lack of visible loyalty to the nation and values of democratic Ireland. When news reached Melbourne of a food crisis in Ireland during 1862, the Irish-born mayor of Melbourne, Robert Bennett, launched a collection for its relief. He noted, 'When people were living in abundance in a plentiful country like this, it was very easy for them to forget the distress which might exist in the land from which they had come.' Bennett, and other Irish leaders, were determined that a sense of duty to those in Ireland would be nurtured throughout nineteenth- century Melbourne.[27]

While the influence of the Young Irelanders was visible in Melbourne, it was more clearly linked to the future of Irish nationalism in the United States through the organising of ex-Young Irelanders John O'Mahony and Michael Doheny. The Fenian Brotherhood, established in 1858, evolved from the Emmet Monument Association, an organisation dedicated to fostering hope for future military resistance in Ireland. The Fenian Brotherhood was the sister organisation of the Irish Republican Brotherhood (IRB) which operated in Ireland from 1857 under the command of fellow former Young Irelander, James Stephens.[28] The parallel and linked organisations facilitated the funnelling of American monetary, political and military support to Ireland. Though the Fenians did not gain large traction in Chicago immediately, the Civil War and Terence Bellew McManus' 1861 funeral gave new inspiration to the movement, coinciding with the city's economic, transport and population booms.[29] The Irish settler populations of Chicago and Melbourne were in flux during the 1840s and 1850s. The trauma of the Famine and emigration combined with the daily grind of rapidly growing towns and cities to move the focus away from Irish nationalism during the early 1850s. By the second half of the 1850s there was a little more stability, the Young Irelander leadership had regrouped in different factions, and organising began again across the diaspora.

1860–1880

The twenty years between 1860 and 1880 witnessed the ascent of both cities along with a new breed of Irish nationalist leader internationally. During these twenty years, there were shifts in constitutional, militant and agrarian organising, with changing priorities, alliances and tactics in Ireland and throughout the diaspora. Changes in transport networks allowed for increased movement around the globe, facilitating lecture tours and the exchange of ethnic newspapers, while relative international peace in Europe and the expansion of colonial conquests by

Britain and the United States led to a renewed focus on domestic issues. Ireland was alive with uprisings and secret societies during the 1860s which were carried out into its diaspora, while the late 1870s witnessed an international renewal of land and labour protest. How these Irish and international concerns were contextualised by local priorities provides an opportunity to consider similarities and differences in organising across the Irish communities of Melbourne and Chicago.

The early years of the 1860s focused on fundraising and organising. While the IRB and Fenian Brotherhood operated behind the scenes, Irish people in Chicago were preoccupied with the Civil War. As explored in other chapters, Irishmen enlisted in the Union Army, while Irish Sisters of Mercy joined with other religious orders to expand the social provisions of the city. Chicago became an economic and transport hub for Union Army supplies, and the associated industries boomed. In Melbourne, the focus was on consolidating the growth of the city's economy and its rising position within the British empire. The city remained relatively untouched by political nationalism in these early years, though a strong thread of civic nationalism remained, tapping into British values of democracy and a particularly Australian value of religious toleration and opportunity.

The ongoing Civil War in the United States prompted renewed discussions on belonging and the responsibilities of government to its people. In 1863 Chicago hosted the Fenian Convention. The Brotherhood used this wartime convention to set out its priorities regarding American loyalty and Irish freedom, amending its constitution to pledge its 'entire allegiance to the constitution and laws of the United States'. The long-term strategy of the Fenian Brotherhood did not alter though, encouraging younger members of the Brotherhood's Circles to study military tactics and the use of arms in order to drill 'so as to be prepared to offer their services to the United States government, by land or sea, against England's myrmidons' in the event of war between Britain and the United States.[30] Irish soldiers would use their position in the United States army to aid the Union while also frustrating the military might of Britain, if required.

The Civil War brought Chicago to national prominence both for its transport networks and its political conflicts over support for the war and slavery. With this new prominence came new fundraising opportunities. The Irish who remained at home in Chicago supported the IRB and Ireland-based nationalist activities through fundraising. The Chicago Irish Fair, also known as the Fenian Fair, was held during Easter week 1864, bringing together material donations from Ireland and monetary donations from the United States. In response to a series of advertisements placed in the *Irish People*,[31] customers were offered stones from Blarney Castle, clay from Wolfe Tone's grave, picks from 1798, and a crowbar 'used by the drummer bailiff when headed the crowbar brigade from the Clonakilty district'.[32] Absent of fighting Irish men, Chicago's women used the skills that they were already familiar with from parish organising to engage with Irish nationalism and ethnicity. Despite delivery problems related to the ongoing war and customs duties, the Chicago Irish Fair of 1864 collected $55,000 for the buying of arms and 'other separatist aims' in the United States and Ireland.[33] This fair was a chance for a variety of people of Irish descent, whether members of the Fenian Brotherhood or not, to demonstrate their Irish identity as well as to provide an economic and morale boost to the organisation. The proceeds may have been going to the Fenian Brotherhood and IRB, but attending the fair did not automatically denote support for armed rebellion against Britain.

The Fenian Fair brought international eyes to the city, while the distance from the Civil War's hostilities allowed for an infrastructural and newspaper boom. Melbourne also experienced an ascent in economy and status by the 1860s. However, without the frequent stimulus provided by nationalist visitors and newspapers, the focus remained on charitable subscription funds which did not threaten the imperial status quo. Despite these attempts to emphasise the loyal and altruistic motives of the Irish communities in Melbourne, the presence of police officers at charity gatherings dedicated to Irish causes demonstrates a colonial worry about the spread of separatist Irish designs. In 1864, Bishop Hynes noted that the people of Victoria had donated £1,000 for a statue of Daniel O'Connell to be erected in Dublin.[34] Commemorating the 'Great Liberator', who helped to extend the franchise and Catholic freedoms through constitutional means, was deemed to be respectable by Catholic clergymen as well as Victorian politicians. Confronted with obstacles of distance and imperial loyalty, Irish people in Melbourne engaged with nationalism most prominently through monetary donations to cultural and religious empowerment in Ireland. In both cities, the Irish Catholic Church hierarchies mused over how to support or control the varied political leanings of their congregations, priests and religious orders while maintaining their growing congregations' allegiance to the Church.

The Irish Fair brought disputes between nationalist and religious allegiances into the public arena.[35] Chicago's priesthood and hierarchy were split on the subject. Bishop Duggan issued a circular, read in all Catholic churches, condemning the Brotherhood, as 'there is an oath and a secret somewhere in the Society that he cannot find out, and which he ought to know as a Catholic Bishop', while also warning of the descent of nationalist political rhetoric from moral force into bloodshed.[36] Peter Sherlock, on behalf of the Catholic Fenians organising the fair, countered that 'there is nothing in the organization which conflicts with the established laws of the church – no oath, grip, sign or password whatever – and they are conscious of this fact, and assured of their political rights'.[37] Foreshadowing future disputes between Irish revolutionary societies and the Catholic Church, Duggan decreed that funeral processions that made their way to the Catholic Cavalry Cemetery would not be allowed into the cemetery if they were accompanied by any members of secret societies, including the Fenians, wearing regalia or carrying banners.[38] In 1865, this decree was expanded when Duggan instructed his clergy not to administer the sacrament to Fenians and to refuse them a Christian burial.[39] Some priests joined with their bishop in disavowing the Fenian Brotherhood as a secret society, despite the vocal protests of its representatives to the contrary. Others argued that it was not inconsistent for Catholics to love their country, Ireland, and 'they cannot, nor shall they, be alienated from either, by the misrepresentations or assaults of those who would be much better and more profitably engaged in the performance of their ecclesiastical duties'.[40] The image of Fenians as anti-clerical was widespread, but falsely homogenising.[41] The attempts of 'Catholic Fenians' to persuade Duggan of their loyalty to the Church is proof of this nuance.

While members of the hierarchy disavowed Fenianism, the parish networks provided by the Church added to the occupational and military networks which facilitated the growth of the Fenian Brotherhood in Chicago. The Fenian Brotherhood, like the IRB in Ireland, recruited heavily from urban tradesmen, labourers and white-collar workers.[42] As the majority of Irish men in Chicago were involved in unskilled trades as labourers and stockyard workers, the fraternal links encouraged by close and precarious working conditions and military service during the Civil War meant that the Fenian Brotherhood leaders had an easily accessible pool of potential members. Jentz and Schneirov have highlighted the ways that the Fenians connected with labour activism from across different nationalities to encourage both mobilisation of people in the North and organised labour.[43] Thomas Brown argued that the Fenian movement in the United States was 'a product, or by-product, of the Civil War'.[44] The movement of large numbers of Irish and Irish-American men into different units, and particularly into ethnic regiments, facilitated networks of Irishmen across the United States. Nationalist leaders had new and expanded means of communication for their message of Irish independence and exile. However, these expanded networks also led to splits in the motivations and ambitions for action: for many, the Fenian Brotherhood was a social organisation. By 1866, an interested reader of the city directory could find out that the Fenian Brotherhood met every Tuesday and Friday at its Hall at the northwest corner of Wells and Randolph, and that L. H. O'Connor was the Center and Dennis O'Connor the treasurer.[45] The Fenian attempts to invade Canada in 1866 and 1867, combined with the failure of an IRB-sponsored uprising in 1867, led to the collapse of the Fenian Brotherhood in the United States.[46] Despite this setback, Irish nationalism continued to grow in other forms.

If Irish nationalist activity is only judged by American standards of Fenianism, the arguments about Irish-Australian nationalism being negligible are persuasive. However, if the local colonial context and the restrictions on activities are taken into account, Irish nationalism is visible in Melbourne during the 1860s. The armed Fenian rebellions in Ireland and Canada during 1866 and 1867, and the British response to those involved, led to fears of uprisings throughout the British empire, a period known as the 'Fenian scare'. While Irish middle-class leaders in Melbourne were quick to condemn the actions of physical-force nationalists, there was a concern for those affected by British retribution. A letter from Mrs Molly O'Donovan Rossa and Mrs Letitia Clarke Luby requested support for the 'wives, sisters, and little children' of those arrested in Ireland.[47] Their public letter, republished in Sydney's *Freeman's Journal*, was met with debate and efforts to help through the State Prisoners' Relief Fund across the Australian colonies. However, this support came with caveats.

In July 1866, a meeting of seven to eight hundred people was held in Melbourne to raise funds for the distressed families of 'young men who might place themselves in very awkward positions'.[48] It was clearly noted that the meeting was not held to express any sympathy with Fenianism. Mr James Murphy, a prominent land surveyor, observed that he had 'never before taken part in any political or public movement, and that he was unwilling to come forward on the present occasion lest motives by which he was not actuated should be attributed to him.'[49] However, 'This was not a Fenian movement, and it was not intended to send the money home, as some had said, for "physical force purposes".'[50] This was fundraising for women and children who had lost their breadwinner through widespread, and sometimes unfounded, arrests. The mixed religious backgrounds of those attending the meeting were emphasised by newspapers, mirroring the dominance of the SPS's message in Melbourne at the time: people were united by ideology, not religion. Despite the explicitly non-political nature of the meeting, police officers attended in order to stop any speeches deemed to be inciting treason.[51] The high population of Irish men in Melbourne's police force was undoubtedly of use during these moments of tension. A limited amount of £500 was raised for the State Prisoners' Relief Fund.[52] It was at this time that the Winter brothers rose to prominence in Melbourne's Irish nationalist movement, becoming influential in shaping Irish identity in Melbourne through the Irish Catholic newspaper *The Advocate* and their international contacts in Irish nationalist organisations.

The Fenian scare reached Australia's shores in early 1868. Henry O'Farrell, born in Ireland but raised in Victoria, attempted to assassinate Prince Alfred, Queen Victoria's son and the Duke of Edinburgh, on his visit to Sydney.[53] Coming five days before St Patrick's Day, O'Farrell's claim that he was acting as part of an international Fenian conspiracy led to hyper vigilance surrounding the planned festivities. Responding to rumours of a mock funeral for the 'Manchester Martyrs',[54] the Victorian police and soldiers increased their precautions against demonstrations: soldiers were ordered to defend the city's gaol and powder magazine, while foot and mounted police spread throughout Melbourne armed with carbines and revolvers. Sectarian tensions were observed throughout the city: crowds of men and boys feared to be members of the Orange Order sang the National Anthem outside St Francis' Cathedral, while 'detachments of well-known Fenians' were dispersed.[55] Accusations of 'religion, Duffyism and Fenianism' were levelled at Irish Catholics, uniting popular fears about Catholic education, Irish politicians and physical-force nationalism.[56] However, the good reputation of the colony remained at the forefront of the newspaper commentary and the SPS dinner speeches.[57] In this way, the Irish leaders in Melbourne were following a similar pattern to their compatriots in Canada, showing by their responsible and civil behaviour that Irish people could be trusted with self-governance.

Though the middle-class leaders of the SPS were keen to emphasise their innocence of any relationship to Irish nationalists, the rise of the Winter brothers and the establishment of the *Advocate* newspaper led to more vocal interest in Irish nationalist issues in Melbourne. After Gladstone's 1869 reprieve of Fenian prisoners left thirty-four Fenians in Western Australia with no funds to return to Ireland, and the Influx of Criminal Prevention Act precluded Irish political prisoners from landing in Melbourne, a number of prominent Irishmen within Victoria established a new subscription fund.[58] The Released State Prisoner Fund declared support for those who had been arrested and transported for Irish nationalist activities. Fundraising committees were established throughout Melbourne, its suburbs and in other towns in Victoria, with the *Advocate* office acting as a collection point. The newspaper ran subscription lists for two months during mid-1869, detailing the men and women who donated their pounds, shillings and pence to help the released prisoners in Western Australia. Edmund Finn and Edward Ievers, prominent members of the SPS, joined 'A Fenianess', 'Irish Tyranny', 'An Irish girl with an Irish heart' and a 'Scotch Fenian'. These pseudonyms, alongside frequent references to a subscriber's county or town of origin, demonstrate a clear allegiance to ideas of Irish nationhood within Melbourne's Irish communities.[59] The Melbourne CYMS donated a total of £7 10s., as did the men who worked in Patrick Cooney's boot factory on Little Lonsdale Street. Pubs around the city also held collections for the cause, continuing their important role in secular Irish culture.[60] Importantly, female subscribers make up roughly half of the names.[61] A mixture of Melbourne's middle and working classes raised a total of £5,000, a clear divergence from £500 raised for the State Prisoners' Relief Fund four years earlier.

Both cities built upon links between labour, land and Irish nationalism during the 1870s. The rise of ethnic fraternalism that accompanied the post-Civil War years was reflected internationally and coincided with an influx of Irish religious teaching orders into both Chicago and Melbourne. These networks worked within wider webs of communication facilitated by improved telegraph, postal and newspaper links. Through the printing and reprinting of opinion pieces from the Anglophone ethnic press, it was possible to universalise and internationalise experiences of anti-Irish and anti-Catholic discrimination. Concurrently, a sense of solidarity was encouraged between those within labour movements and nationalism, both transnationally and locally, resulting in law-and-order worries about a slide into anarchy.[62] Middle-class leaders balanced respectability and nationalism, and connected with the labouring classes through education, information and organisation, as the 1870s continued.

Bishop Duggan declared in 1868 that his stand against the Fenian Brotherhood had led to its declining popularity in Chicago.[63] However, disillusionment with the Fenians had not led to a waning of nationalist activity. Instead, Chicago's Irish separatists switched allegiance to the Clan na Gael. By 1871 there were branches in most of the Irish districts within Chicago, making the city the organisation's stronghold outside the Northeast.[64] Unfortunately for Duggan and his hopes for ending secret societies in Chicago, the Clan's leadership placed a much higher value on secrecy than the Fenians had, disguising the numbered camps with public names like the Emmet Literary Society. This secrecy did not last for very long, however, as the transient lifestyles of many Irish labourers in Chicago meant regular movements between camps, and the social aspect of Irish nationalism often resulted in drunkenness and a loosening of secrecy codes.[65] The fraternal element of Irish nationalism continued to boost and hinder the cause in Chicago.

While the Clan grew quickly, Chicago's Irish communities remained affected by the daily struggles of the city. The Chicago Fire of 1871 resulted in a need to prioritise family finances over the struggles of the homeland, even if only temporarily. While the fire's devastation slowed the Clan's development, the 1873 economic crisis had the alternative result of raising class awareness and solidarity amid dropping wages and rising redundancies for labourers. A fresh enthusiasm for the 'consciousness of being Irish and downtrodden' emerged, linking labour radicalism with Irish nationalism across class lines.[66] It became a focus for working-class organisations like the Knights of Labor, which held high Irish memberships, and would later provide new organising opportunities for Irish women.[67] As an alternative, the Ancient Order of Hibernians (AOH) emerged as a religious and non-political alternative to the Clan, though it often supported the organisation in parades and rallies. While the AOH has become synonymous with Irish associational culture, particularly in the United States, it does not appear in Chicago's directories until 1875.[68] The AOH helped to connect the labouring classes with the middle classes through shared religious loyalty. The Irish middle classes in Chicago were confronted with a decision: seek new world respectability on a class basis or prioritise the struggles of the old world by connecting with those of a shared heritage regardless of class. Some found a middle way, encapsulated by the 'New Departure' of 1878.[69]

The Winter brothers made use of the increasingly affordable telegraphic technology to create a deeper knowledge of political change in Ireland and Great Britain within Melbourne society during the 1870s. Others encouraged alternative engagements with Ireland's tribulations.[70] The Irish-born Mayor of Melbourne, George Meares, followed his predecessor Robert Bennett in demonstrating Melbourne's solidarity with the Irish food crisis of winter 1879–80. Meares bypassed nationalist organisations and wrote directly to his counterpart in Dublin expressing sympathy for the 'distress now unhappily prevailing in Ireland'.[71] Patrick Naughtin argues that the success of the non-political and non-sectarian

Irish Famine Relief Fund was due to its charitable appeal to non-Irish members of Melbourne society.[72] However, the success of the earlier Released State Prisoner Fund indicates that there was already a move toward more vocal support of Irish nationalism within the colony. While the Winter brothers dominated nationalist politics, the involvement of Irish-born mayors allowed for widening engagement with Irish society through a lens of civic duty and respectability.

The New Departure signalled a temporary Irish move away from physical-force tactics. The belief that social justice would only be achieved through the use of violence, however, increasingly connected labour and nationalist organisers in the diaspora. For Irish nationalists in Chicago, this resulted in the Skirmishing and Emergency Funds, public subscriber funds organised to support the armed overthrow of British rule in Ireland. These funds were promoted within the ethnic press, particularly Patrick Ford's *Irish World*, which was renamed the *Irish World and American Industrial Liberator* by 1878 in recognition of these merging class and nationalist priorities.[73] The economic challenges of the 1870s linked labour and Irish nationalism in the shape of the Land League. However, it also brought the Irish communities of Chicago into more direct class conflict. Men and women like William Onahan, who had been in Chicago for decades, were at odds with men like Alexander Sullivan who received their support from more recent migrants who believed in radical responses to British, and capitalist, control. Similarly, the Catholic Church in Chicago was split at a parish level, with priests supporting and condemning labour and nationalist activity depending on the occupational make-up of their congregation. In Melbourne, tensions between the Catholic Church and labour organising were rare.[74] This may have been due to the lack of Irish representation in leading union roles before the 1870s and the continuing anti-Catholic sentiment in unionised occupations. However, support for labour activism was also a feature of Australian Catholicism. By 1911, American archbishops wrote to their counterparts in Australia for assurances that the 'Australian church was not in "alliance" with socialists'.[75]

Labour radicalism and the Clan na Gael, together with the remnants of the Fenian Brotherhood, found working- and lower-middle-class support. However, there were still attempts to present a unified, and middle class-led, spectacle of Irish nationalist activity in Chicago. The Ogden Grove demonstration and picnic, which usually took place in August, became a political alternative to the ethnic and civic nationalism of the St Patrick's Day parade. As the years progressed, more Irish organisations became involved in the day, and speakers often came from Ireland to speak to a large crowd of picnickers. Despite fictional southside bartender Mr Dooley's misgivings that, 'Whin we wants to smash th' Sassenach an' restore th' land iv th' birth iv some iv us to her thrue place among th' nations, we gives a picnic', these picnics were vital in the promotion of certain messages of Irish nationalism, which were subsequently reported by newspapers in Chicago and the ethnic press of the wider United States.[76] Nationalist activities in Chicago made their way into the Melbourne imagination through the reprinting of anti-Irish cartoons and articles in the *Melbourne Punch*, helping to rouse fears of a global Irish uprising.[77] The *Advocate* and similar mass gatherings in Melbourne provided a counter to the anti-Irish sentiment that was spreading across the city in response to events elsewhere in the world. This claiming of a space, literal and print, for Irish nationalism abroad was an important step in promoting a sense of unification for Irish people in the diaspora.

By the late 1870s, labour radicalism blended with constitutional nationalism internationally to unite the moderate Irish communities of Melbourne and Chicago in the fight for Irish self-rule. The Land League garnered similar support and rhetoric in Melbourne and Chicago, undermining the argument that those who went to Australia were fundamentally different in experience and background to those who emigrated to the United States. These organisations were linked to each other through the *Freeman's Journal* in Dublin. However, the political structures of the British empire and the United States created differing tensions in Irish nationalism up to that point. The American War of Independence and subsequent Civil War had revealed the potential of violence as a means to achieve change in the United States and Ireland. In Melbourne, conversely, geographical distance from Ireland prioritised monetary donations and education of Irish history.

1880–1900

Studies of Irish nationalism in both Melbourne and Chicago, as well as in Ireland, have frequently focused on the 1880s. This was a decade of turmoil and almost success. The decade saw the rise in prominence of the Irish Parliamentary Party (previously the Home Rule League) and Charles Stewart Parnell, and the public support of Irish home rule from the British Prime Minister, William Ewart Gladstone. The growth of the Land League combined the labour activism and fight against economic inequality across the world with the desire for Irish political autonomy.[78] The First Home Rule Bill was introduced in 1886 and, though it was beaten in the House of Commons, signalled a change in British mentalities regarding Irish self-government. While constitutional nationalism witnessed an uplift, the decade saw an international swing toward the use of physical force to achieve change. The actions of each branch of Irish nationalism influenced each other, with the actions of physical-force separatists occasionally creating an atmosphere of fear and restrictions for constitutional nationalist speakers. The splits in Irish nationalism that emerged during the 1880s had ongoing influences on diasporic engagement with Irish politics for the next thirty years.

Chicago continued its rise in national prominence. Economically it thrived, while its Irish community increasingly controlled the direction of Irish-American nationalism. Parnell and John Dillon visited the city during their 1880 tour of the United States. They were greeted by children from the Catholic orphanage and a parade of Chicago's Catholic and Irish societies, with the Clan na Gael dominating proceedings.[79] A year later, the city hosted the Irish Race Convention, which sought to heal the fractures between physical-force republicans and moderate and conservative nationalists. The Chicago Clan na Gael's Alexander Sullivan became arguably the most important leader in Irish-American nationalism, or a close second to John Devoy, over the next decade, and under his leadership Chicago was the site of a public dispute between the Clan and Michael Davitt in 1886. It also saw a slide into criminal enterprise with the murder of Sullivan's Clan rival, Dr Patrick Henry Cronin, making its way into the British courts through the spy Henri Le Caron (aka Thomas Beach) in the Parnell Special Commission of 1889.[80] Ely Janis has declared the Midwest 'a hotbed of physical-force nationalism' during the 1880s and, in 1882, John F. Finerty established the *Chicago Citizen* newspaper as an alternative to the New York-based ethnic press.[81] It is tempting to document the wider changes within Irish-American nationalism through the lens of Chicago. However, this section will focus on the changes that took place within Chicago society itself, highlighting the range of Irish nationalist activities which emerged in the city.

The links between labour radicalism and Irish nationalism forged in the 1870s found a home in the American Land League (ALL) and Ladies' Land League (LLL), established in 1879 and 1881 respectively. The cause of land and social reform in Ireland and the United States found support from men and women within the city, with both leagues being led by journalists, lawyers and their relatives.[82] The women who led the LLL in Chicago, at least in the Tenth Ward, were predominantly children of the Famine, women who had left Ireland as young children. Journalist Alice Quinn was an exception to this and represented the importance of social reform internationally in encouraging involvement in the Land League.[83] As Tara McCarthy notes, the LLL provided an important avenue for Irish-American women to enter wider reforming circles, an influence that would continue across the next forty years.[84]

The 'No Rent Manifesto', issued by the arrested Irish leaders of the Land League, called for the boycott of English goods in Ireland and abroad, attacking Britain economically. Women in the LLL enthusiastically supported the No Rent Manifesto in the United States, using their position as controller of the family economy to show their nationalist allegiances.[85] The Eighth Ward Land League pledged 'not to buy, use, or wear any goods manufactured in or the product of [English] manufactures'.[86] The No Rent Manifesto created tensions within the Land League, reflecting wider splits in the Irish community in Chicago between the rising middle classes and the working class. It also divided those who prioritised countering economic inequality in Ireland and the United States from conservative nationalists who feared a slide into radicalism. While the Land League spread across Chicago, another element of nationalist activity emerged. After years of fundraising, Irish nationalists in America grew tired of waiting for the surge for Irish independence to come from Ireland. Launched by the Skirmishing Fund under Jeremiah O'Donovan Rossa, the Irish-American Dynamite Campaign began on 14 January 1881 with an explosion in Salford Barracks, Manchester.[87] A competition for dominance soon broke out between Rossa's New York-based Skirmishers and Sullivan's Chicago Clan na Gael. The Land League worked in tandem with the efforts of physical-force separatists to hamper British power in Ireland and capitalist inequality more widely: one through economic means, the other through terror.

Irish nationalism in Chicago gained the tacit approval of the city's Catholic clergy during the 1880s. Chicago's Archbishop Feehan was described as 'perhaps the most vehement defender of the Clan-na-Gael and other Irish groups' in the city.[88] Other Catholic priests supported the aims of the Land Leaguers, but fought against the growing power of the Clan, and specifically Alexander Sullivan.[89] Sullivan was believed to also have control of the AOH in the city through his friendship with national delegate Henry Sheridan.[90] Irish Protestants who may have joined in the fight for Irish nationalism were hindered by 'a very natural fear of the intolerance of the Roman Church'.[91] The link between Irish and Catholic in Chicago was thereby encouraged by the lack of strong clerical resistance to Irish nationalism, alienating prospective Protestant allies and encouraging further socialising between priest and congregant.

Fundraising for Irish relief continued in Melbourne, uniting issues of land reform with constitutional nationalism, while retaining an encouragement of cross-religious cooperation. At the same time as funds were being raised for the Irish poor in the Irish Relief Fund, the *Advocate* announced a subscription fund for the legal defence of Parnell and other Land Leaguers. The Parnell Land League Defence Fund was established in November 1880, headed by Joseph Winter and Thomas Fogarty, the popular Mayor of Hotham. It was expected that people of all nationalities who held 'liberal views on the land question' would donate.[92] Seizing upon the monetary support provided to Parnell's legal defence, Irish Land League organiser John Walshe visited Victoria in mid-1881 to promote the League. He was received enthusiastically in the particularly Irish areas of Hotham, Richmond and Collingwood, all areas with thriving Irish ethnic fraternities and subscriber lists for Irish causes during the 1870s. The *Age* and *Argus* united in their attempts to discredit the Land League, the former through fear-mongering about sectarianism and the latter through snobbery at its largely labouring-class membership. By mid-October 1881, there were thirty branches of the Land League in Victoria, mostly in rural and regional areas, along with fifteen branches of the Ladies' Land League, thirteen of which were outside of Melbourne.[93]

The rapid expansion of Land League branches in Victoria led to tension between nationalist organisers in rural and urban areas. On 18 October 1882, the Melbourne Central Committee adopted formal resolutions that they would be responsible for representing all Victorian Land League branches on the advice of Joseph Winter. Melbourne's nationalist leaders were officially charged with speaking for 'all adherents to the cause and sympathisers with it, of whatever religion or nationality they may be'.[94] It provided a link between promoters of Irish nationalism in different settlements around Melbourne and rural Victoria. These donations added to spiritual support being sent to Ireland through the Catholic school sodalities' prayers for the peace and prosperity of Ireland. Following the positive reaction to Walshe in Melbourne, John and William Redmond visited the colony in 1883, beginning a connection that was cemented by their marriages to two cousins from New South Wales.[95] Despite a hopeful start, their lecture tour was marked by dissent and displeasure.

The news of the Invincibles murders[96] and the Irish-American Dynamite Campaign led many of Melbourne's leading Irishmen to condemn all Irish nationalist orators.[97] It was recommended that John Redmond did not visit Ballarat, 'owing to the strong opinions of the local press, which goes as far as to say that loyal citizens should unite and drive him out of the town'.[98] Similar responses had greeted the efforts of Irish Victorians the previous year when five MLAs and two prominent barristers signed an address from 'the Irish People in Victoria and Their Descendants' to their brothers in Ireland to commemorate the centennial celebration of Grattan's declaration of Irish independence.[99] The Grattan Address caused a crisis in the Victorian Legislature.[100] A year later, the Redmonds' vision of a British empire of 'mutually interdependent nations underpinned by liberal political ideas' should have found a welcoming audience within conservative Melbourne.[101] However, the Redmonds' lectures were avoided by men of means, men who John Redmond denounced as 'cowardly Irishmen who hadn't the common manliness to stand by their side and adhere to the principles which they professed to hold'.[102] Charles Gavan Duffy's son John rebuked Redmond, saying that while he understood Irish Australians who supported the Irish National League, he also understood that many prioritised their lives in Melbourne, and their links (no doubt economic as well as social) to non-Irish neighbours.[103] Despite the mixed reception to the Redmonds' visit, their tour brought in a total of £14,657 10s. 3d. to the Irish National League in Dublin, their travelling expenses of over £2,500 being offset by the Australasian organisation.[104] Melbourne's Irish ethnic organisers provided a consistent message of Irish loyalty to the British empire, their enthusiasm only marginally tempered by criticism of Westminster policies in Ireland. However, there was a recognition that Melbourne's Irish communities needed more than letters asking for money from nationalist leaders in Ireland. In 1884, John Redmond wrote to Joseph Winter, 'I suppose the Austr-Irish feeling has very much moderated since I left.'[105] Aided by this knowledge and the increased ease of travel to Australia during the 1880s, there was an intensification in visits from Irish envoys to the city, as well as the relocation of Irish informers by the British Government.[106]

For Chicago's men, the differing social and economic opportunities offered by Irish nationalist organisations led to a crossover in membership. The decline of the Land League in the aftermath of the No Rent Manifesto led to a transition of membership in Chicago. While constitutional nationalists were reorganised into the Irish National League of America (INLA), supporting Parnell's fight for a Home Rule Bill, the Land League's more radical members split themselves between the Clan na Gael and the Knights of Labor. The LLL had an international proclivity toward radicalism, stronger than in the men's movement, and as a result of this competition was shut down by the Land League's male leadership.[107] Women were forced out of political nationalist organising for a time, often opting for greater influence in labour unions.[108] The opportunities provided by public events and membership of nationalist organisations facilitated networks which transcended class boundaries, bringing together state legislators with bricklayers.[109] The Lady Day Ogden Grove demonstrations continued in earnest throughout the decade, and in 1883 it was estimated that 10,000 'Celtic people' gathered, of whom many were 'outspoken in their hate of England and everything English'.[110] The potential for nepotism was an incentive to participation in Chicago Irish nationalism, particularly in a city where city politics and jobs were decided by ethnic competition. Therefore, despite the thousands of attendees, the Ogden Grove picnics were a mixture of supporters of the Land League, Clan na Gael and members of the Irish community with little interest in political nationalism.

By 1885, the dynamite campaign had resulted in the imprisonment or death of many Irish Americans of a 'soldier standard', with no visible results for the establishment of an independent Ireland. Concurrently, Gladstone regained office, Parnell continued to rise in popularity and the campaign for Irish home rule gained traction. The battle for control of the Chicago Clan and the funds raised for the next fight for Irish freedom resulted in a conflict between two factions, known as the Triangle (led by Alexander Sullivan, Michael Boland and Denis Feeley) and anti-Trianglers (led by John Devoy and Patrick Cronin). In 1886, there were two rival Lady Day demonstrations, with the Triangle supporters in Ogden Grove and their opponents in the West Side Driving Park. The militarised organisations of the Hibernian Guards and Clan na Gael attended the former, while the AOH, the Parnell Aid Association, the Palmer House Committee and a committee of ladies selected by the Sisters in charge of St Joseph's Catholic Orphan Asylum attended the latter.[111] The split between secular and religious organisations, as well as secret and public, was clear. The 50 cents that patrons paid to attend the Triangle event was pledged to the armed fight for Irish independence, whereas the alternative demonstration was to split the proceeds between the orphanage and the Parliamentary Fund. As the years progressed, the Triangle's reach left the confines of the Clan, extending throughout most of the city's Irish nationalist organisations under the umbrella of the United Irish Societies of Cook County.[112]

The Haymarket bombing of 4 May 1886 has been credited with dampening Chicago's appetite for dynamite and the associated tools of anarchist and socialist movements.[113] However, the Irish physical-force adherents who spoke at the Ogden Grove demonstration that year did not heed this change in mentality.[114] John F. Finerty, one of the organisers, pledged that the demonstration was to 'furnish aid to Ireland, so that she may avail herself of the privilege of self-defence'.[115] He was followed on stage by the equally vehement lawyer Matthew P. Brady, who declared that the Home Rule Bill was 'unauthorized, and a violation of his sacred trust'.[116] However, despite the strong words from the Irish-American speakers, the visiting speaker Michael Davitt refused to be drawn into the violent rhetoric that would have enthused his audience. In a moment of rebuke, he observed, 'It was easy to set up an ideal Irish Republic by patriotic speeches 3,000 miles away, they could not do it on the hills and plains of dear old Ireland.'[117] The subsequent support of Davitt's argument from Devoy, the anti-Trianglers and many of the Home Rulers based in Ireland signalled a disconnect between nationalist activity in Ireland and in Chicago. Finerty accused those who did not agree with him of cowardice.[118] The split between constitutional nationalists and radical separatists was, on the surface, complete. However, the links between labour radicalism and Irish nationalism were not as easy to break. Three weeks after the Davitt–Finerty debacle, an estimated 13,000 men and women of the labouring classes participated in a demonstration at Ogden Grove. Congressman and labour organiser Frank Lawler, the brother-in-law of Michael Scanlan, spoke at the demonstration alongside Judge Prendergast and Delia Parnell. Prendergast's speech allied the labour movement with support for Parnell, further complicating the narrative of Irish nationalism within Chicago.[119]

There was also a shift in the priorities of Melbourne's established organisations, demonstrating the growth of respectability of the home rule cause. The SPS established branches of the Irish Members' Fund in 1886, transferring some of its power into the local parish. The subscription list was to assist the eighty-six home rule members 'defray their expenses in going to England until they shall have obtained a Parliament of their own in College Green'.[120] Laurence Buckley, who established the Brunswick Irish Members' Fund branch, had been a member of the Brunswick CYMS and later acted as the honorary secretary of the Ladies' Association of Charity of St Vincent de Paul. He joined other leading members of Melbourne's Irish organisations, spread throughout the main institutions of Irish Catholic life, in campaigning for Irish political representation.[121] By 1887, Australia had sent 'a continuous stream of gold to Ireland to carry on the struggle' for the Irish national cause.[122] That year the Celtic Club was organised to support the home rule cause in Ireland. It was named the Celtic Club rather than the Irish Club because 'Ireland's aspirations for self government had the support of a great body of opinion which had no Irish ancestral affiliations'.[123] The organising committee brought together stalwarts of the SPS, politicians and supporters of Irish language and cultural nationalism, as detailed in Chapter 3.

As the 1880s closed, Chicago's Irish nationalist organisations imploded. Faced with the murder trial of Patrick Cronin, one of Sullivan's fiercest critics, the Clan na Gael's secrets were exposed to the world.[124] Irish physical-force nationalism in the city was forced into relative silence during the 1890s. By 1893, the Ogden Grove demonstration had taken on a new tone as the 'Shamrock, Rose, and Thistle' came together to support home rule, and denunciation of England was declared out of order.[125] However, although the links between Ireland-based nationalists and Chicago's Clan na Gael events weakened, Chicagoans continued to read publications like John F. Finerty's *Citizen*.[126] Internal divisions had pushed the city's Irish nationalists to the limit, and some struggled to find a place in a world where home rule was prized and militant nationalism ridiculed. Chicago had always demonstrated strong support for constitutional change and reform of social inequality. For those who demanded physical-force action, the decade that had started with a bombing campaign ended in infamy. The Irish National Alliance was formed in Chicago in 1895 and maintained a strong opposition to home rule largely through its mouthpiece the *Irish Republic*, though it only lasted until the end of the decade.[127] Irish organising in Chicago remained quiet for the rest of the century, with a brief uptick in nationalist rhetoric during the Boer War.[128]

During the 1880s, Melbourne's Irish middle-class leaders encouraged and consolidated the different branches of nationalist organisations so that the centre of power was in Melbourne, not in rural Victoria. Society columns in newspapers brought about a sense of unification, which was enhanced by an annual meeting of all the Irish nationalist organisations in the city convened by leading members of Irish Melbourne society.[129] By 1889, there was another 'successful' Irish envoy to Melbourne. John Dillon's mission, which stopped off in Melbourne, was more widely supported by the leaders of Irish society there.[130] It was now socially acceptable to be linked with Irish nationalism. Archbishop Carr of Melbourne noted that 'here at least hopes are higher that Gladstone's speedy return to office will end the long chapter of the Irish struggle' and hoped that the lecture tour would collect around £30,000.[131] Links between Ireland and Melbourne were protected and promoted at a social, nationalist and religious level. Melbourne's Irish society embraced elements of the Gaelic Revival and, led by Winter and Nicholas O'Donnell, brought the

Irish societies under one roof. They received a visit from Michael Davitt in 1895[132] and continued to support the United Irish League financially throughout the 1890s, while engaging with cultural nationalism through encouraging the learning of the Irish language. The 1880s was a decade of awakening for Irish nationalists in Melbourne, which would continue to evolve until Archbishop Daniel Mannix captured the attention of the world with his focusing of an Irish-Australian nationalist feeling in the aftermath of the First World War.

1900–1922

During the early months of 1900, rumours began circulating in Chicago that five thousand Clan na Gael men were preparing to sail to South Africa to defend the Transvaal.[133] While the AOH supported the mission, it was the United Irish Societies of Chicago who bought and equipped an 'ambulance unit' to enable a much smaller number of fifty-eight Irish Americans to go to Pretoria under the auspices of being paramedics with the American Red Cross. On arrival, the American Ambassador in Pretoria declared the 'Irish American ambulance almost all preparing to fight'.[134] While few from Chicago actually fought, Chicago became a strong fundraising source for Boer fighters, supported by the *Chicago Tribune*, which commended the Irish-American fighters as 'warriors' on their return to the city.[135] Instead of militant nationalism, Chicago's prominent Irish Americans turned their eyes to a rejuvenated constitutional nationalism. The Gaelic Revival found a home in the city, buoyed by tours of the Gaelic League in 1905–6, 1910–12 and 1914–15.[136] John F. Finerty, who had been so vehement in his support of the dynamite campaign, was elected as president of the United Irish League of America (UILA), which replaced the Irish National Federation of America in pushing for home rule in 1901. Alongside his renewed support for constitutional efforts, Finerty voiced his support for women's involvement in the movement.[137] A year after the UILA was established, an elite club for prominent Irish Chicagoans, many of whom had been involved in the now defunct St Patrick's Society, emerged in the Irish Fellowship Club.[138] Irish militant nationalism took a back seat, still there but operating behind the scenes of organisations focused on exerting political and diplomatic power through Chicago's patronage networks. The focus of militant nationalist organising may have moved to New York, and come under the control of John Devoy, but Chicago's Irish citizens were gaining in political influence, largely through its networks of voluntary organisations.[139]

In Melbourne, interest in the Gaelic Revival continued into the new century. By 1902, Nicholas O'Donnell asked for Irish-language promoter Thomas O'Donnell to be sent on a lecture tour to Australia as a 'large number of Melbourne natives attend the classes conducted under the auspices of the local Gaelic League and they are making good progress with their studies'.[140] O'Donnell was also heavily involved in the United Irish League, while working-class men were active in the Self-Determination for Ireland League.[141] In both Melbourne and Chicago, activists who rose in nationalist prominence during the 1880s reinvented themselves to continue to claim leadership roles in the 1900s, Nicholas O'Donnell and John F. Finerty in particular. In Melbourne, however, there was a 'new impetus for Irish affairs' coming from clerks and lawyers who had grown up in CYMS, the Australian Catholic Federation or the Labor Party.[142] This new generation of leaders, men like R. S. Warming and Frank Brennan who led the Young Ireland Society and the Self-Determination for Ireland League, were often the sons of manual workers who, through access to education, gained places in the rising middle class. They were able to bring together different elements of Melbourne's Irish community as well as contextualising Irish nationalism within wider labour activism.

A renewed Catholic confidence in Melbourne connected with Irish nationalism during the First World War under the guidance of Archbishop Mannix. The Easter Rising and the conscription crisis brought these ties even closer, while also highlighting splits between cultural nationalists and republicans.[143] The blessing of Archbishop Mannix gave Catholic associations the confidence to shrug off their non-political stances and embrace nationalist rhetoric. The anti-conscription crises of 1916 and 1917 brought these splits into closer focus.[144] In November 1917, the CYMS, HACBS and the Catholic Workers' Association drew 100,000 Melbournians together at the Richmond Racecourses to hear Mannix speak, while Catholic organisations increasingly flew Sinn Féin flags and slogans from 1918, as discussed in the next chapter. The outbreak of the War of Independence and the failure of home rule brought about further ruptures in Melbourne Irish nationalist organising, with the collapse of the constitutional nationalist organisations that had previously dominated the city and the rise of a proudly Irish Catholic republicanism.[145]

By 1921, the character of Irish nationalist organising in each city had fundamentally shifted. Where Chicago had been a hotbed of militant nationalism throughout the nineteenth century, by the second decade of the twentieth century the declining number of recently arrived Irish migrants and the increasingly powerful place of the Chicago Irish community had led to changed priorities. In Melbourne, conversely, the often conservative, non-religious and, practically always, constitutional flavour of Irish nationalism had become proudly Catholic and increasingly militant under the leadership of Mannix. Distance was no longer a reason for loss of Irish identity. Instead, 'Irishness had become a characteristic, not of the Irish-born, but of the Catholic worker and his sons and daughters'.[146] The Irish communities of Melbourne and Chicago had become increasingly similar in their nationalism by the start of the Irish Civil War. The trauma of the Easter Rising mixed with tight-knit parish communities with distinct labour contexts to reshape Irish nationalist organising. The outbreak of the Irish Civil War, however, brought confusion to both cities and most nationalist organisations simpered away.

CONCLUSION

Irish nationalist organisation and thought in Melbourne and Chicago evolved over the latter half of the nineteenth century. In both cities the middle classes sought to dominate the direction of nationalist activity. Their success depended on who they had to appeal to for support, and how they framed the fight for Irish political freedom. In Melbourne, the principal organisers were journalists, politicians and the Irish-born mayors of the city and suburbs who accessed their secular transnational networks of influence by communication with their Irish counterparts. Many of these men had grown up attending CYMS and SPS events. They articulated the foundational and loyal identities of these organisations. In Chicago, conversely, nationalist organisations dominated Irish secular life from the late 1850s. Members of the middle class, like James Mulligan, may have been the organisers in the mid-century, but the chaos of the American Civil War and Chicago Fire dispersed control of ethnic life across the classes.

As the decades progressed, the messages of nationalist leaders in Melbourne and Chicago diverged. In Melbourne, Irish nationalism was consistently framed as an Irish problem which those abroad could support through setting an example of Irish respectability and order. In Chicago, the industrialised nature of the city allowed for Irish land reform and disenfranchisement priorities to be blended with American labour disputes. This was partially enabled by the differences in geography. In Victoria, radical politics and action was found principally in the goldfields of rural Victoria. This was true in 1854 and can be seen in the location of most Land League branches during the 1880s. While Melbourne's middle classes sought to bring everyone under the control of the urban conservatives, distance enabled a separation in motivations. In industrialised Chicago, however, there was a mix of radical and conservative Irish nationalist thought within one city. Radicalism was not, as in Melbourne and Victoria, spread into wider Illinois. In order to exert power and control in Chicago, middle-class organisers were required to respond to and represent a range of views, splitting the Irish middle class between physical force and constitutional activities.

While there were many differences, there were similarities in how the Irish communities of Melbourne and Chicago responded to Irish nationalism. The influence of the Catholic Church in each city was important to the progress of Irish nationalism, and the form that it took. As Chapter 3 explored, Chicago's hierarchy sought to curb the spread of the Fenian Brotherhood through threats of excommunication in the first decades of the mid-century. Later, the rise of the Clan na Gael and the Land League was facilitated by a sympathetic archbishop and parish priests. By the 1920s it was not the Catholic Church which hindered Irish nationalist organising in Chicago, it was ego and splits in the organisations themselves. In Melbourne, Goold worked within colonial law and order structures to condemn Irish threats to the British empire. However, his successor Carr was influenced by the participation of respected citizens in nationalist endeavours. The role of Archbishop Mannix catapulted the shape of Irish nationalism through a mixture of Catholic advocacy, labour activism and horror at the Easter Rising. The Catholic Church's parish structures, and dependence on female fundraising, benefited Irish nationalism in Melbourne and Chicago by utilising the skills of women in organising fairs, dances and collecting committees. Diasporic Irish communities built upon the foundational identities created by the Catholic Church, education and parish life to evolve a spectrum of Irish nationalist activity acceptable to both Irish society and the ideological and global power positions within which they were placed.

NOTES

1. Timothy G. Lynch, '"A kindred and congenial element": Irish-American nationalism's embrace of republican rhetoric', *New Hibernia Review*, 13:2 (2009), pp. 77–91.
2. Belchem, *Irish, Catholic and Scouse*; Belchem, 'Liverpool-Irish'.
3. Diner, *Erin's Daughters*; Thomas N. Brown, *Irish-American Nationalism 1870–1890* (Philadelphia, PA: J. B. Lippincott Company, 1966), p. 23.
4. The limited work on Irishwomen's nationalism in the diaspora continues to focus on the American context: McCarthy, *Respectability & Reform*; Janis, *A Greater Ireland*.

5. Jane G. V. McGaughey, *Violent Loyalties: Manliness, Migration, and the Irish in the Canadas, 1798–1841* (Liverpool: Liverpool University Press, 2020).
6. Miller, *Emigrants and Exiles*, pp. 404–9.
7. Matthew Frye Jacobson, *Special Sorrows: The Diasporic Imagination of Irish, Polish, and Jewish Immigrants in the United States* (Berkeley: University of California Press, 2002), p. 21.
8. Campbell, *Ireland's New Worlds*, pp. 104–5.
9. Ibid., p. 94.
10. John Belchem, 'Nationalism, republicanism and exile: Irish emigrants and the revolutions of 1848', *Past & Present*, 146 (1995), pp. 103–35; James S. Donnelly Jr., *The Great Irish Potato Famine* (Stroud: Sutton Publishing, 2007), pp. 209–45; James S. Donnelly Jr., 'The administration of relief, 1847–51', in W. E. Vaughan (ed.), *A New History of Ireland. V: Ireland Under the Union, I 1801–70* (Oxford: Oxford University Press, 1989), pp. 316–31, 329–30.
11. John Savage, *Fenian Heroes and Martyrs* (Boston, MA: Patrick Donahoe, 1868), pp. 51–2.
12. James Quinn, *Young Ireland and the Writing of Irish History* (Dublin: University College Dublin Press, 2015), p. 2.
13. O'Farrell, *Irish in Australia*, p. 214.
14. Quinn, *Young Ireland*, pp. 15–17, 92–3; R. V. Comerford, 'Churchmen, tenants, and independent opposition, 1850–56', in W. E. Vaughan (ed.), *A New History of Ireland. V: Ireland Under the Union, I 1801–70* (Oxford: Oxford University Press, 1989), pp. 396–414.
15. Chicago Directory, 1844; David Sim, *A Union Forever: The Irish Question and Foreign Relations in the Victorian Age* (Ithaca, NY: Cornell University Press, 2013), pp. 14–16.
16. Brundage, *Irish Nationalists*, pp. 30–1. This cooperation was seen across the Irish diaspora: Kyle Hughes and Donald M. MacRaild, 'Irish politics and labour: Transnational and comparative perspectives, 1798–1914', in Niall Whelehan (ed.), *Transnational Perspectives on Modern Irish History* (London: Routledge, 2014), pp. 45–68.
17. Raffaello Carboni, *The Eureka Stockade: The Consequence of Some Pirates Wanting on Quarter-Deck a Rebellion* (Melbourne: J. P. Atkinson, 1860).
18. Geoffrey Serle, *The Golden Age: A History of the Colony of Victoria 1851–1861* (Cambridge: Cambridge University Press, 1968), p. 165.
19. Ibid., pp. 155–69.
20. C. H. Currey, *The Irish at Eureka* (Sydney: Angus & Robertson, 1954); Hogan, *Irish in Australia*, pp. 65–78.
21. Jill Blee, *Eureka: The Story of Australia's Most Famous Rebellion* (Woolombi: Exisle Publishing, 2007), p. 73.
22. James Fintan Lalor, 'A new nation: Proposal for an agricultural association between the landowners and occupiers', in John O'Leary and

James Fintan Lalor, *The Writings of James Fintan Lalor* (Dublin: T. G. O'Donoghue, 1895), p. 19.
23. Suttor, *Hierarchy and Democracy*, p. 225.
24. Peter Lalor, in an open letter to the *Argus*, asked if the harsh repression of civil force at Eureka was to 'prove to us that a British Government can never bring forth a measure of reform without having first prepared a font of human blood in which to baptise that offspring of their generous love?' Lalor later became a member of the Victorian Parliament. *Argus*, 10 April 1855; Paul A. Pickering, '"Ripe for a republic": British radical responses to the Eureka Stockade', *Australian Historical Studies*, 34:121 (2003), pp. 69–90.
25. O'Farrell, *Irish in Australia*, p. 200.
26. Keith Amos, *The Fenians in Australia, 1865–1880* (Kensington: NSW University Press, 1988), p. 286; MacDonagh, 'A general view'.
27. *Argus*, 5 September 1862.
28. *Irish American Weekly*, 29 December 1855; James Stephens, *James Stephens, Chief Organizer of the Irish Republic. Embracing An Account of the Origin and Progress of the Fenian Brotherhood* (New York: Carleton Publisher, 1866); McGarry and McConnel (eds), *Black Hand*.
29. Thomas J. Brophy, 'Rivalry between Irish associations in San Francisco over the second funeral of Terence Bellew McManus, 1861', in Jennifer Kelly and R. V. Comerford (eds), *Associational Culture in Ireland and Abroad* (Dublin: Irish Academic Press, 2010), pp. 67–84; R. V. Comerford, 'Conspiring brotherhoods and contending elites, 1857–63', in Vaughan (ed.), *A New History of Ireland. V*, pp. 415–30.
30. Jenkins, *Between Raid and Rebellion*, p. 193; *Proceedings of the First National Convention of the Fenian Brotherhood, Held in Chicago, Illinois, November 1863* (Philadelphia, PA: James Gibbons, 1863), p. 32.
31. The *Irish People* was an Irish newspaper funded by the Fenian Brotherhood in the United States and operated from Dublin. Established by James Stephens in 1863, the newspaper was managed by Jeremiah O'Donovan Rossa and Thomas Clarke Luby and was suppressed by the British Government in 1865. Catherine Shannon, 'Thomas Clarke Luby', *DIB*; Matthew Kelly, 'The *Irish People* and the disciplining of dissent', in McConnel and McGarry (eds), *Black Hand*, pp. 34–52.
32. Brian Griffin, '"Scallions, pikes and bog oak ornaments": The Irish Republican Brotherhood and the Chicago Fenian Fair, 1864', *Studia Hibernia*, 29 (1995–7), pp. 85–97.
33. Griffin, 'Scallions, pikes'; Kevin J. Quigley, 'American financing of Fenianism in Ireland 1858–67' (MA: Maynooth, 1983), p. 138.
34. Hynes to Goold, 24 August 1864 (Goold Correspondence, folder 2, MDHC).
35. Clarence McCarthy to Brownson, 16 April 1863 (CBRO, I-4-b A.L.S. 1p 8vo. 2, Notre Dame Archives (NDA)), original emphasis.

36. *Chicago Tribune*, 9 February 1864, 26 February 1864; Church of the Immaculate Conception, unsigned, to Col. Mulligan, 27 February 1864 (Mulligan Papers, Box 3, Folder 2, CHMRL).
37. *Irish People*, 23 April 1864.
38. Burial indenture between James Duggan, Bishop of Chicago, and Patrick Leigh and Patrick Nolan, 25 August 1863 (Madaj Collection, Box 2, 1-1863-C-1-1, ACA).
39. *Chicago Evening Journal*, 5 December 1865.
40. F. K. Barrett to James Mulligan, 9 February 1864 (Mulligan Papers, Box 3, CHMRL).
41. Brian Jenkins, *The Fenian Problem: Insurgency and Terrorism in a Liberal State 1858–1874* (Liverpool: Liverpool University Press, 2008), p. 327.
42. Brundage, *Irish Nationalists*, p. 89.
43. John B. Jentz and Richard Schneirov, 'Chicago's Fenian Fair: A window into the Civil War as a popular awakening', *Labor's Heritage*, 6:3 (1995), pp. 4–19.
44. Brown, *Irish-American Nationalism*, p. 43.
45. Chicago Directory, 1866.
46. Female correspondents in the *Irish Republic* also credited misogyny as a reason for Fenianism's failure, arguing that the Fenian leadership were slow to summon 'to their aid a power which is all but omnipotent on the earth – the power of women?', thereby weakening the movement. *Irish Republic*, 20 July 1867.
47. *Freeman's Journal* (Sydney), 7 July 1866.
48. *Age*, 12 July 1866; *Argus*, 14 July 1866.
49. *Argus*, 14 July 1866.
50. *Freeman's Journal* (Sydney), 14 July 1866.
51. *Argus*, 14 July 1866.
52. Amos, *Fenians in Australia*, p. 29.
53. Gordon Pentland, 'The indignant nation: Australian responses to the attempted assassination of the Duke of Edinburgh in 1868', *English Historical Review*, (2015), pp. 57–88.
54. Niall Whelehan, *The Dynamiters: Irish Nationalism and Political Violence in the Wider World, 1867–1900* (Cambridge: Cambridge University Press, 2012), pp. 56–7.
55. *Illustrated Australian News*, 23 March 1868.
56. *Age*, 17 March 1868.
57. *Illustrated Australian News*, 23 March 1868.
58. Carnarvon Papers, MS 60807/51/f83, British Library; Amos, *Fenians in Australia*, pp. 176–89.
59. Similar county allegiances can be seen in the American Skirmishing Fund. Whelehan, *Dynamiters*, pp. 201–5.
60. Belchem, *Irish, Catholic and Scouse*, pp. 167–9.

61. *Advocate*, 19 and 26 June 1869; 10, 17, 24 and 31 July 1869.
62. Eric Foner, *Politics and Ideology in the Age of the Civil War* (Oxford: Oxford University Press, 1980), pp. 150–200.
63. Abp Duggan to Abp Cullen, 2 February 1868 (Cullen Papers 334/8/iv/4, Dublin Diocesan Archives (DDA)).
64. Funchion, *Chicago's Irish Nationalists*, pp. 28–9.
65. O'Brien, *Blood Runs Green*, p. 24.
66. Brown, *Irish-American Nationalism*, p. 74.
67. Foner, *Politics and Ideology*, p. 151; Jacobson, *Special Sorrows*, pp. 27–8; McCarthy, *Respectability and Reform*, p. 35.
68. Chicago Directory, 1875.
69. Carla King, *Michael Davitt: After the Land League, 1881–1906* (Dublin: University College Dublin Press, 2016), p. 9; Brundage, *Irish Nationalists*, pp. 111–12; Donnelly, *Great Irish Potato Famine*, p. 229.
70. Michael Palmer, 'The British press and international news, 1851–99: Of agencies and newspapers', in George Boyce, James Curran and Pauline Wingate (eds), *Newspaper History from the Seventeenth Century to the Present Day* (London: Constable, 1978), pp. 205–22; Naughtin, 'The Melbourne Advocate'.
71. *Advocate*, 31 January 1880.
72. Naughtin, 'The green flag', p. 52.
73. Whelehan, *Dynamiters*, pp. 70–137.
74. Pescod, 'Irish participation'.
75. Elizabeth Malcolm and Dianne Hall, 'Catholic Irish Australia and the labor movement: Race in Australia and nationalism in Ireland, 1880s–1920s', in Greg Patmore and Shelton Stromquist (eds), *Frontiers of Labor: Comparative Histories of the United States and Australia* (Urbana: University of Illinois Press, 2018), pp. 149–67.
76. Finley Peter Dunne, *Mr. Dooley in the Hearts of His Countrymen* (Boston: Small, Maynard & Company, 1899), p. 61.
77. Malcolm and Hall, *A New History*, p. 187.
78. Deirdre M. Moloney, 'Land League activism in transnational perspective', *US Catholic Historian*, 22:3 (2004), pp. 61–74.
79. *Daily Inter Ocean*, 24 February 1880; *Cincinnati Daily Gazette*, 28 February 1880.
80. O'Brien, *Blood Runs Green*.
81. Janis, *Greater Ireland*, p. 169.
82. In December 1880 there were three branches of the American Land League [ALL] in Chicago, and by April 1881 there were branches in six city wards with a membership of around 1,260. *Daily Inter Ocean*, 9 December 1880, 28 April 1881.
83. Alice May Quinn got into a series of spats with male members of the Land League, particularly Richard Prendergast. *Chicago Tribune*, 24 April 1882; *Daily Inter Ocean*, 24 June 1882; US Federal Census 1880 data

for Alice M. Quinn; Janis, *Greater Ireland*, pp. 145–6; *Chicago Tribune*, 29 December 1903.
84. By March 1882 there were eleven branches of the LLL in Cook County, focused around South Chicago and the Stockyards, working-class and predominantly Irish areas. *Daily Inter Ocean*, 31 March 1882; McCarthy, *Respectability and Reform*, p. 93.
85. Ely M. Janis, 'Petticoat revolutionaries: Gender, ethnic nationalism, and the Irish Ladies' Land League in the United States', *Journal of American Ethnic History*, 27:2 (2008), pp. 5–27.
86. *Daily Inter Ocean*, 9 February 1881.
87. Whelehan, *Dynamiters*; Shane Kenna, *War in the Shadows: The Irish-American Fenians who Bombed Victorian Britain* (Dublin: Merrion Press, 2013); Sophie Cooper, '"A policy of terrorism is not one to which Englishmen will succumb": British policing and the Irish-American Dynamite Campaign, (MPhil: Trinity College Dublin, 2011).
88. McMahon, *What Parish*, Chapter 1; Funchion, *Chicago's Irish Nationalists*, p. 38.
89. Janis, *Greater Ireland*, p. 169.
90. Funchion, *Irish American Voluntary Organisations*, p. 55.
91. *Chicago Tribune*, 14 August 1881.
92. *Advocate*, 31 January 1880; *Age*, 4 August 1880; *Argus*, 14 August 1880; *Advocate*, 27 November 1880.
93. Naughtin, 'Green flag', pp. 68–78.
94. Ibid., p. 74.
95. Charles Parnell to John Redmond, 1 December 1882 (Redmond Papers, MS 15220, NLI).
96. On 6 May 1882, a group of Irishmen acting under the name of the Invincibles attacked Lord Frederick Cavendish and Thomas Henry Burke, the newly appointed Chief Secretary for Ireland and the Permanent Undersecretary, in Phoenix Park, Dublin. Patrick J. P. Tynan, *The Irish National Invincibles and Their Times* (London: Chatham & Co., 1894); Whelehan, *Dynamiters*, p. 117.
97. Malcolm Campbell, 'John Redmond and the Irish National League in Australia and New Zealand, 1883', *History*, 86:283 (2001), pp. 348–62.
98. Daniel Brophy to Joseph Winter, 3 March 1883 (Winter Papers MS 8622, Box 1798/1, State Library of Victoria (SLV)).
99. *Advocate*, 27 May 1882.
100. Sophie Cooper, 'Melbourne visions of an Irish future in the 1880s', in Richard Butler (ed.), *Dreams of an Irish Future in the Nineteenth Century* (Liverpool: Liverpool University Press, 2021), pp. 133–52.
101. Kelly, 'Irish nationalist opinion'.
102. Quoted in Campbell, 'John Redmond'.
103. October 1882 signalled the end of the Land League and its replacement with the broader Irish National League which had ambitions outside,

but including, land reform. T. W. Moody, *Davitt and Irish Revolution, 1846–82* (Oxford: Clarendon Press, 1984), pp. 542–5.
104. J. Harrington to J. Winter, 7 February 1884, and Receipt signed by J. W. Redmond, William K. Redmond, John W. Walshe, 13 December 1883 (Winter Papers, 1798/1, SLV).
105. J. E. Redmond to J. Winter, 2 June 1884 (Winter Papers, Box 1798/1, SLV).
106. *Gippsland Times*, 24 August 1883; *Age*, 23 August 1883; *Advocate*, 23 May 1885.
107. Meredith Tax, *The Rising of the Women: Feminist Solidarity and Class Conflict, 1880–1917* (New York: Monthly Review Press, 1980), pp. 38–51; Janis, 'Petticoat revolutionaries'; Meagher, *Inventing Irish America*, pp. 185–93.
108. McCarthy, *Respectability and Reform*.
109. For example, Judge Richard Prendergast, one of the most powerful Irishmen in Chicago and a member of Clan na Gael, was introduced to bricklayer and IRB organiser Andy Foy's wife at an Ogden Grove picnic in 1882. Elizabeth Foy's typed recollections (John Devoy Papers, MS 18,058(3), NLI).
110. *Chicago Tribune*, 19 August 1883.
111. *Irish American Weekly*, 21 and 28 August 1886. This split between the AOH and Hibernian Rifles is interesting considering they were part of the same parent organisation, the Chicago divisions of both organisations appearing next to each other in the *Directory of the Ancient Order of Hibernians, 1884–85*.
112. *History of the Ancient Order of Hibernians, From the Earliest Period to the Joint National Convention at Trenton, New Jersey, June 27 1898* (Cleveland, OH: T. F. McGrath, 1898), pp. 73–4. Pat Grant found that the Board of Erin Ancient Order was the 'true order': *Daily Inter Ocean*, 16 September 1890.
113. Cowan, 'Immigrants, nativists', pp. 203–4.
114. *Irish American Weekly*, 28 August 1886.
115. *Citizen*, 14 August 1886, quoted in *The Queen's Enemies in America Assembled in Convention at Chicago* (London: William Ridgway, 1886), p. 20. Revolutionary nationalists promoted the idea of the Irish as helpless slaves during the Famine as a criticism of constitutional nationalists. Donnelly, *Great Irish Potato Famine*, p. 240.
116. *The Queen's Enemies*, pp. 22–3.
117. *Irish American Weekly*, 28 August 1886.
118. Ibid.; *Kansas City Times*, 16 August 1886; *Irish Nation*, 26 August 1886.
119. *Chicago Tribune*, 7 September 1886.
120. *Advocate*, 6 February 1886,
121. *Advocate*, 30 June 1883, 18 February 1888; *Age*, 1 March 1890.
122. *Advocate*, 8 January 1887.

123. Buggy, *Celtic Club*.
124. O'Brien, *Blood Runs Green*.
125. *Daily Inter Ocean*, 16 August 1893.
126. In 1889, the paper's Saturday edition had a circulation of around 14,500 per week nationwide. By 1894, this circulation had increased to 16,350. N. W. Ayer & Son, *American Newspaper Annual* (Philadelphia, PA: N. W. Ayer & Son, 1889), p. 88; N. W. Ayer & Son, American Newspaper Annual (Philadelphia, PA: N. W. Ayer & Son, 1894), p. 125.
127. Brundage, *Irish Nationalists*, p. 132.
128. Funchion, *Chicago's Irish Nationalists*, p. 33.
129. *Advocate*, 8 November 1890.
130. *Advocate*, 13 April 1889.
131. Carr to Abp Walsh (Dublin), 20 September 1889 (uncatalogued, DDA).
132. King, *Michael Davitt*, pp. 382–404.
133. Donald P. McCracken, *MacBride's Brigade: Irish Commandos in the Anglo-Boer War* (Dublin: Four Courts Press, 1999), p. 102.
134. Charles Callan Tansill, *America and the Fight for Irish Freedom, 1866–1922* (New York: Devin-Adair Press, 1957), p. 115.
135. *Chicago Daily Tribune*, 17 November 1900.
136. Úna Ní Bhroiméil, *Building Irish Identity in America, 1870–1915: The Gaelic Revival* (Dublin: Four Courts Press, 2003), p. 10. For more on the role of Irish language in America, see Bobbie Nolan, 'Language and identity amongst Irish migrants in London, Philadelphia and San Francisco, 1850–1920' (PhD: University of Edinburgh, 2019).
137. Brundage, *Irish Nationalists*, p. 137.
138. Funchion, *Irish American Voluntary Organisations*, pp. 173–5.
139. Elizabeth McKillen, *Chicago Labor and the Quest for a Democratic Diplomacy, 1914–1924* (Ithaca, NY: Cornell Press, 1995), p. 23.
140. O'Donnell to O'Brien, 2 June 1902 (Redmond Papers, MS15,235/1, NLI).
141. McConville, *Croppies, Celts*, p. 111.
142. Ibid., p. 116.
143. Ibid., p. 109.
144. Niamh Gallagher explores the impact of the wider Irish-Australian Catholic Church on anti-conscription feeling throughout the Australian colonies in *Ireland and the Great War: A Social and Political History* (London: Bloomsbury, 2020).
145. McConville, *Croppies, Celts*, pp. 111–13.
146. Ibid., p. 117.

7

St Patrick's Day and the Public Performance of Identity

The celebration of St Patrick's Day on 17 March was a particularly diasporic phenomenon in the nineteenth century. While in Ireland the emphasis was on religious devotion, the diaspora used the day in a multitude of ways. For some, the Catholic Church loomed large, though occasionally the Protestant churches claimed the day for their Irish parishioners. Others took the opportunity to claim space in the city, declaring their right to be there and the power that they wielded with those who supplied parade permits. At times it was a moment to declare solidarity with political movements, and at others to celebrate the Irish community's networks of ethnic organisations and pride in cultural nationalism. Mostly, they were a mix of all of these elements. This chapter uses St Patrick's Day celebrations to understand how diasporic communities prioritised the image of Ireland and the United States or Australia and their distinct identities through different generations and domestic circumstances. Building upon the themes of previous chapters, it explores the rhetoric used by leading Irish organisers in Melbourne and Chicago on that most public Irish holiday. The language of belonging and loyalty used at St Patrick's Day dinners and demonstrations brought together diverse communities, encompassing distinct educational, religious and political identities. These celebrations were opportunities to present certain images of diasporic Irishness within and outwith the Irish community. It explores the role that St Patrick's Day played in shaping Irish identity as a national identity and, conversely, the extent to which the day reflected the concerns of those already involved in Irish community life.[1]

The importance of St Patrick's Day to the perception of Irishness in different contexts should not be overestimated, but it should be considered as one of the ways that groups of people portrayed themselves to a large audience. Mike Cronin and Daryl Adair present St Patrick's Day as an 'arbiter ... of the "progress" and "destiny" of the Irish' and therefore as an annual opportunity for advocacy on different issues.[2] However, they warn that the position of St Patrick's Day as an 'Irish' day can distort the impression of the Irish communities in a particular context, creating a false sense of homogeneity and ignoring the 'silent majority'.[3] While St Patrick's Day celebrations did not claim to represent each Irish person in the diaspora, they did provide Irish people around the world with the opportunity to select the elements of Irishness that would form the Irish 'story' of that community. St Patrick's Day was used by Irish people in the United States and Australia to frame their lives within a proud cultural Irish heritage. This chapter examines the ways that Irish organisations and leaders used memory to legitimate 'a particular image of its present and its future, and a particular structure of power and social relations'.[4] The deployment of art, oratory and ritual, combined with institutional history and presence – the St Patrick's Hall and Irish clubs among others – provided diasporic communities with an Irish tradition steeped in the history of Melbourne and Chicago. This chapter is organised into four sections which track changes in the public and private celebration of St Patrick. They broadly echo the time periods of the previous chapter due to the influence of Irish nationalist organisations on the shape of St Patrick's Day events. The impact of the First World War and subsequent Irish Revolution on parading and public expenditure is reflected in the final section which focuses on 1914 to 1922.

Just as the study of Irish nationalism has been dominated by men, St Patrick's Day processions in Melbourne and Chicago during the nineteenth century present an image of predominantly middle-class male involvement. Through the careful application of invitation and admission charges, an organiser-led distinction of who was deemed to be respectable or worthy of participating in and claiming particular Irish identities emerged. While St Patrick's Day was often a stage for middle-class men, there were other groups involved in the wider events: in the religious ceremonies, in the streets and at the fairs. These people influenced and were influenced by the middle-class culture brokers who were central to defining Irishness abroad.[5] Parades were male-only affairs for the first decades of each city. However, the crowds that lined the streets and those who attended picnics were a mix of gender, age and background, allowing for a family-friendly celebration of Irish identity and power. Outdoor events permitted the inclusion of men, women and children from a range of classes to come together and celebrate Ireland's patron saint. In this way, they brought together the themes of this book, primarily ethnic affinity, education, religion and associational culture.

1840–1860

Chicago and Melbourne's societies had similar priorities in the 1840s and 1850s. They were cities of immigrants, rapidly increasing in wealth but without the requisite institutions to support them. As previous chapters have noted, the secular and religious parishes were expanding, creating organisations to occupy, improve and entertain their expanding populations. St Patrick's Day provided an opportunity for the Irish in both cities to come together to celebrate Ireland and its heroes, as well as to reach out to their non-Irish neighbours. These events were often informal gatherings. However, as the 1840s and 1850s progressed, particular societies took charge of formal events, allowing for the promotion of a select group's priorities as the voice of the Irish community. The St Patrick's Day commemorations of early years were important elements in the creation of a sense of stability and culture within the professional classes, if not further afield. In both cities, the themes that emerge consistently are loyalty to their new homes, the mass migration of people from Ireland and their sense of belonging or exile, and the need for charity within Irish communities.

St Patrick's Day in Melbourne was dominated by the St Patrick's Society (SPS) from its establishment in 1842 until the end of the nineteenth century. The men of this organisation, Irish-born and -descended politicians, doctors and businessmen, used the opportunity provided by the attendance of journalists at their dinners to prove their loyalty to their new colonial home and their social peers. Between 1842 and 1845, the leadership of Fr. Geoghegan resulted in a strong correlation between the Catholic Church and Irish nationality, with religious services featuring heavily in the St Patrick's Day celebrations of 1843 and 1844.[6] This resulted in heightened tensions between the Catholic and Orange elements of Melbourne society. The Party Processions Act of 1846, initiated in response to these tensions, banned the public celebration of sentiments that 'may create religious and political animosities between different classes of her Majesty's subjects'.[7] Bowing to this new requirement, the SPS re-emphasised its dedication to being 'open to all and influenced by none' and moved its celebrations inside.

The final parade of the 1840s took place in 1846, when four hundred people marched, a high level of participation in a city of 4,500.[8] The move from public celebrations to private signalled a change in audience, from a parade which anyone could participate in to a select party of the middle class. To gain access to the now indoor SPS ball, revellers had to pay 6s., with wine presenting an extra expense.[9] The numbers of participants in these events ranged from 120 to 250 during the 1850s, an increasingly small number relative to an Irish-born population of between 4,500 and 17,500 over the decade.[10] This was one of the events of the season and a chance to access the membership of 'one of the most influential society's [sic] in this province'.[11] The SPS events held in Melbourne between 1845 and 1860 emphasised the separation of religion and ethnicity of its members. Within Melbourne, to be Catholic was to be Irish, but to be Irish was not necessarily to be Catholic. This was reflected in the city's St Patrick's Day celebrations.

Though the SPS organised the formal celebrations in Melbourne, there were a number of unofficial events for those who could not afford or did not have the contacts to attend. In 1852, Melbourne's streets were filled with domestic servants and diggers from the goldfields, racing around in 'almost every description of vehicle' with long green ribbons streaming from their hats.[12] Swept up in the excitement of the gold rushes, the SPS was keen to note its continued remembrance of Ireland. An address of thanks to John O'Shanassy mourned the suffering of Ireland at the 'capriciousness of a dark and cruel Destiny' before praising the luck of Irish men and women in the 'bright and golden land of Victoria'.[13] By blaming destiny, not the actions of the British Government, the SPS made sure that its sorrow was not viewed in conflict with its loyalty to the colonial governance of the Australian colonies. The 1851 granting of 'responsible government' in Victoria created an image of the colony as a testing ground for possible improvements to the governance of Ireland. Charles Gavan Duffy described Australia, and more specifically Melbourne, as an experiment in enlightenment.[14] The new freedoms enjoyed by Irish Catholics in Melbourne led to the promotion of an identity which reflected Daniel O'Connell's[15] more than that of militant nationalists: that of the loyal British subject who was also proud of his Irish Catholic heritage.

Loyalty to the British empire and Crown at the same time as loyalty to the memory of Ireland was a key theme throughout Melbourne's St Patrick's Day celebrations. The 1850 ball demonstrated this, with organisers hanging a banner of St Patrick next to one of St George and the Dragon, lent for the occasion by the St George's Society. The scene was described as 'the Rose and Shamrock side by side (as they should forever be)'.[16] Edmund Finn noted in 1851, 'it appeared to him that nothing could be more appropriate or truly patriotic than a holy alliance of the fine dear old country they still so ardently loved and the newborn blooming land in which they then lived'.[17] The organisers proudly declared the compatibility of Irish and British-Australian priorities, maintaining the people of Ireland's place in the continued progression and prosperity of Victoria. While St Patrick's Day was celebrated as the national day of Ireland, a moment for declaring an identity distinct from a wider British identity, a conscious effort was made to gain respectability and acceptance from the wider Melbourne society.

The SPS provided links with other class- and ethnicity-based organisations, and through newspaper publicity it was able to forge links with organisations elsewhere in Victoria and the Australian colonies. These men were contributing to an image of separate but linked nations, a family of nations, encouraged by the attendance of representatives from the city's other ethnic clubs. Those involved in organising St Patrick's Day events joined the leaders of the St Andrew's and St George's societies in contributing to a public image of Irish identity based in middle-class priorities.[18] At this stage, however, these celebrations were led and enjoyed by only a small number of people within Melbourne society, with speeches aimed at peers in politics and business. As such, there were themes of loyalty and imperialism that may not have been echoed in other social clubs. However, these speeches were reported in newspapers across Victoria, influencing the views of people from all social classes and backgrounds. The SPS was making a case for Irish involvement in Melbourne society and colonial life more generally.

Unlike Melbourne, the early years of Chicago were not shaped by legislation banning processions. Parades took centre stage, demonstrating the place of Irish people within the city. However, weather conditions frequently hampered the public promotion of Irish identity. Not for Chicago the sunshine of Melbourne. Instead, Chicagoans were treated to snowstorms and floods leading to cancellations, postponements, and complaints about weather-appropriate clothing for participants and observers alike. In 1849, St Patrick's Day events were cancelled due to a devastating flood which caused the loss of around £250,000 worth of property (in 1849 money) as well as the sweeping away of bridges and the loss of at least two children's lives.[19] Similarly, St Patrick's Day in 1858 was described as having 'Premium weather for suicide and the "blues"'.[20] The 1850 parade, however, was 'large and well conducted'. Led by the Montgomery Guards in uniforms and juvenile musicians with flutes, the procession of the St Joseph's Temperance Society had 'quite a gala day appearance' due to the badges and banners.[21] These difficult conditions served as a test of ethnic loyalty, and large turnouts in spite of bad weather were noted with pride in newspaper reports.

While the main focus of the day was the public parade, Irish societies also held their own evening balls and banquets. These events were attended by the city's establishment and were used to promote themes of loyalty to state and country, as well as loyalty to Ireland and Irish heroes. Chicago's ball organisers, just as in Melbourne, ensured the attendance of people of influence and respectability by the charging of a fee for admittance.[22] The Chicago Hibernian Benevolent Society banquet in 1850 donated all of its profits to the relief of destitute immigrants.[23] This was the Society's third such festival, and participants toasted the United States, the State of Illinois, the memory of Washington and the signatories of the Declaration of Independence, before toasting the memory of Daniel O'Connell and the patriots of 1798 and 1848. These toasts aligned the Irish citizens of Chicago with the heroes of American and Irish revolutions, similar to the Irish militia units which had emerged over the previous eight years. By framing the American Revolution as sacred and linked to the Irish experience, those at the St Patrick's Day events were contributing to a shared set of presumptions about life and loyalty in America.[24] Though most of the toasts were led by men, women had a role to play in the proceedings of the evening. Just as male toast-makers observed the part of women in keeping the Irish spirit abroad alive, two women raised a glass to the Emerald Isle.[25] The ethnic press emphasised a shared sense of Irish experience by reporting St Patrick's Day events. The New York-based *Irish American Weekly* included a large report on the 1852 St Patrick's Day in Chicago.[26] That year, before the Chicago parades began in earnest, the Montgomery Guards, accompanied by their band, 'took their station before the communion rails in front of the pews' at St Mary's Cathedral.[27] St Patrick's Day 'acted as a memory-site' for Irish Americans, a time when 'Irish-Americans rhetorically and symbolically grounded their present in a remembered and constructed past'.[28] In Chicago, Irish loyalty was both remembered and proven by past and present military power and prowess.

The Catholic Church was represented throughout St Patrick's Day events, with services beginning each St Patrick's Day celebration in Chicago. The day was an opportunity to pledge both religious and ethnic loyalty outside of the parish boundaries. However, organisers acknowledged that Irish people were separated by class, religious denomination and education. Despite the importance of the Catholic Church in celebrating St Patrick's Day and Irish identity in the city, not all events revolved around one particular religion. From 1853, Chicago public celebrations were organised centrally by a committee of representatives from the city's ethnic organisations. As no particular society took control, the committee allowed for multiple images of what it was to be Irish in Chicago. It also resulted in competition between the different elements of Irish parish life. In this way, Chicago and Melbourne's Irish communities worked similarly, with the middle classes trying to claim power and representation with differing success. The importance of the St Patrick's Day parade in claiming public space for the celebration of Irish history, strength and identity in both Irish and non-Irish minds was encapsulated by the competition for the role of chief marshal in Chicago.[29] In Melbourne, conversely, the SPS built upon the social and political dominance of its members to promote a non-religious civic celebration of its namesake.

1860–1880

The 1860s heralded a more vocal and closely knit Irish community in Melbourne. However, in the midst of this increased solidarity, the SPS temporarily split over the Society's direction and this, combined with wet weather, resulted in no formal celebrations between 1860 and 1862.[30] In the absence of SPS events, 'a number of pleasure parties' were held in Melbourne's public gardens and on its coastlines.[31] Alongside these informal events, the Catholic Church exhibited its growing strength and position in the city when Archbishop Goold held a Mass at the partially built St Patrick's Cathedral. This was a celebration of increased Catholic wealth and community, as well as dedication and loyalty to the Catholic faith.[32] The SPS soon regained control of St Patrick's Day, but its temporary absence had opened a space for the Catholic Church in the celebrations. This would grow over time, allowing the Catholic religious identities of Melbourne's Irish communities to share the day with the secular and middle-class control of the SPS. The colonial restrictions of the Party Processions Prevention Act ensured the dominance of a secular elite and the prioritisation of Melbourne's political and social opportunities in the presentation of Irish identity.

In the years that St Patrick's Day fell on a Sunday the separation between religion, charity and ethnicity in Chicago was emphasised. In his welcome to the 250 attendees of the Hibernian Benevolent Society's ball, T. J. Kinsella noted that the Society had been established 'to soften, to subdue, and destroy all these personal and sectarian animosities and prejudices' that had separated the 'sons of old Erin'. It was open to all and had charity and benevolence as its main objective.[33] Religious organisations used the opportunity of St Patrick's Day to raise money for the support of the community while bringing together its elites.[34] The conflict between the Catholic Church and the growing nationalist sentiment in Chicago was usually ignored on St Patrick's Day, with an implicit understanding that the services that began the day were the religious element of the day, while the parades were secular and therefore a venue to express nationalist sentiment. The 1864 parade publicised these conflicts when the 'church party having abandoned the field' left the Fenians to run the event.[35] That year, Irish Catholics with nationalist sympathies were forced to make a decision about which community they prioritised, and very publicly, when the Vicar-General of Chicago declared 'that the Fenians shall not be admitted to any Catholic Church on that day, nor shall any member of a religious society be permitted to walk in procession where a Fenian takes a part'.[36] Originally two parades were to be held, one Fenian parade led by John Comisky, and another 'composed of the Catholics who remain loyal to their spiritual directors' led by Michael Keeley. Though the latter decided to withdraw, it was understood that though all the Catholic societies had declined to march, 'there is no doubt that members of all will be present in plenty'.[37] The following year, representatives of the Catholic Church returned to the streets during the St Patrick's Day parade, a sign of the declining anti-Fenian rhetoric of the Church in Chicago.

Respect shown by and to the Irish of Chicago was a very important element in St Patrick's Day. In 1860 it was angrily noted that the new municipal administration would be inaugurated on St Patrick's Day. This was deemed to be 'Another Insult to the Irish'.[38] Chicago's St Patrick's Day parades were a clear staking of territory and belonging in the city, and to hinder them was to threaten the place and power of a rising city influence. The Civil War provided another element to these celebrations, encouraging ethnic and religious solidarity in Chicago while increasing the influence and visibility of the Fenian Brotherhood and later the Clan na Gael in the city. During the Civil War, parades were largely held in honour of departing regiments, and in 1862 there was no St Patrick's Day parade; instead, ethnic pride was displayed most prominently on 14 June when the Irish Brigade departed the city.[39] When parades were held, however, the influence of wartime imagery can be seen. In 1863 it rained all day: 'Men were dripping and women trailed their bedraggled skirts through the mire, ignoring bedaubed hose and defiled ankles. Equine flanks emitted clouds of steam and the gay cavalcade of the morning might have rivalled a squad of army mules in the afternoon.'⁴⁰ This imagery of grim Irish determination against harsh conditions can be found frequently in stories of Irish-American valour during the Civil War, helping to establish a rhetorical base for Irish pride within American society.

The Irish communities of Melbourne and Chicago were linked by their presence in new cities with transitional populations. Members of both societies sought to recreate middle-class elements of Irish life, and mirror those already in place in other ethnic immigrant communities. This included the establishment of societies such as the St Patrick's Society and Hibernian Benevolent Society, which brought important people of Irish birth and descent together to enjoy balls and banquets for a fee. These banquets provided an opportunity to highlight loyalty to Ireland and new communities, and were reported widely in local newspapers as well as those with national and international readerships. The foundational years of each city had long-term impacts on the shape of St Patrick's Day events. In Melbourne, processions were illegal, automatically restricting who could be involved in moulding public Irish priorities. In Chicago, the formal events retained their class distinctions. However, the processions allowed for a demonstration of Irish power and popularity throughout society. While women had a greater role in Chicago's St Patrick's Day dinners, they remained on the periphery of celebrations in both cities. As the 1860s progressed, public expressions of Irish identity expanded as the Catholic Church's presence became more strongly Irish-based and ethnic fraternalism increased in both cities.

The later 1860s witnessed heightened ethnic and religious tensions in Melbourne and Chicago. Susan Davis argues that parades are 'public dramas of social relations, and in them performers define who can be a social actor and what subjects and ideas are available for communication and consideration'.⁴¹ The organisers of St Patrick's Day events responded to these changes and priorities by expanding, and restricting, who could be involved in the public expression of celebrating Ireland's national hero. In the midst of this change, there was a consistent theme of Irish political freedom and the threat of enslavement, politically and ideologically. The Catholic Church's presence in both cities had expanded to include widespread parish schooling by religious communities and an increase in religious social life provision. This was reflected in the role of the Catholic Church on St Patrick's Day. Irish people at all levels of society were being taught Irish history and, in many cases, about the inequality that had existed between the wealthy and tenants through benefit societies and other aspects of parish life. A tighter community was created in both cities as Irish Catholics united to support parish schools and Irish charities, and were promoted as a cohesive community by the ethnic press. St Patrick's Day provided a moment for Irish religious and secular organisations to come together as an example to Irish people throughout society, as well as to show a united front against their critics. Though they were usually split by geography, St Patrick's Day was an opportunity to demonstrate that Irish organisations were spread across the city, in every ward and suburb, and that together they could have a big impact.

After the apparent success of the Chicago St Patrick's Day parade in 1864, when the Catholic Church had forced its parishioners to choose between nationalism and religious piety, Catholic clerics and societies were visible participants and organisers of events aligned with nationalist societies. While the Catholic Church did not condone involvement in secret societies, Catholic societies often marched and spoke alongside Irish nationalist organisations in Chicago parades, using processions to spread their priorities and mottos to the wider public, and to demonstrate Catholic power throughout the city. In 1867, the Catholic Juvenile Temperance Society joined with the Fr. Mathew Temperance Society during the parade. Around sixty 'little fellows' carried banners with the words 'Our motto is Temperance' on one side, and the emotive 'All is right; Dad is sober' on the other.[42] As the Chicago Catholic Church's priorities were spread throughout society, so did its representatives. At the St Patrick's Society ball in 1867, Rev. Dr. McMullen argued, 'The Irish clergy were a portion of the Irish people, and sympathised with their wrongs, their misfortunes, and their sufferings, and would indorse [sic] a movement for revolution against tyranny if it took a form that promised success.'[43] For the Irish Catholic clergy, the St Patrick's Society banquet and those organised by other societies was a platform from which to connect to their parishioners on an ethnic level as well as a religious one, while parades helped to unite their organisations across class boundaries.

The image of Australia as a land of freedom and opportunity, so often understood to be the pull of the United States, was emphasised in Melbourne Irish political speeches. The settlement of Australia was traditionally divorced from the tools of the British empire which enforced coercive measures in Ireland. This began to change in 1867 when the SPS speeches were tinged with bitterness, influenced by the Victorian political questions of the time as well as by Charles Gavan Duffy's recent return from Dublin.[44] Within a larger criticism of land control in Ireland, Gavan Duffy chose to focus his censure on the landlords of Ireland, not British Government control. However, this anger was unusual for Melbourne's St Patrick's Day events and was balanced by an acknowledgement of the so-called 'wisdom' of the British Government in granting Victoria responsible government. Gavan Duffy concluded his speech by remarking that 'if ever any English friend asked them what would content Ireland, let them reply, in one sentence, that Ireland would be thoroughly contented, thoroughly loyal, when she had the same liberty that they possessed in Australia'.[45] While criticising the action of Irish landlords, Gavan Duffy maintained that the Irish in Victoria and Ireland were loyal citizens of the British empire, uniting Irish identity near and far with the imperial project.

SPS events were widely reported upon, and therefore what orators said reached large swathes of society, presenting a message on behalf of the whole Irish community and consequently protecting Irish people from widespread backlash at times of panic. In Melbourne, this was brought into clear focus in 1868 when Henry O'Farrell shot at Prince Alfred on 12 March. It was remarked that the shooting of Alfred 'had a depressing influence upon the commemoration' of St Patrick and the focus of the celebrations that did happen was chiefly concerned with reiterating the loyalty of the Irish in Melbourne.[46] Despite the claims of newspaper editors that Fenianism existed in Melbourne even at a low level, the attendees of the Melbourne SPS dinner in 1868 were keen to emphasise Fenianism's roots in the United States, and the consequent lack of opportunity for O'Farrell to interact with those involved in the cause. That there were any Fenian, or quasi-Fenian, organisations in Australia was 'an idle fable' in Gavan Duffy's eyes. According to this argument, the Irish in Australia, as opposed to in America, were simply too far away for political intervention in Britain.[47] These sentiments were reprinted in newspapers around Australia and made their way to the United Kingdom. In this way St Patrick's Day events provided an international platform for pledging loyalty and condemning violence, as well as a domestic one. The message of dual loyalty and good citizenship had been, and would remain, the loudest message of the Irish in Melbourne throughout the nineteenth century.

Fenianism's role in shaping St Patrick's Day can also been seen in Chicago. In the years before 1866, it was observed, the city's St Patrick's Days had been 'honored by friendly gatherings, by speech makings, by the interchange of old memories, by processions where the emblems of charitable societies and of trades floated to the breeze'. That year, however, the planned Fenian raids on Canada resulted in these 'merry meetings chang[ing] to loud alarums [sic]'.[48] The rhetoric of Irish slavery and weakness, and the perceived lack of respect received by the Irish abroad, was highlighted as a problem to be resolved. The Fenian Brotherhood in the St Patrick's Day parade took on military formation, in regimental order, led by Colonel James Quirk and then marshalled by the Centers of local Circles, relating the experience of the Irish in the Civil War to the future struggle for Irish freedom.[49] The 'officers of the district' assured their fellow countrymen, 'By the next St Patrick's day we shall either hold our heads erect or slink aside, shamed to flaunt our slavish flags in the light of freedom ... the Fenian Brotherhood is resolved to do or die for Ireland'.[50] Irishmen were urged to go to work, raise money and organise fighting men into companies. Though they were not to wait for inspiring speeches from visiting lecturers, in honour of St Patrick's Day, the president of the Fenian Brotherhood, Col. W. R. Roberts, gave two lectures to raise money for rifles, and the local Fenian Brotherhood invited 'all, rich and poor, high and low, Irish-American, German, the merchant, mechanic, laborer, and teamster' to attend.[51] Immigrant communities and classes were united in the struggle against oppressive forces and with charitable Irish organisations in the city which, by encouraging the improvement of the Irish in America, also contributed to the restoration of Irish liberty.

The benefits of only hosting balls for those in power were brought into question after the celebrations of 1869 in Melbourne. They were male-dominated events, with women eating separately away from the main hall or on the balcony before joining the men for dancing. MacDonagh has argued that two of the main objectives of the organisers of the dinners was to gather as many prominent Irish or Catholics in the colony together, and particularly to get as many of Victoria's leading men, particularly politicians, to respond to the toasts.[52] This was a way of consolidating the position of Irish and Catholics in the higher echelons of Victorian society, and this was reiterated in the speeches of the evenings. This bonding of Irishmen of all creeds but not all classes became a problem for some in Melbourne. By the end of the 1860s it was observed that in not including them, there was a danger of losing the national allegiance of Melbourne's less elite Irish people.[53]

The decade had seen a stabilising of the city's population and the increase of religious education and social organisation of Melbourne's Irish lower classes. In 1869, a letter to the editor of the *Advocate* suggested a change in how Melbourne's Irish community celebrated their patron saint. Until that point, the powerful and influential men of the city had met to listen to each other make speeches on Irish and imperial loyalty, to toast the Queen and to eat the delicacies of the best caterers in the city. The letter requested that events celebrating Irish identity for 'the classes generally who cannot afford to pay high for amusements' were held.[54] There was a younger generation of Irish-descended people who had been raised in Melbourne. The writer enquired whether it would not be more satisfactory if the prosperity of Ireland was toasted, not just in St Patrick's Hall, but 're-echoed in the air by a few thousand voices, and that the children of Irish parents witness ... [and] remember it. This is the purpose that patriotism abroad should have in view.'[55] Organisers were alert to the push for religious and ethnic education in other areas of society and decided that if they wanted to create a sustained and unified ethnic community within Melbourne, they needed to expand their presentation of what it meant to be Irish across generational and class boundaries.

Chicago's parades provided more opportunities for the involvement of non-traditional groups, often through the lens of sympathy with small or oppressed nations and peoples, as well as a shared Catholicism. This was particularly true during the 1870s. As one newspaper editor pointed out in 1872, 'Not to Ireland alone does St Patrick belong. Anyone who brings light into a dark place, who elevates what is low, who refines what is coarse and savage, is a benefactor to all mankind.'[56] In 1870, a 'colored regiment' was to be involved in the procession under the Fenian flag but unfortunately they did not have enough time to organise themselves.[57] The involvement of the Chicago Laboring Men's Benevolent Society and Laborers' Union, and the Horse Shoers' Benevolent and Protective Society had been a standard of the parade since 1867, but during the Panic of 1873, solidarity was sought with the wider working class.[58] The parade was led by the Polish American Guards, a signal of solidarity with oppressed peoples, and an important ally in the pro-liquor stand that the Irish of the city had supported.[59] The Polish Guards were involved again in 1874 when they concluded the organised procession, on that occasion preceded by the Italian Alpine Hunters who had been established in Italy in 1872.[60] The involvement of non-traditional groups shows an international outlook which may have had positive domestic repercussions for the Irish of the city, linking Irish groups with religious and occupational peers from different ethnicities to achieve change.

Another group to be increasingly involved in St Patrick's Day celebrations were the students of parish schools. In 1868 it was noted that the Holy Family School observed the day by taking part in the procession, and then in the evening 'giving an exhibition in the school-room' which included singing, dialogues, and music by the school bands.[61]

The involvement of schoolchildren indicates the important place of education and parochial schools in the Irish community life in Chicago. These events acted as fundraisers for schools and open days of sorts, showcasing the children of Irish Chicagoans to members of the public and instilling an acknowledgement of the importance of celebrating St Patrick's Day and ethnic pride in children. By 1873, the celebration at the Holy Family School brought 350 children together from the four parochial schools in the parish.[62] According to the *Western Catholic* reporter that attended, the 'Tableaux was the crowning feature of the evening'. The first tableau was based on the scriptural history of Joseph and his brothers in the Book of Genesis. This proved the scriptural education and training of the children: their Catholic education was acknowledged. The second tableau proved their training in Irish history, and the nationalist edge of that education. It was a 'descriptive of "The Wexford Massacre" – was divided into three parts, also, viz., "Praying around the cross," "The Massacre," "After the Massacre".'[63] The priorities of the next generation of Irish Chicagoans were clear. These were to be the adults who would become involved in Irish nationalist activities in the city in the 1880s.

Just as John Mitchel had conjured images of Ireland in his lecture tour of 1856, the Fenian Brotherhood tapped into the idea of loyalty to nation being instilled in Irish people from birth, arguing that St Patrick 'is a name ineffaceably engraved in his memory. While he slumbers in the cradle the grandmother croons some wild ditty of Christianized Ireland.'[64] The Chicago St Patrick's Society referred similarly to a love of Ireland and its heroes. The Society banquet was attended by a hundred of the city's elite.[65] These men were joined by representatives of the St George's and St Andrew's Societies, placing the St Patrick's Society alongside longer-established civil societies.[66] Reflecting the audience assembled, prominent newspaper editor James Washington Sheahan declared that those gathered 'met, not to devise schemes or to taunt the Saxon with his stained hands, but to celebrate Ireland as the home we have loved'.[67] Similar to the proceedings of the SPS in Melbourne, Chicago's Society privileged St Patrick above all, before toasting the Catholic hierarchy and clergy of Ireland, the President of the United States, Ireland, the Union and the Constitution, and the State of Illinois. These were men of rank and stature, figures of respect within Chicago and the wider United States, and though they were there to celebrate St Patrick, many of the secular representatives of law and order in the city were not of Irish descent. While the Fenian Brotherhood's events prioritised the freedom of Ireland, the St Patrick's Society emphasised the rapid rise of Chicago from 'a howling wilderness' to 'a mighty State' and the home of Abraham Lincoln.

In 1870, parades returned to the St Patrick's Day celebration. In Melbourne, the processions that took place between 1870 and 1890 were organised by the SPS, later in tandem with the HACBS. While Chicago's parade participants altered with time, reflecting both domestic and international concerns, the Melbourne parade was securely the realm of these two societies. Led by the community's elites in the case of the SPS and the aspiring Catholic working and middle class in HACBS, both societies had invested in promoting the educational and social progression of Irish people in the city and benefited from a respectable image of Irishness which was easier to achieve when the processions were controlled by a select group of people. The collaboration of the HACBS, which had Catholicism at its very heart, and the non-religious SPS led to Catholicism playing a more public part in the festivities.

In the years after 1870, the HACBS attended religious ceremonies and after the service finished, they mustered outside the cathedral and marched slowly down to Swanston Street, where they were met by the SPS division. The two societies then amalgamated and marched together.[68] In 1870, the procession numbered five hundred, with boys running alongside.[69] The colourful 'spectacle' was a proud demonstration of Irish identity, both Catholic and Protestant, and a very visible reminder of the dominant place of the Irish within Melbourne society. By 1871, the St Patrick's Day parade included 1,300–1,400 marchers, made up of five hundred members of the SPS and eight hundred members of thirteen branches of the HACBS. The procession was accompanied by 2,000–3,000 people of all ages, within which there was a 'great prevalence of the emerald colour' and the wearing of the shamrock. The procession ended in the Friendly Societies' Gardens, where around 6,000 people gathered to enjoy the bank holiday.[70] Melbourne's Irish-born community numbered 29,000 that year, indicating a participation level of around 20 per cent in the day's main event.[71] Other people could have participated in the celebrations at evening events organised by the SPS, as well as events that took place at the suburban town halls, parish schools and concert halls.

The Melbourne SPS and HACBS also added a grand fete to the end of the procession proceedings. The Friendly Societies' Gardens acted as host for the joint outdoor fete after the procession each year. Once at the Friendly Societies' Gardens, there was a programme of sports, as well as a fleet of boats on the lake, a stud of donkeys, merry-go-rounds, a company of minstrels and Simpson's Zoetrope Circus. This was an event that was enjoyed by a wider portion of the community than the two hundred 'leading citizens' that were invited to SPS balls. However, the newspaper reports of the day were still sure to include the names of prominent citizens who attended the day's entertainments, as well as emphasising the respectability of attendees. In 1870, although there was a considerable amount of excitement, 'the proverbially excitable temperament of the Irish seemed almost dormant'.[72] The reports of St Patrick's Day celebrations throughout the next years emphasised that the Irish people, well-dressed and thriving-looking citizens, who attended the day events proved to be 'highly creditable to the country', and those who had 'over-indulged' in the past were reduced.[73]

The speeches of Melbourne's St Patrick's Day balls retained their focus on the positives of life in Australia, a place where Irish people had 'the prosperity that was banished from our native country', as well as the 'complete self-government that we desired in our native country'.[74] Joseph Rowan, the vice-president of the SPS in 1872, proposed a toast to 'Kindred Societies' because Irishmen of all creeds should be united on 'a national platform, from which all sectarian differences should be excluded'.[75] Inclusion and unity of Irish people was encouraged across generational and class lines as well as sectarian as the 1870s continued. John Gavan Duffy brought a youthful point of view to the proceedings in 1875. He 'spoke as the representative of a later generation, and was glad to say that the young people of Irish extraction in this country, if Australians, were not the less Irish on that account'.[76] Gavan Duffy and Rowan were both products of the CYMS and Melbourne's Irish Catholic schools. As the second generation of Irish in Melbourne grew towards adulthood, the importance of widening involvement in Irish activities increased. Speakers could not rely on nostalgic imagery of Ireland to incite Irish Australians to tears and anger, for most of the second generation would never set eyes on Ireland's rural landscapes or experience the effects of coercive laws. Instead, the leaders of Melbourne's Irish communities had to manifest elements of Irishness for a new generation to grasp onto. SPS speeches gained a new bitterness with regard to the landlord system in Ireland, while cultural nationalism was visible at St Patrick's Day events after 1870, involving adults and children alike with Gaelic games, lectures on Irish history and culture, concerts of Irish songs and Irish dancing classes. These were often Australians who had grown up benefiting from Irish Catholic education and participation in an increasingly active parish life centred around Irish and Catholic identity. They had the cultural affinity with the Irish community in Melbourne, and the increasing familiarity with

Ireland's problems, encouraged by political and charitable subscription lists, allowed for new ways of expressing love and understanding of 'home' without threatening their loyalty to the British empire or Crown.

The late 1860s and 1870s saw increased inclusivity in both Melbourne and Chicago's St Patrick's Day celebrations. By this time both cities were stabilising as societies, still expanding rapidly but not at the exhausting rate of the previous decade. While Chicago's different organisations competed for favour and power, Melbourne was able to provide an image of Irish unity through an established group of Irish people who ran and participated in Irish life at all levels. Branches of the HACBS were emerging in parishes across the city and complemented the more centralised SPS. As new suburbs gained in prominence, the SPS appointed representatives who would run separate branches, but these societies worked in tandem. Fundamentally this decade saw a closer association between Irish ethnicity and Catholic religious allegiance in both cities. The plight of other oppressed nations, particularly Catholic nations like Poland and Hungary, featured in the St Patrick's Day events of Melbourne and Chicago, alluding to the transnational struggle of the oppressed and religious. While Melbourne's speeches focused on social inequality created by unfair systems, Chicago aimed their fury at England. These distinctions in rhetoric were made manifest by the different atmospheres of the British empire and the United States, but both led to societies which produced popular Land League activism. New forms of St Patrick's Day celebrations also took on culturally nationalist elements. The involvement of children in the celebration of Irish ethnic pride was emphasised, drawing attention to the next generations of Irish Australians and Irish Americans who were being raised to appreciate and enjoy their heritage, and, in some cases, to fight for the rights that their ancestors were denied.

1880–1914

The Irish communities in Melbourne and Chicago celebrated St Patrick's Day in some form or another every year throughout the latter half of the nineteenth century. They were unique within Melbourne and Chicago's immigrant communities in being consistently granted the space within the city for the celebration of their ethnic heritage, providing Irish cultural and political leaders with a position of influence and competition not afforded to others, a benefit of the early Irish dominance of city council boards. The 1880s saw the testing of the limits of Irish identity and loyalty in both cities, bringing together religious and nationalist priorities deemed unacceptable in previous generations. The news of change in Ireland – the Land War, Invincibles murders, the First Home Rule Bill and the establishment of the Gaelic Athletic Association – presented new strands and nuances to Irish identity in the diaspora. How these changes were filtered through Australian and American lenses, and within new generations of immigrants and children, were most clearly articulated during St Patrick's Day celebrations. However, there was a distinction between the celebrations of Irish identity expressed on St Patrick's Day, often an ethnicity based in the long narrative of Irish and Catholic oppression, tradition and romance, and the political speeches which featured at nationalist rallies and lectures. St Patrick's Day, therefore, focused on an inherent ethnic identity as opposed to the conflicting possibilities of political nationalist identities.

Beginning at the Model School and ending with a hurling match, the influence of Ireland's imperial and cultural histories was represented in Melbourne's St Patrick's Day parades of the late 1870s.[77] As the SPS and HACBS members marched, Melbourne's streets were bedecked with green flags with golden harps. When the 1878 procession reached the Treasury, the procession stopped and three cheers were given for the Governor, who appeared and bowed his thanks.[78] The increase in public prominence of Melbourne's St Patrick's Day celebrations was reflected in the expressions of loyalty to Crown and State. The subsequent year, the procession stopped at the Treasury while the bands played the British national anthem, and the members of the societies gave three cheers for the Queen.[79] This custom was henceforth an accepted part of the St Patrick's Day procession. Despite the increased criticism of British rule in Ireland, loyalty to the Queen and representatives of the British empire remained a central element to the promotion of Irish ethnic identity and the enjoyment of St Patrick's Day in the colonial world of nineteenth-century Melbourne. The involvement of community leaders in Irish nationalist activities, particularly the mayors and civic leaders, ensured the continued demonstrations of loyalty to law, order and society in Melbourne. This was especially important in light of improved cabled and telegraphic information transmission which brought news of violence in Europe.[80]

As well as information, the 1880s heralded a new element of St Patrick's Day celebrations. Through the examination of games and activities played at St Patrick's Day events, it is possible to track the changing expectations of traditions and associational sporting cultures that the organisers had of their attendees. By 1881, the open-air fete was attracting crowds of over 10,000 visitors and was therefore having an effect on a wider element of the Melbourne population.[81] The Friendly Societies' Gardens fete incorporated a hurling match as well as the traditional Irish dancing competitions.[82] This move toward a more staunchly Irish cultural nationalism did not become the norm in Ireland until the 1890s. Hurling competitions were not mentioned in Melbourne's St Patrick's Day events after 1884, though that does not mean they did not occur. Instead, in the years after 1884 there was an increased coverage of the Irish dancing, as well as the embrace of a wider Celtic identity, with the Highland fling joining the schedule of events. Informal events continued to be held in Melbourne, most prominently the horse racing which had been a staple since the 1850s, gaining a particularly Irish element with the Erin Hurdle Race and the Shamrock Handicap by 1887.

Balls and banquets that coincided with St Patrick's Day were a useful marketing tool, used by people within the Irish community as well as non-Irish entrepreneurs. However, by using St Patrick's Day to support the building of infrastructure used by the wider Irish society, a sense of cross-class community was attempted. The CYMS held a ball along with the St George's School Committee in 1882 in aid of the St George's School in Carlton. At this ball, songs such as 'Though the last glimpse of Erin', 'Savourneen Deelish' and 'Kathleen Mavourneen' were sung, bringing together a social and national event with institution-building fundraising.[83] Schools were not the only fundraising focus for the Irish communities of Melbourne on St Patrick's Day, as money was also raised in aid of the St Patrick's Cathedral Fund and St Ignatius Church.[84] These fundraising projects involved the coordination of various Melbourne societies, with the useful side effect of publicly demonstrating through newspaper subscriber lists the community spirit and increasing wealth of the Irish in the city. In Melbourne, the St Patrick's Day events became more inclusive as the decades progressed, and while there was an increased association between ethnicity and religion by the 1880s, it did not dominate the celebrations to the extent of exclusion and alienation.

The increase in Irish nationalist activity brought about by the Irish Land War, the Irish-American Dynamite Campaign and constitutional nationalists' progress in Westminster meant that the SPS speeches of the 1880s had a political edge rarely seen in the previous decades. In 1881, Sir Bryan O'Loghlen said that he could hardly trust himself to speak of Ireland. Instead, he 'could only express his hope that God would send its people a safe deliverance'.[85] O'Loghlen would regain his premiership four months later, making these sentiments particularly strident within the British empire. Two years previously, Charles Gavan Duffy argued that Irishmen had 'done their full share in rearing and developing, guiding and directing, the new nation in its [Australia's] peaceful progress'.[86] The role of Irish people in Melbourne as good citizens who had helped to shape the society was again alluded to, placing the Irish as loyal to both the empire and Ireland within the 'friendship of nations' that the Redmond brothers had promoted on their visit to the colony.[87]

Chicago's St Patrick's Day organisers were equally keen to show their loyalty to the country in which they lived, arguing in 1885 that as 'none are more devoted to the land of their adoption than the Irish people they will become more and more influenced by the American spirit'.[88] The St Patrick's Day balls and banquets in Chicago were partly organised to cement existing power structures and social networks, particularly within an atmosphere of dissent and disagreement on Irish nationalism. Senators and members of the State Legislature often sought the support of their Irish voters through attendance at St Patrick's Day, risking the ire of their non-Irish constituents.[89] This irritation increased from 1883, when Irish nationalist tensions emerged in conflict with the priorities of wider Chicago society. The City Council and the Board of Education decided to designate both St Patrick's Day and Good Friday as bank holidays in the Chicago school system. This was deemed 'a very unwise and impertinent thing – unwise, because it drags religious questions into municipal affairs; and impertinent, because it has been done in the face of public sentiment.'[90] The choice of St Patrick's Day was seen as unfair for reasons of religious preference and national privilege, reflecting the continued control of Irish and Irish Catholics on city life, a sentiment encouraged by the presence of senators at their events.

The Chicago Catholic Church retained its position in St Patrick's Day through the involvement of Catholic organisations in the parades and separate school-based events. Just as the parochial school system played a large part in Melbourne's celebrations of St Patrick's Day, Chicago's parish schools remained involved in the St Patrick's Day celebrations, and by 1881 the entertainments that they put on had become established fundraising events. The Holy Family Sunday School Association staged a two-night entertainment which cost 50 cents for admittance, the proceeds of which went to 'educate the Catholic youth of the parish'.[91] Children also dominated public celebrations, both formally and informally, with young boys that 'yelled and plowed through the mud in the wake of the patriotic sons of old Ireland'.[92] By involving children in St Patrick's Day events, a sense of multi-generational continuation was cultivated, bringing parents, teachers and community leaders together with the heroes of their shared Irish past. This shared imagining of Irish pride, past and present, was an important element in the creation of a sustained sense of community and belonging across the generations of Irish-born and Irish descendants. St Patrick's Day celebrations were increasingly staged events, and by the late 1880s some were voicing criticisms of the day's spectacle. Finley Peter Dunne, through the mouthpiece of Mr Dooley, objected to the 'transformation of St Patrick's Day from a cultural to a political event'.[93] This change was largely brought about by the control of the Irish-American Council.

Balls and banquets brought together the power brokers of Chicago society, Irish and non-Irish. These alternative, private and fee-charging balls and dinners circumvented the Clan-controlled Irish-American Council. The St Patrick's Day events which took place behind closed doors tended to be a stage for the leading citizens of the city, an opportunity for clergymen, lawyers, politicians and journalists to gather together and promote their views to a group of like-minded individuals. When it was understood that there would be conflicts at the dinner, people did not attend. This was the case in 1883 when a reporter from the *Tribune* questioned a number of Chicago's leading Irish Americans on the dynamite campaign. John F. Finerty was so disgusted by William Onahan's negative reaction that when asked why he was not at the St Patrick's Society banquet, Finerty replied, 'I was invited, and had fully intended to present until I read Mr Onahan's interview.'[94] St Patrick's Day events were a time to present a unified front and an example to others. For this reason, there was an increasing separation of nationalist rhetoric during the celebrations. After the public splits in 1883, and the continuing disagreements on the best ways to achieve Irish self-government in the mid-decade, the place of nationalist rhetoric moved to the Ogden Grove demonstrations. Thereafter, the Ireland of public St Patrick's Day celebrations was a more inclusive and civil image, of a great and proud past and a hopeful future. How to achieve that future remained out of focus. When parades were held during the 1880s, 'No transparencies or banners indicative of the Irish-American sentiment on the Irish national troubles were visible.' Instead, harps on green backgrounds and the American colours were flown. The headquarters of the Irish-American Club displayed the national colours of both Ireland and the United States.[95] On St Patrick's Day in Chicago, organisations prioritised loyalty to both the United States and the idea and history of Ireland over political infighting.

Parades were not held in Chicago on four St Patrick's Days between 1880 and 1890. In 1881 it was noted that while yellow and green ribbons in buttonholes indicated that the day was an Irish holiday, there were no celebrations other than a High Mass held by Archbishop Feehan. The weather was cited as a reason for this lack of the 'usually lively and hilarious' day, but more important was the organisers' 'inclination to use the money which would be so expended in ameliorating the sufferings and strengthening the bonds of their fellow countrymen across the Atlantic in obtaining what they consider to be their rights as against the oppression of "landlords"'.[96] In 1881, the *Western Catholic* offered its congratulations to the Irish societies for adopting its advice 'in abandoning the useless custom of parading the streets'.[97] This was repeating a sentiment first advocated in 1880, when processions were cancelled throughout the United States in favour of donating the money to Irish relief funds.[98] This custom was mirrored within the banquets and balls in 1880 and 1881, which donated the proceeds of the celebrations to Irish relief funds, and later, the Irish Land League.[99] In 1886, it was decided that holding parades which required 'so heavy an outlay as would be required would be little less than treason to the mother country', and money was instead donated to the Parnell Fund.[100] For the Irish in Chicago, territory was claimed every day through the sheer numbers of Irish people in the power structures of the city: the politicians, the police and the city workers. They did not need to demand space in an increasingly 'Irish' city. Instead, public and financial support for Irish nationalism was prioritised, while the 'civilised' celebrations of the city's 'middle crust' and elites continued behind closed doors.

While in Chicago the 1870s had seen an extension of solidarity and friendship to those outside of the leading Irish communities, to Polish militias and labour unions, the control of the Irish-American Council and greater emphasis on the needs of Ireland meant that by the 1880s, walls had come crashing back down around the Irish community. Chicago's St Patrick's Day organisers became increasingly inward-looking, eschewing solidarity with other ethnic and civic groups in order to force the dominance of certain Irish societies. By the end of the decade, the Irish-American Council voted forty-eight to eighteen not to have a parade on St Patrick's Day. Vice-President Fitzgerald argued for the need to have a parade, citing the disunity and disinterest of Irishmen in Chicago in celebrating their heritage. In the aftermath of the Cronin murder scandals and increased criticism of supposed Irish-American corruption in the newspapers, Fitzgerald pleaded for a parade which would show the city's press a united front and demonstrate to opponents 'that we are alive and mean to stay alive'.[101] His concerns were overruled. The inconsistencies in Chicago's public displays of ethnic pride during the 1880s denote the fluctuating competition for control and priorities in the city. In the years that parades did not take place, the money saved was sent to Ireland in support of nationalist activities there. In other years, the need for a show of power and unity in the American city was prioritised, bringing thousands of marchers and multiple organisations together under the banner of Irish pride.[102]

This attitude changed after 1890. The traumatic splits in Irish Chicago society were papered over for a St Patrick's Day parade in 1891 where, for a change, the sun shone and for a day, 'Men of every nationality on earth ... became Irishmen and united in doing honor to Ireland's patron saint.'[103] Fitzgerald's hope for a united front was realised. Reflecting a wider shift in Irish associational culture, the Ancient Order of Hibernians and temperance societies for men and boys featured strongly in the parade, as did sports teams from the Gaelic Athletic Association.[104] The Robert Emmet GAA Club marched alongside those named after Wolfe Tone, Michael Davitt, William O'Brien and Daniel O'Connell, ensuring representation, in name at least, of Ireland's nationalist heroes. While the Clan na Gael Guards escorted the parade, this was a powerful demonstration of multi-generational engagement with Irish diasporic cultural and religious life. A year later, Fanny O'Grady attended a parade planning meeting – the only woman to attend – calling on the organisers to let women join in the parade.[105] This request was acquiesced to, though the 'Ladies of Chicago' were to join the end of the parade in carriages.[106] This was still a male affair, and the classed dynamics of the day were highlighted in 1896 when a journalist for the *Daily Inter Ocean* noted, 'It was the day when the poor man lost $1.50 of a day's wages for the sake of the revered saint and the rich man drew his salary and loafed for the same cause.'[107] Nevertheless, it remained a day to demonstrate Irish cultural and Catholic pride to all opponents in the city.

As the years progressed and Melbourne's Irish people moved out to the suburbs in large numbers, smaller events were organised by local chapters of the societies. They were, however, reunited in the annual procession. The 1890 parade involved five bands and twenty branches of the HACBS, four branches of the SPS and seven branches of the newly established Irish National Foresters. It was watched by spectators proudly wearing sprigs of 'the dear little, sweet little, shamrock of Ireland', many of which had been dried-pressed and sent from Ireland, a feature also in the coverage of Chicago's celebrations.[108] The evening festivities included an address by Archbishop Carr, who noted, 'The Irish people loved liberty, but the Irish people loved loyalty also', a sentiment which would have no doubt pleased the Governor and Lady Hopetoun who were in attendance. The custom of halting the procession at the Treasury to show loyalty was altered slightly. In 1886, a month before Gladstone's second Home Rule Bill was vetoed by the House of Lords, three cheers were also given for Mr Gladstone who, according to a recently received cable message, had 'devised a scheme for the buying out of the Irish landlords and the restoration of the Irish Parliament'.[109] By 1891, the changes in Irish nationalist allegiance were acknowledged: 'The banner representing Mr Gladstone and Mr Parnell side by side had probably not been revised up to date, unless it was intended to convey an idea that all would end happily, with the characteristic way of looking on the bright side of affairs.'[110] Though the shape of Melbourne's St Patrick's Days changed dramatically, a demonstration of loyalty to the Queen and her representatives, the British empire and to the wider community of Melbourne, as well as the promotion of principles of home rule in Ireland, were fundamental parts of the day throughout the early twentieth century.[111] As associational culture expanded and became more localised, St Patrick's Day provided an opportunity for both local celebration and centralised representation, with delegates from Irish Victoria's religious, cultural, civic and sporting life descending on Melbourne on special trains and trams for the day. The educational and religious successes of the Irish Catholic community were brought together and spotlighted with special prize-givings by Archbishop Daniel Mannix at the Exhibition Hall grounds in the aftermath of the day's public celebrations.[112]

The prospect of war altered the shape of St Patrick's Day celebrations in both Melbourne and Chicago from 1900. For Chicago, war came earlier than in Melbourne when the Boer War brought a political nature back into the day's parades. Ex-officers of the 7th Illinois Volunteer Infantry and the Irish-American Boer Ambulance Corps led the parade with an 'Irish flag that saw duty on seven South African battlefields'.[113] The role of the parade as a performance of Irish-American pride was forefront in the organisers' minds, who proclaimed in 1901, while explicitly disinviting 'Beamish's famous goat', that there was 'to be nothing ridiculous' about the day's parade.[114] As Charles Fanning has explored, the character of Mr Dooley, a fictional southside publican, frequently mocked the lack of horsemanship in the St Patrick's Day parades and the growing role of the 'professional Irishman' in Chicago's celebrations.[115] In the aftermath of the labour unrest of the 1890s and the exploding population of Chicago, the central St Patrick's Day celebrations became one of many, leading to cultural splits based on class. The plea for solemnity was continued and open-air demonstrations were foregone in 1902, exchanged for religious services, 'Celtic operettas' and a focus on 'a patriotic missionary movement in this country in the interest of Ireland', possibly due to the increasingly vocal presence of 'Prominent catholic Chicago' women in the organising committees.[116] The Gaelic League of America's convention, held in Chicago in 1908, coincided with St Patrick's Day, leading to special mention of the Irish language in the city's newspapers. Rev. John J. Carroll, pastor of St Thomas' Church and national librarian of the Gaelic League, gave his sermon in Irish, a further connecting of the Irish Catholic Church in Chicago and cultural nationalism.[117] This mix of cultural activities, including musical, dance and theatrical performances, religious ceremony and the occasional parade, continued throughout the early 1910s.

1914–1922

Between 1914 and 1922, the political worlds of Ireland and the Irish diaspora fundamentally altered. The First World War threw the world into disarray, while the Irish revolutionary period forced Irish communities around the world to reconsider their allegiances both in Ireland and within the diaspora. St Patrick's Day celebrations became battlegrounds within battlegrounds. Parades had always been sites of contestation, with the performative taking of space by a minority group. Between 1914 and 1922 this developed a new layer as Irish groups were forced to reckon with their image of Ireland's future and place within the British empire. While St Patrick's Day parades had frequently been fought over, with different groups competing for primacy, from 1914 the Catholic Church and Irish nationalism came together in Melbourne and Chicago to promote a strong and proud vision of Irish Catholic autonomy. For the leaders of Irish cultural life in Chicago this was not particularly new, but for those in Melbourne this was a break in the tradition of St Patrick's Day compromise and integration.

The St Patrick's Day parades of Melbourne were massive events throughout the early twentieth century, and frequently represented the strong home rule sentiment of the city.[118] As Cronin and Adair note, Australia witnessed 'the most politicised St Patrick's Day parades during this period'.[119] The prospect of the Home Rule Bill's passage was the focus of Melbourne's 1914 celebrations, with the *Advocate* printing a special number of issues 'with features designed to appeal to Irish Nationalist sentiment' in advance.[120] The day featured a large parade, headed by the children of the HACBS, parochial schools, and the orphanage and secondary schools' St Vincent de Paul's bands. After this focus on the new generations of Irish-Melbourne society came the archbishop and priests. The men and women of the SPS, marching sections of the national clubs, HACBS and INF were followed by various floats organised by Melbourne's Irish clubs.[121] When in 1918, members of Sinn Féin gained a majority of votes in Ireland, refused to take their seats in Westminster and formed the Irish Dáil, the Melbourne Irish established the Irish National Association (INA) in solidarity with this new phase of Irish political independence.[122] The presence of the INA and public support for Irish independence fundamentally reshaped the texture of the city's St Patrick's Day parades.

Throughout the First World War, Melbourne's wartime footing could be seen in the St Patrick's Day celebrations, emphasising loyalty to the Allied cause while also acknowledging the changing face of Irish nationalism. In 1915, Belgian flags were waved and the Marseillaise sung alongside the Irish and Catholic flags and songs.[123] While the picnics and sports continued, the traditional St Patrick's Day races were postponed when the racecourses became military camps. The following year, it was argued that the St Patrick's Day celebrations would 'incite the young men to bear their share of the national burden' and encourage those who could not join up to financially support Australia's expenses 'in defence of the Empire'.[124] While maintaining loyalty to the empire and the war effort, the tone of St Patrick's days and Melbourne's Catholic hierarchy shifted dramatically after the execution of the Easter Rising's leaders, with Mannix taking a prominent role.[125] Alongside this shift in Irish-Australian nationalism was 'an unprecedented storm of sectarianism', with Irish Catholics accused of disloyalty to the war effort.[126] In the final years of the war, returned soldiers in khaki featured prominently in the parade and crowds, demonstrating the layered loyalties of people with Irish, Australian and British colonial identities, and the ties between Irish culture, Catholic religiosity and Australian pride.

St Patrick's Day traditionally presented an opportunity for Irish Australians to come together in celebration of their patron saint, of Irish culture and, increasingly, of Catholic pride. The arrival of Mannix and the changing shape of Irish politics and Irish-Australian activism altered who controlled the message of the day. This echoed the reorientation of Catholic attitudes after 1911, which prioritised a more aggressive approach to achieving Catholic aims in the aftermath of repeated political disappointments related to education.[127] In 1918, Catholic groups carried Sinn Féin colours and flags, and a schools display at the Exhibition Gardens included a display by the children attending Sisters of Mercy schools who formed a 'living Shamrock' symbolic of Rome, Erin and Australia with the Papal, Australian and, crucially, Sinn Féin flags flying.[128] The parishioners of the Sisters of the Good Samaritan also carried a Sinn Féin flag bordered in black for the 'dead rebels of Ireland'.[129] The presence of Sinn Féin flags in the parade and at the Exhibition Gardens led to a town hall meeting of 3,000 people in protest of 'enemy' emblems being displayed.[130] This new tone culminated in the 1920 parade masterminded by Mannix, which saw Irish-Australian Victoria Cross awardees lead the parade on white chargers. As Brenda Niall remarks, the day was 'pure theatre', 'it was a tremendous spectacle, with complex, contradictory meanings'.[131]

After years of unity and welcome being at the heart of Melbourne's St Patrick's Day parades, the 1920 parade struck a different tone in the increasingly sectarian atmosphere of the time. The previous year's parade had been cancelled due to the influenza pandemic, and Niall considers 1920 to be 'a confident, noisy, aggressive demonstration' of Irish and Catholic presence and power in the city.[132] The spectacle aroused fears in Melbourne society, including among Australian Catholics who felt that there was a strong spirit of socialism and anti-imperialism in the day. The following year was much calmer, though the carrying of the Union Jack at the head of the procession did cause outrage, and a group of men rushed the flagbearer, temporarily taking the flag, before the police retrieved it and arrested them. For the rest of the parade, the police escorted a 'somewhat scared looking individual bearing the Union Jack' behind the Irish and Australian flags.[133] In 1922, the Melbourne City Council banned the parade.[134] Irish representatives from Ballarat, Bendigo and other Victorian towns descended on Melbourne in protest and joined the parade that went ahead, without council approval and in spite of terrible weather, with Archbishop Mannix at the helm.[135] At the same time, parish societies marched (with council permission) at a local level.[136] The following day, Mannix declared that they did not mean 'to give offence to anybody, but they did not mean to allow anybody to offend them with impunity'. He continued that they 'wanted to live in friendship with their neighbours, but they were not going to allow their neighbours to walk over them that day, or any other day'.[137] The aggressive determination seen in 1920 had not gone away.

In Chicago, the response to Ireland's changing position on St Patrick's Day celebrations was limited. Parades continued to be foregone with preference for charitable works and private banquets and balls. Politicians sought to win favour with their Irish employees by giving all city employees of Irish parentage the day off, unless they were members of the police or fire departments.[138] In the evenings, grand banquets were held by the United Celtic-American Societies, even in 1919 when the threat of the influenza pandemic was not enough to stop 10,000 guests from dressing in green, white and gold before hearing a description of Sinn Féin's policies.[139] The main presence in the streets were fundraising efforts by Chicago Irish girls and women. In 1916, three hundred women sold shamrocks on behalf of the Catholic Woman's League to raise funds for their work with the 'friendless and homeless girls' of Chicago.[140] Leonora Z. Meder, former commissioner for public welfare and future candidate for Chicago mayor, was one of the women selling shamrocks. The following year, large advertisements in the city's newspapers proclaimed St Patrick's Day as a 'tag day' in 1917, with 5,000 'Chicago Irish girls' selling tags in aid of the Irish-American Relief Association and '200,000 hungry women and children' in Ireland.[141] While Melbourne's parades became increasingly contentious throughout the Irish revolutionary period, Chicago's Irish societies retreated into the ballrooms and banqueting halls of the middle and upper classes. Though balls were filled with rousing speeches in support of Irish republicanism, they were behind closed doors. The impact of nationalist infighting and class splits had made its way into the city-wide organising committees of the St Patrick's Day parades. As no compromise could be found, the previously masculine public presence of St Patrick's Day, with its militias and marching bands, became increasingly localised and focused upon less contentious feminine charity work. Attendance at Catholic Mass and a focus on respectability was emphasised by Irish-American and Catholic organisations as Irish nationalist fervour became confused and splintered.

CONCLUSION

Irish diasporic identity, as well as cultural and political nationalism, had to work within the priorities and parameters of the host country. The Irish in Melbourne managed to create St Patrick's Day events which emphasised loyalty to both Irish nationalism and British imperialism. As many speeches detailed, the Irish in Australia had to remain faithful to their home country and not lose their national identity (however they understood that) in order to commit to their Australian brethren. In a similar way, St Patrick's Day events in Chicago emphasised the heritage of the Irish in America and the positive influence they had on the United States' republican history. Irish events in both cities focused on loyalty to Ireland and held up their new home as the ideal for Irish society to aim for. Within this was the way that Irish and Irish Catholic societal and political freedoms should be achieved: in Melbourne it was by setting a good example and proving that Irish people could be trusted with authority and political freedoms; in Chicago it was by supporting the overthrow of imperialism and the 'old' in order to give oppressed peoples time to prove themselves equal to any other. Criticism of the old order was accepted in both societies because it was done with distance from Britain and Ireland, and within the parameters of acceptance in each new context. This fundamentally shifted during the First World War, when criticism of the status quo was unacceptable to many, particularly if it was under a banner of Catholicism. In the war's aftermath, and with the War of Independence in Ireland, Melbourne's St Patrick's Day parades became the site of performative and, in the eyes of many, aggressive anti-imperialism and Catholic pride. Chicago conversely retreated inside for its political speeches, leaving the public space to be claimed by less hostile and usually sober female fundraisers. The claiming of public space for the performance of Irish pride, for so long the focus of Chicago's Irish societies, had effectively switched in Melbourne and Chicago by 1922.

In both cities, public events allowed for the participation of women and children in community events, though processions remained a male-only spectacle for many years. Special church services opened the day, and members of the clergy gave speeches and blessed parade banners. The religious services meant that families could join together to begin the day of celebration. Children were also involved in more public spectacles through Sunday school pageants and sports days expanding Irish pride and identity to new generations. St Patrick's Day was an opportunity for community leaders to present a particular image of Irishness to the wider world, but it was also a time to set an example of what they expected from members of that community. By celebrating in a public space, they were also carving out a space for the Irish communities in the city and demonstrating the power wielded in local politics, which allowed them to be escorted by police officers and close down public routes for the duration of the procession. This power was not wielded by other nationalities on their national days, and while the Irish organisers were proud of this power, it also drew comment from opponents. Organisers used their networks within the religious and Irish secular community to present an Irish identity in each city which incorporated the intersectional connections and affinities of their fellow citizens, aiming to improve the position of Irish people and their institutions within Melbourne and Chicago society and around the world. These were the power brokers who influenced how cultural affinity was translated into an Irish identity for younger generations, Irish people elsewhere and the wider world.

NOTES

1. Kenneth Moss, 'St Patrick's Day celebrations and the formation of Irish-American identity, 1845–1875', *Journal of Social History*, 29:1 (1995), pp. 125–48.
2. Mike Cronin and Daryl Adair, *The Wearing of the Green: A History of St Patrick's Day* (London: Routledge, 2006).
3. David Fitzpatrick, *Irish Emigration, 1801–1921* (Dublin: Economic & Social History Society of Ireland, 1984), p. 36.
4. David Cannadine, 'The transformation of civic ritual in modern Britain: The Colchester Oyster Feast', *Past & Present*, 9 (1982), pp. 107–30.
5. Belchem, 'Liverpool-Irish'.
6. Bourke, *Catholic Church*, p. 10; *Melbourne Times*, 11 March 1843.
7. 'Party Processions Prevention Act' (1846), 10 Vic. No. 1; *Melbourne Morning Herald*, 19 March 1851.
8. *Port Phillip Gazette*, 18 March 1846; Victorian Census, 1841.
9. Ibid., 14 March 1846.
10. *Age*, 26 March 1856, 17 March 1858; *Age*, 19 March 1859.
11. *Port Phillip Gazette*, 18 March 1846.
12. *Melbourne Morning Herald*, 18 March 1852.
13. Ibid., 19 March 1852.
14. Charles Gavan Duffy, *My Life in Two Hemispheres*, II (London, 1898, repr. Dublin: Irish University Press, 1969), pp. 141, 148.
15. James Kelly, '"No dumb Ireland": Robert Burns and Irish cultural nationalism in the nineteenth-century', *Eire-Ireland*, 47:3&4 (2012), pp. 251–68.
16. *Melbourne Morning Herald*, 20 March 1850.
17. Ibid., 19 March 1851.
18. Donald M. MacRaild, '"No Irish need apply": The origins and persistence of a prejudice', *Labour History Review*, 78 (2013), pp. 269–99.
19. *Daily Commercial Register*, 22 March 1849; *Daily Atlas*, 23 March 1849.
20. *Chicago Daily Journal*, 17 March 1858.
21. Ibid., 21 March 1850.
22. *Chicago Daily Times*, 2 March 1855.
23. *Chicago Daily Journal*, 18 March 1850.
24. Sam Haselby, *The Origins of American Religious Nationalism* (Oxford: Oxford University Press, 2015), p. 21.
25. *Chicago Daily Journal*, 23 March 1850.
26. *Irish American Weekly*, 3 April 1852.
27. *Western Tablet*, 20 March 1852.
28. Moss, 'St Patrick's Day celebrations'.
29. *Chicago Republican*, 19 March 1867.
30. The splits of 1860 were due to the Society's fall into political partisanship and financial mismanagement. *Argus*, 10 February 1860.

31. *Age*, 18 March 1861; *Argus*, 18 March 1862.
32. *Argus*, 19 March 1860.
33. *Chicago Daily Times*, 19 March 1855.
34. *Chicago Daily Journal*, 16 and 18 March 1861.
35. *New York Times*, 27 March 1864.
36. *Irish People*, 23 April 1864.
37. *Chicago Tribune*, 17 March 1864.
38. *Chicago Daily Herald*, 11 March 1860.
39. *Chicago Tribune*, 14 June 1862.
40. Ibid., 18 March 1863.
41. Susan G. Davis, *Parades and Power: Street Theatre in Nineteenth-Century Philadelphia* (Berkeley: University of California Press, 1988), p. 6.
42. *Chicago Evening Journal*, 18 March 1867.
43. *Chicago Republican*, 19 March 1867.
44. *Argus*, 19 March 1867.
45. Ibid.
46. *Advocate*, 21 March 1868.
47. *Argus*, 18 March 1868.
48. *Chicago Republican*, 16 March 1866.
49. *Chicago Evening Journal*, 16 March 1866.
50. *Chicago Republican*, 16 March 1866.
51. Ibid.
52. Oliver MacDonagh, 'Irish culture and nationalism translated: St Patrick's Day, 1888, in Australia', in Oliver MacDonagh, W. F. Mandle and Pauric Travers (eds), *Irish Culture and Nationalism, 1750–1950* (London: Macmillan Press Ltd, 1983), pp. 69–82.
53. *Advocate*, 18 March 1868.
54. Ibid., 27 March 1869.
55. Ibid.
56. *Western Catholic*, 16 March 1872.
57. *Chicago Tribune*, 18 March 1870.
58. *Chicago Republican*, 19 March 1867, 18 March 1868; *Chicago Post*, 15 March 1873.
59. *Western Catholic*, 22 March 1873.
60. *Daily Inter Ocean*, 14 March 1874.
61. *Chicago Republican*, 18 March 1868.
62. *Western Catholic*, 22 March 1873.
63. Ibid.
64. *Chicago Republican*, 16 March 1866.
65. *Quincy Daily Whig*, 14 May 1874; *Chicago Evening Journal*, 19 March 1866.
66. The 1866 St Patrick's Day banquet was the second anniversary banquet for the Chicago St Patrick's Society; the St George's Society was established in 1860. The Illinois St Andrew's Society had the oldest vintage,

having been established in 1846. The St David's Society (est. 1852) was not explicitly mentioned in St Patrick's Day celebrations. *Chicago Evening Journal*, 19 March 1866; Tanja Bueltmann and Donald M. MacRaild, *The English Diaspora in North America: Migration, Ethnicity and Association, 1730s–1950s* (Manchester: Manchester University Press, 2017), pp. 34–51; Pierce, *History of Chicago*, vol. 2, p. 17.
67. *Chicago Evening Journal*, 19 March 1866.
68. *Argus*, 18 March 1870, 18 March 1873.
69. Ibid., 18 March 1870.
70. *Age*, 15 March 1871; *Australasian*, 18 March 1871.
71. Victorian Census, 1871.
72. *Argus*, 18 March 1870.
73. *Age*, 18 March 1876; *Argus*, 18 March 1876.
74. *Argus*, 19 March 1872.
75. Ibid. Joseph Rowan was also a member of the CYMS and Sodality of the BVM.
76. *Argus*, 19 March 1875.
77. *Australasian*, 30 March 1878.
78. *Argus*, 25 March 1878.
79. Ibid., 18 March 1879; *Advocate*, 17 March 1883; *Argus*, 19 March 1883.
80. William Davis in Malcolm Campbell, 'Irish nationalism and immigrant assimilation: Comparing the United States and Australia', *Australasian Journal of American Studies*, 15:2 (1996), pp. 24–43.
81. *Argus*, 18 March 1881; *Australasian*, 19 March 1881.
82. *Argus*, 18 March 1881, 18 March 1884.
83. Ibid., 18 March 1882. In 1886 there was also a concert of Irish music at the South Melbourne Town Hall to raise money for the St Peter's and St Paul's School: *Argus*, 18 March 1886.
84. *Age*, 18 March 1882; *Argus*, 18 March 1885.
85. *Argus*, 18 March 1881.
86. Ibid., 18 March 1879.
87. Cooper, 'Melbourne visions'.
88. *Hyde Park Herald*, 23 March 1885.
89. *Daily Illinois State Journal*, 17 March 1885.
90. *Chicago Tribune*, 17 March 1883.
91. *Western Catholic*, 12 March 1881. In 1883 the average wage for a labourer in Chicago was between $5.50 and $9: *Biennial Report of the Bureau of Labor Statistics* (Sacramento: Office of State Bureau of Labor Statistics, 1884), p. 252.
92. *Western Catholic*, 22 March 1884.
93. Charles Fanning, *Finley Peter Dunne and Mr Dooley: The Chicago Years* (Lexington: University of Kentucky Press, 1978), p. 167.
94. *Chicago Tribune*, 17 March 1883.

95. *Western Catholic*, 22 March 1884.
96. *Daily Illinois State Register*, 18 March 1881.
97. *Western Catholic*, 26 February 1881.
98. *New York Times*, 9 February 1880.
99. *Daily Inter Ocean*, 17 March 1881.
100. *New York Times*, 9 February 1886.
101. *Morning Star*, 18 February 1890.
102. *Daily Illinois State Register*, 18 March 1884.
103. *Chicago Herald*, 18 March 1891.
104. Quinn, *Father Mathew's Crusade*, p. 9.
105. *Daily Inter Ocean*, 2 February 1892.
106. Ibid., 13 March 1892.
107. Ibid., 18 March 1896.
108. *Argus*, 18 March 1890.
109. Ibid., 18 March 1886.
110. *Weekly Times*, 21 March 1891.
111. McConville, *Croppies, Celts*, pp. 101–3.
112. *Age*, 18 March 1918.
113. *Chicago Daily News*, 16 March 1901.
114. Ibid.
115. Fanning, *Finley Peter Dunne*, p. 166.
116. *Chicago Daily News*, 15 March 1902.
117. Ibid., 17 March 1908.
118. McConville, *Croppies, Celts*, pp. 101–3.
119. Adair and Cronin, *The Wearing of the Green*, p. 103.
120. *Advocate*, 21 March 1914.
121. Ibid., 14 March 1914.
122. Dianne Hall, 'Irish republican women in Australia: Kathleen Barry and Linda Kearns's tour in 1924–5', *Irish Historical Studies*, 43:163 (2019), pp. 73–93.
123. *Argus*, 15 March 1915.
124. *Age*, 14 March 1916.
125. Malcolm Campbell, 'Emigrant responses to war and revolution, 1914–21: Irish opinion in the United States and Australia', *Irish Historical Studies*, 32:125 (May 2000), pp. 75–92.
126. O'Farrell, *Catholic Church*, p. 229.
127. Ibid., pp. 196, 211.
128. *Tribune*, 21 March 1918.
129. *Zeehan and Dundas Herald* (Tas.), 22 March 1918.
130. Ibid.
131. Brenda Niall, *Mannix* (Melbourne: Text Publishing, 2016), p. 146.
132. Ibid.
133. *Age*, 21 March 1921.
134. *Herald*, 21 February 1922.

135. *Age*, 2 March 1922; *Advocate*, 2 March 1922; *Geelong Advertiser*, 20 March 1922; *Advocate*, 23 March 1922.
136. *Record* (Emerald Hill), 11 March 1922.
137. *Advocate*, 23 March 1922.
138. *Chicago Daily News*, 16 March 1917, 17 March 1919.
139. Ibid., 17 March 1919.
140. Ibid., 17 March 1916.
141. Ibid., 16 March 1917.

8

Conclusion

In 2019, the Irish Government released referendum legislation on the extension of voting rights to the Irish abroad. An Oireachtas *Spotlight* report noted that the extension of voting rights to citizens residing outside of the state 'confronts a fundamental theoretical question regarding how to appropriately conceptualise a political community'.[1] The conceptualisation of an Irish political and cultural community was a constant concern of culture brokers in nineteenth- and early twentieth-century Melbourne and Chicago, as they tried to balance adjusting to a new life abroad while retaining a shared sense of Irish identity. As this book has emphasised, the different financial resources available to Irish migrant groups led to the uneven evolution of community institutions in the two cities. While Melbourne's Irish prioritised compromise and good relations with other settlers for most of the nineteenth century, Chicago became a hotbed of short-lasting civil associations and a dedicated strand of Irish nationalism. By the turn of the twentieth century, Chicago's passion had largely coalesced around American priorities of political power. Meanwhile in Melbourne, that quest for political power coincided with more militant Catholicism and a renewed interest in the position of Ireland within the British empire. The establishment of the Irish Free State and the subsequent Civil War in 1922 threw Irish diasporic organising into confusion, prompting Irish communities in Melbourne and Chicago to refocus with a renewed emphasis on the needs and aspirations of Irish life within the diaspora. Indeed, this had been the advice of Éamon de Valera in 1922 when he noted that the diaspora had 'primary obligations to those lands' that they were now citizens of, and the Dáil would therefore expect nothing from them.[2]

The Irish diaspora today is a key policy area for the Irish Government. The diaspora provides a key resource for Ireland's economy, tourism and international standing. In the nineteenth century, Ireland acted as a crucial resource for the building of cities and communities abroad. Irish women left Ireland as members of religious orders, as hopeful emigrants and as forced exiles, establishing schools and hospitals, joining trade unions, and bringing up their children surrounded by Irish and Irish Catholic neighbours, teachers and religious leaders. Irish men joined them, in the community halls, stockyards and increasingly the Catholic Church. Between these men and women, strong and multi-generational communities in Melbourne and Chicago were established which, though frequently prioritising Catholicism, maintained a strong connection to Ireland, both its reality and what it represented to those who had grown up hearing stories of a faraway homeland.

This book has considered the influences on Irish community life and the promotion of a particular Irish identity in two distinct cities: Melbourne and Chicago. Using Nancy Green's call to 'understand both the structural constraints and individual cultural choices framing the migration experience',[3] it has utilised a contrasting comparative methodology to complicate the narrative of Irish community-building abroad. These structural and individual contexts have been explored through four central themes: ethnic and religious associational culture, educational provision, nationalism and public performance. Across all of these themes, tensions between the individual, institution and the state impacted how ideas of belonging to an 'Irish' community abroad could be articulated at different times. While these local tensions ultimately shaped the articulation of Irishness, the tools for creating an affinity with Irishness were passed throughout the diaspora, via newspapers, the spread of tradition and the migrant experience itself. Organisations like the Land League spread throughout the diaspora to fundraise for Irish nationalist and land reform objectives, but how these objectives were understood and 'sold' was framed differently. In Chicago, for example, land reform was aligned with the struggles of an international industrial working class, while in Melbourne, a less industrialised city, support for the Land League was brought into a wider fight for home rule. In both instances, however, the language of boycott was deployed. The press allowed news of international Irish nationalism to be spread, to inspire and to warn. In doing so, distinct Irish communities were able to advance their own understandings of Irish 'progress' and belonging by pointing to the activities of other communities within the Irish diaspora. Irish community leaders operated within a world which spread physically and mentally across national boundaries. Their positions within global cities like Melbourne and Chicago provided them with a multitude of tools to support the production, reproduction and promotion of an 'Irish' community which responded to the specific needs of that locale.

Urban centres have never been *just* part of a national history. Global and urban history approaches have demonstrated the multitude of influences that flow in and out of cities, pushing the city limits outwards while focusing on the networks that keep people tied to particular neighbourhoods. The city is inherently global, and ethnic communities within cities are caught between layers of the local, national and international. The Irish communities in Melbourne and Chicago were simultaneously part of multiple worlds, while the cities that they inhabited acted as intricate webs of financial, mercantile, cultural, social and political ties. An Irish person in nineteenth-century Melbourne may have sent their child to an Irish Catholic parish school and attended St Francis' Catholic Church, but they may have bought groceries from an Italian, chatted to a Scot on the tram, or shopped for herbs in Chinatown. We know that they lived on land which had been taken from its original indigenous inhabitants and probably dressed in clothes which had been made in mills in Lancashire using cotton grown in India and dyes from America. An Irish person in Chicago operated in a similarly global city. Both peoples were probably unaware of the myriad international influences on their everyday world, focusing on the explicitly articulated connections that still made them part of the 'Irish' diaspora. It is these consciously articulated connections that this book has focused upon to draw out the transnational tools that linked the Irish diaspora across national and city borders, as well as the differences in how Irish community life emerged, was sustained and adapted in the two cities.

As Anthony King notes, the city as a static and fixed entity is largely a fiction.[4] In the nineteenth century, particularly as Melbourne and Chicago were settled and transformed by hundreds of thousands of immigrants, what constituted 'the city' was constantly in flux. Migrants moved around the expanding settlement as city limits sought to find and fix a boundary. Religious parishes were one of these attempts at boundary-laying, both in terms of geography and identity. In Chicago, the white Catholic parish retained its prominence in organising life until well into the 1950s,[5] while in Melbourne, where ethnic parishes were less vital, the suburb became a key tool in exclusion and inclusion. This book provides an ethnic history perspective on the development of these parish organisations, beginning thirty years before most studies of the Irish in Chicago. Chicago's ethnic parishes were established to combat a particular situation in the 1840s, and they maintained their power for over a century. The seemingly disjointed network of local communities which both bonded and excluded Chicago citizens became a focus of both urban historians and sociologists with the Chicago School in the 1920s and 1930s.⁶ Across the nineteenth and early twentieth centuries, parish schools and networks knitted together disparate groups of Irish and Irish-descended people across multiple generations, helping to connect them through employment, political nepotism and parish life. These were complemented by city-wide organisations often rooted in politics and middle-class ideas of respectability and culture. The connection between religious and ethnic association was built into the foundations of Chicago's Irish community life from the establishment of the ethnic parish, fashioning belonging as a trifactor of faith, ethnicity and race.

In Melbourne, the parish or suburb also retained an important role in the organisation of associational culture, particularly as friendly and benefit societies spread across the city. As in Chicago, class played a vital role in the development of associational culture and people, Irish and not, became increasingly separated geographically by class and economic resources. In Melbourne, ethnic identity was celebrated by secular and religious organisations for most of the nineteenth century. The arrival of Catholics from southern Europe and, later, from across Asia, complicated the assumption that to be Catholic was to be Irish. This lack of a plural Catholicism in Melbourne lasted well into the twentieth century and was integral to the shape of both ethnic and religious life in the city during the nineteenth. It was this Irish dominance of the Catholic Church which allowed for an ethnically religious 'safe space' and, consequently, encouraged the multi-denominational celebration of associational 'Irishness'. Though the Catholic Church in Melbourne continued to be dominated by Irish leaders until the end of the twentieth century, the loss of state funding for separate Catholic Irish activities forced a shift in the wider ethnic associationalism of the city, bringing Irish and Catholic identities together more explicitly in the civil and political sphere as well as the religious.

In both cities, Avtar Brah's concept of the diaspora space is particularly interesting in considering the ways that parish boundaries sequestered Irish Catholics from other inhabitants of each city, while wider discrimination, both religious and ethnic, simultaneously encouraged cooperation. St Patrick's Day parades in Chicago, for example, included Polish and Italian marchers, providing both a symbol of Catholic solidarity and the perpetuation of a collective memory of exile and trauma. The claiming of public space allowed for the display of Irish power, while also encouraging connection with a wider story suited to the concerns of the day – often related to small nation struggle, religious and ethnic persecution, and exile. As Brah notes, 'there is traffic within cultural formations of the subordinated groups, and . . . these journeys are not *always* mediated through the dominant culture(s)'.[7] Of course, as Irish Catholics increasingly controlled city, union and religious power, we must also consider the moment that Irish Catholics became part of the dominant culture in both cities.

This book began with the Redmond brothers speaking about a 'Unity in Trinity', a concept which would support the idea of a 'Greater Ireland' that connected Irish diaspora spaces across the globe. This was an abstract idea but found tangibility in the transnational networks that Irish people maintained. Edmund Dwyer wrote to his father in Co. Limerick in 1862 with delight. Dwyer, a labourer in Chicago, had received a letter from his mother's relative in Melbourne, the Victorian Premier John O'Shanassy.[8] Dwyer had been encouraged by his siblings, who lived throughout Illinois and Massachusetts, to write to O'Shanassy after reading about him in newspapers that their father had sent from Ireland to the United States.[9] O'Shanassy recommended that 'Australia is on the whole a good country for an honest hardworking man, or a man of capital . . . [but] He does not like to recommend me to leave Chicago', fearing that Dwyer would not be able to gain permanent work in Melbourne. Letters, newspaper reports and family networks enabled this sense of a Greater Ireland much more than the words of a politician. These networks were maintained at all levels of society, with women religious swapping stories of diaspora life with sisters, both religious and familial, in other parts of the world, and Jesuits frequently writing back to Dublin. Formal and informal networks united Irish people in a shared sense of belonging. However, this sense of belonging was articulated in very distinct ways.

While the historiography of the Irish in both cities has traditionally privileged male experiences, this book has emphasised the overlapping spheres of feminine and masculine influence. Male associational culture and politics feature heavily in newspapers and government documents. However, it is the contention of this book that scholars of diaspora communities need to look to the influence of women and pay attention to the position of children in community life in order to more fully understand how Irish societies abroad were sustained and expanded. As David Emmons writes, for Irish Americans, the '"truth" of the story was in its ability to tether one generation to those that came before it, to keep the past alive and lively'.[10] Schools staffed by Irish women and men, many of which were funded by charity and community fundraising, were part of this tethering. Including children in

St Patrick's Day parades and celebrations such as the 1851 Victorian separation festivals helped solidify this link between the past, present and future, writing an Irish presence into the histories of these cities while simultaneously emphasising the community ties which bound the Irish abroad together.

Throughout *Forging Identities*, I have proposed and employed the concept of 'foundational identities' to explore the multiple influences on the Irish communities of Melbourne and Chicago. This concept provides important opportunities for scholars of identity from across disciplines. There is still much work to be done on the experiences of Irish women in the diaspora, and the role that they had on the shaping and persistence of Irish ethnic identity. One way of approaching this is to bring the growing historiographies of women religious and the history of education together with more mainstream histories of the Irish diaspora. This book adds to that growing knowledge, but there is still much more to be done. The role of laywomen has also been understudied, partially due to a lack of records but potentially because of the ease in which certain other voices have been raised and documented. There has been a surge in important work on Irishwomen's activism, in Ireland and the diaspora, recently, building upon the landmark work of Margaret Ward, Louise Ryan and Linda Connolly.[11] It is my hope that researchers continue to look to newly available or underutilised records to find the place of women, alongside their husbands, brothers and friends, in the story of Irish ethnic identity abroad and at home.

In drawing together men and women in this book, the concept of 'culture brokers' as priest, publican and politician is complicated and expanded to include teacher and nun – men *and women* with cultural authority who had the ability to move between classes, to access the highest echelons of power and to distribute it, through education, charity and community networks. In doing so, they helped to shape connections based on ethnicity and religion, and to sustain them across cities booming with people and resources, and across multiple generations and periods of migration. This book has focused on the Irish communities in Melbourne and Chicago. It does not seek to make grand statements about the Irish diaspora generally, but to explore the myriad ways that community organisers adapted visions of Irish identity to suit the needs of specific local groups of the Irish diaspora. In doing so it has utilised Alan O'Day's 'mutative ethnicity'. As mutative ethnicity is often adapted unconsciously, the role of education was vital in shaping ideas from a young age and sending these ideas back into the community through children's parents, neighbours and the parish organisations that they became involved with. Identification with Irish belonging and community therefore became more than just a symbol to be engaged with on St Patrick's Day. It was a part of everyday life.

NOTES

1. *Spotlight: Overseas Voting in Presidential Elections: Representative Democracy, Electoral Integrity and the Situation in EU States* (Oireachtas Library & Research Service: 2019), p. 4.
2. Quoted in Keown, 'The Irish Race Conference, 1922'.
3. Nancy L. Green, 'The comparative method and postmodern structuralism: New perspectives for migration studies', *Journal of American Ethnic History*, 13:4 (1994), pp. 3–22.
4. Anthony D. King, 'Boundaries, networks, and cities: Playing and replaying diasporas and histories', in Thomas Bender and Alev Cinar (eds), *Urban Imaginaries: Locating the Modern City* (Minneapolis: University of Minnesota Press, 2007), pp. 1–16.
5. Barrett, *History from the Bottom Up*; McMahon, *What Parish*.
6. Tom Hulme, *After the Shock City: Urban Culture and the Making of Modern Citizenship* (Woodbridge: Boydell Press, 2019).
7. Brah, *Cartographies of Diaspora*, p. 209.
8. Edmund Dwyer Jr to Edmund Dwyer Sr, Chicago, 6 April 1862. Illinois 23rd Infantry, Co. B, Civil War (Pensions Records, Fold3.com).
9. Ibid., 23 September 1860.
10. Emmons, *Beyond the Pale*, p. 337.
11. McCarthy, *Reform and Respectability*; Niall Whelehan, 'Sacco and Vanzetti, Mary Donovan and transatlantic radicalism in the 1920s', *Irish Historical Studies*, 44:165 (2020), pp. 131–46; Dianne Hall, 'Irish republican women in Australia', pp. 73–93; Mary McAuliffe and Liz Gillis, *Richmond Barracks 1916: We Were There. 77 Women of the Easter Rising* (Dublin: Dublin City Council, 2016); Louise Ryan and Margaret Ward (eds), *Irish Women and Nationalism: Soldiers, New Women and Wicked Hags* (Dublin: Irish Academic Press, 2004); Marie Coleman, 'Compensating Irish female revolutionaries, 1916–1923', *Women's History Review*, 26:6 (2017), pp. 915–34; Linda Connolly, *The Irish Women's Movement: From Revolution to Devolution* (Abingdon: Palgrave, 2002); Margaret Ward, *Unmanageable Revolutionaries: Women and Irish Nationalism* (London: Pluto Press, 1995).

Bibliography

PRIMARY SOURCES

Manuscripts Collections

Chicago

Abraham Lincoln Presidential Museum and Library, Springfield, IL (ALPML)
    J. Alonzo Leonard Papers
Archdiocese of Chicago Archives (ACA)
    Bishops Quarter and Van de Velde Diary
    Historical Records – Various Bishops
    Madaj Collection
    St Vincent de Paul Society Administrative Records
    William Onahan Diary and Papers
Chicago History Museum and Research Library (CHMRL)
    Henry W. Magee Papers
    Mulligan Papers
Sisters of Mercy Heritage Center, Belmont, NC
    Chicago Regional Community Papers
University of Notre Dame Archives, South Bend, IN (NDA)
    Orestes A. Brownson Papers

Melbourne

Melbourne Diocesan Historical Commission (MDHC)
    Irish National Foresters Papers
    Archbishop Goold Papers and Diary
Public Record Office of Victoria (PROV)
    Inward Overseas Passenger Lists (British Ports)

State Library of Victoria Archives (SLV)
    John Winter Papers

Dublin

Dublin Diocesan Archives (DDA)
    Cardinal Cullen Papers
    Uncatalogued letters
Irish Jesuit Archives (JAD)
    Melbourne Collection
    The St Patrick's College Gazette
National Library of Ireland
    John Devoy Papers
    John Redmond Papers

United Kingdom

British Library
    Carnarvon Papers

Online

Ancestry.com
    Australia, Death Index, 1787–1988
    Illinois, Databases of Illinois Veterans Index, 1775–1995
Fold3.com
    Civil War Pensions Records

City and National Publications

Chicago

General Directory and Business Advertiser of the City of Chicago for the Year 1844 (Chicago: Ellis & Fergus Printers, 1844)

The Chicago City Directory, and Business Advertiser (Chicago: Robert Fergus Book & Job Printer, 1855)

T. M. Halpin, *Chicago City Directory, for the Year 1861–62* (Chicago: Halpin & Bailey Publishers, 1861)

— *Chicago City Directory, for the Year 1863–4* (Chicago: Halpin & Bailey Publishers, 1863)

Edwards' Chicago Business Director: Embracing a Classified List of all Trades, Professions and Pursuits in the City of Chicago, for the Year 1866–7 (Chicago: Edwards, Greenough & Deved, 1866)

Edwards' Chicago Business Director: Embracing a Classified List of all Trades, Professions and Pursuits in the City of Chicago, for the Year 1868–9 (Chicago: Edwards & Co. Publishers, 1868)

Edwards' Chicago Business Director: Embracing a Classified List of all Trades, Professions and Pursuits in the City of Chicago, for the Year 1869–70 (Chicago: Edwards & Co. Publishers, 1869)

Edwards' Chicago Business Director: Embracing a Classified List of all Trades, Professions and Pursuits in the City of Chicago, for the Year 1870–71 (Chicago: Richard Edwards Publishers, 1870)

The Lakeside Annual Directory of the City of Chicago, 1875–6 (Chicago: Donnelly, Loyd & Co., 1875)

The Lakeside Annual Directory of the City of Chicago, 1878–9 (Chicago: Donnelly, Loyd & Co., 1878)

The Lakeside Annual Directory of the City of Chicago, 1880 (Chicago: Chicago Directory Company, 1880)

The Lakeside Annual Directory of the City of Chicago, 1882 (Chicago: Chicago Directory Co., 1882)

The Lakeside Annual Directory of the City of Chicago, 1885 (Chicago: Chicago Directory Co., 1885)

Rand McNally & Co.'s pictorial guide to Chicago: what to see and how to see it (Chicago: Rand McNally & Co., 1886)

The Lakeside Annual Directory of the City of Chicago, 1889 (Chicago: Chicago Directory Co., 1889)

Chicago Social Service Directory (Chicago: Burmeister Printing Co., 1918)

United States:

Sixth Census of the United States, 1840 (Washington, DC: Norman Ross, 1990)

Seventh Census of the United States, 1850 (Washington, DC: Robert Armstrong, 1853)

Eighth Census of the United States, 1860 (Washington, DC: Government Printing Office, 1864)

Ninth Census of the United States, 1870 (Washington, DC: Government Printing Office, 1872)

Tenth Census of the United States, 1880 (Washington, DC: Government Printing Office, 1886)

Eleventh Census of the United States, 1890 (Washington, DC: Government Printing Office, 1892)

Thirteenth Census of the United States, 1910 (Washington, DC: Government Printing Office, 1910)

Fourteenth Census of the United States, 1920 (Washington, DC: Government Printing Office, 1920)

Melbourne

Sands & McDougall Melbourne City Directory, 1869 (Sands & McDougall Publishers, 1869)
Irish-Australian Almanac and Directory (Winter & Co., 1888)
Victorian Parliamentary Debates (Victorian Hansard)
'Superintendent Summary Report', *Census of Victoria, 1854* (Melbourne: John Ferres Government Printer, 1855)
Census of Victoria, 1857 (Melbourne: John Ferres Government Printer, 1858)
Census of Victoria, 1861 (Melbourne: John Ferres Government Printer, 1861)
Census of Victoria, 1871 (Melbourne: John Ferres Government Printer, 1871)
Census of Victoria, 1881 (Melbourne: John Ferres Government Printer, 1884)
Census of Victoria, 1891 (Melbourne: Robert S. Brain Government Printer, 1892)

Australia:
The First Commonwealth Census, 1911 (Melbourne: J. Kemp Government Printer, 1911)
— *The Second Commonwealth Census, 1921* (Melbourne: H. J. Green Government Printer, 1921)

Printed Material

Anon., *General Laws of the Irish National Foresters' Benefit Society: Executive Council of Australasia* (Melbourne: 'The Reformer' Printing Company, 1888)
Anon., *Hibernian Australasian Catholic Benefit Society: 2nd Biennial Meeting of Deputies from States of Australia and New Zealand* (Sydney: Finn Brothers, 1903)
Anon., *History of the Ancient Order of Hibernians, From the Earliest Period to the Joint National Convention at Trenton, New Jersey, June 27 1898* (Cleveland: T. F. McGrath, 1898)
Anon., *Illustrated Souvenir of the Archdiocese of Chicago: Commemorating the Installation of the Most Reverend Archbishop George W. Mundelein, D.D., February 1916* (Chicago: R. H. Fleming Publishing Company, 1916)
Anon., *Manual of the Children of Mary for the Use of all Establishments, Schools and Orphan Asylums of the Sisters of Charity* (New York: P. J. Kennedy & Sons, 1867)
Anon., *Proceedings of the First National Convention of the Fenian Brotherhood, Held in Chicago, Illinois, November 1863* (Philadelphia: James Gibbons, 1863)
Anon., *Some of the Fruits of Fifty Years: Ecclesiastical Annals ... Since the Erection of Each* (Melbourne: A. H. Massina & Co., 1897)
Anon., *The Queen's Enemies in America Assembled in Convention at Chicago* (London: William Ridgway, 1886)
Anon., *Third Annual Directory of Ancient Order of Hibernians of the United States, Containing the Names and Addresses of all National, State, County,*

and Division Officers: 1884–1885 (Dayton, OH: Sweetman's Book & Job Printing House, 1884)
Abbot, Willis John, *Carter Henry Harrison: A Memoir* (New York: Dodd, Mead & Company, 1895)
Andreas, A. T., *History of Chicago from the Earliest Period to the Present Time in Three Volumes*, v2 (Chicago: The A.T. Andreas Company: 1884)
Ayer, N. W. and Son, *American Newspaper Annual* (Philadelphia: N. W. Ayer & Son, 1889)
Carboni, Raffaello, *The Eureka Stockade: The Consequence of Some Pirates Wanting on Quarter-deck a Rebellion* (Melbourne: J. P. Atkinson, 1860)
Carter, Charles Rooking, *Victoria, the British 'El Dorado' ... a Field for Emigration* (London: E. Stanford, 1879)
Clacy, Ellen, *A Lady's Visit to the Gold Diggings of Australia in 1852–53* (London: Hurst & Blackett, 1853)
Coughlin, Mary Foote, *A New Commandment: A Little Memoir ... 1859–1909* (Chicago: Sisters of the Good Shepherd, 1909)
Colbert, Elias and Everett Chamberlain, *Chicago and the Great Conflagration* (Chicago: J. S. Goodman & Co., 1872)
Dunne, Finley Peter, *Mr Dooley in the Hearts of His Countrymen* (Boston: Small, Maynard & Company, 1899)
Duffy, Charles Gavan, *My Life in Two Hemispheres*, II (London, 1898, repr. Dublin: Irish University Press, 1969)
Finn, Edmund, *The Chronicles of Early Melbourne, 1835 to 1852, Historical, Anecdotal and Personal* (Melbourne: Fergusson & Mitchell, 1888)
Flinn, John F., *History of the Chicago Police: From the Settlement ... The Mayor and Superintendent of the Force* (Chicago: Police Book Fund, 1887)
Ffrench, Charles (ed.), *Biographical History of the American Irish in Chicago* (Chicago: American Biographical Publishing Co., 1897)
Goodman, George, *The Church in Victoria During the Episcopate of Charles Perry, First Bishop of Melbourne* (London: Seeley & Co. Ltd, 1892)
Harmon, Thomas L., *Fifty Years of Parish History: Church of the Annunciation, Chicago, Ill., 1866–1916* (Chicago: D. B. Hansen & Sons, 1916)
Hogan, James Francis, *The Irish in Australia* (London: George Robinson & Co., 1888)
Howard, John W., *The First Thirty Years' Rise and Progress of the Hibernian Australasian Catholic Benefit Society* (Melbourne: John Howard, 1896)
Illinois Constitutional Convention, *Laws of the State of Illinois Enacted by the Thirty-Third General Assembly* (Springfield, IL.: H. W. Bokker, 1883)
— *The Constitution of the State ... July 2d*, A.D. *1870* (Chicago: Western News Co., 1870)
Lalor, James Fintan, 'A new nation: Proposal for an Agricultural Association between the landowners and occupiers', in John O'Leary and James Fintan Lalor, *The Writings of James Fintan Lalor* (Dublin: T. G. O'Donoghue, 1895)

McGirr, John E., *Life of the Rt. Rev. Wm. Quarter, D.D.: First Catholic Bishop of Chicago* (orig. 1849, reprinted Chicago: St Mary's Training School Press, 1920)

Milner, John and Oswald W. Brierly, *Cruise of H.M.S. Galatea, Captain ... the Duke of Edinburgh in 1867–1868* (London: Wm. H. Allen and Co., 1869)

Mulkerins, Thomas M., *Holy Family Parish Chicago: Priests and People* (Chicago: Universal Press, 1923)

Savage, John, *Fenian Heroes and Martyrs* (Boston: Patrick Donahoe, 1868)

State Bureau of Labor Statistics, *Biennial Report of the Bureau of Labor Statistics* (Sacramento: Office of State Bureau of Labor Statistics, 1884)

Stephens, James, *James Stephens, Chief Organizer of the Irish Republic. Embracing An Account of the Origin and Progress of the Fenian Brotherhood* (New York: Carleton Publisher, 1866)

Superintendent of Public Instruction, *Twelfth Biennial Report of the Superintendent of Public Instruction of Illinois: 1877–1878* (Springfield, IL: Weber & Co. State Printers, 1879)

Sweetman, Edward, Charles R. Long and John Smyth, *A History of State Education in Victoria* (Melbourne: Critchley Parker, 1922)

Tynan, Patrick J. P., *The Irish National Invincibles and Their Times* (London: Chatham & Co., 1894)

Newspapers

Chicago

Chicago Daily Journal (1844–1922)
Chicago Daily Times (1853–5)
Chicago Evening Journal (1861–96)
Chicago Post (1871–2)
Chicago Republican (1865–72)
Chicago Tribune (1847–1922)
Daily Inter Ocean (1879–1902)
Irish Citizen (1868)
Irish Republic (1867)
Leader (1855)
Pomeroy's Democrat (1869–76)
Sunday Times (1875)
Western Catholic (1872–84)
Western Tablet (1852)

United States

Cincinnati Daily Gazette (1880)
Daily Atlas (1849)

Daily Commercial Register (1849)
Daily Illinois State Register (1868–85)
Daily National Intelligencer (1854)
Irish American Weekly (1852–86)
Irish Nation (1882–6)
Irish People (1863–4)
Kansas City Times (1886)
Morning Star (1890)
New-York Freeman's Journal and Catholic Register (1842)
New York Herald (1873–89)
New York Times (1864–86)
New York Tribune (1890)
Sangamo Journal (1862)

Melbourne

Advocate (1868–1922)
Age (1854–1922)
Argus (1846–1922)
Australasian (1864–1922)
Catholic Magazine (1890)
Herald (1861–1922)
Illustrated Australian News for Home Readers (1867–75)
Independent (1883–1922)
Melbourne Courier (1845)
Melbourne Morning Herald (1850–2)
Melbourne Times (1842–3)
Port Phillip Gazette (1842–6)
Port Phillip Patriot and Melbourne Advertiser (1842–6)
Record (1922)
Standard (1908)
Tribune (1915)
Weekly Times (1891)

Australia

Ballarat Courier (1873)
Coburg Leader (1894)
Freeman's Journal (1887–1905)
Geelong Advertiser (1841–1922)
Gippsland Times (1883)
Portland Guardian and Normanby General Advertiser (1859)
Sydney Morning Herald (1891)
Zeehan and Dundas Herald (1918)

Ireland

Freeman's Journal (Dublin) (1888)

SECONDARY SOURCES

Abbott, Carl, 'Civic pride in Chicago, 1844–1860', *Journal of the Illinois State Historical Society*, 63:4 (1970), pp. 399–421

Aiken, Síobhra, '"Sinn Féin permits … in the heels of their shoes": Cumann na mBan emigrants and transatlantic revolutionary exchange', *Irish Historical Studies*, 44:165 (2020), pp. 106–30

Akenson, Donald H., *The Irish Diaspora: A Primer* (Toronto: P. D. Meany Co., 1996)

— *Small Differences: Irish Catholics and Irish Protestants 1815–1922. An International Perspective* (Montreal: McGill-Queen's University Press, 1988)

— *The Irish Education Experiment: The National System of Education in the Nineteenth Century* (Abingdon Routledge, 1970, repr. 2012)

Allen, Maree G., *The Labourers' Friends: Sisters of Mercy in Victoria and Tasmania* (West Melbourne: Hargreen Publishing Company, 1989)

Allen, Matthew, 'Sectarianism, respectability and cultural identity: The St Patrick's Total Abstinence Society and Irish Catholic temperance in mid-nineteenth century Sydney', *Journal of Religious History*, 35:3 (2011), pp. 374–92

Amos, Keith, *The Fenians in Australia, 1865–1880* (Sydney: New South Wales University Press, 1988)

Anbinder, Tyler and Hope McCaffrey, 'Which Irish men and women immigrated to the United States during the Great Famine migration of 1846–54?', *Irish Historical Studies*, 39:156 (2015), pp. 620–42

Anderson, Benedict, *Imagined Communities: Reflections on the Origin and Spread of Nationalism*, revised edn (London: Verso, 1991)

Arthure, Susan, 'Being Irish: The nineteenth century South Australian community of Baker's Flat', *Archaeologies*, 11 (2015), pp. 169–88

Bailey, Craig, *Irish London: Middle-class Migration in the Global Eighteenth Century* (Liverpool: Liverpool University Press, 2013)

Bairner, Alan, 'Ireland, sport and empire', in Keith Jeffery (ed.), *An Irish Empire? Aspects of Ireland and the British Empire* (Manchester: Manchester University Press, 1996), pp. 57–76

Barker, Hannah, *Newspapers and English Society 1695–1855* (London: Routledge, 2014)

Barr, Colin, *Ireland's Empire: The Roman Catholic Church in the English-Speaking World, 1829–1914* (Cambridge: Cambridge University Press, 2020)

Barr, Colin and Hilary M. Carey (eds), *Religion and Greater Ireland: Christianity and Irish Global Network, 1750–1950* (Montreal: McGill-Queen's University Press, 2015)

Barrett, James R., *History from the Bottom Up and the Inside Out: Ethnicity, Race, and Identity in Working-Class History* (Durham, NC: Duke University Press, 2017)
— *The Irish Way: Becoming American in the Multiethnic City* (London: Penguin Books, 2012)
— *Work and Community in the Jungle: Chicago's Packinghouse Workers, 1894–1922* (Urbana: University of Illinois Press, 1990)
Barth, Gunther, *Instant Cities: Urbanization and the Rise of San Francisco and Denver* (Oxford: Oxford University Press, 1975)
Bayly, C. A., *Empire and Information: Intelligence Gathering and Social Communication in India, 1780–1870* (Cambridge: Cambridge University Press, 1996)
Bayor, Ronald H. and Timothy Meagher, *The New York Irish* (Baltimore: Johns Hopkins University Press, 1996)
Beckert, Sven, 'Institution-building and class formation: How nineteenth-century bourgeois organized', in Graeme Morton, Boudien de Vries and R. J. Morris (eds), *Civil Society, Associations and Urban Places: Class, Nation and Culture in Nineteenth-Century Europe* (Aldershot: Ashgate, 2006), pp. 17–38
Belchem, John, 'Hub and diaspora: Liverpool and transnational Labour', *Labour History Review*, 75:1 (2010), pp. 20–9
— *Irish, Catholic and Scouse: The History of the Liverpool Irish, 1800–1939* (Liverpool: Liverpool University Press, 2007)
— 'The Liverpool-Irish enclave', in Donald M. MacRaild (ed.), *The Great Famine and Beyond: Irish Migrants in Britain in the Nineteenth and Twentieth Centuries* (Dublin: Irish Academic Press, 2000), pp. 126–46
— 'Nationalism, republicanism and exile: Irish emigrants and the revolutions of 1848', *Past & Present*, 146 (1995), pp. 103–35
— 'The Irish in Britain, United States and Australia: Some comparative reflections on labour history', in Patrick Buckland and John Belchem (eds), *Irish in British Labour History: Conference Proceedings in Irish Studies* (Liverpool: University of Liverpool Press, 1993), pp. 19–27
Belich, James, *Replenishing the Earth: The Settler Revolution and the Rise of the Anglo-World, 1783–1939* (Oxford: Oxford University Press, 2009)
Bew, Paul, *Land and the National Question in Ireland, 1858–82* (Dublin: Gill & Macmillan, 1978)
Blainey, Geoffrey, *A History of Victoria* (2nd edn, Cambridge: Cambridge University Press, 2013)
Blee, Jill, *Eureka: The Story of Australia's Most Famous Rebellion* (Woolombi: Exile Publishing, 2007)
Bourke, D. F., *A History of the Catholic Church in Victoria* (East Melbourne: Catholic Bishops of Victoria, 1988)
Bowen, Desmond, *Paul Cardinal Cullen and the Shaping of Modern Irish Catholicism* (Dublin: Gill and Macmillan, 1983)

Brah, Avtar, *Cartographies of Diaspora: Contesting Identities* (London: Routledge, 1996)

Breathnach, Ciara, 'Irish Catholic identity in 1870s Otago, New Zealand', *Immigrants and Minorities*, 31:1 (2013), pp. 1–26

Bressey, Caroline, 'Surfacing black and brown bodies in the digital archives: domestic workers in late nineteenth-century Australia', *Journal of Historical Geography*, 70 (2020), pp. 1–11

Broome, Richard, *Aboriginal Victorians: A History Since 1800* (Crows Nest: Allen & Unwin, 2005)

Brophy, Thomas J., 'Rivalry between Irish associations in San Francisco over the second funeral of Terence Bellew McManus, 1861', in Jennifer Kelly and R. V. Comerford (eds), *Associational Culture in Ireland and Abroad* (Dublin: Irish Academic Press, 2010), pp. 67–84

Brosnan, Kathleen, 'Public presence, public silence: Nuns, bishops, and the gendered space of early Chicago', *Chicago Historical Review*, 90:3 (2004), pp. 473–96

Brown, Thomas N., *Irish-American Nationalism 1870–1890* (Philadelphia: J. B. Lippincott Company, 1966)

Brown-May, Andrew, 'A charitable indulgence: street stalls and the transformation of public space in Melbourne, c. 1850–1920', *Urban History*, 23:1 (1996), pp. 48–71

Bruce, Susannah Ural, '"Remember your country and keep up its credit": Irish volunteers and the Union Army, 1861–1865', *Journal of Military History*, 69:2 (2005), pp. 331–59

Brundage, David, *Irish Nationalists in America: The Politics of Exile, 1798–1998* (Oxford: Oxford University Press, 2019)

— 'American Labour and the Irish Question, 1916–23', *Saothar*, 24 (1999), pp. 59–66

Buckley, Anthony D., '"On the club": Friendly societies in Ireland', *Irish Economic and Social History*, 14 (1987), pp. 39–58

Bueltmann, Tanja, *Clubbing Together: Ethnicity, Civility and Formal Sociability in the Scottish Diaspora to 1930* (Liverpool: Liverpool University Press, 2015)

Bueltmann, Tanja and Donald M. MacRaild, *The English Diaspora in North America: Migration, Ethnicity and Association, 1730s–1950s* (Manchester: Manchester University Press, 2017)

Buggy, Hugh, *Celtic Club. A Brief History, 1887–1947* (Melbourne: Celtic Club, 1948)

Burchell, R. A., *The San Francisco Irish, 1848–1880* (Berkeley: University of California Press, 1980)

Campbell, Malcolm, *Ireland's New Worlds: Immigrants, Politics, and Society in the United States and Australia, 1815–1922* (Madison: University of Wisconsin Press, 2008)

— 'John Redmond and the Irish National League in Australia and New Zealand, 1883', *History*, 86:283 (2001), pp. 348–62

— 'Emigrant responses to war and revolution, 1914–21: Irish opinion in the United States and Australia', *Irish Historical Studies*, 32:125 (May 2000), pp. 75–92
— 'Irish nationalism and immigrant assimilation: Comparing the United States and Australia', in *Australasian Journal of American Studies*, 15:2 (1996), pp. 24–43
— 'The Other Immigrants: Comparing the Irish in Australia and the United States', *Journal of American Ethnic History*, 14:3 (1995) pp. 3–22
Candeloro, Dominic, 'Chicago's Italians: A survey of the ethnic factor, 1850–1990', in Melvin Holli and Peter d'A. Jones (eds), *Ethnic Chicago: A Multicultural Portrait* (Grand Rapids: Wm. B. Eerdmans Public Co., 1995), pp. 229–59
Cannadine, David, 'The transformation of civic ritual in modern Britain: The Colchester Oyster Feast', *Past & Present*, 9 (1982), pp. 107–30
Central Statistics Office, 'Life in 1916 Ireland: Stories from Statistics Emigration', available https://www.cso.ie/en/releasesandpublications/ep/p-1916/1916irl/people/emigration/#d.en.97639 [Accessed 23 April 2021]
Chatelain, Marcia, *South Side Girls: Growing Up in the Great Migration* (Durham, NC: Duke University Press, 2015)
Clark, Peter, *British Clubs and Societies 1580–1800: The Origins of an Associational World* (Oxford: Oxford University Press, 2000)
Clarke, Brian P., *Piety and Nationalism: Lay Voluntary Associations and the Creation of an Irish-Catholic Community in Toronto, 1850–1895* (Montreal: McGill-Queen's University Press, 1993)
Clear, Catriona, *Nuns in Nineteenth-Century Ireland* (Dublin: Gill & MacMillan, 1987)
Codell, Julie (ed.), *Imperial Co-Histories: National Identities and the British and Colonial Press* (London: Associated University Presses, 2003)
Coleman, Marie, 'Compensating Irish female revolutionaries, 1916–1923', *Women's History Review*, 26:6 (2017), pp. 915–34
Coleman, Patrick, '"In harmony": A comparative view of female Orangeism, 1887–2000', in Angela McCarthy (ed.), *Ireland in the World: Comparative, Transnational, and Personal Perspectives* (Abingdon: Routledge, 2015), pp. 110–36
Comerford, R.V., 'Deference, accommodation, and conflict in Irish confessional relations', in Colin Barr and Hilary M. Carey (eds), *Religion and Greater Ireland: Christianity and Irish Global Networks, 1750–1950* (Montreal: McGill-Queen's University Press, 2015), pp. 33–51
— 'Churchmen, tenants, and independent opposition, 1850–56', in W. E. Vaughan (ed.), *A New History of Ireland. V: Ireland Under the Union, I 1801–70* (Oxford: Oxford University Press, 1989), pp. 396–414
— 'Conspiring brotherhoods and contending elites, 1857–63', in W. E. Vaughan (ed.), *A New History of Ireland. V: Ireland Under the Union, I 1801–70* (Oxford: Oxford University Press, 1989), pp. 415–30

Connolly, Gerard, 'Irish and Catholic: Myth or reality? Another sort of Irish and the renewal of the clerical profession among Catholics in England, 1791–1918', in Roger Swift and Sheridan Gilley (eds), *The Irish in the Victorian City* (London: Croom Helm, 1985), pp. 225–54

Connolly, Linda, *The Irish Women's Movement: From Revolution to Devolution* (Abingdon: Palgrave, 2002)

Connolly, Mary Beth Fraser, *Women of Faith: The Chicago Sisters of Mercy and the Evolution of a Religious Community* (New York: Fordham University Press, 2014)

Conzen, Kathleen Neils, David A. Gerber, Ewa Morawska, George E. Pozzetta and Rudolph J. Vecoli, 'The invention of ethnicity: A perspective from the USA', *Journal of American Ethnic History*, 12:1 (1992), pp. 3–41

Cooper, Frederick, *Colonialism in Question: Theory, Knowledge, History* (Berkeley: University of California Press, 2005)

Cooper, Sophie, 'Melbourne visions of an Irish future in the 1880s', in Richard Butler (ed.), *Dreams of an Irish Future in the Nineteenth Century* (Liverpool: Liverpool University Press, 2021), pp. 133–52

— 'Something borrowed: women, Limerick lace and community heirlooms in the Australian Irish diaspora', *Social History*, 45:3 (2020), pp. 304–27

— '"English, yet essentially un-English": Female constructions of imperial belonging in Melbourne, 1850–1870', in Sutapa Dutta (ed.), *British Women Travellers: Empire and Beyond, 1770–1870* (London: Routledge: 2019), pp. 189–204

Cowan, Mimi, '"We know neither Catholics, nor Protestants, nor Free-Thinkers Here": Ethnicity, religion, and the Chicago public schools, 1837–94', in Colin Barr and Hilary M. Carey (eds), *Religion and Greater Ireland: Christianity and Irish Global Networks, 1750–1950* (Montreal: McGill-Queen's University Press, 2015), pp. 187–205

Cronin, Mike and Daryl Adair, *The Wearing of the Green: A History of St Patrick's Day* (London: Routledge, 2006)

Cronon, William, *Nature's Metropolis: Chicago and the Great West* (London: W. W. Norton & Co., 1991)

Crosbie, Barry, *Irish Imperial Networks: Migration, Social Communication and Exchange in Nineteenth-Century India* (Cambridge: Cambridge University Press, 2012)

Cummings, Kathleen Sprows, *New Women of the Old Faith: Gender and American Catholicism in the Progressive Era* (Chapel Hill: University of North Carolina Press, 2009)

Currey, C. H., *The Irish at Eureka* (Sydney: Angus & Robertson, 1954)

Davidoff, Leonore and Catherine Hall, *Family Fortunes*, revised edn (London: Routledge, 2002)

Davis, Richard P., 'Loyalism in Australasia, 1788–1868', in Allan Blackstone and Frank O'Gorman (eds), *Loyalism and the Formation of the British World, 1775–1914* (Woodbridge: Boydell Press, 2019), pp. 223–40

Davis, Susan G., *Parades and Power: Street Theatre in Nineteenth-Century Philadelphia* (Berkeley: University of California Press, 1988)
Davison, Graeme, 'Gold-rush Melbourne', in Iain McCalman, Alexander Cook and Andrew Reeves (eds), *Gold: Forgotten Histories and Lost Objects of Australia* (Cambridge: Cambridge University Press, 2001), pp. 52–66
— 'Colonial origins of the Australian home', in Patrick Troy (ed.), *A History of European Housing in Australia* (Cambridge: Cambridge University Press, 2000), pp. 6–25
— *The Rise and Fall of Marvellous Melbourne* (Melbourne: Melbourne University Press, 1979)
Dearinger, Ryan, *The Filth of Progress: Immigrants, Americans, and the Building of Canals and Railroads in the West* (Berkeley: University of California Press, 2016)
de Búrca, Marcus, 'The Gaelic Athletic Association and Organized Sport in Ireland', in Grant Jarvie (ed.), *Sport in the Making of Celtic Cultures* (Leicester: Leicester University Press, 1999), pp. 100–11
Delaney, Enda, 'Diaspora', in Richard Bourke and Ian McBride (eds), *The Princeton History of Modern Ireland* (Princeton: Princeton University Press, 2016), pp. 490–508
— 'Our island story? Towards a transnational history of late modern Ireland', *Irish Historical Studies*, 37 (2011), pp. 599–621
— 'The Irish diaspora', *Irish Economic and Social History*, 33:1 (2006), pp. 35–45
Delaney, Enda and Donald M. MacRaild (eds), *Irish Migration, Networks and Ethnic Identities since 1750* (London: Routledge, 2007)
Delaney, Enda and Fearghal McGarry, 'Introduction: a global history of the Irish revolution', *Irish Historical Studies*, 44:165 (2020), pp. 1–10
Delay, Cara, *Irish Women and the Creation of Modern Catholicism, 1850–1950* (Manchester: Manchester University Press, 2019)
de Nie, Michael, *The Eternal Paddy: Irish Identity and the British Press, 1798–1882* (Madison: University of Wisconsin Press, 2004)
Dennis, Richard, *Cities in Modernity: Representations and Productions of Metropolitan Space, 1840–1930* (Cambridge: Cambridge University Press, 2008)
Dickson, David, Justyna Pyz and Christopher Shepard (eds), *Irish Contexts in the Origins of Modern Education* (Dublin: Four Courts Press, 2012)
Diner, Hasia, *Erin's Daughters in America: Irish Immigrant Women in the Nineteenth Century* (Baltimore: Johns Hopkins University Press, 1983)
Dobson, Miriam and Benjamin Ziemann (eds), *Reading Primary Sources: The Interpretation of Texts from Nineteenth- and Twentieth-Century History* (London: Routledge, 2009)
Dolan, Jay P., *The American Catholic Experience: A History from Colonial Times to the Present* (Garden City: Doubleday & Company, 1985)

Donlon, Regina, *German and Irish Immigrants in the Midwestern United States, 1850–1900* (Abingdon: Palgrave Macmillan, 2018)

Donnelly Jr., James S., *The Great Irish Potato Famine* (Stroud: Sutton Publishing, 2007)

— 'The administration of relief, 1847–51', in W. E. Vaughan (ed.), *A New History of Ireland. V: Ireland Under the Union, I 1801–70* (Oxford: Oxford University Press, 1989), pp. 316–30

Dowd, Christopher, *Rome in Australia: The Papacy and Conflict in the Australian Catholic Missions, 1834–1884* (Leiden: Brill, 2008)

Doyle, David Noel, 'The Irish in North America, 1776–1845', in J. J. Lee and Marion R. Casey (eds), *Making the Irish American: History and Heritage of the Irish in the United States* (New York: New York University Press, 2006), pp. 171–212

— 'The Irish in Australia and the United States: Some comparisons, 1800–1939', *Irish Economic and Social History*, 16 (1989), pp. 73–94

— 'The Irish in Chicago', *Irish Historical Studies*, 26:103 (1989), pp. 293–303

Doyle, Joseph, 'Cardinal Cullen and the system of national education in Ireland', in Dáire Keogh and Albert McDonnell (eds), *Cardinal Paul Cullen and his World* (Dublin: Four Courts Press, 2011), pp. 190–204

Dyrenfurth, Nick, '"A terrible monsters": From "employers to capitalists" in the 1885–86 Melbourne Wharf Labourers' strike', *Labour History*, 94 (2008), pp. 89–111

Edmonds, Penelope, *Urbanizing Frontiers: Indigenous Peoples and Settlers in 19th Century Pacific Rim Cities* (Vancouver: UBC Press, 2010)

Emmons, David M., *Beyond the American Pale: The Irish in the West, 1845–1910* (Norman: University of Oklahoma Press, 2010)

— *The Butte Irish: Class and Ethnicity in an American Mining Town, 1875–1925* (Urbana: University of Illinois Press, 1990)

Erie, Stephen P., *Rainbow's End: Irish-Americans and the Dilemmas of Urban Machine Politics, 1840–1985* (Berkeley: University of California Press, 1990)

Fanning, Charles, *Finley Peter Dunne and Mr Dooley: The Chicago Years* (Lexington: University of Kentucky Press, 1978)

Ferriter, Diarmaid, *The Transformation of Ireland, 1900–2000* (London: Profile, 2005)

Fitzgerald, Maureen, *Habits of Compassion: Irish Catholic Nuns and the Origins of New York's Welfare System, 1830–1920* (Urbana: University of Illinois Press, 2006)

Fitzpatrick, David, 'Exporting brotherhood: Orangeism in South Australia', in Enda Delaney and Donald M. MacRaild (eds), *Irish Migration, Networks and Ethnic Identities since 1750* (London: Routledge, 2007), pp. 129–62

— 'Ireland and empire', in Andrew Porter (ed.), *The Oxford History of the British Empire: The Nineteenth Century* (Oxford: Oxford University Press, 1999), pp. 494–521

— 'Emigration, 1871–1921', in W. E. Vaughan (ed.), *New History of Ireland. VI: Ireland Under the Union, II, 1870–1921* (Oxford: Clarendon Press, 1996), pp. 606–55

— *Oceans of Consolation: Personal Accounts of Irish Migration to Australia* (Cork: Cork University Press, 1994)

— 'The Irish in Britain: Settlers or transients?', in Patrick Buckland and John Belchem (eds), *The Irish in British Labour History: Conference Proceedings in Studies* (Liverpool: University of Liverpool Press, 1993), pp. 1–10

— 'Emigration, 1801–70', in W. E. Vaughan (ed.), *A New History of Ireland, Volume V: Ireland Under the Union, I, 1801–1870* (Oxford: Clarendon Press, 1989), pp. 562–622

— 'Irish emigration in the later nineteenth century', *Irish Historical Studies*, 22:86 (1980), pp. 126–43

— '"A share of the honeycomb": Education, emigration and Irishwomen', *Continuity and Change*, 1:2 (1986), pp. 217–34

— *Irish Emigration, 1801–1921* (Dublin: Economic and Social History Society of Ireland, 1984)

Flanagan, Maureen A., *Seeing with Their Hearts: Chicago Women and the Vision of the Good City, 1871–1933* (Princeton: Princeton University Press, 2002)

Foner, Eric, *Politics and Ideology in the Age of the Civil War* (Oxford: Oxford University Press, 1980)

Foster, R. F., *Paddy and Mr Punch: Connections in Irish and English History* (London: Penguin Books, 1995)

Fraser, Lyndon, 'Irish women's networks on the west coast of New Zealand's South Island, 1864–1922', *Women's History Review*, 15:3 (2006), pp. 459–75

Funchion, Michael F., 'Irish Chicago: Church, homeland, politics, and class – the shaping of an ethnic group, 1870–1900', in Melvin Holli and Peter d'A. Jones (eds), Ethnic Chicago: A Multicultural Portrait (Grand Rapids: Wm. B. Eerdmans Publishing, 1995), pp. 57–92.

— *Irish American Voluntary Organisations* (New York: Greenwood Press, 1983)

— *Chicago's Irish Nationalists, 1881–1890* (New York: Arno Press, 1976)

Galenson, David W., 'Economic opportunity on the urban frontier: Nativity, work, and wealth in early Chicago', *Journal of Economic History*, 51:3 (1991), pp. 581–603

Gallagher, Niamh, *Ireland and the Great War: A Social and Political History* (London: Bloomsbury, 2020)

Gallman, J. Matthew, *Receiving Erin's Children: Philadelphia, Liverpool, and the Irish Famine Migration, 1845–1855* (Chapel Hill: University of North Carolina Press, 2000)

Garraghan, Gilbert J., *The Catholic Church in Chicago, 1673–1871* (Chicago: Loyola University Press, 1921)

Geary, Laurence M., 'Australia *felix*: Irish doctors in nineteenth-century Victoria', in Patrick O'Sullivan (ed.), *The Irish World Wide: Vol. 2: The Irish in the New Communities* (Leicester: Leicester University Press, 1993), pp. 162–79

Gellner, Ernst, *Conditions of Liberty: Civil Society and its Rivals* (London: Hamish Hamilton, 1994)

Gilley, Sheridan, 'The Roman Catholic Church and the nineteenth century Irish diaspora', *Journal of Ecclesiastical History*, 35:2 (1984), pp. 188–207

Gleeson, David, *The Green and the Gray: The Irish in the Confederate States in America* (Chapel Hill: University of North Carolina Press, 2013)

Grant, James and Geoffrey Serle, *The Melbourne Scene, 1803–1956* (Melbourne: Melbourne University Press, 1956)

Greefs, Hilde, 'Clubs as vehicles for inclusion in the urban fabric? Immigrants and elitist associational practices in Antwerp, 1795–1830', *Social History*, 41:4 (2016), pp. 375–95

Green, Nancy L., 'The comparative method and postmodern structuralism: New perspectives for migration studies', *Journal of American Ethnic History*, 13:4 (1994), pp. 3–22

Griffin, Brian, '"Scallions, pikes and bog oak ornaments": The Irish Republican Brotherhood and the Chicago Fenian Fair, 1864', *Studia Hibernia*, 29 (1995–7), pp. 85–97

Haines, Robin, *Emigration and the Labouring Poor: Australian Recruitment in Britain and Ireland, 1831–60* (Basingstoke: Macmillan Press Ltd, 1997)

Hall, Catherine, *Civilising Subjects: Metropole and Colony in the English Imagination 1830–1867* (Chicago: University of Chicago Press, 2002)

Hall, Dianne, 'Irish republican women in Australia: Kathleen Barry and Linda Kearns's tour in 1924–5', *Irish Historical Studies*, 43:163 (2019), pp. 73–93

— '"Now him white man": Images of the Irish in colonial Australia', *Australian Historical Association*, 11:2 (2014), pp. 167–95

Hall, Dianne and Elizabeth Malcolm, '"English institutions and the English race": Race and politics in late nineteenth-century Australia', *Australian Journal of Politics & History*, 62:1 (2016), pp. 1–15

Hall, Stuart and Paul du Gay (eds), *Questions of Cultural Identity* (London: Sage Publications Ltd, 1996)

Handlin, Oscar, *The Uprooted: The Epic Study of the Great Migrations that made the American People* (New York: Little, Brown & Company Ltd, 1951)

Harkin, Frances, '"Where would we be without the GAA?": Gaelic games and Irishness in London', *Irish Studies Review*, 26:1 (2008), pp. 55–66

Harper, Marjory and Stephen Constantine, *Migration and Empire* (Oxford: Oxford University Press, 2010)

Haselby, Sam, *The Origins of American Religious Nationalism* (Oxford: Oxford University Press, 2015)

Hatfield, Mary, *Growing Up in Nineteenth-Century Ireland: A Cultural History of Middle-Class Childhood and Gender* (Oxford: Oxford University Press, 2019)

Haupt, Heinz-Gerhard and Jürgen Kocka, *Comparative and Transnational History: Central European Approaches and New Perspectives* (New York: Oxford University Press, 2009)
Hickman, Mary, *Religion, Class and Identity: The State, the Catholic Church and the Education of the Irish in Britain* (Aldershot: Avebury, 1995)
Hickman, Mary, Nicola Mai and Helen Crowley, *Migration and Social Cohesion in the UK* (Abingdon: Palgrave Macmillan, 2012)
Holli, Melvin and Peter d'A. Jones (eds), *Ethnic Chicago: A Multicultural Portrait* (Grand Rapids: Wm. B. Eerdmans Publishing, 1995)
Hooper, Carole, 'Access and exclusivity in nineteenth-century Victorian schools', *History of Education Review*, 45:1 (2016), pp. 16-27
Howe, Stephen, *Ireland and Empire: Colonial Legacies in Irish History and Culture* (Oxford: Oxford University Press, 2000)
Hoy, Suellen, 'The Irish girls' rising: Building the women's labor movement in Progressive-Era Chicago', *Labor*, 9:1 (2012), pp. 77–100
— *Good Hearts: Catholic Sisters in Chicago's Past* (Urbana: University of Illinois Press, 2006)
— 'Caring for Chicago's women and girls: The Sisters of the Good Shepherd, 1859–1911', *Journal of Urban History*, 23:3 (1997), pp. 260–94
Hughes, Kyle and Donald MacRaild, *Ribbon Societies in Nineteenth-Century Ireland and Its Diaspora: The Persistence of Tradition* (Liverpool: Liverpool University Press, 2018)
— 'Irish politics and labour: Transnational and comparative perspectives, 1798–1914', in Niall Whelehan (ed.), *Transnational Perspectives on Modern Irish History* (London: Routledge, 2014), pp. 45–68
Hull, Terence H., 'The strange history and problematic future of the Australian census', *Journal of Population Research*, 24:1 (2007), pp. 1–22
Hulme, Tom, *After the Shock City: Urban Culture and the Making of Modern Citizenship* (Woodbridge: Boydell Press, 2019)
Hunt, Thomas C., 'The impact of Vatican teaching on Catholic educational policy in the United States during the late nineteenth century', *Paedogogica Historica*, 24:2 (1984), pp. 437–60
Inglis, K. S., *The Australian Colonists: An Exploration of Social History 1788–1870* (Melbourne: Melbourne University Press, 1974)
Jackson, Alvin, 'Ireland, the union, and the empire, 1800–1960', in Kevin Kenny (ed.), *Ireland and the British Empire* (Oxford: Oxford University Press, 2005), pp. 123–52
Jacobson, Matthew Frye, *Special Sorrows: The Diasporic Imagination of Irish, Polish, and Jewish Immigrants in the United States* (Berkeley: University of California Press, 2002)
Janis, Ely M., *A Greater Ireland: The Land League and Transatlantic Nationalism in Gilded Age America* (Madison: University of Wisconsin Press, 2015)

— 'Petticoat revolutionaries: Gender, ethnic nationalism, and the Irish Ladies' Land League in the United States', *Journal of American Ethnic History*, 27:2 (2008), pp. 5–27
Jeffery, Keith (ed.), *'An Irish Empire'? Aspects of Ireland and the British Empire* (Manchester: Manchester University Press, 1996)
Jenkins, Brian, *The Fenian Problem: Insurgency and Terrorism in a Liberal State 1858–1874* (Liverpool: Liverpool University Press, 2008)
Jenkins, William, *Between Raid and Rebellion: The Irish in Buffalo and Toronto, 1867–1916* (Montreal: McGill-Queen's University Press, 2013)
Jentz, John B. and Richard Schneirov, *Chicago in the Age of Capital: Class, Politics, and Democracy during the Civil War and Reconstruction* (Urbana: University of Illinois Press, 2012)
— 'Chicago's Fenian Fair: A window into the Civil War as a popular awakening', *Labor's Heritage*, 6:3 (1995), pp. 4–19
Jupp, James, *From White Australia to Woomera: The Story of Australian Immigration* (Cambridge: Cambridge University Press, 2002)
Kantowicz, Edward R., 'Cardinal Mundelein of Chicago and the shaping of twentieth-century American Catholicism', *Journal of American History*, 68:1 (1981), pp. 52–68
Kanya-Forstner, Martha, 'Defining womanhood: Irish women and the Catholic Church in Victorian Liverpool', in Donald M. MacRaild (ed.), *The Great Famine and Beyond: Irish Migrants in Britain in the Nineteenth and Twentieth Centuries* (Dublin: Irish Academic Press, 2000), pp. 168–88
Karamanski, Theodore J., *Rally 'Round the Flag: Chicago and the Civil War* (Oxford: Rowman & Littlefield Publishers, 2006)
Keating, Ann Durkin, *Chicagoland: City and Suburbs in the Railroad Age* (Chicago: University of Chicago Press, 2004)
Kehoe, S. Karly, *Creating a Scottish Church: Catholicism, Gender and Ethnicity in Nineteenth-Century Scotland* (Manchester: Manchester University Press, 2010)
Kelleher, Patricia, 'Class and Catholic Irish masculinity in antebellum America: Young men on the make in Chicago', *Journal of American Ethnic History*, 28:4 (2009), pp. 7–42
— 'Young Irish workers: Class implications of men's and women's experiences in Gilded Age Chicago', *Éire-Ireland*, 36:1&2 (2001), pp. 141–65
Kelly, James, '"No dumb Ireland": Robert Burns and Irish cultural nationalism in the nineteenth century', *Eire-Ireland*, 47:3&4 (2012), pp. 251–68
Kelly, Mary C., *The Shamrock and the Lily: The New York Irish and the Creation of a Transatlantic Identity, 1845–1921* (New York: Peter Lang, 2005)
Kelly, Matthew, 'Irish nationalist opinion and the British empire in the 1850s and 1860s', *Past & Present*, 204 (2009), pp. 127–54
— 'The *Irish People* and the disciplining of dissent', in Fearghal McGarry and James McConnel (eds), *The Black Hand of Republicanism: Fenianism in Modern Ireland* (Dublin: Irish Academic Publishing, 2009), pp. 34–52

Kenna, Shane, *War in the Shadows: The Irish-American Fenians who Bombed Victorian Britain* (Dublin: Merrion Press, 2013)
Kenny, Kevin, 'Twenty years of Irish American historiography', *Journal of American Ethnic History*, 28:4 (2009), pp. 67–75
— 'Diaspora and Irish migration history', *Irish Economic and Social History*, 33:1 (2006), pp. 46–51
— 'Labor and labor organizations', in J. J. Lee and Marion R. Casey (eds), *Making the Irish American: History and Heritage of the Irish in the United States* (New York: New York University Press, 2006), pp. 354–63
— (ed.), *Ireland and the British Empire* (Oxford: Oxford University Press, 2005)
— (ed.), *New Directions in Irish-American Historiography* (Madison: University of Wisconsin Press, 2003)
— 'Diaspora and comparison: The global Irish as a case study', *Journal of American History*, 90:1 (2003), pp. 134–62
— *The American Irish: A History* (Harlow: Longman, 2000)
— *Making Sense of the Molly Maguires* (Oxford: Oxford University Press, 1998)
Keown, Gerard, 'The Irish Race Conference, 1922, reconsidered', *Irish Historical Studies*, 32:127 (2001), pp. 365–76.
Kibler, M. Alison, *Censoring Racial Ridicule: Irish, Jewish, and African American Struggles over Race and Representation, 1890–1930* (Chapel Hill: University of North Carolina Press, 2015)
Kirsch, George B., Othello Harris and Claire E. Nolte, *Encyclopedia of Ethnicity and Sports in the United States* (Westport: Greenwood Publishing Group, 2000)
King, Anthony D., 'Boundaries, networks, and cities: Playing and replaying diasporas and histories', in Thomas Bender and Alev Cinar (eds), *Urban Imaginaries: Locating the Modern City* (Minneapolis: University of Minnesota Press, 2007), pp. 1–16
King, Carla, *Michael Davitt: After the Land League, 1881–1906* (Dublin: University College Dublin Press, 2016)
Laidlaw, Zoë, *Colonial Connections 1815–1845: Patronage, the Information Revolution and Colonial Government* (Manchester: Manchester University Press, 2005)
Lake, Marilyn and Henry Reynolds, *Drawing the Global Colour Line: White Men's Countries and the International Challenge of Racial Equality* (Cambridge: Cambridge University Press, 2008)
Larkin, Emmet, 'Paul Cullen: The great ultramontane', in Dáire Keogh and Albert McDonnell (eds), *Cardinal Paul Cullen and his World* (Dublin: Four Courts Press, 2011), pp. 15–33
— 'The devotional revolution in Ireland, 1850–75', *American Historical Review*, 77:3 (1972), pp. 625–52
LeFebvre, Henri, *The Production of Space*, trans. Donald Nicholson-Smith (Oxford: Basil Blackwell, 1991)

Lindberg, Richard C., *To Serve and Collect: Chicago Politics and Police Corruption from the Lager Beer Riot to the Summerdale Scandal, 1855–1960* (Carbondale: Southern Illinois University Press, 1998)

Logan, John, 'The national curriculum', in James H. Murphy (ed.), *The Oxford History of the Irish Book, Volume IV: The Irish Book in English* (Oxford: Oxford University Press, 2011), pp. 499–517

Luddy, Maria, 'Women and philanthropy in nineteenth-century Ireland', *Voluntas: International Journal of Voluntary and Nonprofit Organizations*, 7:4 (1996), pp. 350–64

— *Women and Philanthropy in Nineteenth-Century Ireland* (Cambridge: Cambridge University Press, 1995)

Lynch, Timothy G., '"A kindred and congenial element": Irish-American nationalism's embrace of republican rhetoric', *New Hibernia Review*, 13:2 (2009), pp. 77–91

MacDonagh, Oliver, 'The Irish in Australia: A general view', in Oliver MacDonagh and W. F. Mandle (eds), *Ireland and Irish-Australia: Studies in Cultural and Political History* (London: Croom Helm, 1986), pp. 155–74

— 'Irish culture and nationalism translated: St Patrick's Day, 1888, in Australia', in Oliver MacDonagh, Oliver, W. F. Mandle and Pauric Travers (eds), *Irish Culture and Nationalism, 1750–1950* (London: Macmillan Press Ltd, 1983), pp. 69–82

— 'The Irish in Victoria, 1851–91: A demographic essay', in T. D. Williams (ed.), *Historical Studies VIII* (Dublin: Gill and Macmillan, 1971), pp. 67–92

MacDonagh, Oliver, W. F. Mandle and Pauric Travers (eds), *Irish Culture and Nationalism, 1750–1950* (London: Macmillan Press Ltd, 1983)

MacRaild, Donald M., '"No Irish need apply": The origins and persistence of a prejudice', *Labour History Review*, 78 (2013), pp. 269–99

— *The Irish Diaspora in Britain, 1750–1939*, 2nd end (Abingdon: Palgrave Macmillan, 2011)

— 'Crossing migrant frontiers: Comparative reflections on Irish migrants in Britain and the United States during the nineteenth century', *Immigrants and Minorities*, 18:2–3 (1999), pp. 40–70

Magee, Gary B. and Andrew S. Thompson, *Empire and Globalisation: Networks of People, Goods and Capital in the British World, c. 1850–1914* (Cambridge: Cambridge University Press, 2010)

MacIntyre, Stuart, *A Concise History of Australia* (Cambridge: Cambridge University Press, 1999)

Malcolm, Elizabeth and Dianne Hall, *A New History of the Irish in Australia* (Cork: Cork University Press, 2019)

— 'Catholic Irish Australia and the labor movement: Race in Australia and nationalism in Ireland, 1880s–1920s', in Greg Patmore and Shelton Stromquist (eds), *Frontiers of Labor: Comparative Histories of the United States and Australia* (Urbana: University of Illinois Press, 2018), pp. 149–67

Mangion, Carmen M., *Contested Identities: Catholic Women Religious in Nineteenth-Century England and Wales* (Manchester: Manchester University Press, 2008)

Mangione, Thomas, 'The establishment of the Model School system in Ireland, 1834–1854', *New Hibernia Review*, 7:4 (2003), pp. 103–22

Mannion, Patrick, *A Land of Dreams: Ethnicity, Nationalism, and the Irish in Newfoundland, Nova Scotia, and Maine 1880–1923* (Montreal: McGill-Queen's University Press, 2018)

McAuliffe, Mary and Liz Gillis, *Richmond Barracks 1916: We Were There. 77 Women of the Easter Rising* (Dublin: Dublin City Council, 2016)

McCaffrey, Lawrence, Ellen Skerrett, Michael F. Funchion and Charles Fanning, *The Irish in Chicago* (Urbana: University of Illinois Press)

McCarthy, Angela, '"In prospect of a happier future": private letters and Irish women's migration to New Zealand, 1840–1925', in Lyndon Fraser (ed.), *A Distant Shore: Irish Migration and New Zealand Settlement* (Dunedin: University of Otago Press, 2000), pp. 105–16.

McCarthy, Tara M., *Respectability and Reform: Irish American Women's Activism, 1880–1920* (Syracuse: Syracuse University Press, 2018)

McCartin, James P., *Prayers of the Faithful: The Shifting Spiritual Life of American Catholics* (Cambridge, MA: Harvard University Press, 2010)

McClaughlin, Trevor (ed.), *Irish Women in Colonial Australia* (St Leonards: Allen & Unwin, 1998)

— *Barefoot and pregnant? Female Orphans who Emigrated from Irish Workhouses to Australia, 1848–50* (Melbourne: Genealogical Society of Victoria, 1991)

McConville, Chris, *Croppies, Celts and Catholics: The Irish in Australia* (Caulfield: Edward Arnold, 1987)

McCracken, Donald P., *MacBride's Brigade: Irish Commandos in the Anglo-Boer War* (Dublin: Four Courts Press, 1999)

McGarry, Fearghal and James McConnel (eds), *The Black Hand of Republicanism: Fenianism in Modern Ireland* (Dublin: Irish Academic Press, 2009)

McGaughey, Jane G. V., *Violent Loyalties: Manliness, Migration, and the Irish in the Canadas, 1798–1841* (Liverpool: Liverpool University Press, 2020)

McGrath, Patrick, 'Secular power, sectarian politics: The American-born Irish elite and Catholic political culture in nineteenth-century New York', *Journal of American Ethnic History*, 38:3 (2019), pp. 36–75

McGreevy, John T., *Catholicism and American Freedom: A History* (New York: W. W. Norton & Company, 2004)

McKenzie, Kristen, *Scandal in the Colonies: Sydney and Cape Town, 1820–1850* (Melbourne: Melbourne University Press, 2004)

McKillen, Elizabeth, *Chicago Labor and the Quest for a Democratic Diplomacy, 1914–1924* (Ithaca: Cornell Press, 1995)

McMahon, Cian, *The Global Dimensions of Irish Identity: Race, Nation, and the Popular Press, 1840–1880* (Chapel Hill: University of North Carolina Press, 2015)

McMahon, Eileen, *What Parish Are You From? A Chicago Irish Community and Race Relations* (Lexington: University of Kentucky Press, 1995)

McMahon, Timothy, Michael de Nie and Paul Townend (eds), *Ireland in an Imperial World: Citizenship, Opportunism, and Subversion* (London: Palgrave Macmillan, 2017)

Meagher, Timothy J., *Inventing Irish America: Generation, Class, and Ethnic Identity in a New England City, 1880–1928* (South Bend: Notre Dame Press, 2001)

Merriner, James L., *Grafters and Goo Goos: Corruption and Reform in Chicago* (Carbondale: Southern Illinois University Press, 2008)

Miller, Kerby A., Ellen Skerrett and Bridget Kelly, 'Walking backward to heaven? Edmond Ronayne's pilgrimage in Famine Ireland and Gilded Age America', in Enda Delaney and Breandán Mac Suibhne (eds), *Ireland's Great Famine and Popular Politics* (London: Routledge, 2016), pp. 80–141

Miller, Kerby A., 'Class, culture and immigrant group identity in the United States: The case of Irish-American ethnicity', in Virginia Yans-McLaughlin (ed.), *Immigration Reconsidered: History, Sociology, and Politics* (Oxford: Oxford University Press, 1990), pp. 96–129

— *Emigrants and Exiles: Ireland and the Irish Exodus to North America* (Oxford: Oxford University Press, 1985)

Moloney, Deirdre M., 'Land League activism in transnational perspective', *US Catholic Historian*, 22:3 (2004), pp. 61–74

Moody, T. W., *Davitt and Irish Revolution, 1846–82* (Oxford: Clarendon Press, 1984)

Morris, R. J., 'Introduction: Civil society, associations and urban places: Class, nation and culture in nineteenth-century Europe', in Graeme Morton, Boudien de Vries and R. J. Morris (eds), *Civil Society, Associations and Urban Places: Class, Nation and Culture in Nineteenth-Century Europe* (Aldershot: Ashgate Publishing, 2006), pp. 1–16

Morgan, Patrick, *Melbourne before Mannix: Catholics in Public Life 1880–1920* (Ballarat: Connor Court Publishing, 2012)

Morton, Richard Allen, *Justice and Humanity: Edward F. Dunne, Illinois Progressive* (Carbondale: Southern Illinois University Press, 1997)

Moss, Kenneth, 'St Patrick's Day celebrations and the formation of Irish-American identity, 1845–1875', *Journal of Social History*, 29:1 (1995), pp. 125–48

Mulrooney, Margaret M., *Black Powder, White Lace: the du Pont Irish and Cultural Identity in Nineteenth-Century America* (Lebanon: University Press of New England, 2002)

Murphy, David H., 'Irish Jesuit schooling in Victoria, Australia', *Irish Journal of Education*, 25:1/2 (1991), pp. 52–8

Nadel, George, *Australia's Colonial Culture: Ideas, Men and Institutions in Mid-Nineteenth Century Eastern Australia* (Melbourne: F. W. Cheshire, 1957)

— 'The Melbourne Advocate, 1868–1900: bastion of Irish nationalism in colonial Victoria', in Ciara Breathnach and Catherine Lawless (eds), Visual, Material and Print Culture in Nineteenth-Century Ireland (Four Courts Press, 2010), pp. 223–33
Niall, Brenda, Mannix (Melbourne: Text Publishing, 2016)
Ní Bhroiméil, Una, Building Irish Identity in America, 1870–1915: The Gaelic Revival (Dublin: Four Courts Press, 2003)
Nolan, Janet A., 'Women's place in the history of the Irish diaspora: A snapshot', Journal of American Ethnic History, 28:4 (2009), pp. 76–81
— '"The nun who stopped traffic" and "the Patrick Henry of the classroom": Justitia Coffey, Margaret Coffey, and Chicago's school wars', Radharc, 5/7 (2004–6), pp. 33–52
— Servants of the Poor: Teachers and Mobility in Ireland and Irish America (South Bend: University of Notre Dame Press, 2004)
— Ourselves Alone: Women's Emigration from Ireland 1885–1920 (Lexington: University of Kentucky Press, 1989)
Noone, Val, Nicholas O'Donnell's Autobiography (Ballarat: Ballarat Heritage Services, 2017)
— Hidden Ireland in Victoria (Ballarat: Ballarat Heritage Services, 2012)
O'Brien, Gillian, Blood Runs Green: The Murder That Transfixed Gilded Age Chicago (Chicago: University of Chicago Press, 2015)
O'Brien, John and Pauric Travers (eds), The Irish Emigrant Experience in Australia (Dublin: Poolberg Press, 1991)
O'Day, Alan, 'A conundrum of Irish diasporic identity: Mutative ethnicity', Immigrants and Minorities, 27:2–3 (2009), pp. 317–39
O'Farrell, Patrick, 'The Irish in Australia and New Zealand, 1791–1870', in W. E. Vaughan (ed.), A New History of Ireland. V: Ireland Under the Union, I, 1801–70 (Oxford: Oxford University Press, 1989), pp. 661–81
— 'The Irish in Australia and New Zealand, 1870–1990', in W. E. Vaughan (ed.), A New History of Ireland. VI: Ireland Under the Union, II, 1870–1921 (Oxford: Clarendon Press, 1996), pp. 703–24
— The Irish in Australia: 1788 to the Present (Randwick: New South Wales Press, 1987)
— The Catholic Church in Australia: A Short History, 1788–1967 (London: Geoffrey Chapman, 1969)
Ó Gráda, Cormac, The Great Irish Famine (Cambridge: Cambridge University Press, 1995)
Oireachtas Library and Research Service, Spotlight: Overseas Voting in Presidential Elections: Representative Democracy, Electoral Integrity and the Situation in EU States (Dublin, 2019)
O'Kane, Frances, A Path is Set: The Catholic Church in the Port Phillip District and Victoria: 1839–1862 (Melbourne: Melbourne University Press, 1976)

Ó Maolfabhail, Art, 'Hurling: An old game in a new world', in Grant Jarvie (ed.), *Sport in the Making of Celtic Cultures* (Leicester: Leicester University Press, 1999) pp. 149–65
O'Neill, Ciaran, *Catholics of Consequence: Transnational Education, Social Mobility, and the Irish Catholic Elite 1850–1900* (Oxford: Oxford University Press, 2014)
Otto, Kristin, *Capital: Melbourne when it was the Capital City of Australia, 1901–27* (Melbourne: Text Publishing, 2009)
Pacyga, Dominic, *Slaughterhouse: Chicago's Union Stock Yard and the World It Made* (Chicago: University of Chicago Press, 2015)
— *A Biography: Chicago* (Chicago: University of Chicago Press, 2011)
— 'To live amongst others: Poles and their neighbors in industrial Chicago, 1865–1930', *Journal of American Ethnic History*, 16:1 (1996), pp. 55–73
Palmer, Michael, 'The British press and international news, 1851–99: Of agencies and newspapers', in George Boyce, James Curran and Pauline Wingate (eds), *Newspaper History from the Seventeenth Century to the Present Day* (London: Constable, 1978), pp. 205–22
Parkes, Susan M., '"An essential service": The National Board and teacher education, 1831–1870', in Brendan Walsh (ed.), *Essays in the History of Irish Education* (Abingdon: Palgrave Macmillan, 2016), pp. 45–83
Pašeta, Senia, *Before the Revolution: Nationalism, Social Change and Ireland's Catholic Elite, 1879–1922* (Cork: Cork University Press, 1999)
Pentland, Gordon, 'The indignant nation: Australian responses to the attempted assassination of the Duke of Edinburgh in 1868', *English Historical Review*, 130:542 (2015), pp. 57–88
Pescod, Keith, 'Irish participation in Victoria's union movement, 1850–1900', *Australasian Journal of Irish Studies*, 11 (2011), pp. 7–27
Pickering, Paul A., '"Ripe for a republic": British radical responses to the eureka stockade', *Australian Historical Studies*, 34:121 (2003), pp. 69–90
Pierce, Bessie Louise, *A History of Chicago* (Chicago: A. A. Knopf, 1940)
Platt, Harold L., *Shock Cities: The Environmental Transformation and Reform of Manchester and Chicago* (Chicago: University of Chicago Press, 2005)
— *The Electric City: Energy and the Growth of the Chicago Area, 1880–1930* (Chicago: University of Chicago Press, 1991)
Poovey, Margaret, *Uneven Developments: The Ideological Work of Gender in Mid-Victorian England* (Chicago: University of Chicago Press, 1988)
Proudfoot, Lindsay and Dianne Hall, *Imperial Spaces: Placing the Irish and Scots in Colonial Australia* (Manchester: Manchester University Press, 2011)
— 'Memory, place and diaspora: Locating identity in colonial space', *Journal of Irish and Scottish Studies*, 4:1 (2010), pp. 47–64
Quinn, James, *Young Ireland and the Writing of Irish History* (Dublin: University College Dublin Press, 2015)

Quinn, John F., *Father Mathew's Crusade: Temperance in Nineteenth-Century Ireland and Irish America* (Amherst: University of Massachusetts Press, 2002)
Rae, John, 'The eight hours day in Victoria', *The Economic Journal*, 1:1 (1891), pp. 15–42
Redmond, Jennifer, *Moving Histories: Irish Women's Emigration to Britain from Independence to Republic* (Liverpool: Liverpool University Press, 2018)
Regan-Lefebvre, Jennifer, *Cosmopolitan Nationalism in the Victorian Empire: Ireland, India and the Politics of Alfred Webb* (Basingstoke: Palgrave Macmillan, 2009)
Reid, Robert L. (ed.), *Battleground: The Autobiography of Margaret A. Haley* (Urbana: University of Illinois Press 1982)
Reynolds, Frank L., 'The Ancient Order of Hibernians', *Illinois Catholic Historical Review*, 4:1 (1921), pp. 22–33
Ridden, Jennifer, 'Britishness as an imperial and diasporic identity: Irish elite perspectives, c. 1820–1870s', in Peter Gray (ed.), *Victoria's Ireland? Irishness and Britishness, 1837–1901* (Dublin: Four Courts Press, 2004), pp. 88–105
Ridge, John T., 'Irish county societies in New York, 1880–1914', in Ronald T. Bayor and Timothy J. Meagher (eds), *The New York Irish* (Baltimore: Johns Hopkins University Press, 1996), pp. 275–300
Roddy, Sarah, *Population, Providence and Empire: The Churches and Emigration from Nineteenth-Century Ireland* (Manchester: Manchester University Press, 2014)
— 'Spiritual imperialism and the mission of the Irish race: The Catholic Church and emigration from nineteenth-century Ireland', *Irish Historical Studies*, 38:152 (2013), pp. 600–19
Ronayne, Jarlath, *First Fleet to Federation: Irish Supremacy in Colonial Australia* (Dublin: Trinity College Dublin, 2002)
Rouse, Paul, *Sport and Ireland: A History* (Oxford: Oxford University Press, 2015)
Ryan, Louise and Margaret Ward (eds), *Irish Women and Nationalism: Soldiers, New Women and Wicked Hags* (Dublin: Irish Academic Press, 2004)
Sanders, James W., *The Education of an Urban Minority: Catholics in Chicago, 1833–1965* (Oxford: Oxford University Press, 1977)
Sargent, Paul, *Wild Arabs and Savages: A History of Juvenile Justice in Ireland* (Oxford: Oxford University Press, 2013)
Schneirov, Richard, *Labor and Urban Politics: Class Conflict and the Origins of Modern Liberalism in Chicago, 1864–97* (Urbana: University of Illinois Press, 1998)
Schrader, Ben, *The Big Smoke: New Zealand Cities, 1840–1920* (Wellington: Bridget Williams Book, 2016)
Schrover, Marlou and Floris Vermeulen, 'Immigrant organisations', *Journal of Ethnic and Migration Studies*, 31:5 (2005), pp. 823–32
Serle, Geoffrey, *The Golden Age: A History of the Colony of Victoria, 1851–1861* (Cambridge: Cambridge University Press, 1968)

Shaikh, Fariha, *Nineteenth-Century Settler Emigration in British Literature and Art* (Edinburgh: Edinburgh University Press, 2019)

Shanabruch, Charles, *Chicago's Catholics: The Evolution of an American Identity* (South Bend: University of Notre Dame Press, 1981)

Shiell, Annette, *Fundraising, Flirtation and Fancywork: Charity Bazaars in Nineteenth Century Australia* (Newcastle: Cambridge Scholars Publishing, 2012)

Shiels, Damian, *The Irish in the American Civil War* (Dublin: THP Ireland, 2013)

Shorten, Ann R., 'The legal context of Australian education: An historical exploration', *Australia New Zealand Journal of Law Education*, 1:1 (1996), pp. 2–32

Sim, David, *A Union Forever: The Irish Question and Foreign Relations in the Victorian Age* (Ithaca: Cornell University Press, 2013)

Sinclair, Georgina, 'The "Irish" policeman and the Empire: influencing the policing of the British Empire – Commonwealth', *Irish Historical Studies*, 36:143 (2008), pp. 173–87

Skerrett, Ellen, 'Chicago's Irish and "brick and mortar Catholicism": A reappraisal', *US Catholic Historian*, 14:2 (1996), pp. 53–71

— 'The development of Catholic identity among Irish Americans in Chicago, 1880–1920', in Timothy J. Meagher (ed.), *From Paddy to Studs: Irish-American Communities in the Turn of the Century Era, 1880–1920* (New York: Greenwood Press, 1986), pp. 117–38

Sleight, Simon, *Young People and the Shaping of Public Space in Melbourne, 1870–1914* (London: Routledge, 2013)

Smyth, William J., *Toronto, The Belfast of Canada: The Orange Order and the Shaping of Municipal Culture* (Toronto: University of Toronto Press, 2015)

Suttor, T. L., *Hierarchy and Democracy in Australia: 1788–1870* (Melbourne: Melbourne University Press, 1965)

Swan, James B., *Chicago's Irish Legion: The 90th Illinois Volunteers in the Civil War* (Carbondale: Southern Illinois University Press, 2009)

Sweeney, Loughlin, *Irish Military Elites, Nation and Empire, 1870–1925* (Basingstoke: Palgrave, 2019)

Taaffe, Edward James, Howard L. Gauthier and Morton E. O'Kelly, *Geography of Transportation*, 2nd edn (Englewood Cliffs: Prentice-Hall, Inc., 1996)

Tansill, Charles Callan, *America and the Fight for Irish Freedom, 1866–1922* (New York: Devin-Adair Press, 1957)

Tax, Meredith, *The Rising of the Women: Feminist Solidarity and Class Conflict, 1880–1917* (New York: Monthly Review Press, 1980)

Theobald, Marjorie R., 'Women, leadership and gender politics in the interwar years: the case of Julia Flynn', *History of Education*, 29:1 (2000), pp. 63–77

— *Knowing Women: Origins of Women's Education in Nineteenth-Century Australia* (Cambridge: Cambridge University Press, 1996)

Thomson, Kathleen and Geoffrey Serle, *A Biographical Register of the Victorian Legislature: 1859–1900* (Canberra: Australian National University Press, 1972)

Trait, Ruth, 'Rev. Patrick Joseph Aylward 1849–1898', *Footprints*, 15:2 (1998), p. 33
Twomey, Christina, 'Gender, welfare and the colonial state: Victoria's 1864 *Neglected and Criminal Children's Act*', *Labour History*, 73 (1997), pp. 169–86
Urban, Andrew, *Brokering Servitude: Migration and the Politics of Domestic Labor during the Long Nineteenth Century* (New York: New York University Press, 2017)
Vapnek, Lara, *Breadwinners: Working Women and Economic Independence, 1865–1920* (Urbana: University of Illinois Press, 2009)
Vertigan, Tas, *The Orange Order in Victoria: Origins, Events, Achievements, Aspirations, and Personalities* (Melbourne: Loyal Orange Institution of Victoria, 1979)
Wade, Louise Carroll, *Chicago's Pride: The Stockyards, Packingtown, and Environs in the Nineteenth Century* (Urbana: University of Illinois Press, 1987)
Walch, Timothy, 'The Catholic press and the campaign for parish schools: Chicago and Milwaukee, 1850–1885', *US Catholic Historian*, 3:4 (1984), pp. 254–72
Walsh, Patrick, 'Education and the "universalist" idiom of empire: Irish National School books in Ireland and Ontario', *History of Education*, 37:5 (2008), pp. 645–60
Ward, Margaret, *Unmanageable Revolutionaries: Women and Irish Nationalism* (London: Pluto Press, 1995)
Waugh, John, *First Principles: The Melbourne Law School, 1857–2007* (Melbourne: Melbourne University Publishers, 2007)
Waugh, Max, 'The national system of education in Victoria, 1849–1862: Sir Richard Bourke and the Irish connection', in Philip Bull, Frances Devlin-Glass and Helen Doyle (eds), *Ireland and Australia, 1798–1998: Studies in Culture, Identity and Migration* (Sydney: Crossing Press, 2000), pp. 102–12
Weinbren, Dan and Bob James, 'Getting a grip: The roles of friendly societies in Australia and Britain reappraised', *Labour History*, 88 (2005), pp. 87–103
West, Martin R. and Ludger Woessmann, '"Every Catholic child in a Catholic school": Historical resistance to state schooling, contemporary private competition and student achievement across countries', *Economic Journal*, 120:546 (2010), pp. 229–55
West, T., *The Bold Collegians: The Development of Sport in Trinity College, Dublin* (Dublin: Lilliput Press, 1991)
Whelan, Bernadette, 'Women on the move: A review of the historiography of Irish emigration to the USA, 1750–1900', *Women's History Review*, 24:6 (2015), pp. 900–16
Whelan, Irene, 'Religious rivalry and the making of Irish-American identity', in J. J. Lee and Marion R. Casey (eds), *Making the Irish American: History and*

Heritage of the Irish in the United States (New York: New York University, 2006), pp. 271–85

Whelehan, Niall, 'Sacco and Vanzetti, Mary Donovan and transatlantic radicalism in the 1920s', *Irish Historical Studies*, 44:165 (2020), pp. 131–46

— *The Dynamiters: Irish Nationalism and Political Violence in the Wider World, 1867–1900* (Cambridge: Cambridge University Press, 2012)

Wiley, Shaun, Krystal Perkins and Kay Deaux, 'Through the looking glass: Ethnic and generational patterns of immigrant identity', *International Journal of Intercultural Relations*, 32:5 (2008), pp. 385–98

Young, Linda, *Middle Class Culture in the Nineteenth Century: America, Australia and Britain* (Abingdon: Palgrave Macmillan, 2003)

Yuval-Davis, Nira, *The Politics of Belonging: Intersectional Contestations* (London: Sage Publications, 2011)

Theses

Akthar, Shahmima, '"A public display of its own capabilities and resources": A cultural history of Irish identity on display, 1851–2015' (PhD: University of Birmingham, 2019)

Bateson, Catherine, 'The sentiments and culture of Irish American Civil War songs and music' (PhD: University of Edinburgh, 2018)

Cooper, Sophie, 'Irish migrant identities and community life in Melbourne and Chicago, 1840–1890' (PhD: University of Edinburgh, 2017)

Cooper, Sophie, '"A policy of terrorism is not one to which Englishmen will succumb": British policing and the Irish-American Dynamite Campaign (MPhil: Trinity College Dublin, 2011)

Cowan, Mimi, 'Immigrants, nativists, and the making of Chicago, 1835–1893' (PhD: Boston College, 2015)

Naughtin, Patrick, 'The green flag at the antipodes: Irish nationalism in colonial Victoria during the Parnell era, 1880–91' (PhD: University of Melbourne, 2011)

Nolan, Bobbie, 'Language and identity amongst Irish migrants in London, Philadelphia and San Francisco, 1850–1920' (PhD: University of Edinburgh, 2019)

Quigley, Kevin J., 'American financing of Fenianism in Ireland 1858–67' (MA: Maynooth, 1983)

Index

American Civil War, 41, 59, 61, 65–7, 98–9, 103, 144, 159, 161–2, 193–4
Ancient Order of Hibernians, 70, 111, 113–14, 165, 169, 175, 208
anti-Catholicism *see* nativism
Australian Labor Party, 80, 113, 146

balls, 65, 69, 99, 186, 189, 191, 195–7, 199–201, 204, 206–7, 212–13
benefit, benevolent and friendly societies, 63–4, 75, 77, 81, 97
  Chicago Hibernian Benevolent Society, 63, 70, 191–4
  Hibernian Australasian Catholic Benefit Society, 81, 96, 105, 109, 113, 145, 176, 200–2, 210
  Illinois Catholic Order of Foresters, 111–12
  Irish National Foresters Benefit Society, 77–8, 211
  St Francis' Benefit Society *see* Hibernian Australasian Catholic Benefit Society
  United Sons of Erin Benevolent Society, 63, 66, 70
  Women's auxiliaries, 109, 110, 112
Boer War, 174–5, 209

Carr, ArchbishopThomas, 174, 208
Catholic Church
  adult education provision, 96, 105, 109
  and St Patrick's Day, 188, 191–3, 200–2, 204–8, 210
  approach to nationalism, 66, 108–9, 160–1, 164, 166, 169–70, 174, 176, 193, 195, 201, 210–11
  attendance, 45–6, 111, 113, 160
  church building, 62, 92–3, 97, 105–6, 128–9, 145, 204
  hierarchy *see* Carr, Archbishop Thomas; Cullen, Cardinal Paul; Duggan, Bishop James; Feehan, Archbishop Daniel; Goold, Archbishop James; Mannix, Archbishop Daniel; Mundelein, Cardinal George; Quarter, Bishop William; Quigley, Archbishop James; Van de Velde, Bishop James
  inter-ethnic competition, 94, 145–6
  intervention in secular society, 62, 76, 80, 146, 176, 188
Catholic Federation, 80, 113, 146, 176
Catholic Young Men's Society, 95, 105, 109, 176–7, 201
Celtic Club, 77, 173–4
Chicago Federation of Labor, 80, 198
Chicago Fire, 41–2, 70, 74, 103, 165
Chicago Relief and Aid Society, 71, 103
Chicago Teachers' Federation, 2, 80
Chicago Women's Trade Union League, 80
children, 67, 91, 94, 99, 102, 122–47, 170, 187, 198–202, 210, 224–5
  youth organisations, 104, 195, 208
Clan na Gael, 164–6, 168–9, 171–2, 174–5, 193, 206
Cullen, Cardinal Paul, 7, 17, 95, 110, 129–30, 134

culture brokers, 9, 59, 122–3, 146–7, 153, 187, 220, 225

dancing, 99, 201, 204, 210
Democratic Party, 76–7
domestic service, 43, 48, 69, 142
Dublin, 95, 110, 123–4, 129–30, 134, 165, 167
Duggan, Bishop James, 160–1, 164–5

education legislation,124–6, 133–4, 137–43, 146–7, 163, 197, 223
education tax, 131, 134, 137–8, 141–2, 144
emigration schemes, 29–31, 36–8, 69
 Earl Grey orphan girls, 94
environment, 39, 190, 193–4, 212
ethnic collaboration, 39, 60, 93, 189–90, 197–9, 201–2, 223–4
ethnic/racial competition, 33–5, 37, 42–3, 46, 93
Eureka Stockade, 40, 156–7

Federated Seamen's Union of Australasia, 68
Feehan, Archbishop Daniel, 169, 207
Fenian Brotherhood, 66, 73–4, 158–62, 164, 166, 193, 196–9
 Fenian Dramatic Club, 73–4
 Fenian Fair, 159–61
Fenian scare, 163, 167, 196
female reform institutions, 100, 127
First World War, 146, 176, 187, 210
foundational identities, 2, 10, 116, 123–4, 128, 130, 133–4, 138, 142–3, 146–7, 153–4, 199, 221–5
fundraising, 99–102, 105, 128–9, 131, 134, 160–6, 170, 172–3, 195, 197, 204, 207
 fairs and bazaars, 99, 102, 108, 112, 159–60
funerals, 158, 161

Gaelic Athletic Association, 79, 208
Gaelic League, 175–6, 210
Gaelic Revival, 79, 174–6, 201
Gavan Duffy, Sir Charles, 65, 131, 155, 189, 195–6, 204–5
Geoghegan, Father Patrick, 62–3, 93–4, 188
gold rushes, 29, 156–7
Goold, Archbishop James, 126, 129, 192
Grattan Address, 171

Haley, Margaret, 146
hotel *see* pub

instant cities, 13–14, 28, 58
inter-faith cooperation, 63, 70, 77, 93, 99, 136
Irish-American Club, 76, 79, 81, 206
Irish-American Republican Club, 76
Irish history, 105, 130, 135, 145, 167, 187, 194, 201–3
Irish National League, *see* Land League
Irish National School, 125, 129–30, 133, 136
Irish Republican Brotherhood, 158–62

Knights of Columbus, 114
Knights of Labor, 68, 80, 165, 171

labourers, 43, 58, 73, 161, 165, 168, 172, 176
 labour organising, 74, 164–8, 173, 207
 Catholic, 80, 146, 161
 information, 69, 78
 inter-regional mobility, 78, 165
 strikes, 40–4
 trade unionism, 43, 68, 77, 80, 112, 198
Ladies' Land League, 154, 168–72
Land League, 77, 111, 166–72, 202, 207
Land War, 59, 75, 203
language
 Catholic parish, 93–5, 142
 English, 43, 48, 93–4
 Irish, 79, 174–6, 204, 219
libraries, 40, 60, 64, 77
literary societies, 70, 74, 81, 83
loyalty, 60–1, 67, 92, 105, 123, 141, 145, 160, 163, 186, 188–91, 196, 199, 201, 203–6, 208–9, 211

male religious orders, 107–8, 127–8, 131, 135, 137, 139–40, 145, 164, 194
Manchester Martyrs, 163
Mannix, Archbishop Daniel, 113, 146, 175–6, 178, 209, 211–12
mayors, 91, 158, 165, 170, 203
migrant care, 69, 81, 127
military, 65–6, 72–3, 209–11
militia, 60–1, 111, 172, 190–1
Mundelein, Cardinal George, 146

INDEX

national parish, 93, 128, 142, 222
nativism, 39, 57, 62–4, 66, 114, 130–1, 139–41, 144, 146, 163–4, 167, 193
networks, 12–13, 110–11, 161–2, 164, 205, 224
nun, 8–9, 17–18, 93–4, 98–103, 108–9, 122–4, 126–9, 131–5, 138–40, 145–7, 159, 164, 172, 194, 211–12, 221, 224–5

O'Brien, Mother Agatha, 127
O'Connell, Daniel, 60, 156, 160, 189, 191
O'Farrell, Henry, 163, 196
Ogden Grove, 166, 172–4, 206
Onahan, William, 75–6, 166, 206
Orange Order, 62, 68–9, 163, 170–1, 188
original landholders
    Aboriginal landholders, 29
    Native American landholders, 28–9
orphan asylums, 99, 103, 122, 127, 135, 168, 172
O'Shanassy, Sir John, 2, 65, 189

papal decrees, 106, 132, 141, 144
parades, 62, 78, 91, 161, 166, 186–214
parish, 12, 17–18, 47, 91, 97, 99, 105–6, 113–14, 128–9, 131, 142, 161, 188, 222
Party Processions Act (1846), 62, 188, 192
picnics, 166–7, 187, 200–1
police, 45, 60, 160, 163, 212
politics, 44, 46–7, 65, 67, 76, 135–6, 160, 172, 193, 197, 202, 205–6, 224
priests, 62, 66, 77, 92, 95, 101, 111, 133, 160–1, 166, 169, 195, 225
Protestantism, 124–5, 131–2, 145, 147, 169, 200
    Protestant churches, 46, 83, 93, 186
public space, 63, 91, 97, 160–1, 166–7, 186–90, 192–5, 200–4, 207–8, 210–13, 223
pubs, 64–5, 78, 154, 164

Quarter, Bishop William, 93, 126, 128
Quigley, Archbishop James, 155

radical thinkers (non-Irish), 156–7, 177
regionalism, 62
religious competition, 94, 137, 162–3

Repeal Association, 60, 136, 156
respectability, 47, 57, 60, 65, 100, 102, 127, 142, 163, 200–1, 209–10
riots, 42, 62, 68

St Patrick's Day, 2, 35, 72, 78, 104, 163, 166, 186–214, 226
St Patrick's Society of Australia Felix, 59–63, 77, 79, 81, 83, 91, 173–4, 177, 188–90, 192, 194–6, 200–2, 211
St Patrick's Hall, 64, 69, 187
St Patrick's Society, Chicago, 75, 81, 194
St Vincent de Paul's Society, 71, 95, 97, 99, 103, 109, 134, 173, 210
saloon *see* pubs
schooling, 114, 122–47, 224–5
    and nationalism, 198–9, 201, 204–6, 210
    convent fee-paying schools, 99–100, 107–8, 128, 139
    fundraising, 100–4, 134, 197–8, 204, 206
    national schools, 125, 132
    parish schools, 18, 80, 102, 107, 114, 126, 128, 130, 132, 139–43, 145, 194, 198–9, 222
    state schools, 126, 130–1, 139–41, 146
    Sunday schools, 101, 103
social advancement, 48–9, 61, 63, 101, 108, 129, 136–7, 142, 154
social Catholicism, 114, 165
sodality, 98, 104–5, 107–9, 124, 170
speaking tours *see* visiting lecturers
sport, 71–3
    athletics, 72
    cricket, 71–2
    Gaelic games, 68, 72–3, 79, 203
    hurling, 62, 72, 203–4
    rugby, 71
state prisoners, 162–4
Sullivan, Alexander, 166, 168–9, 172, 174

temperance, 64, 70, 91, 114, 190–1, 195, 208
trade, 28, 40–1
transport
    canals, 29, 41
    city transit, 75, 112, 158, 209, 212
    railways, 29, 41
Trinity College Dublin, 45–6, 71–2

United Irish League of America, 175
United Irish Societies of Chicago and Cook County, 76, 172, 175

Van de Velde, Bishop James, 94
Victoria, separation of, 64, 91
visiting lecturers, 71, 79, 81, 105, 153, 156, 166–8, 170–6

Winter, Joseph, 2, 163, 165–6, 170–1, 174
women
  and associational culture, 58, 62, 83, 92, 98, 100–2, 110, 112–13, 164, 166–9, 221; *see also* benefit societies, women's auxiliaries
  and emigration, 30–1, 69, 123, 127, 154, 221, 225
  and fundraising, 98–9, 102, 129, 138, 160, 164, 178, 224
  and labour organising, 80, 83, 112, 146, 165–6, 169, 173, 178; *see also* Chicago Teachers' Federation, Chicago Women's Trade Union League, Knights of Labor, Margaret Haley
  and lay teaching, 43–4, 122, 124, 129–34, 136, 142–3, 145–6, 221, 225
  and nationalism, 8, 73, 80, 108, 153–4, 160, 164, 166, 168–9, 172–3, 175; *see also* Ladies' Land League, women religious
  and St Patrick's Day, 187, 191, 193–4, 197, 208, 210–11, 213–14
women religious *see* nun

Young Irelanders, 65, 155–8
youth, 30–2, 132, 156, 198, 201

EU representative:
Easy Access System Europe
Mustamäe tee 50, 10621 Tallinn, Estonia
Gpsr.requests@easproject.com

www.ingramcontent.com/pod-product-compliance
Lightning Source LLC
Chambersburg PA
CBHW052047220426
43663CB00012B/2478